Bread, Knowledge and Freedom: A Study of Nineteenth-Century Working Class Autobiography

UNIVERSITY OF WINNIPEG
LIBRARY
Portage Avenue
Winnipeg, Manitoba R3B 2E9
DISCARDED

Bread, Knowledge and Freedom

A Study of Nineteenth-Century Working Class Autobiography

HD
8393
. A1-
U56 .
1982

David Vincent

Methuen

London and New York

First published in 1981 by
Europa Publications Ltd

First published as a University Paperback in 1982 by
Methuen & Co. Ltd
11 New Fetter Lane, London EC4P 4EE

Published in the USA by
Methuen & Co.
in association with Methuen, Inc.
733 Third Avenue, New York, NY 10017

© 1981 David Vincent

Printed in Great Britain at the
University Press, Cambridge

All rights reserved. No part of this book may be
reprinted or reproduced or utilized in any form or by
any electronic, mechanical or other means, now known
or hereafter invented, including photocopying and
recording, or in any information storage or retrieval
system, without permission in writing from the
publishers.

British Library Cataloguing in Publication Data
Vincent, David
Bread, knowledge and freedom. – (University paperbacks 790).
1. Labour and labouring classes – Great Britain
– History – 19th century   2. Labour and
labouring classes – Great Britain – Attitudes
I. Title
305.5′6   HD 8388

ISBN 0–416–34670–7

Library of Congress Cataloging in Publication Data
Vincent, David, 1949–
Bread, knowledge and freedom.

(University paperbacks; 790)
Bibliography: p.
Includes index.
1. Labor and laboring classes – Great Britain –
Biography – History.   I. Title.
[HD8393.A1V56 1982] 305.5′62′0941 82–14163
ISBN 0–416–34670–7 (pbk.)

For my parents

Contents

Preface

This study makes use of a category of source material which hitherto has received insufficient attention from historians of the working class. It is in part a bibliographical exercise, and I am grateful to the Social Science Research Council for their support in the search for material. Many colleagues, including Dorothy Thompson, John Burnett, Edward Royle, P. E. H. Hair, Chris Gregory, Colin Richmond, John Briggs, Victor Neuburg and Eddie Frow, have kindly supplied me with references to autobiographies, and I must pay tribute to the County and Borough Librarians from Lerwick to Truro, who have answered my enquiries with such patience and expertise. Stella Lynde provided invaluable assistance in the task of processing the volume of correspondence and material generated by my pursuit of autobiographies, and Anne Ridgewell, Pam Seddon and Carolyn Busfield typed the completed manuscript. The book is a revised and extended version of a Cambridge Ph.D. thesis, and I am grateful to my former supervisor, Neil McKendrick, for his continued interest in the project. Some of its errors of fact and judgement have been removed with the help of John Burnett, Marjory Cruikshank, Geoff Eley, Scott Bennett, Anna Davin and Marguerite Dupree, who read drafts of various chapters. My especial thanks to Margaret Spufford for her encouragement and advice, and to Jim Walvin, who first set my feet on this road and was there at its conclusion to make a detailed reading of the final manuscript. I have been greatly dependent upon the support and critical skills of my wife, who, in the midst of attending to the needs of a young family, has found the time to work over every sentence of this book.

Keele
January 1981

Chapter One

Introduction

"I James Bowd of Swavesey in Cambridgeshire have now Reached to my 66th Anivarsary day and beign unable to go out to Labour I was sitting at home alone My Mind was taken back to the Early stages of my Life . . .",[1] thus a farm labourer, born in 1823, began to set down one of the hundred and forty-two working class autobiographies which form the basis of this study. Bowd was clearly not used to wielding a pen, but the fragment of formal schooling he had received as a child had endowed him with just enough literacy to leave a record of his memories for his descendants. It was a most ordinary life. He had lived where he was born and had followed the calling of his parents and of their parents. With old age approaching, he had little to show for a lifetime's toil, and little to look forward to except increasing ill-health and poverty. Yet he thought it worthwhile to commit to paper the events and experiences which had mattered to him and had made him the man who sat looking back to his childhood. He wrote of the illness he had suffered at the age of seven which had left him lame; of his early introduction to manual labour; of his marriage; of his reactions to the birth of five children and the death of two; and of his endless struggles to keep in work and out of debt. As he sought to find a pattern in his life so the historian can stand at his side and gain a privileged insight into the unfolding of his personality. The purpose of this study is to attempt to discover how these working men and women whose autobiographies cover some part of the period between 1790 and 1850, understood their lives, and thereby to reach a better understanding of the working class as a whole during the industrial revolution.

(i)

The works included in the main group of autobiographies have satisfied three broad conditions. As a first step it is necessary to distinguish between life-

---

[1] Bowd, p. 293. Here and in all subsequent references, the title of the autobiography is abbreviated to the author's surname. If an author wrote more than one autobiography, some part of the title is also given. Unless specified in the first reference, the work cited is the first edition. For full details, see the Bibliography, part I.

histories which are genuine autobiographies and those which are either biographies or fictional autobiographies. This is a more difficult problem than might at first appear. The word "autobiography" was not in use at the beginning of the period, and of the works used here only thirty-one have the term somewhere in the published title; the rest rely on the more traditional titles composed of words such as "Recollections", "Reminiscences", "Memoirs", "Adventures", and "Life of", which were frequently used to describe biographies as well as autobiographies in the nineteenth century.[2] Autobiography was only one amongst many genres of nineteenth century literature, and the form was susceptible to appropriation by practitioners in other fields. It was attractive to the few, inexperienced, working class novelists who found in its structure an acceptable solution to the considerable technical difficulty of constructing a novel.[3] The form was seen by Charles Kingsley in *Alton Locke* as the ideal medium for preaching to the working class about the dangers of violence and to the middle class about the need to alleviate the condition of the poor.[4] In this, Kingsley, himself an ordained Anglican minister, was extending the flourishing tradition of "conversions" of convicted prisoners, whose thoughts and repentance were guided by prison chaplains or visiting ministers and published in order to encourage potential sinners to keep to the paths of righteousness by threatening them with the consequences of transgression.[5] As much as the genuine autobiographies contained the writer's definition of his situation in society, so the form could be used by those who wished to impose their definition upon him.

The second condition is that the autobiographer should have been the child of a working man and should have remained a member of the working class until the composition of his memoirs. Such a condition poses difficulties with those who have "retired", and with those who develop their literary talents to such an extent that they can supplement or even supplant their earnings from manual labour with those from writing, teaching, or becoming what might be termed "professional agitators", on behalf of various causes. The evolving status of these occupations will be discussed later in the book; at this stage I have adopted the procedure of including any autobiography in which the author attempts to present himself as a working man, whatever he might mean by that term.[6] The only categories which have been excluded are those of

[2] The first known use of the word recorded in the *Oxford English Dictionary* is by Southey in a book review in the *Quarterly Review* in 1809; the earliest entry in a dictionary is in 1847. The first autobiography used in this study which is actually so-called is the *Autobiography of an Artisan*, by Christopher Thomson, published in London in 1847.
[3] See, for instance, the most widely read of the very few novels written about the working classes by members of that class during the period, *Johnny Robinson*, by Thomas Wright ("The Journeyman Engineer") (2 vols; London, 1867). The novel is devoid of plot and is only held together by the continuing presence of the first person narrator. See also P. J. Keating, *The Working Classes in Victorian Fiction* (London, 1971), ch. 1.
[4] Charles Kingsley, *Alton Locke* (London, 1850). The novel was originally presented simply as "An Autobiography" of "Alton Locke, Tailor and Poet". There was no outward indication that it was a novel or that Kingsley had anything to do with it. The model for the novel is thought to have been Thomas Cooper, who eventually wrote his own autobiography in 1872.
[5] See, for instance, *The Autobiography of a Reformed Thief* (London, 1863).
[6] Thus, for instance, by the time Joseph Arch came to write his memoirs he had long since left the land to become a full-time trade-union leader and later a Liberal M.P., but nonetheless he announced in the preface that his narrative is "the life story of an English agricultural labourer"

soldiers and sailors where the narrative is confined to the writer's military career, and those of ordained ministers whose voluminous body of memoirs merits a study of its own.

The third condition concerns the period covered by the autobiographies. For each work there are clearly two relevant dates, the year in which the writer was born and the year in which the autobiography was written.[7] All autobiographies which cover at least part of the period between 1790 and 1850 have been included. For reasons which we shall examine in the following chapter, working class autobiographies began to appear as the class as a whole took its first steps towards self-consciousness in the 1790s, and 1850 has been chosen as a terminal date for two reasons. The first is that as we move into the second half of the century, we start to encounter individuals whose lives stretched well beyond 1900, and whose access to the social mobility provided by formal education and the modern trade union and Labour Party bureaucracies transformed the significance of both the pursuit of knowledge and the pursuit of freedom. The second reason is that if the scope of the research is widened to include works published after the First World War, the increase in the volume of material would render impracticable the type of comprehensive study attempted here. There is, indeed, an important sense in which the relevance of an autobiography's contents is always conditioned by two dates, making it impossible to begin or end the study at a fixed point. Some of the autobiographers were born as early as the 1750s, and all were discussing their experiences in what is, in many respects, a discrete period of working class history, from a range of dates which stretch well beyond 1850. Consequently, whilst the focus of our analysis will be on the period which saw the birth and early struggles of the working class, we shall be constantly concerned with both the past of that period, and its future.

The hundred and forty-two autobiographies which are listed in the first part of the Bibliography have been assembled partly by gathering together items which were separately already known to historians, and partly by undertaking a more systematic search for texts which lay hidden in private possession or in the holdings of public libraries and other archives.[8] In addition I have looked at a sample of works which fall outside the various criteria to assess more accurately the particular characteristics of the structure and contents of the main group of autobiographies.

(ii)

At first sight it is perhaps surprising that such a rich vein of source material has yet to receive the serious attention of English historians. A number of the

(Arch, p. 1), and throughout the succeeding account he makes it clear that despite the situations he has held, he still regards himself, and wishes to be regarded, as a working man.

[7] As the content and significance of autobiography is, as we shall see, determined by the fact that they are a single interpretation of a life from a fixed point in time, they should be sharply distinguished from diaries which, although a valuable form of source material in their own right, have not been included in this study.

[8] I am grateful to the Social Science Research Council for providing financial assistance for this part of the research. A full annotated bibliography of nineteenth century working class autobiography is currently being compiled by Professor John Burnett and myself.

works have been republished recently, but apart from John Burnett's anthology *Useful Toil*,[9] historians have restricted themselves to raiding a handful of well-known works for isolated pieces of evidence. By contrast, the genre of American slave autobiography, which entered its most fertile phase at much the same time as the British working class autobiographies and has many features in common, has long been recognized as an essential point of departure for the study of slave history.[10] The much slighter traditions of French[11] and German[12] working class autobiography have been studied, and in this country personal testimony in the form of oral history has become a major industry during the last decade, complete with its own journal and basic text-book.[13] Yet amongst the most obvious limitations of oral history is that its scope will shortly become confined to the twentieth century. As we look back down the silent centuries from the end of the nineteenth, it is to the attempts of working men and women to write down their life-histories that we must turn if we are to hear their own judgements on their past. The neglect is at least in part a product of unresolved doubts about the "truth" and "relevance" of works which are necessarily subjective in form and limited in number. How can we trust the autobiographer to tell the truth about himself, and even if we can establish ways in which he is doing so, to what extent can his memories be taken as representative of his class as a whole?

St. Augustine, the author of the first recognizable autobiography, sought to overcome the first of these difficulties by appealing directly to his readership: "They wish to hear and they are ready to believe; but can they really know me? Charity, which makes them good, tells them that I do not lie about myself when I confess what I am, and it is this charity in them that believes me".[14] The historian's natural charity stems from the fact that in the autobiographies, it is precisely the element of subjectivity which is of the greatest value. To a point they share this characteristic with all other types of source material. Newspaper reports, eyewitness accounts, minutes of meetings, letters and commissions of enquiry, are all forms of literature, and their structure and content are inescapably moulded by the conventions of the specific literary form and the preconceptions of their authors. They are all in some way selective and no matter how lengthy can only represent a fragment of the total event.

[9] John Burnett, ed., *Useful Toil. Autobiographies of Working People from the 1820's to the 1920's* (London, 1974). Professor Burnett is currently compiling a second anthology of autobiographical treatment of family experience. There is also a valuable unpublished Ph.D. thesis by Bernard Sharratt, which applies the "close reading" techniques of literary criticism to the autobiographies of Bamford, Somerville, Frost and Burn: *Autobiography and Class Consciousness. An attempt to characterise nineteenth-century working class autobiography in the light of the writer's class* (Cambridge Univ., Ph.D., 1974).

[10] See especially John F. Bayliss's anthology, *Black Slave Narratives* (New York, 1970) and John W. Blassingame's influential study, *The Slave Community* (New York, 1972). His methodological chapter, pp. 227–235, contains a clear and forceful defence of the historical importance of autobiography. These autobiographies should be distinguished from the so-called slave "autobiographies" collected by the Federal Writers Project in the 1930s. Although a valuable and extensive archive, they are mostly a form of oral history. See *The American Slave: A Composite Autobiography*, 18 vols. (Westport, Conn., 1972) and the 12 volume *Supplements*, Series 1 (Westport, Conn., 1978).

[11] See Michel Ragon, *Histoire de la Littérature Prolétarienne en France* (Paris, 1974), pp. 75–101;

[12] Wolfgang Emmerich, *Proletarische Lebensläufe*, 2 vols. (Reinbeck bei Hamburg, 1974, 1975).

[13] See *Oral History*, 1975–, and Paul Thompson, *The Voice of the Past* (Oxford, 1978).

[14] St. Augustine, *Confessions*, translated by R. S. Pine-Coffin (Harmondsworth, 1971,) p. 209.

They are written after the event, perhaps only a day or so if a newspaper report, much longer if a parliamentary commission. They are subject to problems of factual accuracy. They are, in short, forms of communication, and the inter-action between the writer and intended audience means that a historian is always concerned with not one but two distinct events—the historical event which he is studying and the event of communication which has produced his evidence.

An assessment of the subjectivity of all types of source material is a necessary precondition of their analysis, and can yield useful information on the state of knowledge amongst individuals and groups, and on how they formulate and transmit their experience. The subjectivity of autobiography, however, encap-sulates rather than merely qualifies its meaning. When an individual sets down a record of his life, he does more than provide an account of a series of actions. We are presented not with a collection of remembered facts, but rather with a pattern of recollected experiences. Inevitably these do contain a number of separate, verifiable "facts", such as the attendance at meetings or the dates of various events, but these are incidental to the main value of the accounts. The distinction between the factual accuracy and the "truth" of a memoir was clearly recognized by one of the earliest autobiographers, James Donaldson: "As I have written wholly from recollection, it can scarcely be expected that I could remember names of places and dates very correctly; but this will be of little consequence, as the public are already in possession of them through other sources. For the main point, namely the truth of the narrative, I can con-fidently appeal to all who served with me".[15] Thus although matters such as misremembered or unrecorded dates can cause occasional problems and demand further research, it is possible to undertake a historical analysis of the works without embarking on the sort of detailed background investigation into the lives of each autobiographer which, in view of the number of individuals involved, would be impossibly time-consuming.[16]

Up to a point we can accept the guarantee offered by James Donaldson as to the more general truth of the narratives. The extent to which the auto-biographers felt themselves to be subject to the critical scrutiny of those who had shared their experiences clearly varied according to the form of publica-tion and the nature of the intended audience. Those, for instance, who wrote for their local community upon whose subscriptions they were dependent, were likely to have every moment of their autobiographies interrogated by a reader-ship far more informed than any subsequent student can hope to be. Those, on the other hand, who were attempting to communicate the condition of a section of the working class to a middle class audience, had a readership in some respects more distant from their experiences than a modern historian might expect to become. At the very least all would be constrained by the same feeling as the Scottish hawker and street-singer William Cameron, who con-fessed at one point: " . . . if I go beyond the truth I am aware that it would mak me the loast character in existance, as every town and village in my perigreenations can judge for itself as for what has taken pleas between me

---

[15] Donaldson, pp. vi–vii.
[16] The research I carried out for my edition of James Burn's autobiography revealed some unreliability in the matter of dates and chronology, but great accuracy in his recollections of social conditions.

and my congregations on the street".[17] In the end, however, the truth of an autobiography is not dependent on a certain relationship, however it is controlled, between the autobiographer's statements and the reality of the outside world, but rather on the quality of the relationship which he establishes between the various aspects of his personality as he seeks to reconstruct its development. It is not a matter of honesty or deceit, but rather of a capacity to grasp imaginatively the complexity of the life-long interaction between the self and the outside world. Providing composition takes place before senility sets in, what is to be feared is not a physical deterioration of memory,[18] but rather a failure to make full use of its powers. As Roy Pascal has written, "The most fatal error, in all types of autobiography, is not untruthfulness, but triviality of character".[19] What is required above all is energy of insight, an ability to comprehend fully the significance and coherence of past experiences, together with the literary skill to transmit an account in such a way as to make the widest connection with the experience and imagination of the readership. Therefore, whilst the reader of autobiographies, like the reader of any source material, must always be assessing the possibility of error and bias, and attempting to counteract it by searching for internal consistency, making cross-references between the autobiographies and checking particular points against external evidence, he is really looking for the intensity of the author's recollections and the ambition and control of his interpretation. More than any other form of source material, autobiography has the potential to tell us not merely what happened but the impact of an event or situation upon an actor in the past. The Kendal spinner William Dodd explained his principle of selection at the beginning of his autobiography: "I shall, therefore, confine myself in the following narrative to such facts as may serve to show the *effects* of the system upon my mind, person, and condition".[20] Where a working man would normally appear before the historian only in the monochromatic glare of a riot, or a passing organization or movement, now he can be seen as a man who received a certain education, went to work at a particular age, is now trying to raise a family, is in prosperity or debt, good health or bad, has accompanying beliefs and interests, has previously been active in some fields and not in others, and has a future which has already happened. As the autobiographer, who usually, though not invariably, is writing towards the end of his life, comes face to face with himself first as a child and then as a maturing adult, we are always viewing specific situations and actions in the context of change and movement. The historian feels charity towards the autobiographer because he is trying to comprehend himself over time. If we wish to understand the meaning of the past we must first discover the meaning the past had for those who made it and were made by it.

At one level, the problem of the representative quality of what must be a finite number of works is no different than that posed by any other form of literary evidence. Few men exist in any generation, in any sector of society,

[17] Cameron, p. 115.
[18] I. M. L. Hunter, *Memory* (Harmondsworth, 1964), pp. 225–8.
[19] Roy Pascal, *Design and Truth in Autobiography* (London, 1960), p. 78. See chs. I and XII for the general argument in this paragraph. Also, James Olney, *Metaphors of Self* (Princeton, 1972), pp. 1–43.
[20] Dodd, p. 5.

with the ability to communicate in an organized form the truths which all experience, and the relevance of an individual's record is not necessarily diminished by the intensity of his perceptions or his desire to articulate them. The argument is all the more powerful in the case of autobiography, for whereas the composition of fiction or poetry, whether published or not, is likely to be the prerogative of only a minority of any community, there is a sense in which all men and women are autobiographers. As Wilhelm Dilthey, who was one of the first to point out the importance of autobiography for the historian, emphasized, "Autobiography is merely the literary expression of a man's reflection on the course of his life. Such reflection, though it may be limited in extent, is frequently made by every individual. It is always present and expresses itself in ever new forms".[21] The mere fact, therefore, that the action of recollection was translated into a written form and then, in the majority of cases, published, does not in itself isolate the contents of an autobiography from the experiences of those who have remained silent. Rather the autobiographies can be seen as projecting a pencil of light into the darkness of the unspoken memories of men and women whose lives were conditioned by the same social experience.

Difficulties may arise, however, if it can be shown that the conditions surrounding the composition and publication of autobiographies are such as to confine the practice to certain categories of individuals within the working class. One obvious qualification for an autobiographer is that he or she should be literate, although the authors of some of the manuscript autobiographies were clearly unaccustomed to the act of composition.[22] The syntax and spelling of, in particular, the manuscript autobiographies of the Yorkshire shoemaker, Robert Spurr, the London cabinet maker Henry Price, the Northumbrian waggonway-wright Anthony Errington, and James Bowd, are consistent only with the speech forms in which the works must have been conceived, and as such can better be understood if they are read aloud. At this level the distinction between oral and written communication is near to collapse. These writers demonstrate just how slight a command of literacy was required in order to make, in all four cases, a successful attempt at autobiography, and as, by 1800, at least one in three of the most illiterate occupational groups within the working class, labourers and servants, possessed sufficient literacy to sign the marriage register,[23] it is perhaps not surprising that the group of autobiographers we are studying here is an extremely diverse collection of individuals. There is a slight bias towards the non-industrial skilled trades, but it is no more than that; only a quarter of the autobiographers actually served apprenticeships, and their numbers are almost balanced by those whose lives were spent at or near the very bottom of the ladder of income and status—eleven farm labourers, ten servicemen, seven beggars and hawkers, five servants and two navvies. It is

[21] Quoted in H. P. Rickman, ed. and intro., *Meaning in History. W. Dilthey's Thoughts on History and Society* (London, 1961), p. 86.

[22] Three of the autobiographies, those of Cameron, "Bill H.", and Marsh were dictated rather than written, and although Cameron was certainly literate, "Bill H.", and particularly Marsh, who appended his mark to his account, may not have been. Two more autobiographers, Thomas Davies and James Downing, though literate, had lost their sight and must have dictated their memoirs.

[23] Lawrence Stone, "Literacy and Education in England 1640–1900", *Past and Present*, no. 42, (1969), pp. 110–111; Roger Schofield, "Dimensions of Illiteracy 1750–1850", *Explorations in Economic History*, vol. 10, no. 4 (Summer 1973), p. 450.

7

possibly to be expected that the trades of shoemaking and printing are over-represented, but at least fifteen others wrote of their experiences in the harsh early days of the first factories. If the group is not a statistically accurate cross-section of the working class in this period, neither is its membership confined to the most skilled and prosperous of that class.

The geographical distribution of the autobiographies is equally wide. In common with the rest of their class, most of the autobiographers moved frequently, if only short distances, and consequently it is difficult to be precise about the residential characteristics of the group. On the whole the only distortion in the pattern would appear to be a not unexpected concentration on the urban areas,[24] especially London and the northern industrial towns, and a slight over-representation of Scotland, which presumably reflects the lead of the Scottish elementary education system in the early part of the period. The almost complete absence of Welsh autobiographies can partly be explained by the exclusion from the group of Welsh language (as well as Gaelic) works,[25] but otherwise remains something of a mystery.

The one major silence is that of women. When I began to collect these works I expected to find at least a sizeable minority of autobiographies by working women covering the period; in the event I have located just those of the cotton weaver Catherine Horne, the domestic servant Janet Bathgate, the Fen child worker Mrs Burrows, the 97 year old widow Elspeth Clark, the straw-plait worker Lucy Luck and the servant and teacher Mary Smith. There is a scattering of works by humble eighteenth century poetesses,[26] and an increasing volume of material from later in the nineteenth century, but for this period the composition of autobiographies seems to have been very largely a male prerogative. Why this should be the case is an interesting question. It cannot be explained merely by differentials in literacy,[27] and there was a relative equality of opportunity within the very low levels of education open to working class children at this time.[28] The answer must lie, in general terms, in the absence among women of the self-confidence required to undertake the unusual act of writing an autobiography, and in particular from the increasing exclusion of women from most forms of the working class organizations, especially self-improvement societies, which provided the training and stimulus for self-

---

[24] Only ten of the autobiographers can be said to have lived all their life in the countryside, but many more were brought up in rural areas before moving into the towns, and others spent periods in the countryside during their adult lives.

[25] I am grateful to a number of Librarians of Welsh Public Libraries, particularly Mr O. Iowerth Davies of Haverfordwest, for information on what appears to be a flourishing tradition of Welsh language autobiography which merits the attention of a more qualified historian than I. Problems of language, distance and cultural difference have deterred me from looking at Ireland.

[26] See in particular Mary Collier, *Poems, on Several Occasions . . . With some remarks on her life* (Winchester, 1762).

[27] On average female literacy rates were between ten and fifteen points behind male rates, and were slowly closing. There is some evidence, however, that in the areas of high working class female employment, the rate could be very low—there was an 84 per cent female illiteracy rate in Oldham in 1846—but this would still not explain the nationwide absence of female autobiographers. See Roger Schofield, art. cit., p. 453.

[28] See Pauline Marks, "Femininity in the Classroom: An Account of Changing Attitudes", in Juliet Mitchell and Ann Oakley, eds., *The Rights and Wrongs of Women* (Harmondsworth, 1976), pp. 176–198.

expression for so many of the male autobiographers.[29] The silence may also be a reflection of the subordinate position of women within the family; the husband was the head of the family and as such thought to be responsible for communicating its history to future generations. The consequence of the silence is that here, as in so much of written history, women can rarely be seen, except through the eyes of the fathers, husbands, lovers and sons.

Even amongst the men, the composition of autobiography was an uncommon activity, and as a mode of expression was more accessible to those who had prior experience as writers, particularly as journalists or poets, or as activists in the spectrum of working class organization in the period. At least twenty-five autobiographers wrote published or unpublished poetry at some point in their lives, and over a quarter held some position of official or unofficial leadership within the working class community. Most, but not all, led honest and fairly sober lives, and a great many read books and attempted to improve themselves. But, as the next chapter will demonstrate, it is a characteristic of nineteenth century working class autobiography that composition and publication were not limited to a group defined in terms of a narrow range of beliefs and practices. Where almost the only working people to write their life-histories had been Puritans and later Methodists, the genre now became the property of individuals from widely different backgrounds who wrote from an equally varied set of motives. Thus, whilst the group includes such established figures as William Lovett, Samuel Bamford and Thomas Cooper, the proportion of figuratively and at times literally anonymous writers has steadily increased as the search for working class autobiographies has widened. Men such as George Ayliffe, William Hanson, Joseph Haynes and George Marsh, left little mark on their own times and none on the body of written history. Due attention will be paid at appropriate points in the forthcoming analysis to the clusterings of outlook and behaviour that are to be found in this group, but, providing a proper caution is exercised, we can legitimately attempt to use the contents of the autobiographies to explore a wide variety of themes in the history of the nine-teenth century working class.

A final problem which should be considered is the extent to which the manner of publication exercised a distorting influence on the type of individual who might succeed in getting into print. The great majority of the autobiographies already known to historians were issued by commercial London publishers, whose concern for their profits and consequent sensitivity to the values of a largely middle class readership might be expected to lead to a bias in the type of manuscript accepted and possibly to the censoring of the accepted texts. The first point to be made here is that inasmuch as the wider search for auto-biographies has limited the predominance of the public figures, so it has in-creased the proportion of works which by-passed the metropolitan publishers. About a third of the sample went through the London firms,[30] but an equal

---

[29] Dorothy Thompson has drawn attention to the presence of women in political disturbances from Peterloo to Chartism, but the female friendly societies, trade unions and political organizations which can be located were shortlived and few in number and she finds it "incontrovertible" that women were withdrawing altogether from working class organizations from the 1840s onwards. Dorothy Thompson, "Women and Nineteenth-Century Radical Politics: A Lost Dimension", in Mitchell and Oakley, op. cit., pp. 112–138.

[30] No one firm specialized in these works, the most active in the field being the temperance

proportion were either published by the author himself or were still in manuscript at the time of his death. The remainder were published by small provincial firms, or first appeared in radical journals and local newspapers. The
publishing history of the autobiographies introduces us to one of the major
themes of the third section of this book, that in the first half of the nineteenth
century access to literary self-expression was not only dramatically greater
than it had been in the preceding century, but in many respects was more open
than it was later to become, as all forms of publishing became much more
capital intensive. However, the diversification of the forms of publication
multiplies rather than resolves the problems of distortion. The content and
organization of the autobiography would be subject not only to the influence of
publishers or editors, but to the nature of the intended audience and the
structure of the literary form in which it appeared. To take one example, the
fact that John Bezer wrote his *Autobiography of One of the Chartist Rebels of 1848*
for publication in the *Christian Socialist* clearly had an effect both on the selection
and interpretation of his memories, and on the way in which he divided his
life into self-contained episodes to fit the framework of serialization.[31] No single
formula can be devised to eliminate or average out the problem of distortion.
It is a matter of being constantly aware of the possible effects of various factors,
and of using the contrasting forms of publication to clarify the influence of
each.

However many autobiographies are collected, they remain separate literary
works. The larger the group the better are we able to discern the particular
identity of any one item, but although there are times when it is useful to
aggregate certain aspects of the autobiographies in order to gain some idea of
the relationship of the group to known qualities of the working class as a whole,
they are not a statistically accurate sample of the working class and no
truths, either in general or in particular, can be deduced by adding up their
contents and dividing by the total number. It is as units of literature that they
must be studied, and a key to their relevance to the history of the working
class may be found in the connection between the activity of autobiographical
self-analysis and the formation of class consciousness. The nature and significance of class consciousness, and its relationship to the economic "base" has
been the subject of an increasing body of research since Georg Lukacs redis-
covered the philosophical side of Marx half a century ago.[32] The rapidly increasing influence of Antonio Gramsci owes much to his preoccupation with
the fact that class relations are not determined solely by the organization of
production but are deeply affected by the complicated way in which one class
imposes its will upon another. At the centre of his notion of hegemony is the
phrase "the conception of reality". Class consciousness can only exist when a
social group holds a common conception of reality, and the resolution of class
relation is deeply influenced by the content of that conception. His

publisher William Tweedie, responsible for the autobiographies of Burn, Lowery and
Plummer.
[31] See the editorial comments in my republication of the work in *Testaments of Radicalism* (London,
1977), pp. 147–187. It should be added that Bezer transcends the limitations of his form with
great success.
[32] See especially Georg Lukacs, *History and Class Consciousness* (London, 1971 ed.), chs. 3 and 4.
For a useful clarification of the current debate see, Raymond Williams "Base and Superstructure in Marxist Cultural Theory", *New Left Review*, 82, (1973).

approach coincides with our understanding of the nature of autobiography at three levels. Firstly, where Dilthey pointed out that all men are autobiographers, so Gramsci affirmed that " ... everyone is a philosopher, though in his own way and unconsciously, since even in the slightest manifestation of any intellectual activity whatever, in 'language', there is contained a specific conception of the world".[33] Secondly, whereas the content of autobiography is determined by the way in which the writer understands the nature of the world in which he lives, how it has moulded his personality and how in turn he has succeeded in asserting his identity, so, for Gramsci, at the centre of class conflict is the question of whether, " ... the social group in question may indeed have its own conception of the world, even if only embryonic; a conception which manifests itself in action ... ", or whether, " ... this same group has, for reasons of submission and intellectual subordination, adopted a conception which is not its own but is borrowed from another group".[34] Finally, this conception, which is the organizing constituent of the realm of "superstructure" cannot be predicted from a study of the "base", but can only be identified by an examination of its actual occurrence in history. The insights the autobiographies give us into the formation and content of this conception may be partial and incomplete, but few other forms of source material will bring us closer to this crucial area of class consciousness.

(iii)

Although the scope of the separate autobiographies varies according to the career of the autobiographer and his intentions and success as a writer, the size and diversity of the genre as a whole ensures that, taken together, they can yield information on almost every aspect of working class history in this period. This study, however, does not set out to do justice to the full range of opportunities offered by the autobiographies, and still less does it attempt to find answers to all the questions posed by their contents. Indeed, one of the main purposes of this book is simply to introduce, or to re-introduce, historians to the extent and value of a form of source material which has been unjustly neglected. Many of the individual works demand full-length studies in their own right, and whatever analysis is attempted here, there will remain a need for a great deal more research both on this group of autobiographies and on those of other periods and social groups. Nonetheless, the way in which the preoccupations of the autobiographers intersect with those of contemporary historians of their society suggest a number of areas in which it might be fruitful to begin work.

The following chapter looks more closely at the intentions of the autobiographers and seeks to reach an understanding of why they were attracted to this form of self-expression. Before we evaluate all or any part of their conception of themselves, we must first of all consider how they saw themselves as autobiographers. The historian of the self, like any other historian, must organize his interpretation according to a set of implicit or explicit assumptions

---

[33] Antonio Gramsci, *Selections from the Prison Notebooks*, edited and translated by Quintin Hoare and Geoffrey Nowell Smith (London, 1971), p. 323.
[34] *Ibid.*, p. 327.

about the nature and significance of the past. By contrasting the approach of these writers to those in preceding and contemporary literary traditions of discussing the lives of working men and women, we hope to bring these assumptions to light. It is a matter not only of laying the foundation for the rest of the analysis, but of gaining some insights into the sense of the past within the working class as a whole. If we can establish how and why working men thought their past was important, we can know much more about how they regarded their present and their future.

Whatever occupations and pursuits the autobiographers followed, almost all were brought up as members of a family, and almost all either formed or attempted to form families as adults. The history of the working class family is the history of the private lives of private men and women, and there would appear to be much to be gained from discovering what the autobiographers have to say about their emotional experiences. There is a limit to the insights that can be gleaned from the most subtle analysis of census material, and whilst it is always necessary to place this qualitative evidence in the context of the statistical data now available, it should be possible to use the memories and observations of these writers to help tease out the skein of human relationships that is family life. Furthermore, it is here that the autobiographers are most likely to discuss the crucial connections between their material lives, their existence as workers, both as children and adults, and the other basic areas of experience to which they attach significance. When we come to what are often assumed to be the direct responses to their material conditions, such as various forms of political activity, these connections are usually either implicitly assumed, or treated at a very generalized level. In Part Two we shall be discussing the interrelationship between the emotional and material considerations of working class family life at three levels. Firstly, we shall examine the autobiographers' treatment of the major experiences of love and death, and how their responses were qualified by the physical problems of existence. Then we will look more closely at the meaning they attached to participation in their family economy; in particular at how they regarded the evolving balance between the role of the family as a unit for maximizing income and its role as an institution for nurturing its members. Finally, we will consider their changing ideas about the nature of childhood, and how these ideas were influenced by, and in turn informed, their response to both their family economy and the development of institutional education. In this way it is hoped to explore some of the links between three basic elements of the autobiographer's view of the world: work, family and the actual and potential development of the working man's personality.

Part Three is concerned with the uses of literature in the working class community. Together with the volumes of poetry, a number of which were prefaced by these autobiographies, the works we are studying constitute a large proportion of all the books written by the working class in this period. Wherever we look, we are likely to find the autobiographers employing books as a means of entertainment, or instruction, or intellectual exploration, or self-improvement, or monetary gain, or, finally, as a means of self-expression. There are again three chapters, the first of which, chapter six, confines itself to the practical problems of acquiring literature and examines the characteristics imparted to the pursuit of knowledge by the attempts which the readers made to overcome the difficulties which beset them. Chapter seven is a case study of communication: through a detailed comparative study of the meaning that was attached to a single phrase, "useful knowledge", we attempt to evaluate the success with which an advanced group of the middle class transmitted its view of the role of literature in the new industrial society to the sector of the working class that was potentially most receptive to it. At the centre of this debate was the question not only of the uses of literature, but of the nature and future of class relations in general. Chapter eight explores the dilemmas and achievements of those who attempted to use literature to comprehend, evaluate and respond to the world in which they lived. The final chapter returns to the autobiographies as a whole and makes a concluding assessment of their contribution to the history of the working class of this period.

Chapter Two

The Sense of the Past

Most autobiographies must begin their existence in the same way as James Bowd's brief memoir, with the author turning over the events of his life in a moment of quiet and realizing that it was possible to link the fragments of memory into a continuous narrative. The cabinet maker James Hopkinson described, for instance, the moment when, "As I lay in bed thinking over my past life, on the 2nd morning of the New Year 1888, I was struck with the number of incidents that came before my mind's eye, with a vividness and a power that perfectly astonished me. I appeared indeed to live over again the leading events of my life from my infancy upwards to the present time".[1] He found he enjoyed looking at his past self, and, as Thomas Mann has written, "Love of oneself . . . is the beginning of all autobiography".[2] When the Ettrick shepherd and poet, James Hogg, came to explain the presence of his *Memoir*, he simply stated that "I like to write about myself; in fact, there are few things which I like better; it is so delightful to call up old reminiscences",[3] and seventy-three years later the Cornish tin miner and poet, John Harris, was content to set Hogg's words at the head of his own autobiography.[4] Without a fascination with the self, there can be no autobiography, and the deeper the fascination, the more successful the resulting analysis. However, the act of composition and especially of publication is also conditioned by a number of factors specific to a particular period and culture. All men reminisce, but few write, and fewer still write books. This chapter looks at why these men and women set down their memoirs, and examines some of the implications of the proliferation of working class autobiographies during the nineteenth century.

(i)

The nineteenth-century working class autobiographers inherited two strongly contrasting traditions of self-expression. The first was the elaborate and

---

[1] Hopkinson, p. 3. He was born in 1819. See also another cabinet-maker, Henry Price, who described how he turned to writing his autobiography in the intervals between rocking the cradle of his great-granddaughter (Price, p. 17).

[2] "Goethe und Tolstoi" in *Leiden und Grösse der Meister* (Frankfurt am Main, 1957), p. 45, quoted in Derek Bowman's introduction to, Ulrich Bräker, *The Life Story and Real Adventures of the Poor Man of Toggenburg* (Edinburgh, 1970), p. 40.

[3] Hogg (1972), p. 3.

[4] Harris, p. 1. See also Thomas Cooper's admission: "I have written the book chiefly to please myself. And that, I suspect, is the chief reason why anybody writes an autobiography" (p. 2).

specialized genre of spiritual autobiography which developed during the religious and political crisis of the Civil War period and continued as a recognizable literary form throughout the eighteenth and into the nineteenth century.[5] The second was the diffuse and largely hidden tradition of oral story telling which had at various times surfaced in ballads and broadsides and was to continue alongside the growth of more formal means of recording past experience. Common to both traditions was the presence of ordinary men and women recounting their past, and in some combination their influence pervades the works we are studying.

In 1850 a former pauper, beggar and gaolbird, Josiah Basset, published *The Life of a Vagrant, or the Testimony of an Outcast to the Value and Truth of the Gospel*. "I come not from the seats of learning", he proclaimed, "neither can I boast of my ancestry—nor yet have I to record heroic deeds as a memorial of my own fame,—but from the outcasts of society, I come forth to raise a humble monument to my Saviour's praise."[6] For Basset, as for every one of the line of spiritual autobiographers which stretched back to the Chief of Sinners himself, John Bunyan, the experience of conversion was sufficient justification for the presentation of his life. The existence of the working class autobiographies was dependent upon a number of basic assumptions about the nature of human development which had emerged in the earlier form. All the spiritual autobiographies were rooted in a sense of passing time. St. Augustine's *Confessions*, written in 400 A.D. and separated by almost a thousand years from any known successor, may be regarded as the forerunner of autobiography in that it was the first to be based on the post-classical sense of the movement of time in the life of the individual.[7] For St. Augustine the presence of change and the memory of past events were fundamental to his comprehension and celebration of his existence:

> What, then, am I, my God? What is my nature? A life that is ever varying, full of change, and of immense power. The wide plains of my memory and its innumerable caverns and hollows are full beyond compute of countless things of all kinds. Material things are there by means of their images; knowledge is there of itself; emotions are there in the form of ideas or impressions of some kind, for the memory retains them even while the mind does not experience them, although whatever is in the memory must also be in the mind. My mind has the freedom of them all. I can glide from one to another. I can probe deep into them and never find the end of them. This is the power of memory! This is the great force of life in living man, mortal though he is![8]

The Confessions was not a portrait but a narrative of spiritual development, and this quality is a central characteristic of the religious autobiographies. The religious life of the individual was constantly changing, constantly in movement

---

[5] See Owen C. Watkins, *The Puritan Experience* (London, 1972), *passim*; Paul Delany, *British Autobiography in the Seventeenth Century* (London, 1969), pp. 6–104; John C. Morris, *Versions of the Self* (New York, 1966), chs. II and III.

[6] Basset, p. 1.

[7] For a discussion of St. Augustine's attitude towards memory and his treatment of time, see R. Pascal, op. cit., pp. 21–3; A. R. Burr, *The Autobiography. A Critical and Comparative Study* (London, 1909), pp. 212–213.

[8] St. Augustine, op. cit., p. 224.

between salvation and true grace on the one hand, spiritual fall and eternal damnation on the other; the relationship between the soul and the world in which it found itself could only be understood and communicated in the dimension of time.

Then, although the spiritual autobiographies were, by definition, primarily concerned with the religious life of the individual, they were a product of the assumption that the true state of man's soul could only be known through his experience of external reality. To discover God, man first had to discover himself. As the carpenter's son Thomas Tryon wrote, "The Knowledge of a Man's Self is a Key to the Knowledge of all other things",[9] and such self-knowledge was located in the individual's everyday life. The recollection and interpretation of past actions was both the preliminary and permanent duty of every Christian.

Finally, all the narratives were based upon the assertion of the right of every individual to determine his spiritual identity. All that stood between him and his maker was the Bible. This conviction was important both for the commitment to free speech which it embodied, and for the encouragement it gave to the most humble and non-literate of individuals to analyse and set down their own experiences. Throughout the seventeenth and eighteenth centuries the tradition of spiritual autobiography introduced an entirely new section of the population to the habits of analysis and expression of the continuing exchange between their spiritual life and their day-to-day activity. As the fire of the Puritan sects began to die down, the genre took on a new lease of life in the hands of John Wesley. As part of his attempt to create a literate but highly disciplined network of followers, he commenced publication in the *Arminian Magazine* of a long series of autobiographies of itinerant preachers.[10] Under his tight editorial control, greater emphasis was placed on the role of religious narrative as a guide and comfort for other travellers on the narrow and stony road to salvation, and they were widely read both at the time and later in the nineteenth century when the majority were republished in Thomas Jackson's *The Lives of Early Methodist Preachers*.[11]

In addition to the development of essential ideas about the justification of autobiography, the spiritual tradition continued to influence the working class autobiographies at two levels. In the first instance, the revival of the emphasis on the conversion experience in the Nonconformist churches generated a scattering of works throughout the nineteenth century which were patterned, with varying degrees of fidelity, on the older form. In some cases it was a matter of imitating specific works. There is, for instance, a section towards the end of Robert Butler's *Narrative of the Life and Travels of Serjeant Butler*, first published in 1823, where he gives, at great length, "a retrospect of all my death-like troubles in their order, as we would thereby discover more impressively the preserving care of our heavenly Father, 'to whom belong the issues from death' ", which is almost interchangeable with a passage in Bunyan's

---

[9] Thomas Tryon, *Some Memories of the Life of Mr Tho: Tryon* (1705), p. 51. Tryon was born in 1634.

[10] See Isabel Rivers, ' "Strangers and Pilgrims': Sources and Patterns of Methodist Narrative", in J. C. Hilson, M. M. B. Jones and J. R. Watson, eds., *Augustan Worlds* (Leicester, 1978) pp. 189–203.

[11] 3 vols., 1837–8.

Grace Abounding.[12] Butler's *Narrative* is a hybrid work; the spiritual analysis is tacked on at the end of a straightforward account of his military career, and the same is true of the contemporary autobiography of another ex-serviceman, David Love, who set out to write a serious account of his life of sin and redemption but kept drifting off into what was clearly the more congenial task of describing his adventures as a soldier and travelling bookseller.[13] Some writers, on the other hand, stuck to their last. The Halifax weaver William Hanson, for instance, born in 1803, and writing eighty years later, provides us with a narrative which in its interpretative structure could have been composed at any point in the preceding two centuries. He describes how, "I was led to realize my justification in Christ in the year 1824. And from that time have been enabled to say, that I have passed from death unto life and have been made a new creature in Christ Jesus; old things having passed away and all things become new",[14] and thereafter we are presented with the familiar combination of a precise spiritual self-analysis set in the context of a frustratingly vague account of his family and working life.

In the majority of autobiographies, however, the influence is to be found not in the structure but rather in the tone and general purpose of the works. The meaning of the past is now conceived in secular terms, but in spite of this fundamental change the autobiographers, on the whole, retained a desire to write respectable and above all morally improving pieces of work. The Baptist James Hopkinson is one of the very few to continue to hope that his autobiography might stimulate a conversion: "If these lines", he writes at the beginning of his memoir, "should be the means of pointing out to anyone some of the Shoals and Quicksands of life, I shall be pleased. But if they should be the means of leading *one* to seek after the salvation of their Soul and to love that saviour who gave himself a ransome for them, I shall be amply repaid."[15] In one sense there is no distance between this objective and that of a man like Christopher Thomson, a sometime shipwright, travelling actor, house-painter and self-improver, who dedicated his *Autobiography of an Artisan* "To the Artisans and Labourers of England, Fellow workers in the holy cause of Self Elevation", and defended its existence by asserting, "If he is asked, then why did he write at all? his answer is, with the hope of doing something to benefit his fellow-labourers! For he is not without hope, that with all his faults, by pointing out to his order the various stumbling-blocks that have stood in his way, and by showing how, and where, he fell down, or turned aside, or surmounted them, that the result of such experience may help them to repair the road to learning and domestic comfort".[16] In his career and in his interpretation of it, Thomson is in the mainstream of the autobiographies where Hopkinson is on the fringe, yet the connection between the two scarcely needs underlining. There is a common language, a common concern for moral values and a common didactic purpose in the presentation of the life of a working man.

---

[12] Butler, pp. 349–50; John Bunyan, *Grace Abounding to the Chief of Sinners* (Everyman edn., London, 1969), pp. 9–10.

[13] His autobiography was published in parts in 1823 and 1824. Although he properly dwells at length on his sins as a child, his conversion, which should have been the centrepiece of the book, is abruptly inserted in the midst of an unrelated narrative (p. 91).

[14] Hanson, p. 13.   [15] Hopkinson, p. 3. See also Teasdale, Preface.

[16] Thomson, pp. vi–vii. As the Frontispiece of his *Memoirs of a Working Man*, Thomas Carter wrote, "If I one Soul Improve, I have not lived in Vain".

The spiritual autobiographies can be seen as a response to a particular political, social and religious crisis in seventeenth century England, and their contents continued to reflect many of the developments and conflicts within the society in which the authors lived. Yet it is not surprising that those who have studied the genre have concentrated their attention on the religious content and passed over such information on secular topics as they contain, for this is exactly as the authors would wish their works to be read. The world in all its petty detail had a significance only insofar as it illustrated the changing relationship of the Soul to God. If man's alienation from his Maker was to be overcome, then the pleasures and achievements of his material existence must be set at naught. This was the message John Wesley wished his readers to draw from the autobiographies he published: "Let every Preacher read carefully over the 'Life of David Brainerd' ", he wrote, "Let us be followers of him, as he was of Christ, in absolute self-devotion, in total deadness to the world, and fervent love to God and man".[17] Each autobiographer described his past actions in order to condemn them. Much has rightly been made of the way in which the spirit of Bunyan informed the early radical ideology, but many of those who read his works were led to deny the significance of all participation in external events. "I had often read Bunyan's Pilgrim's Progress", recalled another transitional autobiographer, William Brown, "and considered myself like the apostate in the iron cage, and drew my own conclusions".[18] His conclusions led him to embrace God and reject his past; as he wrote when looking back at his record of sins and errors: "When I reflect on these things, my soul chooses strangling rather than life".[19]

It is at this point that the working class autobiographies part company with the tradition which had nurtured them. Whereas Josiah Basset wrote of his autobiography, " . . . it unfolds many things which are calculated to abase me yet . . . my design is not to exalt myself, but that great Redeemer who called me out of darkness into his marvellous light . . . ",[20] the majority of these men and women wrote to exalt the reality of both their own lives and the society in which they lived. We gain an indication of their approach from the titles under which their works were published. Of the twenty-five autobiographical works which appeared in the first major group from 1840 to 1860, almost all were characterized in terms of the specific occupational or political identity of their authors, using such terms as "Working Man", "Journeyman Printer", "Bookbinder", "Artisan", "Factory Cripple", "Handloom Weaver", "Beggar Boy", "Radical", "Publicist", "Temperance Lecturer", and "Chartist Rebel".[21] By contrast, of the 189 works contained in Watkins' bibliography of Puritan autobiographies published before 1725,[22] only four titles contain any

---

[17] John Wesley, *The Works of the Rev. John Wesley*, ed. T. Jackson (3rd edn., London, 1831), vol. VIII, p. 328, quoted in I. Rivers, art. cit., p. 196.

[18] Brown, p. 136. See the "Supplement" to the autobiography, pp. 130–153, in which he summarizes his religious experience.   [19] *Ibid*, p. 130.

[20] Basset, p. iii. See also William Bowcock's statement of autobiographical intent: " . . . my desire is to set forth the rich reigning Grace of God towards me the vilest of the vile" (p. v).

[21] Respectively, Thomas Carter, Alexander Somerville and the anonymous "Working Man" (ed. Maguire), (all "working men"), Charles Smith, Christopher Thomson, William Dodd, The Dundee Factory Boy, Willie Thom, James Burn, Samuel Bamford, J. C. Farn, Robert Lowery, and John Bezer.

[22] Watkins, op. cit., pp. 241–249.

reference to the social or occupational identity of the writer,[23] and in each case the description is incidental to the information which is intended to be conveyed by the title. Whatever the state of their private religious beliefs, they wrote because they knew, or were trying to know, themselves rather than God. Their moral development could only be understood in relation to the actual society in which they lived. This was certainly the case with Samuel Bamford who, having published a successful political autobiography, set out to write a sequel which would be simultaneously a history of the growth of his personality and a history of the society in which he had spent his childhood. He explained the presence of *Early Days* in its preface:

> That this was asked for by many whose judgement on such matters would be authoritative anywhere, he could readily shew, whilst his own reflections suggested that a book giving an account of the childhood and parental home,—the physical, moral and mental advancement or retrogression of his youth, with a truthful and ingenuous acknowledgement of errors, and of the circumstances which led to them, might also be rendered available for some good, in several ways; that it might be so composed as to form, in addition to his other works, a help to the history of the present, and in some degree of past times, and of the people especially who inhabit these parts of the island of Britain affording views of their manners, habitations, and employments; their traditions, superstitions, politics, factions, amusements, and occasional insurrections.[24]

The working class autobiographies were founded on a secular understanding of the meaning of the past. The relationship between the self and society was seen as a continuous dialectical process rather than one of ultimate transcendence. In this sense they may be described as objective in their treatment of the material world where the spiritual autobiographies were essentially subjective. Such an approach opened up the possibility of both writing real history, and making it.

(ii)

For obvious reasons, it is less easy to trace the outlines of the second major influence on working class autobiography, the tradition of oral reminiscence. The pervasive influence of urban publishers makes it dangerous to assume that the chap-books and broadsides which appear to be the most indigenous forms of the literature of the poor, are a direct reflection of their experience,[25] and the modern school of oral historians has yet to undertake a sustained study of what their respondents knew of their past, and how they had acquired such information. Within the autobiographies themselves, however, there are some clues as to the content of the tradition of story-telling in their communities which had laid the foundation of their knowledge of themselves and the world into which they had been born. At the outset there was the question of the

---

[23] Apart from those, that is, who identify themselves as ministers or preachers.
[24] Bamford, *Early Days*, pp. iii–iv.
[25] See Victor E. Neuburg, *Popular Literature* (Harmondsworth, 1977), pp. 103–5, 139–143; Leslie Shepherd, *The History of Street Literature* (Newton Abbot, 1973), pp. 53–77.

identity of their parents and the history of their own family. William Cameron, for instance, introduced himself thus: "I was born at a place called Plean, in the parish of St. Ninians, in the shire of Stirling, where my mother's forbears were residents for generations unknown, although I can only trace them to the days of Charles the Second".[26] Most of the autobiographers were content with a brief summary of the residential and occupational history of their family, but some allowed themselves the space to recount the more memorable achievements or personalities of their ancestors. Peter Taylor dwelt at length on the exploits of Gregor M'Gregor, the most notorious poacher and smuggler in the district, who courted and married Taylor's great aunt[27] and Samuel Bamford devoted the whole of his second chapter to "My Forefathers". Their values and exploits were of direct relevance to his own character: "Such were the men and women from whom I derived my being", he concluded, "The rebel blood, it would seem, after all, was the more impulsive; it got the ascendancy— and I was born a Radical".[28] Although he was now making a formal record of his family, he himself, like every other working man or woman of his generation, was dependent for his information upon tales passed down through the generations. His source for his account of his great-grandfather James Bamford, who flourished in the second decade of the eighteenth century, was, "According to what was handed down in our branch of his posterity",[29] and there is every reason to suppose that there existed a similarly rich and vital private oral history in those families which had not yet been disrupted, as Bamford's was to be, by the accelerating migration from the country to the towns.

There is no means of assessing the accuracy of all the tales that are told, and indeed it is clear that many were valued as much for the entertainment they afforded as for the information they contained. Alongside and frequently mixed up with the transmission of factual history was the retelling of stories and verse for the amusement or, occasionally, intimidation of a new generation. James Burn recalled that "In the course of my vagrant wanderings on the Borders, I had learned much of its legendary lore, and romantic history. Often while we occupied the chimney nook of a moorland farm-house in a winter's *nicht*, the daring deeds of some border reiver would be related in the broad vernacular of the district, or tales of ghosts, witches, and fairies, would go round until bed-time".[30] It is difficult to draw a firm distinction here between fact and fiction, and it must have been doubly so for the child as he listened to these stories. Equally they were not necessarily wholly oral in their derivation. Many of the tales started life in chap-books once read and half forgotten, and Alexander Somerville and Christopher Thomson both retained a vivid memory of garbled accounts of historical events told to them by old men who had once seen books about them.[31] What matters is that the child grew up in an environment full of story-telling, and that it was expected that in his turn he would

---

[26] Cameron, p. 9. John Thelwall, as was only to be expected of a Free Born Englishman, claimed that he was "descended from a Saxon family of that name, many centuries ago settled in the north of Wales". See also Wood, p. 2; Arch, p. 3.

[27] P. Taylor, pp. 14–18.   [28] Bamford, *Early Days*, p. 22.   [29] *Ibid*, p. 11.

[30] Burn (1978), p. 66. The practice was first described by one of the earliest observers of the habits of the common people, the Newcastle-upon-Tyne curate Henry Bourne, in his *Antiquitates Vulgares* (1725) ed. and revised by John Brand as *Observations on Popular Antiquities including the Whole of Mr Bourne's Antiquitates Vulgares* (1776). See 1890 edn., p. 113.

[31] Somerville, p. 39, Thomson, p. 35.

pass on such stories to his children. In later life most of the autobiographers, having made their own contact with books, became more concerned about the distinction between real and imaginary worlds, and many, including Burn, were very critical of the way in which superstitions had been presented as facts to frequently terrified children, but they retained a deep respect for the education and stimulus to their imagination that they had received from the story-tellers of their youth.

By translating the tradition of oral recollection into formal literature the autobiographers at once extended and transformed its function. Those who intended to write for their family or local community might simply be making permanent a set of memories increasingly threatened with dispersal as the twin forces of industrialization and urbanization disrupted older ways of life. But the truly private autobiography is even rarer than the truly private diary, and by writing down what had previously only been spoken, these men were almost inevitably reaching out into a wider audience. Even a man like Anthony Errington, whose manuscript autobiography can never have been intended for publication, started out with a dual intention; as he wrote at the head of his account, "The reason of my wrighting the particulars of my life and Trans-actions are to inform my famely and the world".[32] Errington's limited command of the techniques of writing make it particularly easy to hear the voice of the story-teller as he presents incidents from his childhood and his harsh and dangerous life as a waggonway-wright in the Northumbrian coalfield. Most of the memories have a central bearing on the formation of his character, but as with many of the autobiographies, a proportion are included for no better reason than that their recollection amuses the writer and may entertain the reader. We see him as a small boy in the company of two others coming across a red-hot cover of a pit fire, and in the way of small boys, seeing what would happen if they made pancakes out of their excrement;[33] we listen to his tale of a visit to Newcastle when he became mixed up in an attempt by a tailor to win a wager of twenty guineas by flinging a tailor's goose "from the half moon battery over the houses and shops to the Bridge End".[34] There are anecdotes about events, such as John Harris's fond recollection of the night his drunken Uncle George fell into his own cesspit,[35] or about characters, such as James Hawker's memory of John Newnham:

> One Dear Old Friend, the first man I ever spoke to in Oadby, and one I shall never Forget, was John Newnham who Lived Next Door. He was so courteous and quiet and would try to Please every one. He would sometimes, like other Men, enjoy himself, but I Have never seen him out of Temper. He was a very Tall Man, with no flesh on his bones, and he looked Hard as Nails. He was a Singer at the Church and out of Church he was a High Kicker. Very Few men was Better than him. I once se him knock a Pipe off the tall mantle shelf in the White Horse Tap Room.[36]

Such a feat might be retold in the pub, or to the narrator's children; in this

---

[32] Errington, p. 1. The wording and pagination of material quoted from Errington's account follow the excellent unpublished transcription of P. E. H. Hair. I am very grateful to Professor Hair for allowing me to make use of his labours, which ought to be published in full.
[33] *Ibid.*, p. 7. [34] *Ibid.*, pp. 19–20. A "tailor's goose" was a smoothing iron.
[35] Harris, p. 20. [36] Hawker, p. 96.

case it happens to be written down. The presence of these anecdotes lightens the task of the historian, but as they reached out from their family to the world, the autobiographers had a number of particular objectives in recounting the seemingly trivial details of their everyday life.

In the first instance the anecdotes were intended simply to convey the basic humanity of the working man. This was especially the case with the political autobiographers who were anxious to demonstrate that they were not the one-dimensional malcontents that they were so often portrayed to be. They too had been children, they too fell in and out of love, they too suffered all the petty pleasures and pains of daily life. The major part of William Lovett's life-story, for instance, consists of a dry and largely humourless narrative of successive meetings, publications, addresses and personality clashes, yet by sharp contrast the account of his childhood is full of relaxed anecdotes. We are told how a local woman triumphantly rescued her father from the clutches of a press-gang, and treated to a long account of how the politician-to-be was shut in the jaws of a rotting shark washed up on the beach of his native Newlyn.[37] Samuel Bamford, who had gained considerable national fame as a martyred politician by the time he came to write *Early Days*, submits us to lengthy stories of the ups and downs of adolescent love affairs, even to the extent of reprinting the texts of valentines which pass between himself and his beloved. Anticipating a possible reaction from his readership, he resolutely defended the inclusion of such trivia: "Let no one despise simple incidents like these. They are the rufflings which mark human existence—the joys and the anxieties—the lights and shadows—of which humble life is composed".[38] The public men wanted to demonstrate that they had private lives, the private men delighted in making their lives public. As the developing laws of political economy reduced their identity to a factor in a supply and demand equation, and as the press translated their protest movements into crude stereotypes, so they seized with avid pleasure the occasional opportunities to reconstitute the wholeness of their lives. "What I have already written", said John Bezer in the midst of his anonymous *Autobiography of One of the Chartist Rebels of 1848*, "and what I shall write for a little time, is not very interesting to the readers of this journal, I dare say—it is merely one of 'the simple annals of the poor'; but as John Nicholls has it 'It may perhaps, appear ridiculous to fill so much paper with babblings of one's self; but when a person who has never known any one interest themselves in him, who has existed as a *cipher* in society, is kindly asked to tell his own story, how he will gossip!' Exactly so".[39]

Already we see the details of daily existence being used as a currency of exchange between working class writers and middle class readers, and there was a group of autobiographers who attempted a much more coherent presentation of their culture. They realized that if some care were taken in selecting and fitting together the various anecdotes, it might be possible to compose a picture of the structure and mores of an entire section of society. They were encouraged in their ambition by the growth of two related literary genres. Works such as James Dawson Burn's *The Autobiography of a Beggar Boy*, or William Cameron's *Hawkie, The Autobiography of a Gangrel*,[40] or William Green's

---

[37] Lovett, ch. 1, *passim*.   [38] Bamford, *Early Days*, p. 174.   [39] Bezer (1977), p. 166.
[40] Although Cameron's autobiography was not published until 1888, it was written during the 1840s. Cameron himself died in 1851.

The Life and Adventures of a Cheap Jack, by One of the Fraternity, had their roots firmly in the longstanding tradition of thieves' tales and confessions from the gallows. In one form or another these had been part of the staple diet of popular literature since at least the seventeenth century, but in the 1830s and 1840s they took on a new lease of life in the flourishing genre of Newgate novels which now displayed a much more detailed interest in the lifestyle and background of the criminals they portrayed.[41] At one end of the market were the broadside confessions which achieved unprecedented sales in the 1830s,[42] and at the other were the industrial novels, and especially Charles Dickens, who began to show how it was possible to incorporate the lowest elements of society into the highest form of literature. Burn dedicated the first edition of his autobiography to Dickens,[43] and Green explained that he was provoked into writing by inaccuracies in Dickens' portrayal of cheap-jacks.[44]

The second genre was that which emerged from the 1830s onwards as a reaction to the growing urban crisis, otherwise known as the Condition of England Question. The middle class responded to the threats posed by the rapidly expanding towns and cities both by commissioning a series of official and quasi-official studies of the conditions of their inhabitants and by establishing a market for a profitable vein of low life reporting in which the more bizarre areas of urban society were visited by journalists and writers, mostly middle class but including some working class writers and autobiographers, particularly Thomas Cooper and Charles Manby Smith. The increasing body of fictional and would-be factual treatments of their community gave confidence to the autobiographers, but they were led to make their own contribution by two particular assumptions about the nature of their world. The first was a deep sense of the separateness of working class life, and a consequent conviction that only those who had grown up within it could know what it was really like. As Bill H. put it, " ... no one can judge of their equals so well as them that lives with them; and I believe I can give my opinion about the ways of a working man, better than a big top gentleman, that has never been brought up amongst them, and can't be so well acquainted with them, as I am, let him be as clever as he will".[45] Of the two gentlemen who might have been exempted from such censure, Engels was not published in England until 1894, and Mayhew does not seem to have been widely read by those whose experiences he recorded.[46] The attitudes of the autobiographers ranged from a quiet pride in the distinctiveness of their way of life to a fierce resentment, especially on the part of William Dodd and the Dundee Factory Boy who were attempting to portray the lives of factory children, at the misrepresentations of their conditions which were to be found in contemporary literature.[47] The second closely

[41] Keith Hollingsworth, *The Newgate Novel 1830–1847* (Detroit, 1963), pp. 14–17.

[42] R. D. Altick, *The English Common Reader* (Chicago, 1957), p. 288.

[43] "I hope, therefore," wrote Burn at the end of the Dedication, "that you will accept this expression of my regard as a small instalment of what I owe you". Emboldened by the success of the first edition of his book, Burn dedicated the second, published the following year, to the Queen.

[44] Green, p. 1. He particularly objected to the character of Dr Marigold.

[45] Bill H., p. 86.

[46] For the development and impact of Mayhew's approach as a social scientist, see E. P. Thompson and Eileen Yeo, eds., *The Unknown Mayhew* (Harmondsworth, 1973), pp. 56–109.

[47] Dodd explained that " ... having witnessed the efforts of some writers (who can know nothing

related assumption was that it was wholly misleading to regard working class life, even in its least respectable forms, merely as an increasingly atomistic and degenerate version of the model of society developed by the middle class. Rather, each section of the working class community possessed its own highly sophisticated structure and morality. "People who look down from the comfortable eminence of social life", wrote Burn, "will necessarily imagine that all class distinctions will cease to exist among the wandering *nomads* who live upon the charity of the well-disposed. In this they are very much mistaken."[48] Thus he attempted to recreate the intricate social organization of the beggars in the Borders and similar services were performed for the disappearing race of travelling players by Christopher Thomson and Harvey Teasdale, for the cheap-jacks by William Green, and for hawkers and street-singers by William Cameron and David Love. These writers both supported and exemplified Burn's further statement that, "I have found that nearly every class of people in the kingdom have a moral code of their own, and every body of men has its own standards of perfection".[49] Above all they were challenging the notion that morality necessarily diminished in proportion as poverty increased. As Christopher Thomson wrote of the actors with whom he had once worked, "The precarious profession, and, as some have it, the *idle* one, of the strolling player, is not, as many suppose it to be, all time mis-spent or thrown away. Oh no! even in its hungriest form, there is to him a morality in its privations".[50] In their different ways these men were weaving together a mass of often highly entertaining material to illustrate two fundamental statements, that the actions of any individual could only be understood within the context of the social structure in which he lived, and that the identity of that invariably complex structure was only fully knowable to its members.

If story-telling could be the basis for a contribution to the very young discipline of sociology,[51] it was also the point of departure for an attack on the established body of written history. There is a scattering of evidence within the autobiographies which suggests that the section of society which neither had access to nor featured in the formal record of its own times was accustomed to transmitting information about its collective past through oral communication. James Burn left us with a fascinating account of the role of the travelling newsvendor in his portrayal of his step-father, an alcoholic ex-soldier called William McNamee, who supported his growing family by peddling or by begging when drink or some other misfortune had consumed the family's capital assets. In either guise he could expect hospitality from the farms and cottages he visited in return for news of the Napoleonic Wars and of more distant historical events.[52] The rural communities had for centuries been dependent upon travelling tradesmen for their knowledge of events which had

of the factories by experience), to mislead the minds of the public upon a subject of so much importance, I feel it to be my duty to give to the world a fair and impartial account of the working of the factory system, as I have found it in twenty-five years of experience" (p. 5). Dodd was encouraged to write by Lord Ashley who employed him to gather material for his Factory Campaign but his efforts do not seem to have reached the Dundee Factory Boy who, nine years later, claimed that he too was writing because no books contained "a true picture of the condition, sufferings and struggles of a Factory Boy, painted by his own pen" (p. 2).
[48] Burn, p. 45. [49] *Ibid.*, p. 52. [50] Thomson, p. 269.
[51] See Philip Abrams, *The Origins of British Sociology 1834–1914* (Chicago, 1968), pp. 31–52.
[52] Burn, pp. 44, 65–6.

taken place outside their immediate experience.[53] Within the communities the past events to which their inhabitants attached significance were passed down from generation to generation. Benjamin Wilson began his *The Struggles of an Old Chartist* with an account of the impact upon his native village of Skircoat Green of the Peterloo Massacre, which took place five years before he was born. His information came from his uncle and his mother who together educated him in the traditions of his village, which, as Wilson noted in his first paragraph, "had long been noted for its Radicalism"[54], and thus provided him with a context for his subsequent career as a Chartist. In this sense both Burn and Wilson were following in the footsteps of their parents, but they chose to write rather than reminisce because in common with the rest of the auto-biographers they were no longer satisfied with the existing channels of communicating the past.

The adequacy of the oral tradition was called into question firstly by the rapidly accelerating pace of change in every aspect of working class life and the consequent danger that the poverty of the formal record would separate the generations altogether. This was the point of departure for Thomas Frost who wrote in the introduction to his account, "So rapid has been the progress of the nation in mental development and political enfranchisement that men not yet old may look upon the days of their boyhood as curiously and as wonderingly as their fathers did upon the age of the Tudors,"[55] and Charles Shaw, writing a few years later, angrily drew an even wider analogy: "This generation might be as far from the time of my youth as the age of the Sphinx. It seems to know as little, too, of the Forties in England as of the condition of Egypt in the time of the early Pharoahs".[56] The problem of comprehending the scale of change was exacerbated by the continuous reconstruction of the towns in which the majority of autobiographers lived. From decade to decade the physical points of reference and memory were transformed or obliterated. Writing in 1887, Benjamin Wilson had constantly to recreate the now vanished topography of the Halifax of his youth in order to make his account of Chartism comprehensible to his readership.[57] As the urban areas grew and were rebuilt so the labouring population moved out of long-established rural communities and into the towns where the autobiographers in common with the rest of their class experienced constant short-distance residential mobility. Those with memories lost contact with those for whom the memories might have some meaning. They had more to tell and less opportunity to tell it.

If the impersonal forces of change threatened to overwhelm the customary means of keeping the past alive, the particular concern of the autobiographers stemmed from the nature of their response to the transformation of their world. It is no accident that the founder of the prototype working class organization, Thomas Hardy, should also be a founder of the tradition of working class autobiography. The London Corresponding Society was an expression of a demand by working men to take part in the history of their nation and in turn

---

[53] For a description of the traditional role of beggars and pedlars as newsvendors see James Russell, "Reminiscences of Yarrow" in J. G. Fyfe, ed., *Scottish Diaries and Memoirs 1746–1843* (Stirling, 1942), p. 553; Martha Somerville, ed., *Personal Recollections from early life to old age of Mary Somerville* (London, 1873), p. 13; Thomas Somerville, *My Own Life and Times 1741–1814* (Edinburgh, 1952), p. 245.

[54] Wilson (1977), p. 195.   [55] Frost, *Forty Years*, p. 1.   [56] Shaw (1903), p. 205.

[57] See, for instance, his account of the arrival of the Plug Plot riots in Halifax on p. 200.

the fortunes of the Society and its provincial counterparts constituted the prologue to the working class's own history. Although Hardy did not complete his *Memoir* until he was on his deathbed in 1832, it was begun almost as soon as the life of the Society was finally snuffed out in April 1798.[58] The composition of his autobiography was both impelled and justified by Hardy's sense of his status as an historical figure: "As every man," he began the account, "whose actions, from whatever cause, have acquired publicity, is sure, in many things, to be misrepresented, such a man has an undoubted right, nay, it becomes his duty, to leave to posterity a true record of the real motives that influenced his conduct. The following Memoir, therefore, requires no apology, and none is offered".[59] His concern was not only to preserve the past but to connect it with the present. As he wrote in the Preface, "A correct history of such a Society, the present generation,—who are likely to reap the fruits of its labours— cannot but highly appreciate. . . ".[60] The efforts and sufferings of the pioneers of the 1790s would lose their meaning if the post-war radicals had no knowledge of them. History could not be made unless it was also recorded.

Despite Hardy's concern, and the more industrious though less conclusive labours of his L.C.S. comrade Francis Place, the first working men to appear in print as self-conscious participants in the nation's history were not radical politicians,[61] but soldiers and sailors who had fought in the Napoleonic Wars. At the height of the struggle, about one man in every ten of military age in Great Britain and Ireland was serving in the army, navy or regular militia, and it has been calculated that loss of life among servicemen was proportionately higher between 1794 and 1815 than between 1914 and 1918.[62] Moreover, the British Government's determination to use the war not only to maintain the European balance of power but to crush domestic discontent by means of officially inspired propaganda and legal repression transformed the prolonged conflict into the first people's war. If radicalism was treason, then enlistment was the highest form of patriotism, and when peace was finally made, the returning soldiers and sailors found a new market for their reminiscences.[63] In the face of a re-born and more vigorous movement of popular radicalism, the middle class public was only too anxious to read accounts of loyal working men risking their lives to defend their country against the heirs of the French Revolution. Most of the memoirs are confined to their authors' military

---

[58] For the convoluted history of the composition and publication of the autobiography, see David Vincent, *Testaments of Radicalism*, pp. 27–9.

[59] Hardy (1977), p. 37.

[60] *Ibid.*, p. 35. Hardy still had hopes that Francis Place, who was collecting documents and eye-witness accounts, would eventually publish a proper history of the period. His account was only intended as a necessarily incomplete contribution.

[61] With the single exception of John Thelwall's autobiographical preface to his *Poems Chiefly Written in Retirement*, published in 1801. The other radical of the period to write an autobiography was John Binns, who emigrated to America and published his *Recollections* in Philadelphia in 1854.

[62] Clive Emsley, *British Society and the French Wars 1793–1815* (London, 1979), pp. 133, 150, 169. If volunteers and local militia are added to the regulars, the proportion of men under arms rises to one in six.

[63] See W. H. Fitchett, ed., *Wellington's Men, Some Soldier Autobiographies* (London, 1900); C. Emsley, op. cit., pp. 172–3. Many regiments in this period started their own schools for privates and N.C.O.s who wanted to learn to read and write.

careers,[64] but a handful are complete life-histories and contain valuable information on the circumstances and outlook of early nineteenth century working men.[65]

The great majority of ex-servicemen, however, were closer in experience to Burn's step-father William McNamee, with no trade, little prospect of secure employment and only members of their own community as occasional audiences for their tales of privation and sacrifice. They had come to believe that they had played a significant part in their nation's victory, yet their only reward was poverty and the continued repression of any organizations they attempted to form. Their resentment fuelled the rising tide of political unrest which culminated in the Reform Bill Crisis and then re-emerged as Chartism, but now their attempts to intervene in the nation's history took place off the record. Taken together, the autobiographers participated in and left some account of almost every radical movement in the first half of the nineteenth century. They wrote from a variety of perspectives but common to all was the fear that their political past was in danger of obliteration. As early as 1801 we find Hardy's co-defendant in the 1794 Treason Trials, John Thelwall, writing a brief account of his life in order to combat what he described as his "intellectual proscription"[66] and when the events of the decade began to enter the history books, Hardy wrote bitterly that "We learn but little from modern histories, for each historian accommodates the facts to his ideas, almost in the same manner as a cook sauces up his dishes to his palate".[67] Little had changed by the time Thomas Frost came to complain in 1880 that Chartism " . . . has been persistently misrepresented by successive writers and therefore very imperfectly and erroneously understood . . . ",[68] and at the end of the century the veteran freethinker, George Holyoake, mourned with almost complete justification that, "The Chartists have made as much noise in the world as they know how—yet to the generation of today they are ambiguous, they have had no historian".[69]

The autobiographers' anxiety was all the more acute as they recognized that it was no longer possible to sustain a satisfactory alternative history through the processes of oral transmission. Even without the obstacles created by the lack of continuity in the working class communities there was the basic problem that from its outset the radical movement had been increasingly dependent on the written word to define and realize its objectives. The societies of the 1790s had been founded upon a text, Paine's *Rights of Man*, and the paper war which commenced when the Government replied by sponsoring the Reeves' Asso-

---

[64] See, *inter alia*, John Green, *Vicissitudes of a Soldier's Life* (London, 1827); "G. B.", *Narrative of a Private Soldier, Written by Himself* (Glasgow, 1829); Anon, *Life on Board a Man-of-War, by a British Seaman* (Glasgow, 1829).

[65] Of the autobiographies in the main group we are studying, those of Brown, Butler, Donaldson, Downing, Lawrence, Love, Martin, Mayett and Miller are by Napoleonic War veterans. Chatterton, McEwan and Somerville spent periods in the army later in the century.

[66] Thelwall, p. xliv.

[67] *Add. MS.* 27818, f.270. Letter to the *Monthly Magazine*, 10 Aug. 1825. His comments were provoked by John Bayley's *The History and Antiquities of the Tower of London with Memoirs of Royal and distinguished persons* (London 1821, 25).

[68] Frost, *Forty Years*, pp. 97.

[69] G. J. Holyoake, *Bygones Worth Remembering* (London, 1905), vol. 1, p. 84. See also Aitken, 9 Oct., p. 3; John Saville, "R. G. Gammage and the Chartist Movement", introduction to 1969 reprint of R. G. Gammage, *The History of the Chartist Movement* (1894).

ciations[70] was but a foretaste of the use both sides were to make of print in the developing class conflict. The mass of broadsides, addresses, letters, pamphlets, newspapers and occasional books were the very fabric of political activity, and it was wholly impossible to preserve or transmit them through spoken reminiscence. This was why Francis Place spent so many years building up his invaluable archive, and why both Hardy and the man who inherited much of his political legacy, William Lovett, devoted so much of their memoirs to reprinting the papers of the movements to which they had belonged. In Lovett's case in particular, their inclusion almost ruined the work as a personal narrative, but as he explained in the preface, they contained so much of the truth about the associations with which he was concerned, and the contemporary press and subsequent histories so little, that he had to reprint them if future historians were to have any reliable material upon which to work.[71]

The autobiographies themselves are evidence of both the existence and the inadequacy of the oral history of the working class. Many of the accounts had begun their existence as spoken reminiscences. Lovett acknowledged that, "The commencement of the following pages I must attribute to the solicitations of some of my radical friends, who, when I had been talking of some of the events of my life, and of the different associations I have been connected with, and of the various political struggles in which I have been engaged, have urged me to write the facts down . . .".[72] Long sections of Hardy's *Memoir* had been read out to two of the meetings to commemorate the acquittal of the defendants of 1794 which were held annually for at least forty years; Watson's account is a transcript of a speech he gave to a Public Tea in honour of his retirement as a radical publisher in 1854; John Snowden entered print when two of his many local speeches on past radicalism were published in the *Halifax Courier*, and another Halifax autobiographer Benjamin Wilson, finally collapsed and died while publicly reminiscing about the late 1830s.[73] Through old men talking to young men, through anniversary dinners and public teas, through funeral processions and orations, a history survived. The existence of a corporate memory was demonstrated by the Halifax historian Frank Peel, who succeeded in writing a lively and accurate history of the Luddites and Chartists by interviewing survivors of the two movements in the late 1870s.[74] However, his example was not imitated; the documents were largely dispersed or lost, and the survivors finally died, although the number still living in the 1880s is evidence of the extent to which Chartism was a young man's movement. All that was left was Gammage's history, which was written too early, and about thirty autobiographies, which yield many insights into the various events but which cannot stand, either individually or collectively for the histories which needed to be written.

Instead they may be read as fragmentary evidence of what was known about the past, of how that knowledge survived, and above all, of how working men regarded the significance of the past. They were a product of a conviction that it was time working men entered history. "All things have a history" wrote the

[70] E. P. Thompson, *The Making of the English Working Class* (Harmondsworth, 1968), pp. 116, 122, 126.
[71] Lovett, p. iv. See also Farish, *Autobiography*, p. 40.   [72] *Ibid.*, p. iii.
[73] See David Vincent, *Testaments of Radicalism* (London, 1977), pp. 27, 105, 191.
[74] Frank Peel, *The Risings of Luddites, Chartists and Plug Drawers* (1st edn., Heckmondwike, 1880).

Ashton-under-Lyne Chartist William Aitken, "and the struggles of many of
the working men of this country, if placed on paper, would read as well, and be
as interesting, as the lives of many a coronetted Lord."[75] They were a product
of a deep sense of the continuity of the past. Most of the writers looked back
over periods which to modern historians appear to encompass major dis-
junctions in the nature of political activity, yet the autobiographers were
concerned to emphasize the connections between the separate elements of the
history they had seen and attempted to make. They had available to them the
still active tradition of viewing life as a pattern of major change, of always
looking for the moment when the individual found the true path and rejected
the misguided and sinful ways of his youth. In his fictional autobiography of
Alton Locke, Kingsley had demonstrated how the model might be used to
explain a rejection of Chartism, but in this respect, if in no other, his novel
stands against the majority of genuine memoirs. The autobiographers were
aware of variety and change, but the separate elements were bound together
partly by the fact that they all represented some form of active response to
the world in which they lived, and partly by the fact that despite all the
defeats and side-turnings, there did appear to be a single tradition of a struggle
for political freedom which had begun with Paine and Hardy in the 1790s
and was still alive as some of the surviving Chartists welcomed the passing of
the Third Reform Bill. The outlook was summarised in John Snowden's
words as he looked back to the day when he joined the Chartist movement:
" . . . he became a member of the association, and from that day to the present
had remained a member of some association or other which had for its object
the enfranchisement of the whole people of this country in accordance with the
ancient constitution of England".[76] The past was still alive, and they wrote in
order to connect it with the future. Lovett composed his autobiography, "so
that the working classes of a future day may know something of the early
struggles of some of those who contended for the political rights they may be
then enjoying . . .".[77] The next generation needed information about the past,
and in particular they needed the example of the lives of those who had devoted
themselves to the long struggle. As Edward Rymer wrote at the beginning of
his *The Martyrdom of the Mine*:

> My objects are to show why every miner is bound by duty and necessity to
> form part of the trades union organisation now existing in every mining
> district over the whole kingdom this side of the Irish Channel, and to give
> advice and encouragement to those who may volunteer, as I have done for
> forty years, to serve actively and honestly in the cause of humanity, and to
> shirk no duty, however unpleasant, difficult or dangerous, in the general
> emancipation of labour.[78]

(iii)

The first public recognition of the emergence of a new voice in the tradition
of autobiography came in the *Quarterly Review* of 28 December 1826. Comment-

---

[75] Aitken, 18 Sept., p. 3. See also Thomson, p. 2.
[76] Snowden, col. 1. See also Wilson, p. 210.   [77] Lovett, p. iii.   [78] Rymer, p. 1.

ing upon the recent publication of ten memoirs of men whose careers ranged from the insignificant to the infamous, it complained bitterly that

> The classics of the *papier mâché* age of our drama have taken up the salutary belief that England expects every driveller to do his Memorabilia. Modern primer-makers must needs leave *confessions* behind them, as if they were so many Rousseaus. Our weakest mob-orators think it a hard case if they cannot spout to posterity. Cabin-boys and drummers are busy with their commentaries *de bello Gallico;* the John Gilpins of "the nineteenth century" are the historians of their own *anabases*, and, thanks to "the march of intellect", we are already rich in the autobiography of pickpockets.[79]

This long and throughly entertaining review is remarkable both for a perceptive description of the new literary genre and a largely unrepresentative response to its implications. It is not only that the memorabilia of cabin boys and drummers were being received, as we have seen, with growing enthusiasm, but that the general principle of men, and sometimes women, in obscure circumstances entering the realm of polite literature was long established and was being increasingly encouraged.

The first working man to make a serious impact upon the literary establishment was the Wiltshire agricultural labourer Stephen Duck. Born in 1705 in the village of Charlton in Wiltshire, his poetry eventually reached the notice of no less a figure than the Reverend Joseph Spence, a close friend of Pope and successively professor of poetry and history at Oxford University. Spence set himself the task of increasing the audience for Duck's poems and rescuing their author from his life of toil. Duck found himself translated in turn into a Yeoman of the Guard, Keeper of the Queen's Library at Richmond, and an ordained Anglican minister, before his mind gave out in 1754 and he committed suicide by drowning himself in the Thames at Reading, a fate, oddly enough, that was later to befall his patron.

As part of his campaign, Spence published in 1731, "A Full and Authentick Account of Stephen Duck",[80] which remained the major source of information on his life throughout the subsequent biographies. It paints a picture of an intelligent son of a poor and illiterate working man who received a smattering of education at a Charity School and who then proceeded to educate himself in a way which bore a remarkable similarity to the nineteenth century autodidacts. As with Cooper and Lovett and Somerville, he had to carry his books to work, hurrying through his labours in order to snatch brief opportunities for reading, and in so doing, often taking risks with his health: "When he did so, his method was to labour harder than any Body else, that he might get Half an Hour to read a *Spectator* without Injuring his Master. By this means he used to set down all over Sweat and Heat, and has several times caught colds by it".[81] Almost all the nineteenth century autobiographers pursued knowledge in the company of a "learned neighbour", normally a fellow working man with

---

[79] *Quarterly Review*, vol. XXXV, 28 Dec. 1826, p. 149. The unsigned article was written by the journal's editor, James Lockhart.

[80] *A Full and Authentick Account of Stephen Duck, the Wiltshire Poet. Of his Education; his Methods of Improving himself; how he first engag'd in Poetry; and his great Care in writing* (London, 1731).

[81] *Ibid.*, p. 11. For the influence of the *Spectator*, see Q.D. Leavis, *Fiction and the Reading Public* (London, 1932), pp. 121–6.

similar inclinations who was perhaps a little further along the road; so did Duck, and whilst it is not essential to the purpose of this work to establish the origin of the phrase "mutual improvement" it is doubtful whether we shall find an earlier reference than the one contained in Spence's description of the value of his friendship:

> He said, He had one Dear Friend, that he mention'd with uncommon Affection. They used to Talk and Read together, when they cou'd steal a little Time for it. I think too, they sometimes studied their Arithmetick together. This Friend had been in a Service at *London* for two or three Years: He had there learn'd a little which were good Books to read. He had purchased some, and *Stephen* had always the use of his little Library; which by the time possibly may be encreas'd to two or three Dozen of Books. This Friend knew no more out of English than *Stephen*: but by talking together they mutually improv'd each other.[82]

The small library which Duck painfully collected was very similar in its scope and content to those of his successors; all that was missing were the works of the Romantic poets and the occasional presence of the theological and political classics of the French Enlightenment and Tom Paine. For Spence, Duck's self-improvement was an integral component of his identity, his "longing after Knowledge" sprang from the same source as his later writings.

To judge from the evidence of the spiritual autobiographies, Duck was participating in an already established tradition of labouring men embarking upon the pursuit of knowledge.[83] There was a sufficient availability of reading matter, a sufficient level of literacy, which even for agricultural labourers in this period was as high as 30 per cent[84], and, particularly with the development of the Charity School system from which Duck himself benefited,[85] a sufficient access to elementary education to ensure that even in rural communities it would be possible to find two or three "uneducated" men who were lovers of books. It was a tradition which nurtured Duck—who was not the only literate man even in his small village—and a succession of peasant poets throughout the eighteenth century.[86] The self-improving working men of the industrial society, who made such a vital contribution to the developing working class culture, were not quite the innovators that they appeared both to themselves and to many subsequent historians. At best they were elaborating and finding new meaning in a pattern of behaviour which stretched back for at least two centuries.

One man who was both aware of a tradition and attempted to foster it was Robert Southey, Poet Laureate since 1813. In his *Lives and Works of the Uneducated Poets*, which first appeared in 1831 as a lengthy preface to the poetry of a new discovery, the servant John Jones, he attempted a biographical summary of a line of poets stretching back to Duck. However, although he was heavily dependent upon the writings of the various patrons of the poets he

---

[82] *Ibid.*, pp. 7–8.
[83] See Margaret Spufford, "First steps in literacy; the reading and writing experiences of the humblest seventeenth century spiritual autobiographies", *Social History*, vol. 4, no. 3, Oct. 1979, pp. 407–435.
[84] Lawrence Stone, art. cit., pp. 102–112.
[85] See M. G. Jones, *The Charity School Movement* (Cambridge, 1938).
[86] See Rayner Unwin, *The Rural Muse* (London, 1954), pp.47–109.

discussed, his essay partially obscured a very significant change which had been taking place in the way in which such men were regarded and treated by the literary establishment. It is possible for the modern critic to see Duck, at least at the outset of his career, as a representative of his culture, but nothing could have been further from the mind of his most influential patron. A constant theme of the *Full and Authentick Account* is the extent to which Duck's persona as the "uneducated poet" was totally dependent upon his contact with the works of the literary figures with whom Spence was professionally concerned. Without Milton and the *Spectator* contributors in particular, Duck would scarcely have been able to talk, let alone write poetry:

> Indeed it seems plain to me, that he has got English just as we get Latin. Most of his language in Conversation, as well as in his Poems, is acquir'd by reading. The Talk he generally met with has been so far from helping him to the manner in which he speaks, that it must have put him even to the difficulty of forgetting his Premier–Language. You see this evidently in conversing with him. His common Talk is made up of the good Stile, with a mixture of the Rustick: tho' the latter is but very small in proportion to the former.[87]

The influence of his literary mentors and various patrons extended not only to his speech and the style of his poetry, but even, Spence claimed, to the selection of the subject matter of Duck's first major poem, *The Thresher's Labour*, which achieved a standard he never succeeded in attaining in later works.[88] Such a topic might have seemed a natural choice for a "peasant poet", but, as Spence explained: "The Composition which was next in order is that on his own *Labours*: That Subject was given him by one of those who first encourag'd his Taste for Poetry: and after this was finish'd and applauded, he was employ'd from the same quarter in his *Shunammite*".[89] Rather than representing an alternative and independent cultural tradition, Duck was paraded as confirmation of the vitality and validity of the metropolitan arcadian culture of Pope and Dryden. To be sure he retained just a little of "the Rustick", and the "very good natural sense" which gave his work its own character, but he was otherwise removed, artistically and later physically, from the culture of his fellow agricultural labourers.

A further reason for his detachment was the conviction held by his patrons that Duck possessed the quality which placed him on a separate level from mere versifiers, the quality of Genius. Spence was not alone in recognizing this: "I need not tell you that the QUEEN, who is always fond of Merit, wherever She finds it, upon seeing his Pieces, and the Genius that appear'd thorough them, express'd a particular Satisfaction in such an Opportunity of doing Good. Her Majesty resolv'd immediately to take him out of his Obscurity, and the Difficulties he had labour'd under".[90] The concept of Genius was an essential component of literary criticism throughout the period.[91] It was a mystical, and at one time explicitly religious endowment, the possession of

---

[87] Spence, op. cit., pp. 10–11.
[88] For a discussion of Duck's poetry, see Raymond Williams, *The Country and the City* (London, 1973), pp. 88–90.
[89] Spence, op. cit., p. 13.   [90] *Ibid.*, p. 14.
[91] See M. H. Abrams, *The Mirror and the Lamp* (New York, 1958), pp. 184–225.

which elevated the poet to the ranks of the timeless tradition of Homer, the Old Testament poets and Shakespeare. It could not be acquired by labour, however great, although Addison isolated two species, of which the lesser, evidently possessed by Duck, required study if it was to find its full expression. The conception was a useful critical weapon for assaulting Locke's empiricist psychology, and as such was incorporated into the Romantic tradition as an integral part of the commitment to natural spontaneity which was developed as a defence against the increasingly mechanical ethos of the industrializing society of the early nineteenth century.[92] By asserting that Duck had been thus endowed, his patrons set the seal on his isolation from the culture in which he had grown up. Genius transcended time and place, and consequently the intellectual development of the poet could not be explained in the context of his particular social background. Conversely the emergence of Duck and his successors need not in any way alter the contemporary perceptions of the character and capabilities of the labouring population as a whole.

Yet despite the continuing presence of the concept of Genius in late eighteenth and early nineteenth century literary criticism, there was to be a distinct change in attitude towards the peasant poets. Hannah More's multifarious activities in the field of the literacy of the lower orders encompassed the support of Ann Yearsley, a poor "milkwoman" from her home town of Bristol. In many respects her activities and attitudes conformed to the established tradition. She collected a list of wealthy and titled patrons, and in her prefatory letter to the poems, earnestly discussed the Genius of her discovery, bringing in Shakespeare and Chatterton as points of reference.[93] But her criteria for assessing the value of Ann Yearsley's poetry were in direct contrast to those of Spence: "If her epithets are now and then bold and vehement, they are striking and original; and I should be sorry to see the wild vigour of her rustic muse polished into elegance, or laboured into correctness".[94] Furthermore, she was extremely anxious lest her activities should corrupt the milkwoman's personality: "Pressing as her distresses are, if I did not think her heart was rightly turned, I should be afraid of proposing such a measure, lest it should unsettle the sobriety of her mind, and, by exciting her vanity, indispose her for the laborious employments of her humble condition; but it would be cruel to imagine that we cannot mend her fortune without impairing her virtue".[95] Whilst her concern that education might disrupt the passivity of the poor reflected the preoccupations of many late eighteenth and early nineteenth century observers, her emphasis on the relevance of Ann Yearsley's cultural background to her creative identity marked an important development.

In his *Lives and Works*, Southey both consolidated the tradition and took it one step further. He was concerned above all to reject the convention of literary criticism which interpreted all writing by means of an abstract notion of excellence, and ignored everything which failed to achieve the preconceived standard. While he recognized that most of the "uneducated poets" possessed only limited talent, he defended their right to be considered as genuine poets, despite their shortcomings:

[92] See Raymond Williams, *Culture and Society* (Harmondsworth, 1963), pp. 56–64.
[93] Hannah More, "A Prefatory Letter to Mrs Montague", in Ann Yearsley, *Poems on Several Occasions* (London, 1785).
[94] Hannah More, op. cit., p. vii.   [95] *Ibid.*, p. xi.

But when we are told that the thresher, the milkwoman, and the tobacco-pipe maker did not deserve the patronage they found,—when it is laid down as a maxim of philosophical criticism that poetry ought never to be encouraged unless it is excellent in its kind,—that it is an art in which inferior execution is not to be tolerated, —a luxury, and must therefore be rejected unless it is of the very best,—such reasoning may be addressed with success to cockered and sickly intellects but it will never impose upon a healthy understanding, a generous spirit, or a good heart.[96]

Moreover, in attempting to rescue the reputation of these men and women he was at the same time hoping to encourage working class poets in his own society. As Poet Laureate he saw it as his duty to foster the writing of poetry for the simple reason that the act of making verse, whatever its quality, deepened the feeling of the individual: " . . . if he is a good and amiable man," he wrote, "he will be both the better and the happier for writing verses. 'Poetry', says Landor, 'opens many sources of tenderness, that lie for ever in the rock without it' ''.[97] His essay was widely read, and stood as both a symptom of and a contribution to the spread of a more relaxed and enthusiastic approach to literary activity amongst the "uneducated" members of society.[98]

By the time the *Quarterly Review* delivered its jeremiad, the expanding middle class reading public which it correctly identified as the market for the works it was reviewing,[99] was looking with increasing favour on attempts by labouring men to depict their surroundings. If the poetry of an uneducated man was to be valued for its reflection of the circumstances of his life, it was but a short step to demand that the author added a direct account of the growth of his personality. As part of his presentation of John Jones, Southey commissioned from his protégé, *Some Account of the Writer, written by himself*, and this autobiography could be added to those written earlier in the century by two genuinely talented rural poets, James Hogg and John Clare.[100] On the surface at least, patrons and poets were in perfect accord; on the one side there was a thirst for information which would validate the poetry of a new discovery, on the other was a growing confidence in the details of their everyday life, a feeling expressed by John Clare in one of his two manuscript autobiographies:

As to the humble situation I have filled in life it needs no apology for all tastes are not alike they do not all love to climb the Alps but many content themselves with wandering in the valleys—while some stand to gaze on the sun to watch the flight of the towering eagle—others not less delighted look down upon the meadow grass to follow the fluttering of the butterflye in

[96] Southey, op. cit., p. 164. The references are to Stephen Duck, Ann Yearsley and John Frederick Bryant.
[97] *Ibid.*, p. 165.
[98] Martha Vicinus concludes, however, that most working class poets received "Distant sympathy rather than distinct encouragement". See *The Industrial Muse* (London, 1974), p. 168.
[99] *Quarterly Review*, art. cit., p. 164.
[100] Hogg's "Memoir of the Author's Life" was first published as the introduction to *The Mountain Bard* in 1807, and revised editions appeared in 1821 and 1832. Clare's two autobiographies were written in 1821 and 1824 at the request of his patrons, but were not published until this century. There was also a brief autobiographical letter by the shoemaker poet Joseph Blacket, which was published together with some of his poetry and other biographical information in 1809.

such a latitude I write not without hope of leaving some pleasure for my readers on the humble pages I have here written.[101]

The line of rural muses continued throughout the nineteenth century, and from the 1840s the voices of poets from the new industrial centres began to reach a wider audience.[102] At first it appeared that the much greater availability of literature in the growing towns merely compounded the threat they posed to the existing established order, but gradually the hope dawned that working men reading and occasionally writing respectable literature might be a means of mediating the increasingly bitter class relations. Through their introduction to the great literary classics the readers would embrace values which transcended their embattled class culture, and by writing about their lives and, in particular, their literary pursuits, an important line of communication would be opened up between the more advanced sections of both classes. The concern now was to stress the ordinariness of the literate working man, to see him in the context of his own culture and to hope that he represented a significant aspect of it. The point was made by Charles Knight, one of the leading publishers of cheap but improving literature, in his preface to the autobiography of the Colchester and London tailor, Thomas Carter, which first appeared in the *Penny Magazine* of 11 May 1844: "The peculiar interest of these 'Memoirs of a Working Man' is in the view which they present of the mode in which the mind of the writer has been formed, under the most adverse circumstances. He makes no claim to any extraordinary powers of understanding; he displays no unwonted energies. He is neither the 'village Hampden', nor the 'mute inglorious Milton', whose 'destiny obscure' was determined by his lot in life".[103] The work was published anonymously, and Carter had written only a little poetry, and that of unusually poor quality. He merited the attention of the middle class reading public for no other reason than he was a working man in love with books.[104] By the time the compositor Charles Manby Smith came to write his *Working Man's Way in the World* a few years later, the battle for public acceptance appeared to be over: "The time has been", he wrote, "when an apology would have been thought necessary for obtruding on the notice of the public these passages in the life of a Working Man: that time is however past, and there are now an abundance of precedents to keep any man in countenance who, for reasons good, bad or indifferent, may choose to draw aside the veil from his personal history, and publish it to the world".[105]

As the new middle class began to exert a formative influence on the book trade, the long-established tradition of encouraging certain forms of literary self-expression among the lower orders, began to take on a new dimension

---

[101] Clare, *Autobiography*, p. 11.   [102] See M. Vicinus, op. cit., pp. 140–179.

[103] Carter, *Memoirs*, pp. vii–viii. The *Penny Magazine* had been founded by the Society for the Diffusion of Useful Knowledge, whose chief publisher was Charles Knight. See below, chapter seven.

[104] The first volume of his autobiography contains detailed references to 108 different books or sets of books to which he had gained access and read.

[105] C. M. Smith, p. v. His autobiography was begun at the instigation of the proprietor of *Taits' Magazine*. In the same vein, Christopher Thomson confidently inscribed the words of Carlyle on his title page: "The common doings and interests of men are boundless in significance; for even the poorest aspect of nature, especially of living nature, is a type and a manifestation of the invisible spirit that works in nature".

and a new meaning. After some hesitation, the market for accounts of the "real life" of the working class rapidly expanded. A respectable readership which had neither the desire nor the courage physically to enter the homes and the neighbourhoods of the urban working class, eagerly seized the opportunity of gaining access through the safer and cleaner medium of the printed word. Some sub-sections of the new genre of working class autobiography, such as the usually fictitious memoirs of condemned criminals, might be catering for the lowest levels of middle class taste, but others, particularly the autobiographies of poets and self-educators stood in direct line of succession to the literary labours of Stephen Duck. The *Quarterly Review* might wrinkle its well-bred nose at the vulgarization of what it considered to be the high art-form of autobiography, but the majority of the middle class readers saw in the invasion a means of assuaging both their curiosity and their fears.

(iv)

The emergence of the working class autobiographies represented and in turn encouraged a major change in the way in which working men viewed their past. They were founded upon the secularization of a long-established tradition of spiritual autobiography and the translation into formal literature of elements of a widespread pattern of oral reminiscence. Although the influence of their antecedents can be traced throughout the autobiographies, their contents were a product of a new and much more self-confident attitude towards the development of the working man's personality. The accounts were based on a proud assertion of the significance of the actions and experiences of a section of society whose rare excursions into the autobiographical form had always been in the form of penitents rejecting the reality of all their daily transactions. The working class autobiographers were committed to the double task of analysing both their own past and that of the working class community. Only by understanding himself could the working man understand the world in which he lived, and conversely, true self-knowledge was impossible without a comprehension of the structure and historical identity of the section of society in which the personality was formed. The search for such knowledge was both a precondition and a result of the growth of class consciousness. The more working men became aware of the historical significance of their own actions, the greater was the necessity and the possibility of defining and controlling their historical identity. As Gramsci has written, the starting point for a genuinely critical conception of the world, "is the consciousness of what one really is, and is 'knowing thyself' as a product of the historical process to date which has deposited in you an infinity of traces, without leaving an inventory".[106] The desire to make such an inventory was the point of departure for all the working class autobiographies.

In this ambition, however, they were not alone. The period which saw the appearance of the first working class autobiographies has been described by Roy Pascal as "the Classical Age of Autobiography", in which the form realized its true potential in the hands of such writers as Rousseau, Goethe and Wordsworth. It is a development which Pascal sees as an integral part of the

[106] A. Gramsci, op. cit., p. 324.

rise of the middle class. The "breakthrough", he writes, may be understood, "as a significant element of the process of self-assertion and self-realisation of the European middle-class, shaking itself free of the values and forms of an aristocratic culture, and boldly probing into its own spiritual foundations".[107] It was for this reason that the *Quarterly Review* felt able to dismiss the early working class autobiographies as corrupt imitations of a middle class art-form, and it was for the same reason that the majority of the middle class extended a welcome to what appeared to be an attempt by the lower orders to borrow their mode of expression. For as it shook itself free of the aristocracy, the middle class was no longer satisfied with the preservation of an exclusive culture and was attempting to develop along lines which would complement and support the new ruling class. Consequently, providing the more overtly political working class writers were excluded, there was every reason to encourage working men, particularly the more intelligent and influential amongst them, to abandon a private tradition of oral reminiscence in favour of a form of self-expression which had been perfected by their social superiors. It raised in a particularly acute form the problem of whether in embracing literature as a means of discovering itself the working class had sacrificed its cultural independence at the very outset.

Thus, rather than resolving the question of class identity, the appearance of the working class autobiographies highlighted the ambiguity of the early working class culture. From one perspective they appeared the essential first steps towards emancipation, from another, they might be the first signs that the culture of the labouring classes could be tamed and subjugated. If we wish to clarify these issues further, we must look more closely at what the autobiographers had to say about their world, but we can, in conclusion, establish two points of reference for the forthcoming analysis. The first is that despite the claims of the early reviewers, there is little evidence that the working class autobiographers were consciously imitating a borrowed form of self-expression. Of the two major traditions which informed their writing the first, spiritual autobiography, was shared by, but was by no means exclusive to, the educated classes, and the second, the oral tradition, was very largely hidden from the gaze of polite society. Apart from occasional references to Franklin and some indication, as we shall see, that Rousseau and Wordsworth had influenced their view of childhood, these writers seem to have been building on what they considered to be indigenous models for recounting their past. Secondly, that whilst the autobiographies did mark an important transition, the break was far from absolute. Not only did the two traditions continue alongside the new genre—the spiritual autobiographies in an increasingly attenuated form, the oral tradition still diffuse and energetic but less and less able to transmit the whole of working class experience—but they continued to influence the way in which working men approached the meaning of their lives. On the one hand we find a continuing moral seriousness, a constant concern with the moral development of the individual and with the possibility of using public self-analysis as a means of encouraging the moral development of others. On the other there was a continuing sense of the unexplored potential of literature as a means of self-discovery. Whether in the case of near illiterates like Errington or Bowd, painfully fashioning sentences in an unpractised hand and occa-

[107] R. Pascal, op. cit., p. 51.

sionally carving memorably direct images and phrases, or experienced writers like C. M. Smith and Burn, delighting in their new skill and occasionally over-reaching themselves, we are always sharply aware of men still exploring the possibilities of the written word.

UNIVERSITY OF WINNIPEG
LIBRARY
515 Portage Avenue
Winnipeg, Manitoba R3B 2E\

PART TWO: THE WORKING CLASS FAMILY

Chapter Three

Love and Death

Samuel Bamford claimed that he wrote *Early Days* partly at the request of a critic of his first volume of autobiography, *Passages in the Life of a Radical*, who had asked that he should, " . . . give a circumstantial account of his childhood, his parents, his home and his family; just in the way and tone in which he had already related the experience of his more mature years".[1] If none of the succeeding working class autobiographers achieved such a sustained and convincing representation of their private lives, the great majority shared Bamford's objective of placing the major events of his adult life in the context of his childhood and family. They wrote of their relationships with their parents and their children, of their schooling, of their participation in their family economy, of their courtship and marriage, and of their reactions to the many births and deaths in their lives, in order that they might be understood as complete human beings, and if we are to respond to their challenge we must devote some attention to their treatment of these topics.

Although, as we shall see, the autobiographers avoided any discussion of some aspects of their private lives, and wrote with difficulty about many others, their attempts to connect the public side of their personalities with their private emotional experiences are of great value. The historiography of the family, and in particular the working class family, is still dominated by studies based on the exploitation of quantifiable data. The poverty and unreliability of much of the available literary material, together with the need to establish a rigorous conceptual basis for the discipline has led to most of the major advances being made by demographers and historical sociologists working on parish records and census material.[2] Yet while it is clearly the case that the functions of the family cannot be understood without a detailed knowledge of its structure, the analysis of structure can itself do no more than sketch the shadowy outlines of what actually happened inside the family. The most sophisticated computer programme can never tell us how much a man loved his wife, or to what extent parents grieved over the death of a child, nor can it establish with any precision the way in which the fundamental emotional experiences were affected

---

[1] Bamford, *Early Days*, p. v.

[2] Michael Anderson's *Family Structure in Nineteenth Century Lancashire* (Cambridge, 1971) remains much the most valuable study of the nineteenth century working class family.

UNIVERSITY OF WINNIPEG
LIBRARY
515
Winnipeg, Manitoba R3B 2E9

by the material circumstances of the family. The central question facing the historian of the working class family is how its reproductive functions, marriage and the raising of children, meshed with its productive functions, its role as the basic unit for acquiring and consuming the means of existence. The more elaborate our knowledge becomes of the range of structural factors to be taken into account, the more urgent is the task of undertaking a careful investigation of how the various members of the family integrated their activities within it. We can now be certain, for instance, that the wife of a domestic artisan was frequently not only her husband's emotional and sexual partner, but also his business partner. We know that his children were not only the repository of his values and his skills, but were also, as Hans Medick puts it, "the capital of the poor man".[3] Yet we still have very little idea of the meaning the actors attached to the frequently conflicting roles they were called upon to play.[4] For this reason a close study of the autobiographers' portrayal of themselves as children and as parents may enable us to make some contribution to the existing body of family history and at the same time establish a context for the later study of the way in which the autobiographers responded to their basic emotional and economic experiences through such activities as self-improvement and political agitation. We shall begin by looking at the part played in their lives by the primary sentiments of love and grief, and proceed, in chapters four and five, to a discussion of their handling of their family economy and childhood.

(i)

At a first glance, the most striking characteristic of the autobiographers' treatment of their family experience is not what is said but rather what is not said. The historian finds himself asking many more questions than the autobiographers are prepared to answer. We should begin therefore, by examining their reticence, partly in order to provide a context for the information which is recorded, and partly because in some respects their silences provide an eloquent testimony to certain fundamental attitudes towards the nature of working class family life.

The most significant silence is that of women, which we discussed in the opening chapter. The six women's autobiographies which have so far come to light contain little information on the authors' private lives, and indeed the Bury cotton weaver Catherine Horne was one of the very few autobiographers of either sex to have chosen to remain single. There is clearly a need to understand the experiences of family life from the point of view of the daughters, wives and mothers, but in this study we shall have to rely very largely on the perspective of the male members of the community. The remaining silences have to do with the form of the autobiography and the nature of the auto-

[3] Hans Medick, "The proto-industrial family economy: the structural function of household and family during the transition from peasant society to industrial capitalism", Social History, 3, Oct. 1976, p. 302.

[4] For a forceful critique of the more arid forms of the structuralist approach, and a demand that more attention be paid to "the actor's definition of his situation", see Michael Anderson, "Sociological history and the working class family: Smelser revisited", Social History, 3, Oct. 1976, especially pp. 326-334.

biographers' intentions. They are a product of the extent to which the auto-biographers felt themselves unable, or felt it improper or unnecessary to write at length, or even at all, about aspects of their family experience. In the first instance a major problem underlying the whole of the treatment of their emotional lives is that of language. Love, grief, and above all sexual activity are not necessarily verbal, let alone written categories of experience; you do not need to be able to read and write to make love or to fall in love, equally you do not need words to feel grief, or even to give some expression to that grief. These observations hold true for all sections of society but clearly are more relevant to the class which was least accustomed to using the written word in its daily transactions.

As readers or as listeners, working men had some access to written treatment of emotional and family life through broadsides and popular melodrama,[5] but as writers their practical experience was limited. The evidence both from studies of marriage registers and from the autobiographies suggests that despite the increasing mobility of the working class population in this period, most courtship took place between couples who were living within an easy walk of each other's homes.[6] Where courtship had to take place over a longer distance, communication was tenuous and frequently broke down altogether. Some of the autobiographers kept up a correspondence and brought their courtship to a successful conclusion, some were employed by less literate members of the community to write on their behalf,[7] but others were unable or unwilling to write frequently or at all, and thus jeopardized their relationships.[8]

When, therefore, the autobiographers were faced with the challenge of writing about the more intense and private incidents in their emotional lives, their command of language frequently proved inadequate. Those still steeped in a religious tradition of self-expression, like the reformed vagrant Josiah Basset, were, when dealing with bereavement, able to import or construct Biblical lamentations which despite the generalized phrases often succeeded in communicating both a sense of a deep grief and a feeling that it had been at least partly assuaged by their employment.[9] But those writing in a more secular tradition were often forced to employ borrowed clichés and literary phrases to give expression to their deeper feelings. Sometimes, as in the case of the compositor J. B. Leno, they appeared as unattributed quotations: "'A good

[5] See Louis James, *Fiction for the Working Man* (Harmondsworth, 1974), pp. 114–134; Martha Vicinus, "The Study of Nineteenth Century Working Class Poetry", in Louis Kampf and Paul Lauter, eds., *The Politics of Literature* (New York, 1972), pp. 322–55; V. E. Neuburg, op. cit., pp. 123–70.

[6] R. F. Peel, "Local Intermarriage and the Stability of Rural Populations in the English Midlands", *Geography* 27 (1942), pp. 23–30; P. J. Perry, "Working Class Isolation and Mobility in Rural Dorset, 1837–1936", *Transactions of the Institute of British Geographers* 46 (March, 1969), pp. 121–141; Edward Shorter, *The Making of the Modern Family* (London, 1976), pp. 153–4; Joseph Lawson, *Letters to the Young on Progress in Pudsey during the Last Sixty Years* (Stanningley, 1887), pp. 10–11.

[7] William Lovett wrote of his early life in Newlyn, "As I could write tolerably well, I had to write love letters for many young neighbours . . ." (Lovett, p. 21). See also Claxton, p. 10; Younger, p. 373; Horler, p. 8.

[8] See, for instance, the anonymous Printer's Devil who did not learn to write until his early twenties and previously experienced great difficulty in his courtship through his inability to correspond with his girl (p. 22) and the soldier Robert Butler whose fiancée married another when the one letter he wrote home went astray (Butler, (1853) p. 14).

[9] Basset, p. 36.

mother, an affectionate partner, a wise counsellor, a model of industry'" is the sentence he imports to describe his opinion of his wife.[10] Elsewhere, incidents and states of emotion are described in stilted and unspecific language which transmits only a limited sense of the personalities involved or the relationship which existed between them. Even the many published and unpublished poets in the ranks of the autobiographers found it much less easy to write in prose about their private lives. It was a rare autobiographer who could fashion his own language of emotion. When the barely literate farm labourer James Bowd suddenly writes, "for I was as fond of my wife Has a Cat is of New Milk",[11] we know exactly what he means; the same can rarely be said of the other accounts we have.

A second obstacle was that the autobiographers felt it would be out of place for them to discourse at length on their private lives, and quite improper to discuss any aspect of their sexual experience. Despite the diverse range of circumstances which gave birth to these autobiographies, all the writers were united in their desire to produce respectable and in one way or another, improving literature. The danger of overstepping the mark in this respect was made very clear in the article on autobiography in the *Quarterly Review* of 1826. Attacking disclosures of the private conduct of families contained in the works under review, it concluded that, "The mania for this garbage of Confessions and Recollections, and Reminiscences, and Aniliana, 'is indeed a vile symptom.' It seems as if the ear of that grand impersonation 'the Reading public' had become as filthily prurient as that of an eavesdropping lackey".[12] If we may take as a yardstick the publishing history of J. D. Burn's *The Autobiography of a Beggar Boy*, whose few passing references to sex and the bodily functions were minutely excised when the 1855 edition was republished in 1882,[13] standards appear to have become even more rigid as the century progressed. It was not merely that the autobiographers may have been intimidated by middle class opinion or by middle class editors. Those published in working class journals for a working class readership were no more explicit than those appearing under the imprint of a major London publisher. The writers seem to have believed that revelations of marital disharmony or of sexual activity were at the very least undignified, and might well conflict with their deep desire to in some way improve and not degrade their readership.[14] Even the handful of men who wrote private manuscript autobiographies appear to have been constrained either by this attitude or by a wish not to embarrass their children, to whom they usually addressed their memoirs.

We have, therefore, nothing to compare with the detailed and convincing account of an unsatisfactory marriage contained in the remarkable late eighteenth century autobiography of the "poor man of Toggenburg" Ulrich Bräker.[15] The one exception is that of the former knife grinder and music hall artist Harvey Teasdale, who was forced to give an account of his marital

---

[10] Leno, p. 30.   [11] Bowd, p. 297.   [12] *Quarterly Review*, art. cit., p. 164.

[13] For details of the excisions, see my introduction to Burn, p. 31. When William Cameron's autobiography, which was originally written between 1840 and 1850, was finally published in 1888, the editor deleted "some *spicy* bits here and there . . . applying to the standard of to-day". Cameron, pp. 6–7.

[14] See also the contemporary genre of American slave autobiography, where "a discussion of sex was taboo and family secrets were too sacred to reveal". John W. Blassingame, op. cit., p. 228.

[15] See Ulrich Bräker, op. cit., pp. 159, 182, 198–9.

troubles which culminated in his imprisonment for attempting to shoot his estranged wife in order to explain the meaning of his subsequent conversion experience which was the focal point of his autobiography.[16] Equally, the autobiographers' treatment of sexual matters is in absolute contrast, for instance, to the two autobiographies of Robert Roberts, whose relaxed and unsensational account of such topics as incest, masturbation, prostitution and sexual activity inside and outside the marriage provides a far more rounded picture of the family life of the early twentieth century working class than is to be found in any of the works we are studying.[17] We glean from these pages that at least three of the autobiographers were born out of wedlock,[18] and that at least three more fathered children outside the marriage bed,[19] but the evidence is too fragmentary to permit any serious analysis.

There was a sense in which the autobiographers found themselves unable to write easily about their family life, or felt that they ought not to refer to some aspects of it, and there was also a sense in which they simply thought it was unnecessary to dwell at length on a number of topics. The treatment of any aspect of an autobiographer's life is dependent upon the significance he attaches to it, and the connection he wishes to make between that aspect and the overall development of his personality. Thus what these writers had to say about each facet of their family experience was controlled by how they conceived its relationship to the structure of the life history they were attempting to communicate. In this respect most of the autobiographers considered that the details of their emotional lives were not a matter of interest to their readership, or, for that matter, to future historians, for whom many were consciously writing. As Leno bluntly stated: "With my home life, I am not desirous of dealing. The fact is that it would fail to prove interesting to strangers, and it was with no conception that it would that I commenced this autobiography".[20] This attitude was not derived from any desire to restrict attention to their private lives. As a group these autobiographies were founded on the assertion that the whole of working class life, in all its mundane detail, was as real and as important as that of any other section of society. It was rather that the autobiographers saw only a limited connection between their family experience and what were the general themes of their life-histories, the development of their moral and intellectual personality. Charles Knight, the publisher of instructive works for the working class, advised the Colchester tailor Thomas Carter, whose autobiography he published in 1844, to cut down "particulars which could only be interesting to himself and his family . . . but on no account to suppress what would be interesting to all—the history of the formation of his habits of thought, and thence of his system of conduct—the development of his intellectual and moral life".[21] There is every reason to suppose that not only did the other middle class publishers concur with Knight's advice, but

[16] Teasdale, pp. 81–6.
[17] See Robert Roberts, *The Classic Slum* (Manchester, 1971); *A Ragged Schooling* (Manchester, 1976).
[18] James Murdoch, James Burn and Henry Price.
[19] Samuel Bamford, John Clare and William Heaton.   [20] Leno, p. 29.
[21] Carter, *Memoirs*, p. xi. Carter's autobiography first appeared in Knight's *Penny Magazine*, 11 May 1844. In the autobiography, Carter occasionally chafed at the restriction. See, for instance, p. 219; "I now had much additional proof of the value of a thoughtful and affectionate domestic partner. I must not, however, enlarge upon this topic".

that the other autobiographers agreed with Carter's acceptance of his publisher's opinion, whether or not they themselves were under similar editorial pressure.

The reason for what is, on the face of it, a surprising disconnection between their family experience and their intellectual and moral selves is partly to be found in their attitude towards women. In very few instances do they seem to have regarded their sweethearts and wives or any other women in the community as equal partners in the search for reason and truth which occupied so much of their lives and autobiographies.[22] William Lovett suggested that "much of the bickerings and dissensions often found in the domestic circle had their origin in the wife's not understanding and appreciating her husband's political or literary pursuits" and blamed the men for not enlightening the women.[23] Christopher Thomson entered a lengthy plea that women should be allowed to join mutual improvement societies.[24] Both seem to have been arguing against the prevailing standards of working class behaviour, and in general the autobiographers considered that they achieved their feats of learning in spite of rather than because of their family life.

Their conception of the relationship between their families and their moral development and achievement was a little more complicated. In particular there was a marked disparity between their attitude towards their own childhood and towards the bringing up of their children. We are given only tantalizing glimpses of how they raised their children and of what became of them in later life, but there is, on the other hand, a relative abundance of material on their own experiences as children. The autobiographers' treatment of their own childhood was conditioned by a general acceptance of the Wordsworthian view of the impact of childhood on the formation of adult personality.[25] A few were still writing in the Puritan tradition and dismissed the whole period as a record of sin and moral failing from which the adult eventually escaped, but for the great majority the child was very much the father of the autobiographer. As such it merited a lengthy discussion, touching on wide areas of their family economy and the factors influencing their physical, moral and intellectual development, and this will form the basis of the following two chapters.

The evidence of their response to the death of their children, which we shall discuss later, suggests that their reticence on the part they played in bringing up their children, and the part the rearing of their children played in their own lives, is not just a reflection of a lack of affection for their children. At one level it is merely that they do not appear to regard the general topic of childrearing as a matter of burning interest to the working class community and accordingly they do not feel constrained to compare notes on the matter. If their wives had written it is possible a different picture would have emerged. More than this they do not seem to feel that their interaction with their children had any measurable effect on their moral personality, or conversely

[22] It was, on the other hand, part of the standard pattern of self-improvement for a "reader" to form a close, mutually supportive, friendship with another male "reader" in the community. (See below, pp. 125–8). There were, however, examples of influential mothers, particularly in the case of Joseph Arch and the surprisingly numerous political autobiographers who lost their fathers when young—see, for instance, William Lovett, Thomas Cooper, Thomas Hardy, Robert Lowery, James Watson and Thomas Dunning.

[23] Lovett, p. 38.   [24] Thomson, pp. 379–382.   [25] See below, pp. 87–9.

44

that the fortunes of their children, both as children and as adults was any serious reflection of the autobiographer's moral strength and weakness. Significantly, they have no wish to use the adult careers and personalities of their children to either validate their own lives or compensate for any deprivation or shortcomings in them. It is not just that the combination of late marriages, numerous children and limited lifespan made it unlikely that they would survive to see all their children as adults, although this may have been a factor. Neither were they merely indifferent to what happened to their children as adults—the fact that many of these autobiographies were explicitly written to guide the footsteps of their children in later life demonstrates some continuing concern. Rather they appear to have no desire to live their lives through their children. They wanted their achievements and their failings, their sufferings and their pleasures, to be accepted on their own terms. They were not prepared to abdicate their hopes or their responsibilities in favour of the next generation.

The reticence of these writers, and the cramped and stilted quality of what is said, poses a serious analytical problem. As Lawrence Stone pointed out at the beginning of his study, there is a great danger of the historian confusing a social group's inability to give full expression to its feelings on paper with a similar lack of spontaneity in real life.[26] But the converse of this point is equally true, that faced with what the historian may suspect is the distorting influence of the act of composition, he cannot feel free simply to invent what he thinks the writer would have said had he been able to. In a number of areas the silences have to be treated with respect, and the historian must withdraw from the field.[27] Yet all was not silence, and there were in particular two areas of family experience to which the autobiographers could not escape making some reference, however brief. Almost all the autobiographers were brought up as members of a family unit, and in turn married and attempted to sustain a family as adults. We have two men who were orphaned and spent part of their childhood in institutions,[28] and one example, that of the Scottish vagrant and hawker, William Cameron, of a pattern of sexual and emotional relationships founded on a total disregard for the institution of the family. Here, for instance, he encounters a cockney woman with a child in Northumberland: "She asked me my name, and said, 'If I would keep her and the child, she would make a good wife to me'. I agreed that I would keep her a month, and, if we should cast out, that I never would be bad to the child".[29] Having parted company with her during the day he finds her with another man in the evening, and the "marriage" is terminated forthwith. Throughout the narrative a variety of sexual or travelling partners are casually referred to as "wives" but he neither formed nor attempted to form any permanent relationships or households and ended his days alone in Glasgow Town's Hospital, where he was

[26] Lawrence Stone, *The Family, Sex and Marriage in England, 1500–1800* (London, 1977), p. 13.
[27] For instance, see Anthony Wohl's frustrating attempt to examine the topic of incest: Anthony S. Wohl, "Sex and the Single Room: Incest among the Victorian Working Class", in Anthony S. Wohl, ed., *The Victorian Family* (London, 1978), pp. 197–216.
[28] i.e. Henry Price entered a workhouse at an early age in 1832 and was thus in a position to experience and comment (unfavourably) on the transition from the old to the new Poor Law (Price, pp. 10–14). The anonymous Stonemason spent his third to his eighth year in an orphanage (Stonemason, pp. 2–10).
[29] Cameron, p. 44.

encouraged to put pen to paper. Indirect evidence from other autobiographers, who moved through the same culture (particularly James Burn), suggests that amongst this lowest section of society the forms of marriage had little significance,[30] but at every other level the autobiographers' adult emotional and sexual lives were in one way or another organized around the institution of the family. They rarely lived alone by choice, and where their family life was at variance with the legal form, this was usually a case of the law failing to recognize the reality of their emotional lives rather than the other way about.[31]

Thus there is in the majority of the autobiographies at least some discussion of the formation of the family, how and why a marriage was entered into, and how it prospered. Equally there had to be some treatment of the reverse side of the coin, the destruction of family relationships through death. Bereavement is everywhere in these pages, there are references to at least 220 deaths of parents, siblings, wives and children in this collection of autobiographies and if the statistical summary is itself of little significance it does suggest that here we have the opportunity to study some of the implications of the figures the demographers are beginning to produce. By looking at what the autobiographers do permit themselves to say about the making and breaking of family relationships, and at what in places comes through in spite of their intentions, we can begin to build up a picture which although incomplete and indistinct in much of its detail, does represent some advance on the present state of knowledge about the family life of the working class in the first half of the nineteenth century.

(iii)

In 1846 the Shropshire shoemaker William Smith was introduced to a young lady as he was going into a Methodist class meeting. As he later remembered, "She was dressed in black, having just lost and buried two brothers. She was very dark with long black hair and dark eyes which she modestly fixed on the ground. But she gave me such a shake of the hand that I have felt it hundreds of times since then and sometimes feel it now. I was smitten at once. It was love at first sight".[32] There was no need for him to say any more about why he married his wife, and there is no need for the historian to embroider his account. Other autobiographers were similarly unambiguous about their feelings: the Spitalfields "snob" or unskilled cobbler, John Bezer "fell . . . in love";[33] the aptly named soldier David Love "fell deeply in love . . . "[34], as did the servant Peter McKenzie;[35] the poet John Clare was "head over heels

---

[30] See also T. C. Smout, "Aspects of Sexual Behaviour in Nineteenth Century Scotland", in A. Allan MacLaren, ed., *Social Class in Scotland* (Edinburgh, 1976).

[31] This was particularly the case with the Scottish weaver and poet Willie Thom, whose first wife left him after three years' marriage in 1831, and as divorce was out of the question, he then formed a successful common law marriage with Jean Whitecross until her death in 1840, and then with Jean Stephens until his death in 1848. Despite the eminent respectability of both relationships, he felt it necessary to conceal the existence of his first wife and implied that he was legally married to the mothers of his seven children. See Thom, *passim;* Robert Bruce, *Willie Thom The Inverurie Poet—A New Look* (Aberdeen, 1970).

[32] W. Smith, pp. 182–3.   [33] Bezer, p. 177.   [34] Love, p. 23.   [35] McKenzie, p. 51.

in love";[36] Thomas Cooper referred to "my new passions of love";[37] the cabinet maker Henry Price fondly recollected " . . . the Joy & Bliss of Loving";[38] Samuel Bamford described the time when "the young germs of love [were] beginning to quicken in my heart";[39] and when the Coventry ribbon weaver Joseph Gutteridge found that his emotions overcame his vocabulary and could only write of "a sympathetic feeling that word-painting cannot depict",[40] I think we may assume that he too was afflicted by "affective individualism". The friends and workmates who people the anecdotes recounted in these pages were portrayed as falling in and out of love, and those of the autobiographers for whom the course of true love did not run smoothly, suffered accordingly. It took Bill H., then employed as a farm servant, two years to get over the death of the girl he was courting,[41] and when the future politician William Lovett was forced to break off his courtship, he experienced "the severest anguish": "our parting that evening" he wrote "was to me like the parting of mental and bodily powers".[42] The autobiographers rarely itemized the attributes of those who captured their affections, although it is noticeable that the possession of a "fresh" complexion seems to be highly valued,[43] a reflection perhaps less of an aesthetic preference than of a concern for the present and potential health of a prospective wife. However, there is no doubt that they hoped to fall in love—James Hopkinson, an eminently sober and respectable Baptist, whose autobiography is much concerned with his religious activities, rejected the advances of another chapel-goer because, "the tender passion had never yet entered my heart"[44] and was evidently prepared to wait until it did before becoming engaged—and that many considered that they experienced love when they formed relationships.

But this is not to say that the autobiographers invariably regarded love as a sufficient condition for marrying, or even as a necessary as distinct from a desirable one; neither does it follow that the pattern and outcome of their courtships was conditioned solely by emotional considerations. The proper question is how the autobiographers perceived and experienced the balance between their romantic inclinations, which existed at least as an item to be taken into account, and the limitations placed upon their freedom of action by material or normative forces operating within the working class community. It is clear, to begin with, that a number of features of the autobiographers' occupational and home environment interfered with or at least shaped the course of true love. There was, as we have seen, a problem of communication. There was a problem of finding sufficient time. Few working men had the opportunity of regular contact with the opposite sex during working hours. The only exceptions to the general pattern throughout the period of reducing and segregating women's labour were the early mills and potteries, and here the autobiographers were all concerned to stress the resulting promiscuity.[45] None

---

[36] Clare, *Sketches*, p. 75. [37] Cooper, p. 95. [38] Price, p. 59.
[39] Bamford, *Early Days*, p. 169. [40] Gutteridge, p. 143. [41] Bill H., pp. 10–11.
[42] Lovett, p. 37.
[43] Henry Price, for instance, enthusiastically described his wife-to-be as "a Blooming young Lady fresh and fair" (Price, p. 59). See also Davies, p. 2.
[44] Hopkinson, p. 46.
[45] Charles Shaw wrote of the Pottery in which he worked as a child: "I saw drunkenness and lust in appalling forms in the place where I worked" (Shaw, pp. 8, 50). See also The Dundee Factory Boy, pp. 11, 16–24; Dodd, p. 37.

would consider it a place for serious courting and the extent to which others did has yet to be revealed by demographic research. There was a problem of space. Privacy could only be found in the street or in the countryside; the phrase "to walk out" with somebody was, in these autobiographies, both a figurative and a literal description of courtship. As we have seen, most forms of organized working class activity in the period tended towards male exclusiveness, the one exception being the chapel which provided ample opportunity for the leisurely observation of numerous respectable candidates for matrimony and as such proved a happy hunting ground for a number of the autobiographers. Choice of a partner was further restricted by considerations of age and class. One of only two men to marry a significantly older woman was the Uxbridge compositor and poet J. B. Leno, and his concern to assure the reader that his marriage was a success in spite of the fact he was ten years younger than his wife suggests that by this time the practice was no longer common.[46] None of these autobiographers, nor any I have looked at who later managed to escape from their class, made any attempt to marry outside it.[47]

The pressures and impediments interacted with each other in such a way as to produce an extraordinarily varied set of courtships. Some men walked out with their girls for as much as five years before getting married, others met and were wed within as many weeks.[48] It is possible that a different sort of source material would reveal a more consistent pattern, but the evidence here is that the cumulative effect of these factors was to make courtship an intermittent and uncertain activity, and whilst some were able to maintain long relationships, either through good luck or much persistence, others either could not or thought they would not be able to, and were forced to act with great despatch. The only point in common is that the emphasis is placed on the decision to marry rather than on the wedding itself, which seems to have been of little significance.

It is when we turn to a further characteristic of courtship patterns that we really come face to face with the material considerations which all would-be husbands had to take into account. In common with the rest of their class the autobiographers on average waited some fourteen years beyond the minimum age of marriage, and perhaps ten beyond puberty. These autobiographies are not a statistically accurate sample of their class and are rendered even less so by the vagueness of many of the writers as to dates and ages, but it remains the case that the average age of marriage of the fifty-four who give precise information—twenty-six—exactly matches Outhwaite's calculations which are

---

[46] Leno, pp. 29–30. The other man was the Edinburgh servant William Innes.

[47] Recent studies of marriage patterns in the middle decades of the nineteenth century have revealed that stratification within the working class exercised considerable influence over the choice of a marriage partner. Gray and Crossick have also found a limited amount of marriage of the daughters of middle class parents by skilled artisans. Robert Q. Gray, *The Labour Aristocracy in Victorian Edinburgh* (Oxford, 1976), pp. 111–114; Geoffrey Crossick, *An Artisan Elite in Victorian Society* (London, 1978), pp. 118–126; John Foster, *Class Struggle in the Industrial Revolution* (London, 1974), p. 127.

[48] For instance James Child, a Surrey gardener, wrote, "This is where I first met Fanny Youatt who, after five years happy Courtship, became my dear wife" (Child, p. 3), whereas Henry Price invited a girl to go on an excursion to Salisbury, and reported, "We got on all right, Enjoy'd ourselves immensly and in a few weeks afterwards were married". (Price, p. 59).

based on an analysis of the Registrar-General's statistics.[49] Only two of the autobiographers, Joseph Gutteridge and Robert Lowery, are known to have married below the age of twenty. In some areas, conditions of employment were a direct impediment to early marriage. An apprentice would be deterred from marrying by his articles, and by the inadequacy of his income and possibly by the discipline of his master, but even so would enjoy greater freedom than living-in agricultural or domestic servants who would encounter the hostility of an employer to activities which would at best distract an employee's attention and might lead to a complete loss of service. The servant had little chance of privacy and still less of opposing the employer's authority. When Bill H., then working as a farm servant near Saffron Walden, fell in love with a domestic servant of his employer's wife, he was dismissed, and when the couple persisted, so was the girl.[50] It is scarcely surprising that Michael Anderson has found that the only categories of employees to marry significantly later than the working class as a whole, urban or rural, were those living-in servants.[51]

In the main, however, the decision to delay the age of marriage was taken by the autobiographers themselves. With such a widespread and long-standing practice there may be a sense in which couples were influenced by normative conventions operating within the community, but there can be little doubt that such conventions rested on material foundations. For some it was a matter of waiting until they had accumulated what they regarded as sufficient capital to meet the costs of setting up home. The young engineer Peter Taylor managed to save £30 during a four-year courtship,[52] and the manservant Henry White salted away the colossal sum of £100 before marrying his fortunate wife at the age of twenty-four.[53] Although a single man in his early twenties was in the best possible situation to put by some of his income, saving remained a risky business. Benjamin Brierley saw the whole of his nest-egg wiped out by a sudden ten-week spell of unemployment immediately prior to his wedding,[54] and as a result he found himself in much the same position as the shoemaker and poacher James Hawker who, on emerging from church, "stood with a Brand New Wife and an Empty Pocket".[55] Whether or not the couple used the lapse of time to attempt to insure themselves against future financial hardship, all of them knew that a delayed wedding, or at least a delayed engagement if it was the case that intercourse was practised once an understanding had been reached,[56] was the only certain way of restricting the dependents that the parents would have to support. The later true love was consummated, the greater the chance of protecting such affection as existed between the couple from the corrosive effects of subsequent material deprivation.

[49] R. B. Outhwaite, "Age at Marriage in England from the Late Seventeenth to the Nineteenth Century", *Transactions of the Royal Historical Society*, 5th series, XXIII, 1973, pp. 55–70. According to his figures the average age at first marriage for males in the years 1839–1841 was 25.5. The figure for females was 24.3.

[50] Bill H., pp. 10–11.

[51] Michael Anderson "Marriage Patterns in Victorian Britain: An Analysis Based on Registration District Data for England and Wales 1861", *Journal of Family History*, vol. 1, Aug. 1976, pp. 55–78.

[52] P. Taylor, p. 117.   [53] White, p. 116.   [54] Brierley, pp. 54–5.

[55] Hawker, p. 82. See also Blow, pp. 6–7, who calculated he was worth just eightpence after labouring for fourteen years before his marriage.

[56] Peter Laslett, *Family life and illicit love in earlier generations* (Cambridge, 1977), pp. 129–30; Edward Shorter, op. cit., pp. 86–108.

In spite of all the difficulties, the prevailing theme of the autobiographers' accounts of the resolution of the tensions which beset their courtship is one of freedom of action. In part this was because by delaying the age of marriage, in almost all cases, at least until the legal age of majority and often way beyond, these men to a large extent emancipated themselves from their parents' control over the choice of a partner. Just how significant a factor this could be was illustrated by the experience of the one of the two autobiographers to marry in his teens, Joseph Gutteridge. At eighteen, while still an apprentice ribbon weaver, he decided to marry the girl he loved in spite of fierce family opposition, which was largely based on the poverty of the girl's family. He was first of all forced to leave home and go into lodgings following a bitter row with his step-mother; then his uncle, who was the guarantor of his apprenticeship, threatened him with imprisonment if he broke its conditions, and, when he had the banns called in the local church, his family lodged a formal objection. He finally triumphed by adopting the ruse of having banns called simultaneously in two separate churches and marrying in one whilst his family was protesting in the other. Even then his relatives were in a position to exact retribution. Joseph had planned that as a means of compensating for the inadequacy of his wages, his wife would join him in the sixty-loom mill in which he worked, but as was so often the case in the early mills, recruitment was still largely controlled by kinship networks amongst the employees and his uncle was able to prevent her getting a job and thus condemned the couple to the poverty which the family had predicted would be the outcome of the marriage.[57] The later the son or daughter married, the less the need to display such determination, and indeed where the child was amongst the youngest of parents who had themselves married late, the chances of the parents being both alive and in a position to exercise authority were slim. In only a few cases would the question of inheritance be a factor prolonging parental influence;[58] a son would usually have received the major part of any patrimony available at the age of fourteen when the premium for an apprenticeship had to be found if it was to be found at all.

The sense of freedom induced by an absence of control by parents, and, except in the case of servants and armed servicemen, by employers, was further enhanced by the way in which autobiographers viewed the final balance between the emotional and material pressures with which they wrestled. All were well aware not only of the impediments which the physical environment of the working class placed in the way of their emotional life, but of the incalculable material implications of the decision as to when and whom to marry. A wrong choice, an imprudent or unlucky marriage to a woman who turned out to be either temperamentally or physically incapable of managing the household and mothering an increasing family, would place a life-long financial burden upon the husband which no amount of hard work or success in his trade could hope to overcome. For her part, his fiancée would be taking a similar risk with a man whose capacity to support a family could never be guaranteed.

[57] Gutteridge, ch. 3.
[58] Anderson considers that inheritance of property may have been of some consequence amongst more prosperous labourers in Lancashire, but that it played no part in the lives of the urban working class. Gutteridge's experiences very much support his emphasis on the continuing importance of fathers as job-finders for their children. Michael Anderson, *Family Structure*, pp. 91–9, 121–4.

The autobiographers varied in the extent to which they permitted or were forced to suffer the intervention of material considerations, but if few cases were as simple as Christopher Thomson's defiant summary of the outcome of the inevitable conflict—"Love and poverty were the last to try the issue; the contest was brief, and love prevailed!",[59] in the end the great majority rested their decision on the state of their affections and took a chance on the practical consequences. The only group likely to reverse this calculation were those marrying for a second or a third time. William Hanson, a Halifax weaver, was twice widowed and on each occasion made it clear that the dominant motive in remarrying was the need to find a household manager. He could not afford a housekeeper or cope with his large motherless family by himself, and as he wrote of his third marriage, "It was this that led me to think of another marriage, otherwise I had no thought of such a thing".[60]

There is some evidence that girls were more subject to their parents' influence and, as might be expected, more concerned to enquire into the financial prospects of their suitors. Roger Langdon's future wife only agreed to marry him, as he later recalled, "If I got a permanent situation, either on the railway or in the post office" (he chose the former),[61] and Samuel Bamford's suit was rebuffed by the mother who declared that "no one should marry her daughter who could not fetch her away on his own horse".[62] However, the overall conclusion which must be drawn from these accounts is that as in James Burn's case, it was the "emotions of Love", rather than "mercenary feeling"[63] which determined the outcome of courtship. Indeed, there is a sense in which the very prevalence of material considerations intensified the emphasis they placed on their emotional feelings. The most sober amongst the autobiographers valued such areas of personal freedom and emotional fulfilment they could find in between what for many had been a harsh childhood and what for most would be an even harsher life as parents. For the love of a girl who was to cause him great financial suffering, Joseph Gutteridge found that he could "cheerfully forget all the hardships and misery I had passed through",[64] and like his fellow autobiographers, he cherished his first experience of love not only in spite of but almost because of the difficulties which lay behind and ahead of him.

(iv)

If the autobiographers had preserved any illusions throughout the days of their courtship, these soon evaporated. "Love, Marriage and Beggary" was the title John Bezer gave to the chapter describing this period of his life,[65] and Robert Spurr condensed his experience into two lines: "Then i got married to Miss N. Dewhirst. I then found i had been very foolish for i soon began to learn the cares of the world".[66] He had waited until he was twenty-three, and after a period of poverty, his wife died two weeks before their first wedding

---

[59] Thomson, pp. 162–3.   [60] Hanson, p. 31. See also Spurr, p. 284; Kitson, p. 2.

[61] Langdon, p. 64.   [62] Bamford, *Early Days*, p. 207.   [63] Burn, p. 149.

[64] Gutteridge, p. 45.

[65] Bezer, pp. 177–80. See also Lowery's account of his life of "poverty and love" (1979 edn. p. 62).

[66] Spurr, p. 282.

anniversary. Those who had been more provident found that at best they had only delayed their troubles. The confectioner Edward Davis, who married a baker's daughter at the age of twenty-four, found that his plans were swiftly overcome by the uncertainties of his trade: "By this time", he wrote of his wedding, "I had saved forty pounds, and thought myself well equipped for matrimony. Unfortunately my prosperity did not last, for my wages during the first twelve months of married life only averaged fourteen shillings eight pence".[67] Thereafter it was a constant struggle to reconcile the conflicting goals of feeding his family and keeping it out of debt.

In this struggle the working man's wife and children stood as both the major obstacle to financial security and the chief means of warding off destitution. There was not only the continuing cost of feeding, clothing and probably educating an increasing family, but the unpredictable yet inevitable financial disasters of childbirth, sickness and death.[68] The tenuous balance of the family economy would be threatened by a loss of income if any of the wage earners were affected directly, or indirectly if work had to be given up to take the place of a sick mother,[69] and by a drain on resources caused by expenditure on medicine, medical fees and extra food.[70] It was not just that the adequacy of the wage earner's income would be undermined by the fortunes of his family but that the effects of poverty caused by low wages or unemployment would always be experienced in the context of the family. Willie Thom, then working as a customary weaver, left us a moving account of how the impact of such poverty was intensified almost beyond the point of endurance by the suffering of his dependants:

> Imagine a cold spring forenoon. It is eleven o'clock, but our little dwelling shows none of the signs of that time of day. The four children are still asleep. There is a bedcover hung before the window, to keep all within as much like night as possible; and the mother sits beside the beds of her children, to lull them back to sleep whenever any shows an inclination to awake. For this there is a cause, for our weekly five shillings have not come as expected, and the only food in the house consists of a handful of oatmeal saved from the supper of last night. Our fuel is also exhausted. My wife and I were conversing in sunken whispers about making an attempt to cook the handful of meal, when the youngest child awoke beyond its mother's power to hush it again to sleep, and then fell a whimpering, and finally broke out in a steady scream, which, of course, rendered it impossible any longer to keep the rest

---

[67] Davis, p. 12.

[68] In Preston the average male cotton operative in his thirties would expect to be sick for at least a fortnight once in every three to four years and the incidence was higher for older men. Anderson, *Family Structure . . .*, p. 34.

[69] See Burn, p. 178, for a detailed account of his experiences when his wife fell ill with mastitis after the birth of a child: "Seeing we could not afford a nurse, I had to do the duties of one myself. There were six of us, and out of this number I was the only one that could wait upon myself . . . All our little necessaries of clothing and other things which we could spare went, one after another, into the hands of the obliging relation of the unfortunate and improvident". See also Heaton, pp. xix–xx; Working Man, p. 45; Wright, p. 73.

[70] Gutteridge, after suffering prolonged poverty due to the cost of medicine and doctors to treat his sick children, eventually took the unusual step of buying or borrowing as many medical books as he could and set himself up as a doctor and pharmacist both to his own family and to his friends and neighbours (Gutteridge, pp. 77-8).

in a state of unconsciousness. Face after face sprung up, each with one concern exclaiming, "Oh, mother, mother gie me a piece!" How weak a word is sorrow to apply to the feelings of myself and wife during the remainder of that dreary forenoon!"[71]

Conversely, in times of hardship, a working man would look primarily to members of his own family for material as well as emotional support. The wife was in charge of the household budget and her efficiency, ingenuity and courage in a crisis were crucial to the economic survival of the family. The Stonemason, for instance, was full of praise for his wife's contribution during a period of intense poverty: "My wife did her utmost, and in fact, almost more than is credible, to keep our heads above water all through the winter".[72] By the end of this period the opportunities for women and children to directly supplement the family income were diminishing as protective legislation was beginning to take effect and the spread of the factory system was reducing the opportunities for women to assist their husbands at their work.[73] However, in both agriculture, domestic industry and the many non-industrialized urban occupations there were still ample opportunities.[74] Alongside a frequent sense of grievance many of the autobiographers remembered with deep pride being able to make a contribution, no matter how small, to the family budget when still young children, and as adults were sometimes able to render thanks to their wives for assistance on the land, or in particular, at their trades. J. B. Leno owed much to his wife in his early days as a compositor: "How she laboured at the press and assisted me in the work of my printing office, with a child in her arms, I have no space to tell, nor in fact have I space to allude to the many ways she contributed to my good fortune".[75] There were of course, some alternative sources of material assistance. An increasing minority of the working class, including a number of the autobiographers, belonged to and received benefit from friendly societies,[76] but for the majority it was a matter of looking first to their own household; then to other relations, especially for temporary loans, accommodation, temporary or permanent fostering of motherless or orphaned children, and job-finding for elder children; and then to neighbours, none of whom are ascribed any function in these four areas in any of the autobiographies; and finally to the workhouse, where the family, whose economy had already collapsed, would be finally dismembered.[77]

The problem here is how far the complex and pervasive financial consequences of marriage and parenthood remained subordinate to, or coexisted with, or overran the emotional relationship between husbands and wives. At this point we come up against one of the silences which were discussed at the

---

[71] Thom, pp. 12–13.   [72] Stonemason, p. 206.

[73] For the long-term decline of women's work in the nineteenth century, see Eric Richards, "Women in the British Economy since about 1700: An Interpretation", *History*, Oct. 1974, pp. 337–357.

[74] These are discussed in detail in Sally Alexander, "Women's Work in Nineteenth Century London; A Study of the Years 1820–1850", in Mitchell and Oakley, op. cit., pp. 59–111.

[75] Leno, p. 30. See also Hopkinson, p. 96.

[76] See especially Burn, pp. 153–5, 157–61, 173; Gutteridge, p. 96. For the development of the friendly societies in this period, see P. H. J. H. Gosden, *Self Help* (London, 1973), pp. 11–76.

[77] For a detailed discussion of the crucial role of the family in times of economic adversity, see Anderson, *Family Structure*, pp. 136–161.

beginning of this chapter. The autobiographers did not think it proper to refer to the more intimate and less savoury aspects of their domestic lives, and this is one lacuna in their narratives that cannot be skirted around. Some indication of what might be missing is supplied by Francis Place, who had so prospered as a master tailor that he was able to retire at the age of forty-five,[78] but who had experienced severe poverty in his childhood and again in the early years of his married life. His fortunes reached their lowest ebb when he was black-listed for a period of eight months following his prominent role in an unsuccessful, strike of breeches-makers, during the course of which his small daughter had died of smallpox. He gives a very frank description of the way in which the severe physical hardship the couple endured affected his behaviour towards his wife: "This is the only period of my life on which I look back with shame. My temper was bad, and instead of doing everything in my power to sooth and comfort and support my wife in her miserable condition, instead of doing homage for the exemplary manner in which she bore her sufferings, instead of meeting as I ought on all occasions to have done her good temper and affection, I used at times to give way to passion and increase her and my own misery".[79] It is a very credible account. We cannot know how many of these autobi-ographers yielded in the same way. As a sample they exclude those who retreated from their families into drink and oblivion, but many must have taken steps along the road Place shamefully but understandably trod.

Yet if we are not privy to the daily tensions created by the corrosive effect of prolonged poverty, we are able to gain some impression of the cumulative effect of the life-long interaction between the emotional and material sides to their marriages. Most give some summary of their married lives either at the end of the autobiographies or on the death of their wives, and from these two interesting points emerge. The first is that at the end of the day what very frequently appears to be left is a bond based if not on romantic love then at least on a sense of shared experience. However much true love may have been compromised by subsequent hardships, the couple had struggled jointly to keep the family afloat, nurturing the same hopes, suffering the same disasters, throughout the long years absolutely dependent upon each other's efforts. "For about thirty-seven years now we have struggled through many difficulties and changes", wrote William Hanson,[80] and his words were echoed by the miner Edward Rymer, who like Place had suffered great deprivation through being blacklisted for union activities. When his wife died, he mourned the broken partnership, which as old age and infirmity approached was becoming more rather than less essential: "She lingered and suffered until Jan. 22nd, then sank to rest in my presence, while my very soul seemed to lose its hope somehow, and sent me adrift on a dark and trackless future—lonely and desolate without her. We had braved the storm and ruthless tempest in all its fury for 40 years".[81] It is impossible to disentangle the emotional and material interdependence in

[78] For this reason his work is excluded from the main group of working class autobiographies, but, encouraged by his friends Bentham and James Mill, he was rather more open about domestic and sexual matters than the more conventional working class writers.

[79] Francis Place, *The Autobiography of Francis Place*, edited by Mary Thrale, (Cambridge, 1972), p. 115. See also the comments by Lowery (p. 62) on the relationship between poverty and emotional stress in working class families.

[80] Hanson, p. 31.   [81] Rymer, p. 32. See also Spurr, p. 287, Thom, p. 26.

this brief but moving valediction. The couple had survived, and had survived together.

This frame of mind lay at the root of the second point which emerges from these accounts. Many of these men found relaxation and recreation in the company of their family. The Cornish tin miner John Harris, who had himself gone underground at the age of ten, found the prospect of his own children's company a source of strength: "All day long I struggled and strove far below the sound of the river or the sight of the sun; yet the remembrance of their dear faces cheered me in the conflict, and I shook off the bonds of lassitude and hastened to meet them with sunshine in my soul".[82] Robert Burns' description of the tired labourer coming home to his welcoming family in the *Cotter's Saturday Night*, which is the most frequently quoted and imitated poem in the autobiographies[83], expressed an ideal which they all cherished. Yet few had any illusions about the realities of family life and some went out of their way to attack the middle class stereotype of the home as an escape from the material world outside. The cabinet maker Henry Price was particularly angry:

> The Merry Homes of England Around their fires by night. Some one has sung about them. But they could not have known much about them. The vast majority of them in the Towns and Cities Have no room to be merry in. The Bread Winner has to be up and off early, and home late and too tired to be merry. His little ones are fast asleep. He gets a peep at them. God Bless them is his silent prayer. A look at the wife a painful one. What is the matter dear oh nothing. Poor Dear she has been hard at work too. Trying to earn a bit to keep them decent. If this is the case in ordinary times when employ was regular and dad comes straight home and denies himself a glass of ale till he gets there, his shirt wet with sweat and tir'd with a long walk were does the Merriment come in.[84]

The home was seen not as a refuge but as a cockpit, the arena in which the consequences of exploitation and inequality were experienced and battled with.

It is only amongst those autobiographers who were most preoccupied with the ideal of respectability that we see the beginning of a move to place domestic life on a pedestal, to see it as both the source and repository of all positive values and experiences of working class life. All these men recognized that they stood a marginally better chance of leading a decent existence inside rather than outside a family. Life for a single man, especially if he was in lodgings, was full of temptation and Samuel Bamford was not the only autobiographer to marry in order to save himself from the twin perils of drink and loose women.[85] But this is a far cry from the attitude of the self-improving compositor Charles Manby Smith: "In the case of working-men, it is especially a fact that those who are well married are the most efficient, the most respectable, and the most intellectual and humanised (I cannot think of a better word) of their class".[86] Smith saw family life as a place to which the husband could retreat to nurture

---

[82] Harris, p. 67. [83] See below, pp. 186–7.

[84] Price, p. 67. There is a similar passage on p. 73. Precisely the same point is made in Henry Mayhew's angry article, "Home Is Home, Be It Never So Homely", in Viscount Ingestre, ed., *Meliora, or Better Things to Come* (London, 1853), pp. 258–280.

[85] Bamford, *Early Days*, p. 291. Bill H. wrote of his marriage, "It has kept me out of bad company, and cured me of drinking . . . " (p. 37). See also Downing, p. 107; H. Herbert, p. 96.

[86] C. M. Smith, p. 247.

and display the behavioural traits of the respectable working man. For most of these men, the family was more vulnerable and less protective. Amidst the complex material pressures they might hope to isolate some affection, even love, for their wives, and might survive the inevitable tensions and conflicts to reach a point when they could recognize with gratitude a companion in the struggle for existence, but that was all.

(v)

Themselves the survivors of mortality rates which in the towns were once more rising in the middle of this period, the autobiographers lived on in a world in which their closest emotional relationships were always threatened by the unpredictable and often unannounced visitation of death. Yet although these narratives are peppered with references to bereavement they are far from dominated by the subject, and it might be useful to examine the implications of this apparent capacity to survive experiences which one imagines would have a shattering effect on the personality and family life of anyone thus afflicted in our own society.

We should begin by looking at children. The death of an adult would frequently mean the death of a parent, that of a child the loss of a brother or sister. Almost all bereavement involved children in some way, but it is extremely difficult to form more than a very distant impression of its effect on them. If the event took place in early childhood the adult may have had no clear recollection or understanding of it; all Jonathan Saville could remember of the death of his mother when he was three was "the litter coming for her, when I sat and cried till they came back from the funeral".[87] Where the writer retained a memory of a bereavement his capacity to analyse its impact on his developing personality was hampered by the absence of appropriate language and concepts. Many of the autobiographers gave up the attempt and settled for a brief summary, as in, for instance, Bill H.'s laconic account of his family history: "There was a wonderful large family of us—eleven was born, but we died down to six".[88] Others left us with glimpses of the moment of death or burial—the coachman Joseph Haynes realizing that his brother had died beside him in bed,[89] the engineer Peter Taylor watching the grave of his year-old sister opened and the coffin of his three-year-old sister placed inside—[90] which provoke questions never answered in the subsequent text. Only two of the autobiographers possessed the literary skill and psychological insight to go some way beneath the formal record. At the age of seven, Samuel Bamford lost his brother, sister, grandfather, uncle and finally his mother in a smallpox epidemic: "What a void was around us," he recalled, "what a diminished and unsheltered group we seemed to be! Surely, 'the bitterness of death' is in the lonesome desolation of the living; and this bitterness, notwithstanding my naturally cheerful temper, and all which kindness could do to console me, was long my portion, until it began to be feared whether or not I should ever be called from 'the valley of the shadow of eternity' ".[91] We catch a glimpse here of the child being driven in upon himself by bereavement, responding to the

---

[87] Saville, p. 6. See also Plummer, p. xii. [88] Bill H., p. 1. [89] Haynes, p. l.
[90] P. Taylor, pp. 20–2. Also Harris, p. 2. [91] Bamford, *Early Days*, p. 64.

56

inexplicable destruction of a close relationship by withdrawing himself from the remainder of his family and from the rest of his world, inasmuch as he conceived of its existence. James Burn, whose family life as a child was massively disrupted by a combination of death and desertion, was reduced to a state in which his entire emotional life was trapped within him: ". . . the world had no care for me; yet I had a world of feeling within me which was continually acting and reacting upon itself".[92] In Burn's case the remainder of the autobiography can be read, at one level, as a search for the security and identity which had been taken from him in childhood, but none of the other autobiographers, including Bamford, who thought he had made a full recovery from his sojourn in the "valley of the shadow of eternity", offer any connection, explicitly or implicitly, between their experiences of death in childhood and their subsequent personae as adults.

As adults the autobiographers were in a better position to observe and control their reaction to bereavement, and thus they present a wide range of responses both to the prospect and the event of death. It is clear, to begin with, that whilst historians have rightly stressed the prevalence of death in this and previous periods, those yet living had a tendency to turn the facts of mortality on their head. If, to take an extreme example, 47 per cent of the children born in Preston in the 1840s died before the age of five, 53 per cent were still alive. If two out of five adults alive at the age of twenty-five died before they were fifty, three out of those five did not.[93] If death could be unexpected and often inexplicable in medical terms, so was recovery. There were always grounds for hope. When James Bowd's parents were told by a doctor that "they must not set their Affections on this Child" they ignored him and after great expenditure of time and money which they could ill afford, confounded his pessimism, though it is doubtful if they had any idea how they had done it.[94] Death, when it finally came, was always a surprise, no matter how often it had happened before. When Butler's wife died he found himself "sitting opposite to her corpse, solitary and alone, thinking where we had been, and what she had done, and wondering that such a strong healthy woman was so soon taken away by disease . . .".[95] No past experience or rational calculation could answer him.

Butler, however, subsequently found consolation in religion: "My wife's interment was the next trial I had to meet with; but I found my strength equal to my day, because 'the Lord made his grace sufficient for me, and perfected his strength in my weakness' ".[96] The phrases are echoed in many of the autobiographies[97] and their presence can only partly be explained by the point made earlier in the chapter that such formulas solved the problem of finding their own language of grief. There is no doubt that while the great majority of the autobiographers evaluated and comprehended their daily lives in secular terms, when death came there was some turning back to religion for explanation and solace.

It was always possible to hope that death would not come, and some would find consolation in religion when the blow fell, but it would appear that the key factor controlling the nature and variation of the response to bereavement

---

[92] Burn, p. 73. [93] Michael Anderson, *Family Structure*, p. 34.
[94] Bowd, p. 294. [95] Butler, p. 318. [96] *Ibid.*, pp. 319–20.
[97] See J. Taylor, pp. 14–15; Bowd, p. 297; Basset, p. 36; Carter, *Memoirs*, p. 221; Love, p. 114; H. Herbert, p. 90; Davies, p. 5.

was how death interacted with poverty. In practical terms it was impossible to divorce the two experiences, and in the autobiographies the accounts of bereavement are almost always accompanied by discussion of the material factors which either contributed to or were consequent upon the event. Poverty mediated the impact of death in a number of quite different ways. In the first instance the financial hardship often suffered by a young couple could not only render the birth of a child unwelcome but could cushion the blow of its early death. Look, for instance, at James Bowd's concise history of the life and death of James William Bowd:

> Then we began with Mr. J. Crane Fenstanton and we soon had a very Large Bill with him has flower was three pounds per sack and he was such a man to keep anyone with flower, and now we had another Increace in our family and this proved to be another son and this haded another Expence so that we seemed so shut in we could not see any way of escape but this James William Bowd for that was his name did not Live with us long for he only Lived two years and two weeks. . . [98].

He was not a callous man, and loved his surviving children as best he could, but it is clear that when this child died, relief did battle with and soon overcame his grief.

But if the impact of death could be reduced by poverty, it could also be increased by it. Loss of earning and increased expenditure during the final illness, plus the cost of the funeral could impoverish a family, and the family's financial plight was often made worse by the increased difficulty of getting credit at such a time. Shopkeepers and landlords knew full well that if the breadwinner or even his wife had died, it was in their own interests to force as much repayment as they could. The shoemaker Joseph Blacket remembered with anguish sitting at home with his wife dead in one room, his sister-in-law apparently dying in another, his infant demanding attention he was not properly able to give and creditors hammering on his door.[99] When William Hanson, out of a sense of duty, invited his landlord to the wake following his wife's death, he found himself being threatened in front of the guests with eviction, unless he immediately found six months' back rent.[100] Both men eventually lost both their wives and their homes. And inasmuch as the impact of the death of a child could be modified if it had been a drain on the family's resources, so it could be intensified if it had reached an age when it was contributing to the family economy. When Robert Spurr's son died at the age of three weeks, he merely adds that he had to have the grave dug and a coffin made on credit, but when an elder son Cyrus, "a strong boy, a Child of hope. We was looking to him to ade us in old age" suddenly died, he recorded that the event "filled all our hearts with sorrow".[101] All the labour and sacrifice which had enabled the child to survive the high rates of infant mortality had gone for nothing, as had, quite possibly, the parents' old age pension.

Bereavement and debt went together like marriage and debt. Few of the autobiographers experienced pure grief, in the same way that once the light-

---

[98] Bowd, p. 300. See also Davies, p. 2.   [99] Blacket, pp. 15–16.
[100] Hanson, pp. 14–15. See also John Nicol, an unemployed cooper who had to sell all his possessions to pay for his wife's funeral (p. 207).
[101] Spurr, p. 286.

headed days of courtship were over, few experienced pure love. Almost always their experiences were controlled by the way in which the strands of their emotional and material lives were woven together, and this may provide the key to the most significant way in which they contained the experience of death. The point can be made by looking at what is in many ways an atypical reaction, that of Benjamin Brierley, then running his own paper, to the death of his daughter:

> Business was progressing satisfactorily when the greatest calamity of my life befel me; I lost my only child, then in her nineteenth year. This was a blow that took me a long time to recover from—even if I have recovered yet, though it is nearly eleven years since the sad event occurred. Humorous writing was out of the question for some time, indeed, any kind of writing, as I felt as if I had nothing further to live for, and that the blow might be the means of prostrating my wife. The circulation of the journal went down for a time. My partner's health continued to decline, and we agreed to give up business.[102]

Not many working men could afford the luxury of investing so much emotion in a child that its death, and its death alone, could have such a devastating psychological effect. Many were forced to interrupt work to look after a sick wife or motherless children, but none voluntarily abandoned work just because of grief. Willie Thom was not merely indulging in rhetoric when he wrote in the midst of an account of the death of his daughter, killed, as he thought, by the poverty of his family, "Such a visitation could only be sustained by one hardened to misery and wearied of existence".[103] This was exactly how the majority of the autobiographers did cope. The loss of a close relation was so bound up with the material problems of life that at worst it seemed no more than an intensification of the misery of existence.

(vi)

Two brief points can be made in conclusion. The first is that in an important sense death is not the great leveller, and neither are the other events of family life. Rather, family experience has the effect of differentiating otherwise homogeneous social, economic and occupational sections of the population. A given individual may be an only child or one of a large family, may lose one, both, or neither of his parents, and then as an adult the lottery of family life will be repeated. The outcome of this lottery will in turn determine not only much of his emotional happiness but a good deal of his financial prosperity. This point is obvious enough to anyone who has considered family experience at all, but in view of the preponderant role that demography still plays in the history of the family, with its tendency to aggregate and average out human experience, it is proper to stress that the huge variety of family experience that we find in these autobiographies should not be regarded merely as an obstacle to the pursuit of historical generalization but is rather an essential historical reality.

The second point is that when we are engaged in trying to determine a common set of attitudes towards the fundamental experiences of love and death,

[102] Brierley, p. 77.   [103] Thom, p. 17.

it is very dangerous to get involved in the sort of zero-sum game that we have seen practised in the general histories of the family. There is very little comparable autobiographical evidence covering the period before 1800, but such as there is,[104] makes it extremely difficult to believe that the grandparents and great-grandparents of the working men and women who fill these pages did not, as in their different ways both Stone and Shorter would have us believe, court their wives with love in their hearts, look to retain some affection in their marriages, feel real grief, however they contained it, when wives and children died.[105]

What is at issue here is the precision with which language is employed to describe emotional behaviour. It is not my purpose to argue against change in general or against the impact on family life of industrialization and urbanization. It is, for instance, undoubtedly true that the slight increase in the prosperity of the labouring poor in the second half of the eighteenth century, and the much more rapid increase in the second half of the nineteenth, did facilitate a more "humane" form of family life. It thereby follows that the poorer the family, the greater is the strain on the sensibilities of its members, but that is not the same as arguing that poverty obliterates affection. Willie Thom, to take one example, endured material deprivation as harsh and as primitive as any labouring man in the past, but its effect was to intensify his feelings rather than cauterize them. As the following two chapters will argue, a number of significant changes were taking place in the family economy and in attitudes towards the nature of childhood but the fundamental interconnections within the working class family were long established. In all the agricultural families with which we are dealing, and in artisan and factory families, wives and children had to be both loved and economically exploited.

[104] Although the conventional structure of the Puritan autobiographies discouraged treatment of family life, there is sufficient evidence in those that do dwell on these matters to suggest that Stone's "Close Domesticated Nuclear Family" was not confined to the "upper bourgeoisie" in the period after 1640. See, for instance, Thomas Boston, born 1676, the son of a cooper and maltster, who wrote movingly of his grief at the illness and death of his children, and of his relations with and love for his wife. (*A general account of my life* . . . (Edinburgh, 1908), pp. 137–9, 160, 267, 365); Thomas Tryon, the son of a village tyler and plasterer, who included a long section of advice on the conduct of what would seem to have been a humane and caring family, (*Some Memoirs of the Life of Mr Tho. Tryon* . . . (1705), pp. 70–110); James Fretwell, the son of a small timber merchant, who described the close involvement of his parents in his upbringing, (C. Jackson, et al., eds., *Yorkshire Diaries and Autobiographies in the Seventeenth and Eighteenth Century* (Durham, 1877), pp. 182–7); Arise Evans, a tailor, who was distraught at his father's death, (*An eccho to the voice from heaven. Or a narration of the life, and manner of the special calling, and visions of Arise Evans* (1652), pp. 1–6); Oliver Heywood, born 1634, the son of a fustian weaver, who wrote with great feeling of his love for his wife and grief at her death, ("Autobiography", in J. Horsfall Turner, ed., *The Rev. Oliver Heywood, B.A., 1630–1672; his autobiography and event books* . . . (Brighouse, 1882), pp. 131–2, 167–70, 176–7); John Whiting, born 1656, son of a yeoman, who wrote of his grief at his mother's death, (*Persecution expos'd in some memoirs relating to the sufferings of John Whiting* . . . (1715), p. xi); Oliver Sansom, born 1636, son of a small timber merchant who described his affection for the yeoman's daughter he married, (*An account of the many remarkable passages of the life of Oliver Sansom* . . . (1710), p. 47, 132), and John Bunyan, who included these lines in his *A Book for Boys and Girls*, (*The Works of John Bunyan*, vol. III (1853), p. 762): "How oft, how willingly brake they their sleep/If thou, their bantling didst but winch and weep,/Their love to thee was such they could have giv'n,/That thou mightest live, almost their part of heav'n". I am indebted to Dr Margaret Spufford for these references.

[105] c.f. Shorter, op. cit., p. 140; Stone, op. cit., pp. 476–7.

An inefficient wife or too many children at the wrong time spelt financial disaster in 1800 as it had done in 1700 and was to do in 1900 when Seebohm Rowntree carried out his study of poverty in York and identified the poverty life cycle which every working class family had known about for centuries.[106] The basic problem of balancing financial and affective relationships was neither created nor abolished in this period. If we want to understand the process of change, at least in the early modern and modern period, we must discuss the problem as one of an evolving pattern of material and emotional considerations, neither ever dominant, the balance between them varying as between classes and over time.

[106] Seebohm Rowntree, *Poverty* (London, 1901), pp. 136–40.

Chapter Four

The Family Economy

As the Yorkshire engineer Thomas Wood introduced himself, he began with the structure of the family in which he grew up, and proceeded to a description of his economic function within it: "I was the eldest of the family of four brothers and sisters. Father was a handloom weaver. Mother also worked at a pair of looms. Now weavers must have bobbins to weave. It fell to my lot to have to wind those bobbins full of weft from the hank, so between winding and nursing I had little time left for home lessons, still less for play".[1] Like every other autobiographer he first became conscious of himself as a member of a family, which soon revealed itself as a complex economic unit in which he was always a consumer and would need to be a contributor long before his departure from it. This discussion of the family economy is the reverse side of the previous chapter in two senses. If we are to understand the emotional aspects of the family in the context of its material life, it follows that we should attempt to take an accurate measure of its productive functions, and conversely, the identity of the family economy is to be found in its relation to the reproductive functions of family life. Already we can see Thomas Wood starting to explore the connection between himself as a worker and his actual or unfulfilled role as a schoolboy and playing child, and this chapter will be concerned with the way in which the autobiographers handled the balance between the inescapable duty of acquiring the means of existence and what they considered to be the other essential tasks of the family. We shall be concentrating on the perspective of the child as recalled by the adult because the autobiographers are much more consistent in the attention they give to the early years of their family life. Although the main criterion for selecting these works was that their authors should have spent their lives either at work or attempting to find work, they are nowhere more diverse than in the treatment they accord to their adult occupational experiences either inside or outside the context of their families. As a generalization, the less literate the writer, and the less he was involved in specific activities such as self-improvement or political activity, the greater his preoccupation with the details of his life as a worker. The waggonway-wright Anthony Errington for instance, records a mass of information on the perils and pleasures of the Northumberland pit-men, whereas men like Lovett, or Cooper, relegated work and family to the background once their political careers were under way. For reasons which will be explored in the next chapter however, almost all the autobiographers, from the most humble to the most self-important, dwelt at some length on their childhood, and thus provided a

[1] T.Wood, p. 5.

diverse and detailed body of evidence on the experiences which appeared to have formed .their adult character.

It might be argued that this form of literary source material is least relevant to the study of a topic whose essence is quantity. Although the various items could not always be measured in cash terms,[2] the business of the family economy was to maximize and make the most efficient use of the income of its various members. The complexity of the process of calculating the finances of a family economy over time, together with the poverty of the available data, has stimulated some highly sophisticated quantitative history,[3] yet as a leading practitioner of computerized analysis has stated, we cannot construct a satis-factory picture of the operation of the family economy and the impact of industrialization upon it unless we undertake a careful investigation of the perceptions of the actors involved.[4] If we wish to incorporate the questions of poverty and prosperity into a wider study of the functions of the family economy and the reactions of its members to such changes as were taking place, we must attempt to trace the range of meanings and values which were embodied in their behaviour. In this sense, the scattering of references to wage rates and earnings in the autobiographies takes on a different significance. In themselves the references are too insubstantial to sustain any useful analysis, but a great deal can be learned by asking how the autobiographers can discuss so much of their participation in the economic affairs of their families without men-tioning money, and why, on the other hand, they should at certain points choose to describe the financial implications of their activities in precise detail. It was not just a question of variations in memory or numeracy; when they wanted to the autobiographers were capable of remembering their earnings at different points in their childhood down to the last halfpenny. Rather the form of the autobiography allowed them the freedom to decide when they made such references and in what context, and the manner in which they exercised their discretion reflected much of the changing balance of functions within the family economy.

(i)

From the point of view of the child, the primary function of the family economy was to provide him with security. It was virtually inevitable that he would have to contribute to the material well-being of his family from at least the age of ten or eleven and frequently much earlier, but however short the period of total dependence, and however harsh the subsequent period of labour, the

---

[2] The first observer to recognize the significance and complexity of the family economy was the French sociologist Le Play who, in his attempt to construct a complete picture of the pattern of income and expenditure, demanded of his investigators that they quantify such items as the produce of the kitchen gardens of the families they were studying. His series of case-histories include seven English families. See *Les Ouvriers Européens* (2nd edn., Paris, 1855), vol. 1, pp. 401–440; vol. 3, pp. 273–298, 318–363, 364–400; *Les Ouvriers des Deux Mondes* (Paris, 1857), vol. 1, pp. 263–298, 373–402; vol. 3, pp. 269–312.

[3] See in particular the attempts by Foster (op. cit., pp. 95–9, 255–9) and Anderson (*Family Structure* . . . pp. 29–32) to calculate the poverty life-cycle of mid-nineteenth century working class family economies.

[4] M. Anderson, 'Sociological History', pp. 326, 330–4.

child might expect from his membership of a family economy a number of benefits which were essential to his development as an adult working man.

The first of these was the provision of a sense of identity in the world in which he found himself. Almost as soon as he was aware of his father he would be aware of his trade and usually of how that trade was practised. He was the son not just of a working man but of a farm labourer or a shoemaker, and this knowledge made an important contribution to his notion of who he was and what were the appropriate forms of activity in this strange environment. Often it was the beginning of a sense of pride in the occupational tradition of the sector of the working class in which the child would probably live out his days. James Hogg, for instance, had no difficulty in establishing who he was: "My progenitors were all shepherds of this country. My father, like myself, was bred to the occupation of a shepherd . . .".[5] Such a feeling of continuity could survive and even gain enhanced importance in those trades which were being transformed by industrialization. The Coventry weaver, Joseph Gutteridge, was able to begin his account of his family economy a century and a half before his birth:

> The earliest authentic information I can obtain from our family registers is of Thomas Gutteridge, a Fellmonger and Woolcomber, who came from Austrey, a small township on the borders of Leicestershire, about five or six miles from Tamworth. This was about the year 1676. At that time the wool trade was a very prosperous one, and formed one of the chief staples of commerce in Coventry. Coventry was also noted for its permanent dyes used for this fibre, hence the proverb "True as Coventry blue". Thomas Gutteridge appears to have been a man in good circumstances. His eldest son, Thomas, continued his father's business. But the sons of this second Thomas embarked in the Silk trade, a new branch of commerce just then beginning to be established in Coventry. The Wool trade at this time was rapidly being absorbed by the Yorkshire capitalists, who by the aid of steam and water power for working their improved machinery, soon put an end to the hand trade of Coventry . . . From William, one of the sons of the second Thomas, came my father, Joseph. He was the third of six brothers.[6]

It fell to Joseph the son of Joseph to experience and react against the mechanization of weaving, but amidst the dislocation and hardship, there was a deep sense of continuity. However much he resented the age at which he began work, and the conditions in the factory in which he was employed, he accepted that the place of the Gutteridge family was in the textile industry of Coventry. His respect for the tradition of both his family and their trade lay at the root of the dignity he acquired as an artisan. It is perhaps not surprising that a craftsman should bequeath his children a pride in his particular calling or in skilled manual labour in general,[7] but this form of inheritance could also be found in those occupations to which the rest of society awarded little status and less income. Joseph Arch made no apology for his family's occupational history: "Three generations of Arches sleep the sleep of the just in Barford churchyard. They were, every one of them, honest, upright, hardworking

---

[5] Hogg, p. 4.   [6] Gutteridge, pp. 1–2.

[7] See, for instance, the proud descriptions given by Peter Taylor and W. E. Adams of their fathers' artisan skills (P. Taylor, pp. 19–20; Adams, vol. 1, p. 37).

children of the soil; good men and true, ancestors any man might be right proud to own . . . My father was a sober, industrious, agricultural labourer, steady as old Time, a plodding man, and a good all-round worker, who could turn his hand to anything, like his father before him".[8] Such an inheritance had to be taken up at a very early age, but it made the unfamiliarity, the hardship and often the loneliness of child labour a little more bearable.

If there was a certain psychological security to be gained from a father's occupation, the child would also look to his parents' management of the family economy for material security. The demand for support preceded and continued alongside the period of contribution, and however hard he worked, the child's well-being would be dependent on his father's occupational fortunes at least until the age of thirteen or fourteen. The point becomes clear if we look at the autobiographers' accounts of the numerous periods of strain and collapse in the family economies of their childhood. Although he might be only dimly aware of the circumstances surrounding the ill-health or death of his father, or the collapse of his parents' marriage,[9] the child knew full well that when such events took place his own earnings, such as they were, would be little defence against the impoverishment and possibly the dispersal of his family. If there were not too many children, and the wife possessed sufficient emotional and physical strength, she might be able to keep the family going, albeit at a reduced level. Henry Hetherington was appreciative of his mother's efforts when his father took to drink at the age of thirty-five and died three years later.

> Here was an estimable woman left with four children to provide for—without capital, without friends, without any visible means of sustaining her offspring. Plunged, apparently, into irretrievable ruin by the drunkenness and dissipation of him who should have been her natural protection—what did she do? Did she shrink back at the appalling prospect before her? Far from it— She struck out a new occupation, pursued it with indefatigable industry and provided the necessaries, if not the comforts of life for her family till they were all married and comfortably settled![10]

The larger the family, the less the possibility of such an outcome. When David Love's mother was deserted by his father soon after the birth of their seventh child, there was little she could do: "Being thus distressed, forlorn and destitute, with one babe at the breast, and myself about three years old, she was forced to beg her bread and no doubt told her mournful tale to everyone that it might excite their pity and relieve us in our distressed condition".[11]

In such circumstances all or part of the family might be incorporated into the family of a close relative. The future poet John Plummer, for instance, was removed from his family when his father, a staymaker, fell ill: "My father's

---

[8] Arch, pp. 3, 5–6.

[9] As a formal divorce was out of the question, and legal separation not possible until the Matrimonial Causes Act of 1878, it is impossible to gain a clear picture of marital breakdown. However, these accounts would suggest that it was certainly one of the dangers threatening the family economy. The childhoods of Edward Rymer, David Love and Thomas Dunning were deeply affected by the desertion of their fathers.

[10] Hetherington, pp. 7–8. His fellow radicals William Lovett, Thomas Cooper and Robert Lowery were also brought up by similarly resourceful widows.

[11] Love, p. 3. See also Rymer, p. 13; Marsh, pp. 1–2.

trade was not very profitable; and when I was five years of age a serious illness overtook him, which prevented him from attending to his business, thereby changing his affairs, and breaking up his little connexion. By this blow, the family were reduced to a state of the greatest distress; and I was sent to St. Albans, where an uncle took charge of me for a while".[12] From the frequency of such interventions it would seem that at a time of crisis in the family economy, non-resident kin would feel it their duty to render assistance, even to the extent of taking over a destitute household.[13] However, such an obligation does not appear to have extended further than the brothers, sisters or parents of the mother or father, and could only function when these relatives were alive, still in contact and possessed the resources to support an extra family. Where the mother could not find either a second husband or a relative to act in his stead, the workhouse was the most likely destination. The young Henry Price, whose father went blind, was passed on to his grandparents, and when they emigrated he was sent on to his great-grandmother, before finally running out of relatives and ending up in the workhouse at the age of eight, a fate which befell at least three other autobiographers in their childhood.[14]

Although most of these children were either working or capable of doing so when disaster struck, their earnings, even when added to those of their siblings, would rarely enable the family to survive. Until at least their early teens they could only look anxiously at their parents, and in particular at their fathers, and hope that they possessed the necessary good health, good judgement and good fortune to keep the family economy away from the rocks. Unless a breakdown occurred they might not be aware of the exact nature of the dangers which threatened them, but as they grew older and began to experience some of the more ambiguous features of the family economy, such as the three sided struggle between play, school and work, they knew that they were located in the context of an institution whose essential function was to protect them from the destitution which lay outside it. Thus the occupational past and present of the child's father played a central role in the provision of such security the child enjoyed, and in turn he would look to his father for a major contribution in the arrangement of his own occupational future. Whatever the status of the family, the head of the household retained effective responsibility for the selection and arrangement of work for his children, and on the whole, the longer he exercised that responsibility, the greater the child's prospect of a secure career as an adult. On the land the father automatically brought his children into his profession as soon as they could walk. They would either assist older members of their family, or be found work with neighbouring farmers. "I can well Rem(em)ber" wrote James Bowd, "the first day that I went to work my father was sent to plough and I was to go and Drive for him".[15] When the child was sent away to live and work in another household as a farm servant, the necessary arrangements would be supervised by his parents, as was the case, for instance, of

---

[12] Plummer, p. xi. The family finally went to live with his grandmother in Kettering.

[13] The crucial distinction between neighbours and kin was that whereas the former would often supply invaluable short-term assistance, only kin would be expected to take in your household in time of crisis. See M. Anderson, *Family Structure* pp. 148–9.

[14] Price, pp. 5–22. The other workhouse children were Charles Shaw, William Farish and Isaac Anderson.

[15] Bowd, p. 294. See also Pamela Horn, *The Victorian Country Child* (Kineton, 1974), pp. 71–93.

Bill H. when he left home at the age of twelve.[16] The agricultural child did not normally expect to enter the agricultural labour market as an independent agent until at least his mid teens, by which time it would be assumed that he had acquired a full range of skills and the physical strength to carry them out.

In the domestic industries such as handloomweaving, the child would again be gradually incorporated into his father's employment as he grew up, but in those families with a tradition of skilled labour, the situation was complicated by the institution of apprenticeship which in most cases divided the employment experiences of the sons of the family into two parts. Fourteen had been the most usual age to enter an apprenticeship,[17] but even if he was fortunate enough to have received some formal education, the child would be available for work at least by the age of eleven and often much earlier. The pre-apprenticeship period was generally taken up with whatever odd jobs could be obtained and the child's "career" would not commence until he signed his articles. The variety and brevity of the interim occupations inevitably diminished the role of the child's parents. Christopher Thomson, for instance, who was destined to be apprenticed to his father as a shipwright, left school at the age of eleven and over the next two years was allowed to find himself jobs as a draper's errand-boy, brickyard worker and general assistant in a pottery, before his father intervened and called him to his trade.[18] In other cases the child's course of employment even in this intermediate period was charted by the occupational activities of the father, or, where they existed, elder brothers. Peter Taylor's first job, for instance, came about in the following manner: "By the time I was eleven-and-a-half years of age, my brother Willie, who was message-boy in a shop, turned ill, and I was sent to take his place". After a few months he was dismissed from this job, and thus, ". . . I was sent to school again till something would turn up. My father at length got me a job in a brewery". His father was employed as a mason in this brewery, but he was unable to prevent his son getting the sack after a while for committing a series of minor misdemeanours (which included transforming a brewery vat into a makeshift swimming pool), and it was left to his eldest brother to introduce him to his own trade and finally get him apprenticed: "Well James got me in as an apprentice mechanic, and said, 'if you don't behave this time, I'll never speak for you again' ".[19]

The arrangement and successful supervision of an apprenticeship was much the most important contribution a father could make to his son's future prosperity. Few working class parents had any capital to bequeath to their children, and no matter how much trouble was taken with the child's education, the skills he acquired at school would be of little relevance to his occupational life.[20] If the child could complete his articles, however, he would have privileged access to the upper reaches of status and income within the working class and would be eligible for membership of the only institutions the working class possessed for protecting its members against the ravages of the labour market. The possession of literacy might be a necessary precondition for entry into a trade, but the crucial factor was whether a father was able and willing to find an opening, pay the premium and guarantee his son's conduct over the seven-

[16] Bill H., pp. 11–12. See also Bowcock, p. 1; McKenzie, pp. 25–6; Murdoch, p. 1.
[17] O. J. Dunlop, *English Apprenticeship and Child Labour* (London, 1912), p. 135.
[18] Thomson, pp. 51–6.   [19] P. Taylor, pp. 38, 42–3, 46.   [20] See below, pp. 142–3.

year period. It would be difficult for the child to find a vacancy himself, virtually impossible to save up his own premium, and his articles required the signature either of his father or an adult prepared to act *in loco parentis*. If the child's father or possibly an elder brother or sympathetic relation did not perform these functions, the child was almost certainly excluded from the ranks of the skilled artisans for the rest of his life, unless he had the rare good fortune to be sponsored by a charitable institution or individual.[21] The extent to which the child's preferences were taken into account at this crucial period varied according to the circumstances of his family and the indulgence of his parents. Where it was convenient for the father to apprentice his son to himself, which at the very least would save the cost of the premium, he would probably have no choice in the matter.[22] If this was not to be the case, the child might at least be consulted: "My father gave me a choice of being a carpenter or a white-smith", wrote Timothy Claxton, "I chose the latter . . .",[23] and the parents of Charles Smith and James Hopkinson accompanied their children on visits to masters in various possible trades until a position could be found which suited the interests of all the parties concerned.[24]

The value of such security as the child could find in his family economy becomes more evident if it is set in the context of his likely experience as an adult working man. In a sense, an autobiography, however doubtful its conclusions, represents a victory over the uncertainties of life, yet the accounts which are set before us describe a profoundly unstable material existence. The chronic irregularity of employment amongst the unskilled working class was first described by Henry Mayhew and his observations have been confirmed by many subsequent studies,[25] but what comes across in these autobiographies is that constant financial insecurity was the lot even of those working men who had the good fortune to avoid recruitment into the ranks of the casual labourers or the factory proletariat, and spent their lives in seemingly prosperous and well protected skilled trades. In almost every case the successful completion of a seven-year apprenticeship was followed by a period "on the tramp" during which the unemployed artisan would have to leave his home, family and friends and go off in search of work,[26] and thereafter few years passed without spells of unemployment or underemployment which were frequently accompanied by residential mobility. The more the autobiographers dwell upon the details of their working lives, the more we are made aware of the vulnerability of their

[21] Given exceptional persistence or good fortune it was occasionally possible to make up lost ground. James Burn, after many false starts, managed to persuade "a young lady, who was then verging into that equivocal age where love lingers between hope and despair," to translate her affections for him into a sponsorship for his entry into the hat-making trade at the late age of eighteen (p. 123). The Dundee Factory Boy benefited from the generosity of a benevolent publican who stood security for his entry into the shoemaking trade (p. 60). William Lovett, of course, somehow managed to become President of the Cabinet-Makers' Society despite having served an apprenticeship as a ropemaker.
[22] See in particular the accounts of Thomson, pp. 55–6, and Gutteridge, p. 26. Blacket was apprenticed to an elder brother, and James Child to an uncle.
[23] Claxton, p. 5.   [24] C. M. Smith, p. 6; Hopkinson, pp. 19–20.
[25] Especially Gareth Stedman Jones' *Outcast London* (Oxford, 1971), part 1.
[26] See the experiences of Thomson (shipwright), T. Carter (tailor), C. Smith (compositor), Leno (typesetter), P. Taylor (engineer), Burn (hatmaker), Thomas Wood (engineer), and the anonymous Stonemason. Also E. J. Hobsbawm, "The Tramping Artisan", in *Labouring Men* (London, 1968), pp. 34–63.

various occupations. The eight accounts by pit-workers are a catalogue of violent death and injury,[27] and in the physically safer callings, few years passed without some financial reverse occasioned either by the circumstances of the trade or a malfunction in the artisan's own family economy. Henry Price, for instance, survived the misfortunes of his youth to become a cabinet maker, yet he was rarely fully in control of his business, and even in a good year like 1851 he could only record: "I done a little better as far as Earnings go; but only work'd 42 weeks".[28] At any given moment an artisan might appear to be enjoying an assured prosperity, but the image dissolves as we look at the autobiographers' accounts of their lifetime patterns of employment. Not until the establishment of the major capital concerns of industrial Britain, in particular the railway companies, could an artisan expect an occupation to provide him with a safe and predictable source of income.[29]

Taken together, the experiences set before us vividly confirm the Dundee Factory Boy's summary of the lives of the working class: "The great mass of men and women are like corks on the surface of a mountain river, carried hither and thither as the torrent may lead them".[30] As such it was all the more important that as children the working men were provided by their family economy with as strong a source of identity and as much material security as possible. Some insight into the consequences of an absence of such identity is provided by the experiences of James Burn. His natural father, as we saw in the previous chapter, deserted his mother at the time of his birth and his child-hood family economy was the responsibility of his stepfather, an alcoholic ex-soldier named McNamee under whose protection and guidance Burn reckoned he had been "the inmate of every jail in the south of Scotland" within the first two years of his mother's marriage.[31] Whenever the family had accumu-lated enough capital to turn from begging to peddling, his stepfather would go on a drinking bout and reduce his dependents to destitution once more. McNamee had no trade and none to pass on, and the only training Burn received was in the techniques of mendicancy and petty larceny. The one attempt his parents made to secure his future was to abruptly consign him to the family of his natural father, who had married and was working as a handloomweaver and smallholder in Northern Ireland. Burn neither welcomed his new relations nor was welcomed by them, and after a year's toil in this new family economy he left it, and now aged about thirteen, "wandered forth into the wide world a fugitive from kindred and from home".[32] Without any capital, any skills or any personal connections he spent the next six years travelling around the Borders, performing a variety of casual jobs, until, through a combination of unusual persistence and much good fortune he managed to become apprenticed to a hat-maker in Hexham. He had been economically active, if only as an

[27] See the lives of Errington, Hanby, Horler, Lovekin, Marsh, Mountjoy, Parkinson and Rymer. Also the tin-miners, H. Carter, Harris and Oliver.
[28] Price, p. 56.
[29] One autobiographer, Roger Langdon (born in 1825) did eventually find employment with the South Western Railway, and by contrast to his harsh childhood as a farm labourer's son, led a tranquil occupational life, rising from a station porter to signalman and station master. Burn ended his wandering life as a railway stores-keeper.
[30] Dundee Factory Boy, p. 45.
[31] Burn, p. 43. Burn was vague about dates, but he is between the ages of about seven and nine here.   [32] *Ibid.*, p. 78.

item of public display to attract the charity of the more fortunate, almost as long as he could remember, yet as a child, and later, teenage worker, he was, as he wrote, "kicked about the world", "like a vessel at sea without a rudder", "the slave of circumstances", and "like a feather on the stream . . . continually whirled along from one eddy to another".[33]

The images echo the Dundee Factory Boy's description of the perils and uncertainties of working class life in general, but to be "a feather on the stream" was a much more frightening and damaging experience for the child than for the adult. In his formative years Burn was bewildered by the utter rootlessness of his family's economic activity, battered by its poverty and endowed with the minimum prospects of prosperity as an adult. He later struggled with unusual strength of character to construct a life for himself as a skilled and respectable artisan but he never fully came to terms with the uncertainty of his upbringing. As he wrote at the beginning of the second chapter, "Amid the universal transformations of things in the moral and physical world, my own condition has been like a dissolving view, and I have been so tossed in the rough blanket of fate, that my identity, if at any time a reality, must have been one which few could venture to swear to".[34] Burn was unusual in both the scale of his deprivation and the intensity of his reaction to it, but his account does illustrate the significance of the element of security in the child's family economy. The psychological and material protection of the family economy was essential in childhood, and the endowment of both a sense of identity and a foothold in an occupation would be some slight defence against the vicissitudes of adult life. It was an insubstantial inheritance and one for which the child would be made to labour, but it was all that a working man would ever receive, and as such was properly valued.

There is a timeless quality about the developing child's need for security, yet if we now turn to examine this value in relation to the major economic and social changes which were taking place in this period, its significance in the lives of working men and their families begins to appear a little ambiguous and inconsistent. The ambiguity may always have been present, but as the traditional patterns of child labour began to be disrupted by the introduction of new forms of employment and at least the possibility of more substantial formal education, it began to manifest itself in a more acute form. There was a reverse side to the transmission of occupational identity: the family economy was where the child discovered both the inequality and the rigidity of the society into which he had been born. As he began to work within the family economy he took his place in the stratum of society to which his father belonged, and the nature of the organization of production together with the dominant role played by his father in determining his occupational future ensured that the child's freedom to escape from his inheritance was severely limited. In strong contrast to the Smiles' tradition of industrial biography, the prevailing theme of these accounts is of the gulf that existed not just between working class and middle class occupations, but between the many levels of employment within the class in which they found themselves as children.

In their different ways the public reputations of John Clare and Joseph Arch were closely bound up with their personae as agricultural labourers, yet it is instructive to examine the language they employ to describe their birthright.

[33] *Ibid.*, pp. 108, 109, 121, 137.   [34] *Ibid.*, p. 56.

"In cases of extreme poverty," wrote Clare, "my father took me to labour with him, and made me a light flail for threshing, learning me betimes the hardship which Adam and Eve inflicted on their children by their inexperienced misdeeds, incurring the perpetual curse from God of labouring for a livelihood, which the teeming earth is said to have produced of itself before. But use is second nature, at least it learns us patience . . .".[35] For Joseph Arch, "the dark doom of the labourer's child fell upon me betimes,"[36] and if both writers were adopting a somewhat rhetorical approach, they were expressing a fundamental truth about their situation. In this respect the function of the family economy was to police the imprisonment of the succeeding generations in a particular section of the working class. Clare was later prevented from becoming an apprentice because his father was too poor to afford the "trifle" that was required[37] and when we come to look at those autobiographers who had the good fortune to be born into an artisan family, we find that their prospects were similarly dominated by the state of its economy. The premiums for apprenticeship varied extensively according to the prosperity and status of the particular trade[38], and consequently a family whose head worked at one of the more lowly skills or which had suffered some financial misfortune would have its options severely limited. William Farish's family had slipped down the rungs of the working class occupational hierarchy, and try as he might, his father, now a poor handloomweaver, could not afford the premium required to return his son to the family's traditional trade of joinery. "It was a great trouble to my father", wrote his son who was now forced to begin work at the loom, "that he was unable to apprentice me to the trade of my grandfather which was my mother's fond desire".[39]

John Clare's resentment at the hardship which was inflicted upon him had doubtless been felt by farm labourers' children down the generations since the Fall itself, but there is some reason to suppose that the tensions were increasing in this period. Partly it was a matter of the growth of towns and the increasing range of occupations which were to be found in them. It was not easy for a child who had been at work scaring birds or weeding crops almost as soon as he could walk, even to imagine an alternative way of life, but the town child would witness and might occasionally have the chance to try out practical alternatives to his family's traditions and intentions. The freedom given to Christopher Thomson to find his own short-term employment in the period before apprenticeship had a disruptive effect on the smooth flow of occupational inheritance. He found that he very much liked his third casual job: "There was much to delight me at the pottery, and I was desirous of being apprenticed to the trade. The kindness of William and his repeated lectures on the antiquity and uses of clay-ware—his pictures of Etruria and the famous Terra Cottas—all threw a charm around my labours, that under less favourable circumstances would have made the pot house a mere drudgery".[40] He would require his father's permission and finance to fulfil his ambition, and as his father was

[35] Clare, Sketches, p. 47.   [36] Arch, p. 27.   [37] Clare, Autobiography, p. 18.
[38] In London the premiums ranged from £5 to £10 in the less highly paid manual crafts to £50 or even £100 in the superior branches of shopkeeping. See G. D. H. Cole and Raymond Postgate, The Common People, 1746–1946 (London, 4th edn., 1949), p. 69; O. J. Dunlop, op. cit., p. 139.
[39] Farish, Autobiography, p. 15. See also C. M. Smith, p. 6; Adams, vol. 1, p. 82; Thelwall, p. viii.
[40] Thomson, p. 55.

determined to apprentice his son to himself, Christopher was forced, "to bow to my father's resolve, and, at the expiration of my twelfth year, I bade farewell to the pot house".[41] As the farm labourer's child saw more families moving off the land into nearby towns, and the artisan's child saw new occupations being opened up around him, many with less restrictive forms of entry, so such occupational security as the family offered and was in a position to enforce came to appear more and more of a mixed blessing.

The second disruptive factor was again not new to this period, but potentially posed an even greater threat to the child's acceptance of his situation. Very slowly, and with much regional variation, formal education was becoming more widely available, and having acquired a basic literacy, teenage children were gaining access to an increasing wealth of literature. The implications of these developments will be explored in greater detail in the forthcoming chapters, but their contribution to the strains experienced in this area of the family economy should be noted. A particular example is provided by Thomas Cooper who through a combination of the sacrifices of his widowed mother[42] and his own high innate intelligence enjoyed the longest period at school of any of the autobiographers. Although he had for some time been acting as a junior teacher, he was still at school at the age of fifteen, at which point the expectations aroused by his education collided head-on with the realities of his family economy. "In March 1820", he recalled, "I was fifteen years old, and had not left Briggs' school. My mother had tried, at my entreaty, to get me apprenticed to a painter, and had endeavoured to get me entered as a clerk at one or other of the merchant's establishments; but in every case a premium was demanded and my poor mother had none to give."[43] In his case, his mother was very much on his side, but no amount of goodwill could overcome the absence of the necessary capital, and eventually Cooper, who was becoming increasingly sensitive to the neighbours' criticism of his delayed entry into the labour market, persuaded his mother to abandon their ambitions and apprentice him to a shoemaker. For Clare such an outcome would have been a triumph, but for Cooper, with his education behind him, it seemed like a missed opportunity.[44] In general, however, it is striking how few incidents of this kind are recorded in the autobiographies. The great majority of the complaints about transmission of occupation concern mobility within rather than out of the working class. Once the ladder between elementary and further education had been knocked away at the beginning of the nineteenth century, working class families knew that only in the most exceptional circumstances would a formal education be a passport into the middle class, and consequently whilst such education as was received may have added to the dissatisfactions set in motion by changes in the pattern of employment, it was to play a subsidiary role until the beginnings of secondary education and the growth of the lower-middle class at the end of the nineteenth century.

The growing tensions between the values of continuity and personal freedom threw into sharp relief the extent of the authority of the head of the household.

[41] *Ibid.*, p. 56.
[42] His mother was, crucially, widowed when she still had only one child, and she was able to take up her husband's trade of dyeing and successfully devote her energies to supporting her talented son.
[43] Cooper, p. 39.   [44] *Ibid.*, p. 41.

In one sense the proliferation of casual occupations in the towns could only diminish his influence over his children. If he rebelled against his father's control of his working life, it was easier for an urban child to find some means of keeping himself alive outside the family economy, and a number of the autobiographers left home as early as twelve or thirteen and survived the experience, physically and morally. Yet if we look more closely at the accounts, it becomes clear that the cost of such defiance remained high. Without the active involvement of the child's father or possibly another sympathetic relation, it was still extremely difficult for him to obtain a job which had a secure future. Even when the child was to be employed outside the home in an un-skilled factory or artisan trade, employers would often demand the permission of his parents and some guarantee that they would reinforce their discipline,[45] and where there was a chance of an apprenticeship the father's authority would be extended until his son came of age. The child not only had to submit to his parent's choice of a trade, but once the articles had been signed, the legal obligations imposed upon the father, together with the fact that he had now invested an often substantial sum of money, meant that if the child subsequently rejected either his trade in general or a particular master, he would also have to reject all further support from his family. Such was the experience of William Cameron, who, at the age of twelve was bound apprentice to a tailor in Stirling: "As that trade did not suit my disposition, I entered upon it with reluctance, and continued about five months when, by a pretended dulness of judgment, I made my master as tired of me as I was of him, although I knew more of the trade than he suspected. At last I made off, but durst not go home . . .".[46] There was no middle way; if the child left home before the age of apprenticeship, he almost certainly abandoned any hope of a skilled profession later in life, and if he walked out of his apprenticeship, might also have to sever ties with his parents. Outside the family economy there would always be jobs as pot-boys or labourers, but the child could have given up not only any remaining emotional security but much of his chance of gaining economic independence as an adult.[47] Such examples as we have of children leaving home before the age of sixteen suggest an increased conflict between the generations, but the consequences of these actions confirm the continuing significance of the father as a central agent in the provision of economic security.

At any time the capacity of the family economy to supply its members with such security as they needed was dependent upon its occupational characteristics and fortunes, and this fact, taken together with the growing restriction it placed on its members, ensured that the impact of industrialization upon this area of the family economy was far from straightforward. Where the child was brought up in a family which had an established tradition of employment in a

[45] See Bowd, p. 295; Stonemason, p. 34.

[46] Cameron, p. 12. He later returned to his trade for the paradoxical reason that only by gaining a skill could he become economically independent of his father. See also Thelwall, p. xiii, who was equally unable to go home after walking out of an apprenticeship to a shop-keeper, and William Lawrence, who ran away from a harsh master but dared not return home to his father who had borrowed £20 for his apprenticeship (pp. 4-5). He ended up in the Army.

[47] See, for instance, the career of the 'Cheap Jack' William Green whose wandering, insecure occupational career began when he ran away from his brutal father and thus sacrificed a guaranteed future as a butcher.

relatively prosperous trade, and where that trade either continued alongside the factory system or was incorporated into it without serious damage to its privileges, there need be little disruption. In spite of the mechanization of his trade, Gutteridge's father was still able to secure his son's future as a skilled weaver: "Between the age of thirteen and fourteen, I came out of the school to be apprenticed to my father to learn the art of ribbon weaving . . . As my father worked in a factory, I had to learn the trade under his supervision, paying the owner of the factory one half of my net earnings for the use of machinery and the advantage of an experienced foreman."[48] The novelty and hardships of factory life merely enhanced the significance of the family's occupational tradition, and in this respect men like Gutteridge or the engineer Peter Taylor looked forward to the establishment of the labour aristocracy in the second half of the nineteenth century, a central characteristic of which was the continuing role of the family economy as an instrument for preserving and transmitting the well-being of its members.[49]

Everything depended upon the relationship between industrialization and the economic power of the father. Where, for instance, he was unskilled, was not able to provide adequate financial support for his family and could offer little protection for his children as they entered the labour market, the members of the family economy had little to lose from any change. Where, conversely, the impact of industrialization was such as to destroy a continuity of employment and prevent a father from exercising authority over his son's occupational life, the reaction of those involved was extremely bitter. It is instructive to compare the accounts of two contemporaries who, outwardly, were brought up in very different circumstances. Roger Langdon was the son of a poor Somerset farm labourer, who began to contribute to his family economy at the age of eight: "The state of England at that time was very bad indeed, and the poor were really oppressed, especially in our remote part of the country. Well my father had enough to do to make both ends meet and how he and my mother slaved and toiled to keep out of debt! My brothers and myself were sent to work at a very early age, at whatever we could get . . .".[50] He eventually found a job with a neighbouring farmer: "For the princely sum of one shilling a week I had to mind sheep and pull up turnips in all winds and weathers, starting at six o'clock in the morning".[51] Charles Shaw, who was born seven years later in Tunstall, Stoke-on-Trent, the son of a poor painter and gilder, entered a pottery at the age of seven:

When the Queen came to the throne, work was scarce and food was dear. The Corn Laws were bringing into play their most cruel and evil results. One of these results was that little children had to compete for the decreasing sum of available work. As no Factory Act applied in the district where I began to work, the work of the children could be used as harsh necessity or harsher greed determined. We had an old neighbour, a kindly-disposed old woman full of sympathy for her poorer neighbours, suffering herself, perhaps, a little less than those about her, and so willing to do what she could to help them. She had a son, Jack, who was an apprentice in a "pot-works" as a

[48] Gutteridge, p. 26.   [49] See Crossick, op. cit., p. 117.   [50] Langdon, p. 14.
[51] Ibid., p. 28.

"muffin-maker". His mother, knowing the poverty of my parents, suggested I should become Jack's "mould-runner".[52]

Langdon received so little support from his family economy that he eventually left it at the age of fourteen and after spending the succeeding decade in a variety of employments found in that quintessential product of industrialization, the railway, an occupation which might allow him to provide for his children the sort of secure family economy that he had so conspicuously lacked in his own childhood. For Shaw, however, and for William Dodd, Thomas Wood, and the Dundee Factory Boy, who found themselves working as children in the early textile mills, the experience of industrialization represented the destruction of most of the security which their family economy might have supplied. The occupational background of their family provided them with no frame of reference with which to evaluate the bewildering and hostile factory environment, and their fathers offered them little or no protection as they entered the labour market with the result that they felt, as Shaw wrote, that the determining force in their occupational career was the "harsh necessity or harsher greed" of the *laissez-faire* economy. Rather than heightening the ambiguity of the father's role the introduction of new forms of occupation appeared to abolish it. The children laboured harder than any child had ever done, and received even less security in return.

(ii)

The second function that a family economy might perform on behalf of its members was an extension of the first. The child looked to his parents not only for security but also for training. If his father was to exercise a major influence over the selection of his occupation it was equally important that he supervised its conduct. As the child contributed to his family economy he expected its head to ensure that the demands which were made of him did not run ahead of his growing physical strength and technical skill. While he was living in his own home or in that of a master acting *in loco parentis*, the child was required to work and to learn how to work at the same time, and it is clear from these accounts that the presence of the father, either direct or indirect, was essential if the fragile balance between the exploitation and the nurturing of his children was to be maintained.

In most contexts the institution of child-labour embodied a complex hierarchy of activities, at the bottom end of which it was not always easy to determine whether the child was actually aiding or was merely obstructing the operation of his family economy. The pre-industrial artisan workshops for instance, provided an arena for both work and play. Samuel Bamford described the pattern of activities he was called upon to perform whilst he was living with his uncle who was a handloomweaver:

> . . . my employment was to fetch milk every morning, to run to the well for water when wanted, to go errands generally, and to assist my aunt at times in the bobbin-winding department; all of which suited my disposition

[52] Shaw, p. 12.

and habits most pleasingly, except the latter piece of bondage, which on account of its monotonous confinement, soon became abhorrent to my feelings; and had not my frequent escapades in the way of errand running, allowed me many sweet snatches of freedom, my situation would have been far from happy.[53]

The child found recreation amidst his work, or turned his work into a recreation, or performed his work so badly that from his parents' point of view it might as well have been a recreation. Ben Brierley was careful not to overstate the value of his early career:

> And now came the time that I had to be put to work. I had *played* at pulling the "idle bant" when the clogger's apprentices were cross-cutting timber for soles; I had *played* at turning a handle in the Bower Lane rope-walk until my hands were blistered all over; but now I must *work*, as I was getting too big to run in the fields, or raise dust in the lanes. I was put to the bobbin-wheel. How I hated being chained to the stool! and how I suffered from the effects of having "bad bobbins" flung at my head![54]

In the agricultural occupations there also existed a long scale of activity through which the child could progress as he grew up. Somerville spent much of his early childhood herding cows, Langdon was employed weeding for a local farmer, and Hawker, the Suffolk Farm Labourer, Joseph Arch, and William Mabey commenced their agricultural careers bird-scaring. John Clare's experience illustrates the way in which the family's poverty, together with the demands of the seasons and the capabilities of the young boy interacted to control the nature of his childhood occupation: "I believe I was not older than 10 when my father took me to seek the scanty rewards of industry; Winter was generally my season of imprisonment in the dusty barn, Spring and Summer my assistance was wanted elsewhere, in tending sheep or horses in the fields, or scaring birds from the grain or weeding it . . .".[55] There is little reason to suppose that the pattern changed very greatly in the agricultural areas during this period. The Stonemason's childhood lasted into the early 1860s, and like Clare his first introduction to farming life was through weeding in the fields with the womenfolk:

> All I know is that I started on the nearest farm, along with some women, one or two boys, and some girls. The work was hideously monotonous, especially the first month . . . Fancy pulling couch-grass or wickens (this was the local name) by the hand out of the ground into an apron and then casting them into a heap to be burned! This was our work for a month. After that we had a little more variety, spreading manure in the turnip drills, hoeing and thinning the turnips, and hoeing the potatoes, till the hay season.[56]

As his strength increased, more was demanded of the child, and he would progress through a graded series of jobs, making an increasing contribution to

---

[53] Bamford, *Early Days*, p. 101. See also Duncan Bythell's account of the handloomweaver's domestic economy, which is partly dependent on Bamford's account, in *The Handloom Weavers* (Cambridge, 1969), pp. 36–9.
[54] Brierley, pp. 18–19.   [55] Clare, *Sketches*, p. 48.   [56] Stonemason, pp. 32–3.

the family economy and simultaneously gaining the knowledge necessary to become what Arch described as "a sober, industrious agricultural labourer . . . a good all round worker who could turn his hand to anything . . .".[57] Alexander Somerville, who was brought up in the Lothians, advanced from herding cows to general labouring to walking at the tail of the plough until he reached the peak of the agricultural labourer's career structure in his part of the world, and was given charge of a ploughing team.[58] At the other end of Britain, the Suffolk Farm Labourer was climbing a similar ladder, beginning as a "cowboy" at the age of ten, and moving on to general light duties about the farm and then to working with horses in the fields at the age of about thirteen. "I grew in importance", he wrote, "and the next year was entrusted with a one-horse roll. From rolling with one horse I got to harrowing with two horses, and after some experience of this work I aspired to the plough. My master encouraged the idea, and I was permitted to try my 'prentice hand with a pair of steady-going old horses on a stubble, where defective ploughing would be of little consequence."[59]

In artisan families, the relationship between the acquisition of skill and income was dominated by the institution of apprenticeship. The way in which the autobiographers introduced their accounts of their experiences as apprentices makes it clear that they regarded apprenticeship as the only really significant part of their industrial training. Thomas Carter, for instance, reviewing his state of mind as a twelve-year-old, emphasized the distinction between the odd jobs he had hitherto been employed in, and the coming need to embark upon the process of training for his adult life: "I was indeed still young, being not more than twelve and a half years old; yet I felt that it was high time to be learning something by which to get a living".[60] William Lovett similarly saw apprenticeship as the point at which he commenced his serious occupational education: "The time, however, had now arrived when it was necessary that I should learn some useful employment . . .".[61] The chief characteristic of the educative process which took place in an apprenticeship was that the training was carried out in a paternalistic context in which the apprentice worked either with his father or another skilled working man who was supposed to fulfil that role.[62] In a sense it can be viewed as a formal codification of the practice in agricultural communities, a codification which legally recognized the necessity for the father to maintain the balance between training and practice, for which the apprentice would receive a small but steadily increasing wage over the seven-year period.

It is where the ability of the family economy to maintain the balance between these two roles begins to break down that we start to find complaints about the age at which the children are sent out to work. Roger Langdon, for instance, commences his account of his first job in the following terms: "At the tender age of eight I was sent to work on a farm belonging to Joseph Greenham . . .".[63]

[57] Arch, pp. 5–6.   [58] Somerville, pp. 21, 45, 96.
[59] Suffolk Farm Labourer, ch. III. Depending on his rate of physical development, the agricultural child might expect to be performing the full range of farm duties from the age of fifteen onwards.
[60] Carter, *Memoirs*, p. 67.   [61] Lovett, p. 10.
[62] See O. J. Dunlop, op. cit., pp. 172–3, 180–96; David Wardle, *The Rise of the Schooled Society* (London, 1974), p. 29.
[63] Langdon, p. 28.

That he should have started work at such an age in an agricultural community in 1833 was not unusual, but in Langdon's case the period of employment was spent away from the control of his father and was characterized by continuous persecution and maltreatment by those in authority over him. As with the provision of security, if the father was unable or unwilling to involve himself in the labour of the children, the situation of the child on the land was little better than it might have been in the factory, a point emphasized by Joseph Arch, who suffered in much the same way as Langdon:

> The sickly son of an agricultural labourer had as little chance of growing up to a healthy manhood as had the sickly son of a miner or a mill hand: it was a regular case of extremes meeting in a vicious circle. If he got past the bird-scaring stage he had the carter and the ploughman to contend with and their tenderest mercies were cruel. They used their tongues and their whips and their boots on him so freely, that it is no exaggeration to say that the life of poor little Hodge was not a whit better than that of a plantation nigger boy.[64]

Those who farmed with other members of their family, such as Clare and Somerville, were better placed than Langdon and Arch, and equally, the experience of those children who were involved in the industrial processes varied according to the role played by their parents. Brierley's father despaired of his performance as a bobbin-winder and eventually sent his son, now aged about twelve, to work as a piecer in a nearby spinning factory. When, however, young Benjamin's health began to be undermined by "the atmosphere of the mill", his family was able to remove him, and as soon as it was judged that his legs were long enough for the task, he was set to work at a handloom at home, "on a class of work that could not well be spoiled".[65] Edward Rymer's mother, deserted by her husband and left to bring up four children, was in no position to exercise such nice judgement. In the winter of 1844, when Edward was nine, it was "found necessary" to send him into the pit to work first as a door-keeper and then at "pushing and dragging tubs from the coal face to the 'flats' ". "To this work", he wrote, "I was trained before my limbs were able to bear half the strain which it involved."[66] There was no relief, and ten years later, "both brother John and I were assailed by rheumatism. After suffering this horrible infliction, we both became cripples and knocked-kneed".[67] Jonathan Saville's mother died when he was three, and his father was later killed by a fall of earth in the quarry in which he worked, and as a result the supervision of his occupational life as a child was left to the master of Horton workhouse who so neglected his duties that Saville was permanently lamed by the ill-treatment of the weaver to whom he was hired out.[68]

Where the head of a family economy, sometimes through dereliction of duty but more usually because of insufficient economic power, failed to exercise effective control over the progress of a child through the various grades of

[64] Arch, p. 29.   [65] Brierley, pp. 19, 22. See also J. Wood, p. 4.   [66] Rymer, p. 5.
[67] *Ibid.*, p. 4. Edward recovered sufficiently to return to the pit, but John was sent home from Sunderland infirmary a permanent cripple, thus increasing the necessity of Edward's labour: "With brother John crippled and unable to work,. the struggle for dear life for our family had become terrible". See also the career of the "Factory Cripple" William Dodd (Dodd, *passim*, especially pp. 11–12).
[68] Saville, pp. 6–9.

work within the occupation he had entered, there was little to prevent the child being forced to undertake tasks for which he lacked the necessary skill and strength. As with the more general question of security, the introduction of the factory system intensified a difficulty which occurred in other areas of working class labour, particularly on the land. Fathers who were themselves employed in the factories might alleviate the problem by recruiting their own children as assistants, but the extent to which this was possible was limited, and at the best of times father and son would be subject to the impersonal discipline of the machine.[69] If the balance between exploitation and nurturing were upset completely, the child might find that instead of acquiring physical skills as he contributed to his family economy, he was being permanently deprived of them. Such circumstances called into question the entire relationship between training and child labour. The point was made by Charles Shaw as he described his entry to a pottery factory: "Only just now, after all these centuries, is the training of the millions beginning to be felt as a primal necessity for all true and effective human developments. I began to work, but I could never see in what way my poor bit of education would prepare me for such as came to my hand. This began when I was a little over seven years of age, and it was in this wise . . .".[70] "Training" was now seen as something apart from and opposed to the child's activity in the family economy. Rather than incorporating at least some of the "true and effective human developments" of the child, his life as a labourer was seen to be destructive of them.

(iii)

Except insofar as the provision of elements of security and training was dependent on its overall prosperity, the autobiographers had no need to refer to their own earnings in evaluating these functions of the family economy. The third function was, however, directly concerned with matters of quantity. In return for the range of psychological and material benefits which have been discussed, children were expected to make a growing contribution to the finances of the family. Yet even here we find that the autobiographers conceptualized and measured their participation in terms which were only partly related to the monetary worth of their labour.

An initial difficulty was that some children simply did not know how much they were earning. A proportion of those on the land, and virtually all those who assisted in their fathers' pre-industrial domestic workshops would be working to maximize the income of the head of the family economy, who himself might be paid partly in kind. It is doubtful, for instance, whether any member of Alexander Somerville's family economy was fully aware of his or her daily or even annual wage. In return for the notional rent of their tied cottage the family had to perform certain tasks for the farmer throughout the year, and although some members were occasionally paid cash wages for certain types of labour, they usually worked as a single economic unit. It was just not possible

---

[69] Neil Smelser, *Social Change in the Industrial Revolution* (London, 1959), pp. 188–93; M. Anderson, 'Sociolocial History' pp. 320–6.

[70] Shaw, p. 11. He was only rescued from the pottery when, at the age of ten, his family economy collapsed so completely that all its members were forced to enter the workhouse.

for Alexander, the youngest of twelve children, to discuss his early economic activity in monetary terms, and as he turned to the moment when he and an elder sister began full-time work, he could only state that: "My sister went no more to the school that quarter, having to go to the fields to help work for the family bread. When the summer of 1819 came, I left school also, to herd the farmer's cows".[71] Even if the child were sent away to work for another farmer, he might be paid wholly or partially in kind. When the seven year old James Hogg was hired to herd cows by a neighbouring farmer his first half-year's wages were "a ewe lamb and a pair of new shoes".[72]

There was even less likelihood of the subordinate members of the family economy of a domestic artisan receiving a separate wage. The handloomweavers, for instance, were paid for the total amount of work delivered to the warehouse by the head of the household, yet in most cases the wife and children would have worked in activities, such as carding and bobbin-winding, necessary to service the weaving of the father at the loom. Samuel Bamford who spent some time in his uncle's household performing such tasks, does not mention receiving any money at all. It is only when he leaves home and goes to work as a warehouseman for a non-related employer at the age of fourteen, that he gives details of a small but recognizable income.[73] These arrangements often persisted when the domestic economy broke up and members of the family moved into the factory. In most types of factory work it was customary for the child to work as an assistant to an adult who would be paid for the total amount of work completed and where that adult was his father he might again neither see his wages nor be very certain of their extent.

It was not merely that some of the autobiographers were unable to be as precise about money as they or later historians might wish. The absence of a separate wage raised the question of the meaning of work itself. Most children expect and are expected to perform occasional tasks for their parents, such as running errands or helping with the housework. For the most part such activities will have no economic value, and may indeed be invented just to keep the child amused or out of mischief. In our own society the line between "help" and "work" is usually clearly drawn, although there are still grey areas, such as, in particular, child-minding. In the first half of the nineteenth century, however, it was often much less easy for any of the parties concerned to make such a firm distinction. Bamford's career is a case in point. "Work" in his uncle's family economy included fetching milk, going to the well and running errands "generally". The child may not have realized he was working until he was told that his activities had some economic value—George Marsh, for instance, evidently knew that the blackberries he collected for his mother would be sold[74]—or until the elements of compulsion and monotony came to dominate his activity—in the handloomweaving families the moment at which the child was required to wind bobbins seems to have ended any lingering doubts. Equally, from the point of view of his parents the child might have been economically useful some time before he was aware of being so, especially,

[71] Somerville, p. 21.   [72] Hogg, p. 5.

[73] Bamford, *Early Days*, p. 188. The implications of the difficulty of placing a precise cash value on the activities of the domestic artisan's family economy are explored in H. Medick, art. cit., pp. 298–302.

[74] Marsh, p. 6.

again, in the case of baby-minding, or, conversely, his presence in the workshop may have been counter-productive for rather longer than the child realized.

In this period two forces were at work reducing the confusion between the periods of "help" and "work". The slow growth of elementary education, which will be examined in the following chapter, was beginning to impose a greater rigidity on the period of childhood, relegating the time of "help" to the pre-school age and setting up a sharper antithesis between school and work, and at the same time there was a gradual reduction of the incidence of children working alongside parents, particularly as the domestic workshops came under pressure from the factory system. Yet if these developments ensured that an increasing number of children made an abrupt entry into the world of labour, the notion of help remained, in most contexts, closely and critically allied to the notion of work. Objectively, a cash wage is the measure of the amount of labour sold at the rate which an employer is prepared to pay, but if we look closely at these narratives we discover that the majority of the autobiographers placed a much more complex value on the small amounts of money which they brought into their family economies.

At the centre of their calculation was a clear knowledge of why they were being taken from their games or from school, and being made to work. "It only remains for me to state", wrote Hamlet Nicholson, "that in consequence of the needs of my home, I was put at eight years of age to work side by side with my father at the cobbler's stool".[75] Throughout their time as members of their parents' family economy, the child-labourers were deeply aware that their contributions, no matter how small, could make a significant difference to its well-being. Henry White, the son of a Somerset farm-labourer, was, at the age of ten, managing to earn threepence a day as a cowkeeper: "Small as the sum was, however, I knew it would be very acceptable to my persevering father and mother who were toiling early and late to supply our wants; and the munificent payment was accordingly accepted".[76] They frequently knew, possibly because they were deliberately told by their parents, precisely what item of the family's food would be paid for by their work. In the first half-dozen lines of his autobiography James Hawker presents us with a precise statement of both the cause and the value of his labour as a child:

> I was born in 1836 in Daventry, Northamptonshire, of very Poor Parents. My Father was a Tailor by Trade and my Mother assisted him in this work. Times were very Bad and they found it hard to Live. At the age of six I remember my Father working in a Garrett where I Slept, until ten o'clock at night. At the age of eight I went to work in the Fields, scaring Birds for seven days a week at a wage of one shilling. This sum Bought my Mother a four Pound Loaf.[77]

As a result of this knowledge, the autobiographers were able to see their wages as a measure of their service to the family. Ben Brierley took great pleasure in recounting the way in which a crisis in his family economy enhanced the value of his earnings:

> "Our folks" were put to great shift to keep the cart going. Having no other

[75] Nicholson, p. 3. See also Hampton, p. 21.
[76] White, p. 29. See also Arch, p. 33; Bezer, pp. 162–3. [77] Hawker, p. 1.

work to do I employed myself in dragging a wagon laden with coals from the Limeside coal pits, a distance of nearly a mile; having to go twice for a "tub", for which I received threepence remuneration. On one occasion the threepence thus earned had to provide a dinner for the four of us— twopennyworth of bacon, and one pennyworth of potatoes.[78]

Not unnaturally, the small child felt very proud of his capacity to contribute to the family income. Christopher Thomson well remembered his reaction to his first wages: "Even now, while writing, I feel the self-importance which animated me when, after my first whole week's work, I marched into the house and tendered to my mother half-a-crown, the amount of my wages—adding, 'there mother, we shall soon have another public house, if I keep at work at the brick yard' ".[79] The scattering of evidence confirms Michael Anderson's equally impressionistic conclusion that children would be expected to hand over virtually all of their wages until about the age of fourteen,[80] which seems to have been regarded within the working class communities as an intermediate coming of age for the son of the family, whether or not it was accompanied by the formal act of apprenticeship. The children would then be permitted to retain an increasing proportion of their wage for their own use, and at that point the attitude towards the value of the labour began to change. We find the autobiographers estimating the adequacy of their earnings in their mid and late teens in relation to their needs as individual workers,[81] their wages being seen now as a measure not of their service to their family economies but of their growing independence from them.

Two important consequences flowed from the way in which the young child labourers assessed the value of their work. In the first instance, the financial interdependence of the members of the family economy and the way this was known and accepted by children as young as seven or eight, was clearly a force which bound together, emotionally as well as materially, the family as a whole. No matter how bitter the autobiographers felt about their sufferings as child labourers, no matter how wrong they thought it was that they should have had to work, they very rarely blamed their parents for their experiences. They believed that their parents made them labour because they could not afford to do otherwise, and that as children they were simply trapped in the poverty of the family and the class into which they had been born. For Isaac Anderson, it was the "hard times" and not his parents that caused his sufferings as a child labourer: "Eventually I, with my father and two brothers, went thrashing, and it was indeed hard work. I was a growing lad and was always hungry, as it were. My breakfast consisted of a mess of water and flour, but this was not enough to satisfy nature, and long before dinner time I felt so fatigued and hungered I could have eaten my fingers if it had been possible. I could scarcely walk home at the end of the day's work . . . I could not blame my parents in the least; they were very kind."[82] Many of the autobiographers were angry with their employers who, they considered, possessed the discretion

[78] Brierley, pp. 22–3.
[79] Thomson, p. 53. His family was at the time in the throes of a financial crisis occasioned by the failure of a public house which his father had unwisely taken on.
[80] M. Anderson, *Family Structure* p. 129. See especially the account of C. M. Smith, p. 14.
[81] Carter, *Memoirs*, p. 70; Hopkinson, p. 13; Farn, p. 301.
[82] Anderson, p. 7. See also Bezer, p. 163; Parkinson, p. 6.

to treat them better, and some extended their hostility to an attack on the organization of production in general, but the only criticism we find of the parents is in the occasional instance of a drunkard father who was thought to be squandering the family's finances.[83] There was instead, amidst the hardship of their working lives, a deep sense of satisfaction in their knowledge that as much as they depended upon their parents and other members of the family, the family in its turn, depended on them. Look for instance, at the intricate pattern of adjustment, assistance and dependence presented in Somerville's account of the functioning of his family economy:

> James was too young for the heavy task of cleaning the cow-houses every morning, which had to be done, but as he could make shift, with the assistance of one or two of the other children nearest him in age, to carry straw and turnips to the cattle, and give them water; and as the payment of the few pence per day was an object of importance to the family (I do not now remember what James got per day; it was, however, less than I subsequently got when a boy for the same kind of work, and my wages were sixpence per day), William got up every morning to do part of the work to keep James in the employment.[84]

The second consequence was that as long as they received some support from their family economy in return for their financial contribution, the children were capable of containing their suffering within the framework of the values of security and dependence which we have been examining. Many of the autobiographers dwelt in considerable detail on their hardships, but as long as they saw some purpose in their labour, they accepted their situation, however grudgingly. Not all of them went to work as cheerfully as the anonymous Printer's Devil, but most shared a little of his response to his family's poverty: "Compelled, therefore, partly by necessity, and a natural desire to ease a tender parent of part of a burthen, I eagerly embraced the offer of employment in a branch of the art of whip-cord making, having for my week's services about a shilling".[85] The emotional satisfaction of giving and receiving help could exist alongside and, to a limited extent, could ameliorate the worst forms of child labour. In 1832, at the age of seven, the Dundee Factory Boy was sent into a Dundee spinning mill where he worked a thirteen hour day for 1s. 6d. a week and was subject to extensive physical brutality and moral degradation, yet his experiences drew him even closer to his mother who had been forced to find work for him following the transportation of her husband:

> . . . even amidst our misfortunes, wretchedness, and poverty, rays of felicity sometimes penetrated and relieved our minds from the painful monotony of unceasing misery. I know that when under the olive branches of my mother's affections, I often forgot all the ills of my daily life. She too felt so happy when I came home on the Saturday nights, and laid my small wages in her lap, that the tear would sometimes start to her eye. Perhaps it was a tear of gratitude, or sorrow, excited by wanting the protection of a husband and gaining the premature assistance of a son.[86]

[83] See especially Davis, p. 6. [84] Somerville, pp. 11–12.
[85] Printer's Devil, p. 13. He was aged eight or nine at this point.
[86] Dundee Factory Boy, p. 25. His father, a country shoemaker, had been transported for seven years after killing a man in a drunken brawl. The most comprehensive study of the value of

However, where the family economy proved incapable of providing its dependent members with security and training, the value of service became increasingly attenuated and the child came to see his earnings as a measure not of his pride and satisfaction in making a contribution, but of the degree of his exploitation as an individual worker in the labour market. Charles Shaw, for instance, employed in a pottery from the age of seven and totally separated from the rest of his family economy, confined the narrative of his occupational activity to the inadequacy of his wages and the severity of his working conditions. From the moment of entry, we are presented with a precise account of the size of his income and the length of his working day: "My wage was to be a shilling per week. For this large sum I had to work from between five and six o'clock in the morning, and work on till six, seven or eight o'clock at night, just as Jack pleased".[87] William Dodd began work for the same wage which seemed a pitiful return for his sufferings:

> At my first starting in the works, I had 1s. per week, and got gradually advanced till I was 14 years old, at which time I had 3s. 6d. per week. The average wages are about 2s. 6d.; and thus, for a sum of money varying from one farthing to one halfpenny per hour, a sum not more than half sufficient to find me in necessaries, I was compelled, under fear of the strap and the billy-roller . . . to keep in active employ, although my hands were frequently swollen, and the blood was dripping from my fingers' ends. I was also compelled to listen to, and be witness of almost every species of immorality, debauchery, and wickedness; and finally, to be deprived of the power of those faculties nature had so bountifully supplied me with.[88]

As a rule, the weaker the support functions of the family economy, the more we are told about the income of the child labourer. Those who were the victims of the worst excesses of the factory system, Shaw, the Dundee Factory Boy, T. Wood and Dodd, together with those children who went into the mines, Mountjoy, Rymer, Marsh and Errington, provide us with detailed balance sheets of wages and hours, Dodd even going so far as to present his childhood income in the form of a separate table.[89] Their earnings now expressed and symbolized their isolation and vulnerability as child labourers, and the positive areas of meaning in childhood were increasingly excluded from the functioning of the family economy and placed in the context of other activities such as, in particular, education.

(iv)

Although this chapter has concentrated on the experiences of children, the evidence has a relevance for the family economy as a whole. The child's wants and values are in many respects a reflection of those of his parents, and

family earnings in the textile industry is to be found in Frances Collier, *The Family Economy of the Working Classes in the Cotton Industry* (Manchester, 1964).

[87] Shaw, p. 16. For the value to their family economies of the earnings of wives and children in the pottery industry, see Neil McKendrick, "Home Demand and Economic Growth: A New View of the Role of Women and Children in the Industrial Revolution", in Neil McKendrick, ed., *Studies in English Thought and Society* (London, 1974), p. 187.

[88] Dodd, pp. 10–11. See also T. Wood, p. 7.   [89] Dodd, p. 27.

in general the record has been made by children who have grown into adults and have become, for the most part, responsible for dependents of their own. If the mature perspective perhaps adds some clarity to events which at the time may have appeared more confused, it should underpin the criteria by which they control and respond to their own family economies.

The children of the labouring poor had always had to work, and had always presented their parents with the fundamentally insoluble problem of how to simultaneously nurture their children and exploit them economically. A limited defence against the harsher manifestations of this dilemma, and a degree of compensation for the grief and hardship which it inevitably entailed, were provided by connecting certain economic and non-economic functions of the family. Some satisfaction was gained from the way in which in sending the child out to work, the family might be passing on its traditions to the next generation. If the child could be provided with material security and some training, or control over the training, the parents would still be fulfilling their role as guardians, and if the father could influence the conditions and future prospects of his child's employment, he would retain a small niche of independence in the impersonal labour market. Finally, the pain of sending or being sent out to work could be alleviated by the sense of mutual dependence which could accompany it. In this way it is possible to understand how the fact that a child was made to perform tasks which by our standards he would not have been expected to undertake, even in a modified form, until he was twice the age, did not necessarily mean that the affective relationships between the members of the family had broken down.

These findings bear some relation to the pioneering work of Neil Smelser,[90] but whilst retaining the concern to understand the relationship between the productive and reproductive functions of family life, these conclusions suggest more complex patterns of change than Smelser's model of functional integration and differentiation. In the pre-industrial family economy, the functions were neither as integrated nor as stable as has been suggested. There was a permanent and growing tension between the need for security and the need for independence, and at best, the sense of mutual dependence accompanied rather than obliterated the pain and destruction of child labour. Furthermore, whilst the economic power of the father was the fulcrum upon which the critical relationship between the economic and non-economic functions rested, it is an oversimplification to regard the disagregation of his economic authority and other socializing functions as being itself the "key dissatisfaction". The capacity to be involved in the socialization of a child was certainly an important value. The capacity to exercise influence over the child's occupational present and future was a different, though equally prized value. But the really destructive element of the factory system, and in particular the early mines and mills, was not that it prevented a father from simultaneously performing both roles—in the past he had only done so in some domestic workshops, from which members of the early factory workforce were probably not recruited anyway—but it so destroyed his economic power that it prevented him from performing either

[90] Neil Smelser, op. cit., especially pp. 180–224; also, Neil Smelser, "Sociological History: The Industrial Revolution and the British Working Class Family", in, M. W. Flinn and T. C. Smout, eds., *Essays in Social History* (Oxford, 1974), pp. 23–38.

role at any time. He was unable to prevent his child undergoing such a destructive experience in his workplace as to make any nurturing that either parent might undertake practically useless. The early factories both intensified the hardships of child labour and emptied it of what positive value it had possessed.

Chapter Five

Childhood

The period of childhood offers the autobiographer a particular freedom of selection and interpretation. Whereas the narrative of his adult life may be extensively shaped by the characteristics of the career he has followed, there is no equivalent framework for that part of his life which in itself is private and of no direct consequence to contemporary history. If the writer is true to his own memory, his account will begin with a series of disconnected fragments whose meaning is unclear even to him. Thus Henry Price, one of the least sophisticated and most direct of the autobiographers, opened his account with an alarming and slightly mysterious event which befell him at the age of two: "My earliest recollection is of waking one morning and finding myself in a one room Thatch'd cottage crying and trying to get up the chimny and so finding a way out, failing in that and getting as black as a sweep, and an old woman taping at the window".[1] His next memory was of suffering an attack of measles: ". . . how long I cannot tell however I soon got all right, for a short time after I was todling back and forth in front of the fire from the lap of the good woman in whose care I was to the good man Her Husband previous to going to bed. The next thing I remember was the door being open'd and a young woman looking on–rushing toward me catching me up in her arms and smothering me with kisses".[2] Price had an unusually disrupted home background which complicated and eventually defeated his attempts to establish the meaning of his first recollections, yet in his confusion he succeeded in transmitting the unpredictable and disjointed way in which the memory of childhood works.[3] How the adult responds to the challenge of finding a pattern in these experiences will depend not only on the quality of his recall but on his assumptions about the nature of childhood and its relevance to his mature personality. This chapter sets out to explore how the autobiographers' attitudes to the significance of their childhood were influenced by their experiences at home, at school and at work, and in turn informed their discussion of them.

(i)

John Younger grew up in the remote Border village of Longnewton. He justified his decision to devote the first one hundred and forty pages of his autobiography, which he wrote in about 1840, to this period of his life, on the grounds that

[1] Price, p. 1.   [2] *Ibid.*, p. 1.   [3] See I. M. L. Hunter, op. cit., pp. 269–280.

. . . nice observation might perhaps trace much of the future character of the man as developed in these childish exercises, as perhaps something of future ruling passion and principle may be here formed, or take at least the bent of their future peculiar direction. This is a little in consistence with Wordsworth's idea, when he calls the child "the father of the man" though perhaps not calculating on the same strict degree of phrenological principle.[4]

Wordsworth's celebration of the natural innocence of the child whose spontaneous and creative spirit was ever threatened by the adult world stood in direct contrast to the view of childhood as the period in which original sin might permanently corrupt the moral being if it were allowed to flourish unchecked. Those of the autobiographers who were writing within the spiritual tradition could find little of value in their early years. "The writer of the following words", began William Smith's *Memoir*, "is now 84 years of age, he being born on August 17 1820 in the town of Wellington, Salop, and up to the age of 21 lived a wicked and profligate life far above many men older in years."[5] As soon as he was capable of self-expression the child demonstrated his sinful state—"We soon began to manifest the depravity of our corrupt hearts in acts of mischief and disobedience to our parents, often causing them the keenest sorrow", wrote Josiah Basset of himself and his siblings.[6] The development of a child's personality was merely a matter of the increasing scale of his transgressions: "But as in stature I advanc'd," sang James Downing, "In sin I did proceed".[7] "When about seven years of age", recollected William Bowcock, "my condition as a lost sinner appeared evident", and by the age of eleven he had become "a willing slave of sin".[8] The child's parents were the victims of his evil ways, and often partly responsible for them through their failure to exercise sufficient discipline. "Yes, my dear young reader, it is good for a man that he bear the yoke in his youth.", concluded Robert Butler after recounting the way in which he had been so indulged that he was almost "ruined for time and eternity".[9] Some of the autobiographers who viewed their childhood in a more positive light had nonetheless undergone periods of intense religious guilt, to which they looked back with a mixture of curiosity and profound distaste. James Bezer devoted a whole chapter of his autobiography to the impact on his young conscience of the hell-fire preaching of his Dissenting Sunday school teacher. A particularly eloquent sermon on the wrath to come finally overcame the child's resistance:

> As I went home I felt dreadful, yet a beam of hope shone—oh, if I could only get the opportunity, nobody seeing me, of doing as the *'ancients'* did, I should be saved! So, begging of father and mother (I was not *nine years* old at the time) to let me stay in, while they went to the chapel—I actually undressed myself to the skin, got out of the cupboard father's sawdust bag, wrapped myself in it, poured some ashes over my head, and stretched myself

---

[4] Younger, p. 17. The reference is to a line in the first of a group of Wordsworth's poems known as "Poems Referring to the Period of Childhood". For the development of the idea of childhood in the works of the romantic poets, see Peter Coveney, *The Image of Childhood* (Harmondsworth, 1967), pp. 52–83.

[5] W. Smith, p. 180.   [6] Basset, p. 2.   [7] Downing, p. 2.

[8] Bowcock, p. 1. See also Teasdale, pp. 5, 33.

[9] Butler, pp. 14–15. For the similar treatment of childhood in the Puritan autobiographies, see Owen Watkins, op. cit., pp. 53–7.

on the ground, imploring for mercy, with such mental agony and such loud cries that the people in the house heard me, and told my parents about it, though nobody even then knew the truth. Readers will doubtless laugh at this childish folly,—I marvel if some of them have not committed quite as fantastic tricks, if they would only own it![10]

Such an event was the cause of great suffering and probably left a permanent scar on the adult psyche, but in common with the majority of the autobiographers, Bezer was now capable of opposing this guilt-laden approach with a set of assumptions which stressed the innocence and vulnerability of the child whose qualities were not necessarily interchangeable with those of the adult he was later to become. "There is nothing but poetry about the existence of childhood", wrote John Clare, "real simple soul-moving poetry laughter and joy of poetry & not its philosophy & there is nothing of poetry about manhood but the reflection & the remembrance of what has been."[11] The growing sensitivity to the development of the child was a means not only of reaching a more satisfactory understanding of the autobiographer's personality, but of focusing attention on the relative significance of the two fundamental experiences of every working class child, his education, in the general sense of the term and perhaps in the form of institutional schooling, and his life as a child labourer. The problem now was how far the natural qualities of the child were permitted or encouraged to flourish by his surroundings, and how far they were damaged or repressed by his involvement in the economic life of his parents.

The central theme of John Younger's long account was the resilience of the child's vitality: "Oh! the days of youth were such that even in a condition where family poverty pinched of bread, the ills of the period seldom gave more of trouble than was necessary to correct or rectify the excess of pleasure that touched the young nerves so thrillingly".[12] Elsewhere we have numerous accounts of childhood sports and pastimes carried on amidst or in spite of the hardships of their backgrounds. The pattern of games, adventures, transgressions and punishments, was both private to each child and common to all children. "From the time of my birth until I was seven years of age," wrote the cobbler's son James Child, "I cannot say very much, as my time was chiefly occupied in sleeping, eating and drinking and playing like other boys and getting into mischief . . . My chief companion was my hoop which I was never tired of, although as the seasons came round, peg-tops, hocking, sliding and other games took the place of the hoop."[13] Modern children perhaps play "coach and horses" less frequently than Thomas Dunning and his friends, who used to harness themselves together with ropes, elect a driver, and visit "all the villages for miles around, to the great terror of the quiet boys thereof",[14] and the majority certainly have much less contact with the countryside than even those autobiographers who were brought up in the expanding industrial towns, like Joseph Gutteridge in Coventry, or James Hopkinson in Nottingham, both of whom described playing in fields and streams which had long since been built over by the time they came to write,[15] but in general the evidence here

[10] Bezer, p. 167. His father was a Spitalfields hairdresser. See also Bamford, *Early Days*, pp. 113–4; Cooper, pp. 37–9; Hanson, p. 11.   [11] Clare, *Autobiography*, pp. 44–5.
[12] Younger, p. 61.   [13] Child, p. 1. See also Mabey, pp. 5–13.
[14] Dunning (1977), p. 120. He was living at Newport Pagnell at this time.
[15] Gutteridge, pp. 83–94; Hopkinson, pp. 7–10.

confirms the established picture of the traditional character of much of children's recreations.[16]

Yet if there was an element of timelessness about the games, the context within which they were played belonged very much to this class in this period. In the first instance, the various activities which were recorded were almost invariably dependent on the child's energy and imagination, occasionally assisted by a minimum of equipment. It cost nothing, save wear and tear on clothing, to go bird-nesting, and very little to equip a small boy as a fisherman. Anything more elaborate was out of the question, which particularly affected those children whose inclinations included reading. Many of the more literate autobiographers went out of their way to stress that their love of books began in their childhood, and was as natural a pleasure as running in the fields. As such, however, the opportunities for fulfilling their awakened appetite were constrained by their parents' poverty. The poet John Plummer, for instance, the son of a poor staymaker, described how ". . . I always felt a strange kind of fascination for books; and although I could not read them, yet I would pore for hours over the—to me—mystical letters of the alphabet",[17] but once he had learnt to read, the condition of his parents' finances imposed a severe restriction on his pastime: "It would be too long a task to relate my numerous attempts to procure the books which my parents were too poor to purchase for me; or of my haunting the street bookstalls, where I gazed with sad, longing and despairing features on the literary treasures displayed before me, and which the want of a few pence alone precluded me from possessing".[18]

While he played, or attempted to play, Plummer was finding out about the poverty of his family, and as the autobiographers became more aware that, as Thomas Carter put it, "the human mind generally retains, in mature years, much of the tastes and habits it acquired in childhood," and that, "important consequences may and often do arise out of circumstances or practices which in themselves are of little worth",[19] so they began to realize that amongst the inconsequential pastimes of their childhood they had been learning basic lessons about deprivation and inequality. When a child first becomes conscious of himself, the way of life of his parents and companions will appear both natural and inevitable, but as he grows older and gains some knowledge, however incomplete, of other forms of existence, so he will begin to comprehend the peculiarity of his situation. Edward Davis was brought up in the Aston area of Birmingham in a family whose prosperity was undermined by the drinking habits of his father. As his parents moved from home to home, young Edward began to look about him and draw some conclusions: "At the early age of four my outlook upon life was rather a gloomy one, and it remained gloomy for many years. We removed from Holt Street at about this time, and went to a house in Lister Street. There it began to dawn upon me that I belonged to

---

[16] See Iona and Peter Opie, *Children's Games in Street and Playground* (Oxford, 1969), especially pp. 6–8, and *The Lore and Language of School-children* (London, 1977), especially pp. 27–35. The Opies perhaps place undue emphasis on the element of continuity, but the autobiographies do not contain sufficient material on games to sustain the detailed study of nineteenth century childhood pastimes and their relationship with the rest of family life, which is by now badly needed.

[17] Plummer p. xv. See also Carter, *Memoirs*, p. 20; Harris, p. 9; Leatherland, p. 3; Heaton, p. xvi; Brown, p. 294.   [18] Plummer, p. xvi.

[19] Carter, *Memoirs*, p. 27. Also Aitken, 25 September, p. 3.

what is known as 'the poor class of society', for everything in our home seemed to be more sparsely served out than in our neighbours''.[20] Other children accepted the picture of the world presented to them by their parents until they were shocked into self-awareness by a chance discovery. The process was described with great force by Charles Shaw in a chapter entitled, "First Knowledge of Disadvantage".[21] As a child he had played like any other, and had accepted without much complaint that at the age of seven he should abandon his games and go to work. Then, about a year later, while enjoying a brief moment of leisure during his working day, he came across another boy reading a book:

> Now, I had acquired a strong passion for reading, and the sight of this youth reading at his own free will, forced upon my mind a sense of painful contrast between his position and mine. I felt a sudden, strange sense of wretchedness. There was a blighting consciousness that my lot was harsher than his and that of others. What birds and sunshine, in contrast with my work had failed to impress upon me, the sight of this reading youth accomplished with swift bitterness. I went back to my mould-running and hot stove with my first anguish in my heart. I can remember, though never describe, the acuteness of this first sorrow.[22]

Sooner or later the "blighting consciousness" that he was a member of the working class, and of a particular section of that class, would come upon each of these children. As he came to terms with his knowledge, the child gained a new regard for the period of innocence in which he had played and even worked in ignorance of his lot in life, a regard which became more intense and often more generalized as the boy grew further away from his childhood and entered into his full inheritance as a working man. None of the autobiographers endured more physical and emotional suffering than Willie Thom[23] and none spoke in more glowing terms of his early years:

> Oh the days of childhood! Voyage thereafter as we may on smooth or on broken water, these are the landmarks that will never fade. The blue of our native hills may be lost to the eye for long, long years, yet once again we press their heathery bells; but you ye sunny scenes of infancy, though ye glimmer through every darkness, and at every distance, we never meet again.[24]

The Dundee Factory Boy wrote in much the same vein about what, in retrospect, seemed to be the near idyll of his playing days,[25] and it was those children, either on the land or in the new factories, who were least protected by their family economy, who were most likely to use the notion of childhood innocence as a means of conceptualizing and measuring the destructive character of their experience as child-workers. The first chapter of Roger Langdon's autobiography, entitled, "Why was I born", was organized around a contrast, both stated and implied, between two conflicting versions of his childhood. Although in many respects his working conditions were no worse than those under which agricultural children had laboured down the centuries,

---

[20] Davis, p. 21.   [21] Shaw, chapter 3, pp. 20–26.   [22] *Ibid.*, p. 21.
[23] See above, chapter 3, pp. 52–3, 59   [24] Cited in Robert Bruce, op. cit., p. 19.
[25] Dundee Factory Boy, p. 3. See also C. M. Smith, p. 4.

they now appeared a denial of everything childhood stood for: "I was under Jim's control for five years," he wrote "years of my childhood which I ought to be able to say were the happiest of my life. But they were just the reverse, and if I stated all that I suffered at his hands, no sane person would believe that such things could be done with impunity".[26] This approach was developed to its fullest extent by the "Factory Cripple" William Dodd, who began his account by deliberately emphasizing the projected development of the playing child: "I was born on the 18th of June, 1804; and in the latter part of 1809, being then turned of five years of age, I was put to work at card-making, and about a year after I was sent, with my sisters to the factories. I was then a fine, strong, healthy, hardy boy, straight in every limb, and remarkably stout and active. It was predicted by many of our acquaintance that I should be the very model of my father, who was the picture of robust health and strength, and in his time had been the don of the village, and had carried off the prize at almost every manly sport"[27] and then went on to describe in gruesome detail the ways in which it was his fate ". . . finally to be deprived of the power of those faculties nature had so bountifully supplied me with".[28] Nature and the child were now opposed to labour in a way which would have had little meaning for earlier generations of working children.

To identify the manner in which the conditions of employment had repressed or damaged their moral and physical development was to make a judgement on the organization of production in general, and many of the autobiographers made it clear that as they learned about the world into which they had been born, either through their direct experience or through watching the trials and reactions of their parents, they were forming their basic political and social values. Samuel Bamford was particularly aware of the way in which as a young child, who still had no other business but to amuse himself, he had been receiving lessons about what was right and wrong in his society. One crucial memory was of the day his mother paid a visit to her sister who had married a woollen draper and was living in some comfort in Manchester. His aunt was so proud of her new-found status that his mother, who had married a struggling handloomweaver, was admitted no further than the servants' quarters, and she walked back home through the rain, hurt and angry. "I remember as it were but yesterday," wrote Bamford, "after one of her visits to the dwelling of that 'fine lady', she had divested herself of her wet bonnet, her soaked shoes, and changed her dripping outer garments, and stood leaning with her elbow on the window sill, her hand up to her cheek, her eyes looking on vacancy, and the tears trickling over her fingers".[29] As he sought to understand the relationship between the playing and the learning child, he came back to this event:

> Many of the earliest of my impressions were calculated to make me feel, and think, and reflect; and thus I became, imperceptibly as it were, and amidst all the exuberant lightsomeness of childhood, impressible and observant. The notice I took of my mother's anguish and her tears (as before mentioned), whilst it made me hateful of all wrong,—hateful so far as my young heart could be so,—disposed me, at the same time to be pitiful towards all suffering.

[26] Langdon, p. 33.   [27] Dodd, p. 6.
[28] *Ibid.*, p. 11. See also Farish, *Autobiography*, p. 17.   [29] Bamford, *Early Days*, p. 6.

It was the means of calling into action two of the strongest and most durable impulses of my heart—justice and mercy.[30]

Bamford had yet to begin contributing to his family economy, but this event planted in the mind of the future radical politician the seeds of "an unmitigatable contempt for mere money pride, much of it though there be in the world; and as thorough a contempt . . . for the unfeelingness which Mammonish superiority too often produces".[31] "I verily believe", wrote J. C. Farn, "that the anxieties from which I saw my parents suffering, principally induced me to make long, earnest, anxious, and I will add, honest and disinterested exertions to ameliorate the condition of the working classes",[32] and the miners' leader Edward Rymer located the origin of his commitment to trade unionism in the hardships suffered by his family during the 1849 Durham miners strike, which took place when he was about nine: ". . . and what I heard and saw sunk deep into my very soul, and left the principle and impression stamped in my nature that 'union is strength, and knowledge is power' ".[33] Whether the influence was a particular event or situation, or the general ideological background of the home, as in the case of the Halifax Chartists Benjamin Wilson and John Snowden,[34] the adult autobiographers could identify the "exuberant light-someness of childhood" as the time when they first began to question the distribution of power and privilege in their society.

By concentrating on what Burn called the "under-developed sensibility" of the child, the autobiographers were, in effect, dividing their childhood into two parts. At the outset, it was possible to locate the notion of innocence in their behaviour as playing children. Despite the poverty of their backgrounds and the early age at which they had to begin work, their energy and imagination were able to find expression in a wide range of pastimes. However, as time passed and the demands of the family economy threw a shadow over their recreations, the notion of innocence began to be opposed to their actual experience. The dawning knowledge of alternative versions of childhood and thus of the true identity of the path that the working class child must travel was contrasted with the time when his circumstances had appeared as natural as the fields in which he had played; the damaging effects, of, in particular, work in the new factories, were set against the manifested potential of the growing child; and finally the impact on the naive and spontaneous sympathies of the child of the suffering of those about him was seen as the foundation of his sense of the injustice of the situation of the working class in general. In part the autobiographers were trying to recapture what it had actually felt like to play and then to work, to accept the world into which the child had been born and then to begin to realize that all was not as it might be, and in part they were consciously employing an interpretative framework to evaluate events whose meaning was at best only dimly apparent at the time. A major component of the bridge between the outlook of the child and that of the mature adult was the idea and actual experience of formal education. School was the buffer between play and work and its extent and content would inevitably influence the child's response to the transition, and in turn the adults wrote as men who had, for the most part, received some education and were now making more

---

[30] *Ibid.*, p. 39.   [31] *Ibid.*, p. 7.   [32] Farn, p. 197. See also Arch, ch. 1, *passim.*
[33] Rymer, p. 3.   [34] Wilson, p. 195; Snowden, col. 1.

use of it than their teachers could ever have expected. The remainder of this chapter will be concerned with the nature and implications of the schooling given to these children.

(ii)

Almost all the autobiographers felt bound to devote a section of their account to their education, no matter how transient and superficial it might have been. Few had less schooling, for instance, than John Jones, a servant born in 1774 in the Forest of Dean. His education consisted of a brief period at a dame school, followed by two years of lessons on winter evenings given by a retired stone-cutter. Nonetheless he took pains to record it in his brief autobiography, concluding ". . . and that, Sir, was the finishing of my education".[35] Few were less literate than the farm labourer's son James Bowd, whose school career began and ended in a few months, yet we are presented with a careful assessment of his aptitude as a pupil and of the quality of the teaching he received.[36] At the other end of the scale the "Living Publicist" J. C. Farn wasted no time in getting down to the major topic of interest in his childhood: "The place of my birth was a town in one of the Midland Counties, my parents were in humble circumstances, and my opportunities of improvement few and far between. I well remember the torments children in those days were compelled to undergo in order to master the first rudiments of education . . .".[37] For many of the autobiographers the preoccupation with elementary education continued throughout their adult lives as they themselves became Sunday school teachers, ran elementary classes attached to mutual improvement societies, or in some cases started their own day schools. Christopher Thomson wrote a lengthy introduction to his autobiography outlining the necessity of educating working class children,[38] and William Lovett was co-author of the most comprehensive and influential working class tract on elementary education to appear during this period.[39] If their concern often seems out of all proportion to the meagre schooling they received, we are presented with sufficient information to form a picture of both the consumer's experience of elementary schooling in this period, and the significance which working men attached to the subject.

The most striking characteristic of the treatment of this topic is the general recognition of the subordination of education to the demands of the family economy. We may gain some indication of the autobiographers' attitude by glancing briefly at how they handle the point at which they are finally taken away from such schooling as they have been receiving, and are introduced to permanent employment. It is here that they are able to suggest the relationship of their education to the economic situation into which they have been born. Although many of the accounts include lengthy expositions of various aspects of the educational system, we rarely get more than perfunctory one-line statements on the reasons for the departure. John Harris, for instance, winds

---

[35] Jones, p. 171.   [36] Bowd, p. 293.   [37] Farn, p. 196.
[38] Thomson, pp. 1–25: "A Word to My Class".
[39] William Lovett and John Collins, *Chartism* (London, 1840). See Harold Silver, *English Education and the Radicals 1780–1850* (London, 1975), pp. 78–82.

up a long account of several schools with the brief: "At nine years of age I was taken from school and put to work in the fields, to drive the horses in the plough to Uncle George Harris, Bolennowe".[40] J. C. Farn simply concluded that, "The income of my parents rendered it necessary that I should do something for my living as soon as possible, and accordingly I was sent to work before I was eleven years of age".[41] The sword could fall at any moment, the deciding factor being one of a number of possible events. On occasions a family economic crisis, such as the loss of earnings of an elder sibling or the father, could precipitate the child into a job, as was the case with Edward Rymer: "Squire Clough kindly sent brother John and me to school at Thirsk; but we only attended for a short time, when my father left us, and my mother, though toiling hard to keep the home together, had to avail herself of any small labours we elder boys could render".[42] In the rural areas the seasonal demands of agriculture would interrupt education several times a year until one winter the child would simply not go back to school,[43] and in both the town and the country an unexpected offer of a job could terminate an education literally overnight. Even when the child was destined to take up an apprenticeship at the age of thirteen or fourteen, the normal pattern was to leave school between nine and eleven, and fill the intervening period with a variety of odd jobs. The requirements of the family economy, the possibility that the child would be required to act either as a baby-minder while the parents worked, or as an extra contributor to it, hung over every moment of such education that the autobiographer received. Henry White was taken away from school at the age of eight to look after "several younger brothers and sister", sent back again a year later, and finally, "having reached the mature age of ten years and my parents having to provide for the wants of several other little ones, I had to prepare to take my part in bearing the burden and heat of the day. It was about Harvest time, the middle of August 1832, when I commenced to toil for my daily bread".[44] The conclusion of Thomas Wood's account summarizes the experience of the children of factory workers whose position, in this respect, had changed very little from the children of the agricultural worker: "My school life came to an end when I was about eight years old. Perhaps I hastened the event for what with nursing and winding bobbins I had no time to con my lessons and was often on this account in trouble. I now went to work at John Sharpe's mill at the bottom of the town and quite close to the school I had left".[45]

Education was a commodity which had to be paid for. If the child was a potential income earner, then any week-day education he or she received was an expense to the family, even in the few instances when it was technically

---

[40] Harris, p. 32. See also P. Taylor, p. 38; Thomson, p. 51; Farish, *Autobiography*, p. 11; G. Herbert, p. 7; McKenzie, pp. 25–6; Teasdale, p. 24; Mitchell, p. 24.

[41] Farn, p. 196.

[42] Rymer, p. 3. See also Leno, p. 3, whose education was cut short when his father lost his job; and Lowery, p. 45, whose schooling was brought to an end at the age of nine by the onset of his father's fatal illness.

[43] Pamela Horn, *Education in Rural England 1800–1914* (Dublin, 1978), pp. 123–4, 134–40.

[44] White, pp. 15, 25. His father was a farm labourer in the small village of Bagendon, between Cheltenham and Cirencester. See also Mabey, p. 13.

[45] T. Wood, p. 7.

free.[46] The presence of a son or daughter at school stood to the child and his family as a statement of the economic state of the household. Some of the autobiographers' parents were well able to afford the cost, but others could only do so by making sacrifices elsewhere, and their children were well aware of it. William Adams, for instance, who was brought up by his grandmother, described how his education was financed: "My dear old grandmother was too poor to pay even the small fee required—sixpence or eightpence a week. It was therefore agreed that she and her daughters should do an equivalent amount of laundry work for the schoolmaster and his family".[47] John Clare was conscious of the continual interaction between poverty and his attendance at school ". . . but God help her, her hopeful and tender kindness was often crossed with difficulty, for there was often enough to do to keep cart upon wheels, as the saying is, without incurring an extra expence of pulling me to school, though she never lost the opportunity when she was able to send me, nor would my father interfere, till downright necessity from poverty forced him to check her kind intentions".[48] In the same way William Heaton's education started and stopped as his family exhausted the tiny margin of surplus income. He was taught to read at a local school, but then his father, a journeyman tanner, was unable to pay for him to be sent to a schoolmaster to learn to write.[49] The effect of poverty on school attendance could also be felt in ways which were less quantifiable. Alexander Somerville, for instance, explained why he did not go to school until he was nearly eight: "But the chief reason for not being sent sooner to school, I believe, was the want of clothes, such as the affectionate feelings of my father and mother wished me to go in— simply something else than rags; and these were not to be had until 1818, when markets fell, and food being cheaper, it became possible to get clothes".[50]

The immediate consequences of the subservience of education to the family economy were twofold. In the first instance it imposed a serious limitation on the amount of learning the scholar might acquire. Many of these autobiographers could be numbered amongst the intellectual elite of the working class, yet the most they ever gained from their schooling was what Arch described as the "rudiments" of reading, writing and arithmetic, which constituted a "foundation" upon which he was later able to build up "a solid little structure of knowledge".[51] William Lovett ". . . learned to write tolerably well, and to know a little of arithmetic and the catechism, and this formed the extent of my scholastic acquirements".[52] William Green recorded that ". . . when I left school I certainly had learned to read, make figures and scribble after a fashion",[53] and when John Harris's education ended, he was, "then barely able

---

[46] Although they were committed to a policy of free education, most church schools made a small weekly charge and the private schools charged up to 9*d.* a week. Mary Sturt, *The Education of the People* (London, 1967), pp. 39–41, 161–2; David Wardle, *English Popular Education 1780–1970* (Cambridge, 1970), p. 61; E. G. West, "Resource Allocation and Growth in Early Nineteenth Century British Education", *Economic History Review*, 2nd series, vol. XXIII, 1970, p. 84.

[47] Adams, vol. 1, pp. 75–6. This "small fee" was in fact at the top end of the range charged by elementary schools.

[48] Clare, *Sketches*, p. 47.

[49] Heaton, pp. xvi–xvii. He eventually learnt to write at a Methodist Sunday school.

[50] Somerville, p. 19. Also, Langdon, p. 24; Hanson, p. 25; Pamela Horn, *Victorian Country Child* . . . , pp. 22–4.

[51] Arch, pp. 26–7.   [52] Lovett, p. 5.   [53] Green, p. 10.

to read and write and cast up figures".[54] Another future poet, Robert Story attended the village school at Howtel in Northumberland, where, "I learned nearly all that I ever learned from a Master—namely to read badly, to write worse, and to cipher a little farther, perhaps than to the Rule of Three".[55] The Sunday schools aimed no higher than a basic literacy[56], and the dependence of the church schools on the monitorial system placed a further impediment in the way of the naturally intelligent child, as Thomas Dunning observed: "I was sent to the Church, or National school on Bell's system, to learn but very little. The boys who could read moderately well were appointed to teach the younger or lower classes. I was one of these and I had very little time allowed me for either writing or arithmetic, and none for grammar or geography".[57] The only autobiographers to learn more than "the three R's" were Charles Smith, who attended a grammar school near Bristol for two years where he picked up "small Latin and less Greek", Thomas Wood, who intermittently attended a grammar school for a similar period where he also acquired a little Latin, and the disreputable "Hawkie", William Cameron, who somehow made the acquaintance of the classics during a brief sojourn at a Scottish parish school.[58] Otherwise the general experience provides detailed confirmation of Christopher Thomson's angry summary of the educational opportunities presented to working class children: "Our poverty has been an insuperable bar to admission into any school, save the so-called charity schools, and a mere apology for learning doled out to us—just allowed to learn enough to 'get the catechism', some to write their own names, few to learn the simple elements of accounts—then, with such acquirements, early in life, started to the factory or dung-yard, to earn a few pence to assist in procuring a family bread loaf".[59]

The second consequence was that the forces affecting school attendance were such as to prevent the identification of the period of institutional education with a particular period of childhood. It is impossible to make any firm statement on the basis of these autobiographies about the average length and consistency of attendance, other than it was highly unlikely that the child would be at school after the age of fourteen, the usual age of apprenticeship.[60] The lack of a clear distinction between child-minders and dame schools, and the wide variation in the ages at which the autobiographers went to schools undermine an attempt to establish a general age of entry and the constant vulnerability of the children to the economic demands of the family makes the point of departure equally variable. In the day schools most would have left

[54] Harris, p. 12.   [55] Story, *Poetical Works*, p. v. See also Blacket, p. 14; Farn, p. 196.
[56] For an assessment of their achievements, see T. W. Laqueur, *Religion and Respectability, Sunday Schools and Working Class Culture 1780–1850* (New Haven, 1976), pp. 119–123.
[57] Dunning, pp. 119–20. He entered the school in 1820, four years after its foundation. See also J. B. Leno's similar experience in an Uxbridge National School a decade later (Leno, p. 4). On the monitorial system, see Frank Smith, *A History of English Elementary Education 1760–1902* (London, 1931), pp. 150–2; Mary Sturt, op. cit., pp. 30–7.
[58] C. M. Smith, p. 3; T. Wood, pp. 34–7; Cameron, p. 13.
[59] Thomson, p. 19. He was writing in 1847.
[60] The outstanding exception was Thomas Cooper who was still at school at the age of fifteen, although by this time he had virtually ceased to be a pupil and was acting as assistant to the schoolmaster. No reliable national statistics were collected until the 1880s, but such surveys as were carried out in the 1840s suggested that the average period of attendance for those who attended day schools at all would be between one and two years, frequently with interruptions. See John Lawson and Harold Silver, *A Social History of Education in England* (London, 1973), p. 278; David Wardle, op. cit., pp. 45, 65.

by the age of ten or eleven but in the Sunday schools the situation is again complicated by the propensity of successful institutions to merge into adult education and·for successful pupils to evolve into teachers as time passed. John Bezer, for instance, entered a Spitalfields' Sunday school at the age of five, graduated to the testament class at the age of seven, the top class at the age of eight, thence became "head boy", monitor, and at the age of nine, a "teacher".[61] All we have is a faint suggestion that individual schools or areas observed some local rules of attendance. Arch described how "I began to attend when I was six, the eligible age",[62] and Carter's attendance at a local school in Colchester which was supported by a "congregation of Protestant Dissenters" was circumscribed by the standing regulation that "The period for which the boys were admitted was three years".[63] Otherwise, variation was the rule.

Even where it is possible to establish the boundaries of a child's education, attendance was likely to be anything but continuous. The schooling of most of the autobiographers who grew up in rural areas was controlled by the seasonal fluctuations of agricultural labour. John Clare, brought up in the Northampton-shire village of Helpston, summarized the position occupied by his education: "As to my schooling, I think never a year pass'd me till I was 11 or 12, but 3 months or more at the worst of times was luckily spared for my improvement . . .".[64] Timothy Claxton spent a higher proportion of the year at school, but again he was well aware of the extent to which his education was held on licence from his family economy: "So, although there were five of us, and our labour was of some consequence to them, I (the third), at six years of age, was put to a schoolmaster in the neighbouring market town for two years, excepting harvest-time each season, when I was taken home to aid my industrious mother in gleaning, which in that part of the country, is a great help to the poor".[65]

In both the rural and urban areas there also seems to have been a surprisingly high tendency to change schools during the child's educational career. Over half of those who attended school at all attended at least two, some more. Even Harris and Somerville, who lived in isolated rural areas, managed to change their place of education. In some cases, notably that of Samuel Bamford, who attended no less than four schools, one of them twice, enthusiastic parents were an important factor. There were in addition some more general reasons for changes and interruptions. The private day schools which many attended were usually ephemeral institutions, which opened and closed with great ease. Cooper and Adams both transferred to new schools which were more convenient to the place where they lived. The first half of the century was a period of great personal mobility with large scale migration from rural areas into the new industrial towns, and around the towns themselves as they rapidly expanded. Such movement was often sufficient to terminate a child's education altogether, but given a residue of determination on behalf of either child or parent, it could again mean frequent changes of school. Josiah Basset described how his

---

[61] Bezer, p. 157.

[62] Arch, p. 27. He attended an Anglican parish school in the Warwickshire village of Barford.

[63] T. Carter, *Memoirs*, p. 44.   [64] Clare, *Sketches*, p. 48.

[65] Claxton, p. 2. He does not identify the area in which he was born. For other accounts of seasonal education, see Somerville, p. 15; P. Taylor, p. 11; Stonemason, p. 19. See also I. Pinchbeck and M. Hewitt, *Children in English Society*, vol. II (London, 1973), p. 399; P. Horn, *Victorian Country Child* . . . , pp. 18–19.

family's need to keep one step ahead of the landlord resulted in his attending at least five schools in the Southwark area of London: "My father being often unable to pay his rent was constantly changing the place of his abode. He was anxious, nevertheless, wherever he went, to place us under the care of religious teachers. Thus, in a short time, I was removed from Kent-street to Mint-street, Flint-street, York-street, and Lion-street schools".[66] The interruptions would mean bewildering changes of types of school, and at the very least served to further fragment the educational experience of the working class child.

Industrialization intensified and highlighted the existing vulnerability of children as scholars.[67] William Dodd was not the only autobiographer to receive no day-schooling[68], but as long as a child remained outside a factory it was always possible that his parents might find the time or money to arrange at least a few months' education. The extreme situation of the factory children eventually led to the first formal identification of a period of a working class child's life as being the period in which he or she should receive at least some education. Although the factory acts of 1802 and 1819 contained educational provisions, the first serious attempt to enforce a minimum age of employment in factories came with the 1833 factory act which laid down that no children might be employed in cotton factories below the age of nine, and that those between the ages of nine and thirteen were to receive two hours teaching for each of six working days. In 1844 the teaching was increased to half a day but the minimum age was dropped by a year.[69] However, by the end of the period the legislation affected only a fraction of the potential school population, and the experience of the one autobiographer, Thomas Wood, who actually attended a factory school suggests that the innovations were of limited value: "I well remember" he wrote, "the first half-time school in Bingley. It was a cottage at the entrance to the mill yard. The teacher, a poor old man who had done odd jobs of a simple kind for about 12s a week was set to teach the half-timers. Lest, however, he should teach too much or the process be too costly he had to stamp washers out of cloth with a heavy wooden mallet on a large block of wood during school hours".[70]

At best elementary education remained a fragmentary experience, sub-ordinated to the demands of the family economy and unlikely to endow even the most privileged and intelligent of working class children with any more than Arch's "rudiments" of literacy and numeracy. As such, it would seem scarcely possible that the institutions would be capable of becoming either the

[66] Basset, p. 2. He completed his education in the workhouse. Bamford's perambulations were at least partly due to a move during his childhood from Middleton to Manchester and then back to relations in Middleton. Some discussion of the mobility of schoolchildren is to be found in Mary Sturt, op. cit., pp. 163–4.

[67] Sanderson concludes that in Lancashire the initial impact of the factory system on elementary education was such as to cause a drop in literacy rates which did not begin to pick up again until the early 1850s. Michael Sanderson, "Literacy and Social Mobility in the Industrial Revolution in England", *Past and Present*, no. 56, 1972, pp. 75–89.

[68] At least seven others, mostly those from unusually poor backgrounds, received no day schooling.

[69] For details of the legislation, see F. Smith, op. cit., pp. 106–7, 112, 143, 195; Michael Sanderson, "Education and the Factory in Industrial Lancashire 1780–1840", *Economic History Review*, 2nd ser., vol. XX, 1967, pp. 266–279; A. H. Robson, *The Education of Children Engaged in Industry in England 1833–1876* (London, 1931), chs. 2 & 3.

[70] T. Wood, p. 7.

catalyst for the emergence of a new attitude towards the nature of childhood or a focus for the aspirations which it embodied. There were however, two aspects of the elementary education system in this period which may help to explain the attention that was paid to it. The first of these was that within the severe limitations imposed by their economic situation, working class parents retained considerable involvement in the education of their children.

We can begin to gain some indication of the parents' relationship with the pattern of schooling if we glance at the characters of those who actually taught the autobiographers. Few of the children attended schools controlled by more than one master. Dame and private day schools rarely contained more than twenty or thirty pupils, and were often much smaller, and whilst the church schools were frequently designed to accommodate over two hundred, it was intended that the monitorial system would enable a single master to cope with the increased numbers. Consequently the personal attributes of the teacher, who in the private schools probably would be also the proprietor, was of great importance in determining the nature of the education given and received. Even if we disregard the dame schools which, whether they were merely child-minding establishments or genuinely attempted to impart some education, were run almost invariably by women from within the working class community, it is noticeable how often the individual involved had a background of manual labour.[71] Some had been forced into retirement by ill-health or old age and had turned to teaching to stay alive. John Harris, in common with several other autobiographers, was taught by such a man who ran his own school:

> My next teacher was a miner, a mild pious man, of the name of Roberts. He had met with an accident in his work underground, depriving him of a leg which was badly supplied with a wooden stump. In those days any shattered being wrecked in the mill or the mine, if he could read John Bunyan, count fifty backwards, and scribble the squire's name was considered good enough for a pedagogue; and when he could do nothing else was established behind a low desk in a school. I do not think John Roberts's acquirements extended far beyond reading, writing and arithmetic, and I doubt if he knew what the word geography meant.[72]

William Cameron spent four years at a school run by "an old decrepit man, who had tried to be a sailor, but at that employment he could not earn his bread".[73] A second group was formed by those who still pursued manual occupations alongside their profession as teachers. Thomas Carter, for instance, went to a Dissenting school large enough to support two schoolmasters but

---

[71] There has been no satisfactory study of the teaching profession during this period, but Asher Tropp concludes that in 1846, the majority of teachers ". . . were men who had tried other trades and failed. They had been semi-skilled craftsmen, shopkeepers, clerks or 'superior' domestic servants". *The School Teachers* (London, 1957), p. 10. See also R. W. Rich, *The Training of Teachers in England and Wales during the Nineteenth Century* (Cambridge, 1933), p. 118; R. R. Sellman, *Devon Parish Schools in the Nineteenth Century* (Newton Abbot, 1967), p. 19. For Scotland, see Marjorie Cruikshank, *History of the Training of Teachers in Scotland* (London, 1970), pp. 16–71.

[72] Harris, p. 25. "Those days" were the 1820s and 30s. See also P. Taylor, p. 24; Farish, *Autobiography*, p. 10; Tester, p. 2; Innes, p. 7; Hampton, p. 16.

[73] Cameron, p. 11. At the end of his four years, he " was not four months advanced in learning, although I was so far advanced as my teacher".

neither was full time. One used to spend most of his time surveying, the other was "a good penman, tolerably skilful in arithmetic, and generally attentive to his duties. His proper occupation was that of a shoemaker, and he was accustomed to fill up his spare time, during school hours, by making or mending shoes".[74] A third group were the working men who had somehow gained a reasonable education and were prepared to put their talents at the service of the community. The numbers in this group especially were on the increase during this period as the drive for self-improvement began to yield results, and we shall be looking at them in more detail in chapters seven and eight. There were several patterns here. Some, like Thomas Cooper, abandoned a trade, in his case shoe-making, and became full-time teachers, or like Christopher Thomson, took to teaching during a recession in their occupation and then went back to work; some became local preachers and in this way became school-masters—several of the autobiographers were taught by such men; some, like the stone-cutter who taught John Jones, gave lessons in the winter evenings when there was a demand for them;[75] and finally there were the legions who worked a full six-day week alongside their fellow-labourers, and on Sundays taught in the local Sunday school—Shaw, for instance, was taught by a "butty collier", and Brierley by a journeyman shoemaker.[76]

During this period working class parents normally paid for such education as their children received. Despite the growth of the British and National school systems, and the introduction, in 1833, of State finance of education, up until the 1830s well over half of all elementary education was provided by private day schools. As late as 1850, there were still more private than church schools, although the schools in the church systems, which had expanded rapidly in the late 1840s in response to the political unrest earlier in the decade, tended to be much larger, and now contained about two thirds of the pupils.[77] The private day schools, often run by working men, were totally dependent upon the fees, and thus the goodwill, of the parents in the community, and despite the beginnings of a national system, even the church schools were run by local initiative, and required the support of local parents. For this reason we frequently find references in these accounts to the reputation of the teachers. Thomson describes how his teacher, Mr. Brocklebank, "was very anxious that the boys under his care should become scholars, and by their talents procure for him a good reputation as a teacher".[78] Somerville attended a private day school where the quality of the teacher overcame the apparent disadvantage of not being associated with the church: "It was not a parish school; but he had

[74] Carter, *Memoirs*, p. 53.
[75] Jones, pp. 171–2.
[76] Shaw, pp. 135–6; Brierley, p. 15. The great majority of the 250,000 teachers in 1851 were from the same social class as their pupils. T. W. Laqueur, op. cit., pp. 91–3.
[77] See F. Smith, op. cit., pp. 220–222. The figures are taken from Horace Mann's 1851 education census. It is not possible to be at all precise about the period before the mid-1830s, but research by West into the period between the "Brougham" and "Kerry" returns of 1818 and 1833, a period in which the number of day scholars increased by 89 per cent whilst the total population increased by only 24 per cent would suggest that the bulk of this growth was met by this unofficial private initiative. This was particularly the case in the expanding cities, such as Manchester and Bristol, where the local statistical societies continually emphasized the central importance of this type of schooling. See E. G. West, *Education and the Industrial Revolution* (London, 1975), pp. 59–94.
[78] Thomson, p. 38.

a local fame as a good teacher".[79] Gutteridge was at one stage taught by a Wesleyan preacher, who "had the reputation of being a passable scholar and a good teacher".[80] In the absence of any professional standards or qualifications,[81] and given the complete freedom of anyone to call himself a teacher and his front room a school, word-of-mouth comment on the quality of the school could determine its success or failure. When Thomas Cooper first went into the business at the age of twenty-three, he benefited greatly from his local reputation: "My school was eagerly patronised by the poor; and I had a few of the children of the middle class. People in the little town had been talking for years about the remarkable youth that was never seen in the streets, and was known to wander miles in the fields and woods reading. He was believed by some to be a prodigy of learning; and they would send their children to be taught by him".[82] Equally his subsequent failure was also due to the attitudes of parents who, having sent their children to Cooper mainly because he knew Latin and other esoteric subjects, were not enthusiastic about him actually passing on this knowledge.[83]

The incidence of working men as teachers and the dependence of all types of elementary education on the goodwill of the potential customers meant that the working class community possessed a significant area of initiative in the field of schooling. Education was far from being a commodity that was forced upon the working class community by outside agencies. Although private teachers and especially the teachers and managers of church schools often made strenuous efforts to recruit pupils, the parents were in the last resort free to decide whether to send the child to a school, which school to send him to and when to remove him, the only exceptions being where the child was working in a factory covered by the 1833 or 1844 Acts, in a workhouse after 1834, or lived in a village where the parson in alliance with local employers might be in a position to exercise sanctions against absentees from day or Sunday schools. In the absence of any schools, or any schools thought to be suitable, there is evidence that parents would attempt either to educate their children themselves or appoint a sibling or relation to the task,[84] and it is clear that many of the private day schools were formed as much on the initiative of parents as of the potential teacher. David Love, for instance, found himself unemployed after a twelve month spell as a collier:

[79] Somerville, p. 20.   [80] Gutteridge, p. 7. See also P. Taylor, p. 3.

[81] The first teacher training colleges were set up by the British and National Societies in 1808 and 1812, but few of the teachers employed by either Society would have any more training than perhaps a couple of weeks sitting at the back of a class in another school before being placed in full command of their own institutions. The first national qualifications were instituted under the Pupil Teacher Scheme which began in 1846, however even here only about a quarter of those who completed the five year apprenticeship would be awarded a scholarship to a training college where they could study for a certificate. John Hurt, *Education in Evolution* (London, 1972), pp. 93–106: R. W. Rich, op. cit., pp. 115–145; Asher Tropp, op. cit., p. 11.

[82] Cooper, pp. 72–3. The "little town" was Gainsborough.

[83] *Ibid.*, p. 99.

[84] Hamlet Nicholson, John Wood, Thomas Oliver and Samuel Bamford were taught to read by their fathers (p. 3, p. 5, p. 53); Joseph Gutteridge was helped in his lessons by his father (p. 85); J. B. Leno, the Dundee Factory Boy, William Bowcock and Joseph Mayett were taught by their mothers (p. 4, p. 30, p. 1, pp. 1–2); Thomas Carter was taught by an elder brother and in turn taught a younger sister (*Memoirs*, pp. 21–2, 68); Henry Herbert was taught by an uncle (p. 11); Robert Butler by his grandmother (pp. 11–12); and William Lovett by his great-grandmother (p. 3–4).

I went in search of a master for a week, but could find none, at last I was persuaded by some people in a large village to keep a school to teach their children: they found me a large empty place, somewhat like a barn, with a fire place at the end: they soon furnished it with forms and tables, and the first week I got more than twenty scholars, increasing each week, till I had above forty; but I got no more than a penny each week for readers, and three halfpence for writers, so that my wages were but very small and ill paid. My abode there was short, about five months.[85]

Where the parents were faced with schools which were already established they retained the consumers' choice as to whether to purchase their services. There are odd references to parents exercising somewhat direct methods of control over would-be teachers—William Cameron, like David Love, out of a job, reluctantly agreed to take up a post in a Scottish mining village where the parents had "stoned a number of teachers out of the place before I went"[86]— but in the educational market place such actions, though presumably effective, were not the only means of expressing an opinion about the quality of a teacher. Even in small rural communities, concerned parents were often in a position to discriminate between alternative schools. Joseph Blacket, a day labourer's son in the Yorkshire village of Tunstall, attended one school until he was seven, and ". . . another school being opened, by a man who my parents thought better able to instruct, I was placed by them under his tuition, and continued to write and learn arithmetic till the age of eleven".[87]

The initiative possessed by working class parents should not be overstated. The freedom not to send a child to a teacher the parents disliked, a freedom made all the greater by the lack of any rigid conventions as to when a child should be at school, might amount to a freedom to choose between some education or none at all. The teaching in the private day schools could be of extremely poor quality, and by the mid-1840s these schools were beginning to lose out in competition with the better organized and financed church schools where the parents would have much less control over or affinity with the content and methods of instruction. However, both as individuals and as members of religious or self-improvement organizations, the parents' initiative could be highly constructive. Relative to other important areas of his experience, such as conditions of employment and housing, the working man had a genuine chance to intervene and exercise influence. The teaching supplied by the church schools could be questioned and in some cases replaced by types of schooling, in the form of private day schools and Sunday schools in which the teaching was given by working men and women whose activities were controlled by the community they served. The overwhelming influence in the field of elementary education was not the much publicized and much analysed institutions of the Benthamite and denominational educational reformers but the economic circumstances of the working class families; and within these confines working men retained a real incentive to think about education, to talk about education and to act in the field of education.

[85] Love, p. 14.   [86] Cameron, p. 15.
[87] Blacket, p. 13. For an interesting case study of working class parents discriminating in favour of working class run schools, despite their greater cost, see Phillip McCann, "Popular education and social control; Spitalfields 1812–1824" in Phillip McCann, ed., *Popular education and socialization in the nineteenth century* (London, 1977), pp. 1–49.

The second aspect of the educational experience of the autobiographers which directed their attention towards the subject is the simple fact that despite the problem of cost, despite the demands of the family economy, despite the mobility of their families, despite the erratic provision and uncertain existence of schools, the great majority could record some attendance, no matter how brief or interrupted, at some type of elementary school. There may well be an element of bias in the sample here, but as has been indicated previously, the autobiographers number in their ranks those who were brought up in the poorest and most remote sections of the working class community, and those who achieved during their lifetimes only a minimal command over the basic skills of reading and writing. In the absence of reliable statistics, particularly with regard to the Sunday and private day schools, it is impossible to set these accounts in the context of a firm numerical generalization,[88] but it would seem likely that as a result of the combined efforts of dame and private day schools, Sunday schools and the denominational day school systems, factory and workhouse schools, and schools sponsored by working class organizations, by the mid 1840s the great majority of working class children either received some education, however notional, or were at least in a position to form some estimation of what they were missing. At the most pessimistic reckoning, two thirds of working class children could look back on careers as pupils,[89] and the wealth of detail in the autobiographies suggests that the inadequacies of the teaching and the continuing dominance of the family economy could not altogether obliterate the experience. An alternative definition of the identity of the child had been glimpsed, and in a sense the anarchy of educational standards and patterns of attendance could only intensify the feeling of dissatisfaction with the situation and increase the desire to rationalize their treatment.

The autobiographers' careers as pupils were also sufficient to establish education as an agent of differentiation within otherwise homogeneous communities, which is one of the most characteristic consequences of a fully developed educational system. At the most formative period of their lives many of the autobiographers were singled out from their contemporaries and informed that they stood at the head of a hierarchy of personal merit. The reference group· could be extremely limited—John Harris looked back to a dame school consisting of himself and just six other pupils, but the teaching had sufficient content for the child to be measured against his fellows: ". . . and I was soon considered to be the best scholar in her establishment"[90]—and the period cf attendance might be very brief—James Hogg's schooling ended when he was just six years old, but he could still claim that by the time he left, he "had the honour of standing at the head of a juvenile class".[91] Equally the rewards were in themselves trivial—Ben Brierley remembered winning three marbles as the first prize in spelling at a private day school[92]—and indeed

---

[88] Such statistics as are available suggest that between 1818 and 1851 the number of day scholars in England and Wales increased from 674,883 to 2,144,378 enlarging the proportion of the population at school from 1 in 17 to 1 in 8. See F. Smith, op. cit., p. 220.

[89] See David Wardle, *English Popular Education* . . . , p. 65.

[90] Harris, p. 23.   [91] Hogg, p. 5.

[92] Brierley, p. 6. For other prizewinners, see H. Herbert, p. 13; White, p. 24; Shaw, p. 7; Teasdale p. 21; Oliver, p. 8.

educational achievement could be an altogether mixed blessing, as Anthony Errington recalled:

> When I got lorned to spell, one day Thos Nisbet and severell others was standen to say speling, and I sounded the word "stranger", which he had not done, and I got before him. At 12 Oclock, he struck me and made my nose blead. On which a batel comenced, and I proved Conckerror by thrusting him into a Boghole and made him all dirt. On going to school again and mistress being informed by he, I was sentenced to be hugged as before, mistress not hearing my report. But upon a nibouring woman saying that he gave the first offence, she repented and made a small preasent to me when it was too late.[93]

Nonetheless the importance of the differentiation to the growing child stands out from these accounts. Thomas Carter, for instance, summarized his three year career at a school run by the local Dissenters: "Whenever I was unable to get on without assistance, I asked and always obtained my master's help: by these means I eventually became superior to my schoolfellows in regard to writing and figures, and as I was also tolerably clever at orthography and reading, I was promoted to the first seat in the first form, thus becoming what was called 'head boy' ".[94] The concept of education as a matter of hierarchical attainment was enshrined in the monitorial system used by the church schools, and even at the weekly Sunday schools the identity of the child was shaped in academic competition. Thus, for instance, Emanuel Lovekin: "I went to the Wrockmerdine Wood Primitive Methodist Sunday School a good while learned a little knowlidge and truth, For which I had great cause to thank God, Still by perseverance I got to read fairly well and write a little and Somehow I was looked up to as Something alien to the Common Class of young men".[95] Any achievement was largely symbolic as the elaborate system of prize-giving which characterizes modern education was then in its infancy, there was no national system of examinations until the introduction of the pupil teacher scheme in 1846,[96] and the real element of differentiation—the chance offered to the academically successful working class child to step upon the ladder that led up to the middle class—was still half a century away. However, the brief excursions into institutional education which were made by these autobiographers encouraged them to begin to measure their identity in relation to their occupational and social equals in terms of educational attainment. It was here that they first learnt to regard themselves as "something alien to the common class of young men", and it was a lesson which, as their statements in the autobiographies demonstrate, they did not forget.

(iii)

As industrialization progressed, the experience of childhood became increasingly determined by the child's social class. The grammar schools which had once

[93] Errington, pp. 5–6. "To be hugged" was to be held on the back of a larger boy and beaten with a cat o' nine tails, a fate which had previously befallen Errington for playing truant and going bird-nesting.
[94] Carter, *Memoirs*, p. 55.   [95] Lovekin, p. 3.
[96] One of the autobiographers, the anonymous Stonemason, who also showed great promise as a

offered a limited opportunity to the children of the poor, gradually became the preserve of the middle class.[97] The perspective of the working man's child was confined at best to a brief and inadequate period of elementary education which was subordinated to the child's role as a contributor to the family economy. Yet on examining these accounts it becomes evident that education was neither so alien nor so insubstantial a process as might at first appear. In a sense, the key quality of the education system was that it was itself in its childhood. Like a child its immediate constructive capacity was limited, and equally the scope and character of its future development seemed both un-determined and full of potential. Furthermore the working class community could claim if not sole paternity then at least a significant share in the creation and maintenance of the educational opportunities that were open to their children.[98] They could often teach their own children as much as they would be likely to learn in school, they could come together either informally or through some existing institution to sponsor or organize schools, they often supplied the teachers from their own ranks, and as consumers in what was very frequently a genuine market place, they could exercise some influence over the education their children received. It is not difficult for historians to identify a vigorous and heavily financed campaign to develop elementary education as a means of enforcing the social and occupational values of the middle class,[99] but there is a danger of overstating its impact, particularly before the late 1840s. In some instances, such as Joseph Arch's home village of Barford in Warwickshire, the parson could use the church school as a means of extending the influence of the church-squire axis which had traditionally ruled the community. Arch was well aware of the lessons he was being made to learn as a child, and as a parent in the same village vigorously fought the parson-as-teacher on behalf of his own children. In other rural communities and towns where there was a wider range of actual or potential schooling, the process was much less straightforward, and education could be regarded in a much more positive light both because there were alternatives to the middle class church-based education systems, and because even within the church schools, some value would be placed on the education, irrespective of the dressing of catechism-learning and prayers.

In part it was simply that literacy itself was seen, as we shall see in more detail in the following chapters, as an essential tool for freedom of thought and expression, and in part it was that whatever disciplinary overtones it might have, however inefficient it might be in practice, the idea of education embodied certain notions about the identity of the child which, in view of the develop-

schoolboy, was amongst the earliest entrants to the scheme, but he abandoned his "apprentice-ship" after two years and went to be a grocer's errand boy.

[97] Lawson and Silver, op. cit., pp. 250–6, 335; Michael Sanderson, "The grammar school and the education of the poor, 1796–1840", *Journal of Educational Studies*, vol. II, no. 1, Nov. 1962, pp 28–43. Samuel Bamford (born in 1788) was one of the last to be aware of the possibility of a route to higher education. He attended the junior section of Manchester Grammar School and his father refused to let him accept an opportunity to proceed into the Latin class, and he was "thrust . . . from that portal of knowledge which I never afterwards had an opportunity of approaching" (Bamford, *Early Days*, pp. 92–3).

[98] This was especially true of the Sunday schools, which is the central theme of Laqueur's recent major study.

[99] See, most recently, J. M. Goldstrom, "The content of education and the socialisation of the working class child 1830–1860", in Phillip McCann, op. cit., pp. 93–110.

ments which we traced in the previous chapter, were coming to assume a heightened significance. As it became increasingly difficult to palliate the irreconcilable conflict between the need to nurture and exploit working class children, so as we saw in the first section of this chapter, greater attention was being paid to the characteristics of the growing child. The more emphasis that was placed on his innocence and unfulfilled attributes the more his natural development seemed to be opposed to his actual experience in the working class family economy. In this sense education seemed to supply both a definition of the proper identity of the child as a being still learning and requiring the drawing out of his inherent potential, and a practical, if extremely unreliable alternative to and defence against his experience at work. Charles Shaw entitled the first two chapters of his autobiography "Education" and "Work" and in so doing indicated the conflict between the creative and fundamentally appropriate activity of the school and the destructive and in every sense unnatural life of the factory. John Bezer, another Sunday school scholar and one who was extremely critical of both the spiritual hypocrisy and pedagogic incompetence of many of his teachers, nonetheless relished his education: "I yearned for it; whether it was because my home was not as it ought to have been . . . or because association has ever seemed dear to me, or because I desired to show myself off as an apt scholar, or because I really wanted to learn, or all these causes combined—most certainly I was ever the first to get in to school and the last to go out".[100] As an alternative to his wholly unprotective family economy which was causing and was to cause him intense physical suffering as an exploited child-worker, as a repository of working class aspiration and a degree of working class intervention and control, and as an arena, virtually the only arena, in which he might discover and enlarge basic and essential skills which had a value far beyond their very limited economic application, his schooling was at the centre of his assessment of his experience as a child. The autobiographers had nowhere else to turn but to their games and their schooling, however much of a travesty that experience might have been, if they wished to identify the memory of what they once had a right to expect of their world.

[100] Bezer, p. 157.

Chapter Six

The Pursuit of Books

The title of this book is taken from one of the best known working class auto-biographies, William Lovett's *The Life and Struggles of William Lovett In his Pursuit of Bread, Knowledge and Freedom*. The phrase captures the essence of both Lovett's career and those of the majority of individuals whose accounts we are studying. These were men who struggled for their bread in common with the rest of their class, but who also found in themselves the desire and the energy to embark upon the pursuit of knowledge and freedom. The order in which these objectives were listed reflected the relationship between them. The pursuit of bread was the prime concern of any working man, and the context within which all other activities were conducted. The pursuit of knowledge derived its impetus from the circumstances under which bread was gained, and in turn was seen as the essential pre-condition for the pursuit of freedom. By "knowledge" Lovett and the other autobiographers meant book knowledge, and the reading and on occasions writing of literature lay at the centre of their response to the industrializing society. As we saw in chapter two, the auto-biographies were themselves a product of the invasion of the lives of working men and women by the written word, and their contents record the diverse attempts which were made to use the materials and skills of written communication to come to terms with their situation in the organization of production, and to create the possibility of emancipating themselves from the forces which controlled their lives. Part Three will study the pursuit of knowledge in its relation to the pursuit of bread and freedom at three levels. The present chapter is concerned with books as physical objects. It examines the way in which the profile of the pursuit of knowledge was defined by the efforts made by the readers to resolve the practical problems with which they were faced. The following chapters will look at the debate which took place over the meaning of the notion of "useful knowledge" and at the attempts which were made to connect knowledge with freedom.

(i)

Few homes of the labouring poor in pre-industrial Britain were devoid of literature. In the late 1830s, the Central Society of Education commissioned a series of investigations into the reading habits of the working class, which set out to contrast the situation in the towns with that in the rural areas. The findings show very clearly the traditions of book-owning inherited by those who embarked upon the pursuit of knowledge. An enquiry into the condition of sixty-six families in five Norfolk parishes,[1] for instance, revealed that, "Only six of the whole number of families were wholly without books. In three of the remaining sixty there was only a Hymn book; the rest were provided with Bible, Testament and Prayer-Book, generally with two and sometimes with all three; but there does not appear to have been any other description of book in any one of the cottages".[2] A similar picture was revealed by surveys in Kent, Essex, and Herefordshire.[3] It was uncommon to find a home which lacked any literature, although the size and scope of the cottage libraries were usually extremely limited. There might be a few chap-books, the odd volume of travel and exploration, a few old newspapers and journals, but on the whole secular works were comparatively rare. Instead the tiny libraries were largely composed of works connected with the Protestant religion. There would normally be a Bible and perhaps a Prayer Book, a haphazard collection of religious commentaries and sometimes one of the classic works of religious imagination, particularly *Pilgrim's Progress* and *Paradise Lost*. Even in the more prosperous working class households, the libraries were unlikely to be any more extensive. Looking back to his native Bingley in the 1820s, Thomas Wood recalled that, "Books were a luxury in a decent home. A cottage library in a fairly well-to-do family would seldom exceed half-a-dozen volumes, and consisted of such works as Dodderidge's 'Use and Progress of Religion in the Soul', Bunyan's 'Works' particularly the 'Pilgrim's Progress', Cook's 'Voyages', 'News from the Invisible World' etc. and a volume, or perhaps two, of magazines".[4]

The surveys constantly emphasized, however, that the possession of the books bore little relation to the practice of reading. In Dunkirk in Kent, out of fifty families, "The returns state that in two cottages only did the parents employ their evenings in reading",[5] and in neighbouring Broughton-under-the-Blean, the figure was four out of fifty.[6] In general the situation confirms John Clare's comment that, "The Bible, is laid by on its peaceful shelf, and by 9 cottages out of 10 never disturbed or turn'd to further than the minute's reference for reciting the text on a Sunday".[7] The Bible was less the mediator between man and God than a vague symbol of religious commitment, useful as a primer for young children who were learning their letters, an occasional source of entertainment, even, indeed, a particularly suitable item for pawning in times of need. Before the beginning of the consumer revolution towards the end of the eighteenth century, a family's stock of books would constitute the bulk of its

---

[1] G. R. Porter, "Results of an Enquiry into the Condition of the Labouring Classes in five parishes in the County of Norfolk", in *Central Society of Education, Third Publication* (London, 1839), pp. 368–374. The parishes were Mattishall, East Tudenham, Caveston, Hockering and Elmham. Sixty-one of the heads of households were agricultural labourers, and there was one carpenter, one smith, one shoemaker, one bricklayer and one chimney sweeper.

[2] *Ibid.*, p. 372.

[3] *Ibid.*, pp. 87–139; *Central Society of Education, First Publication* (London, 1837), pp.342–59; *Second Publication* (London, 1838), pp. 259–60.

[4] T. Wood, p. 9. See also Joseph Lawson, op. cit., p. 42.

[5] *Central Society of Education, Third Publication*, p. 118.

[6] *Ibid.*, p. 122.   [7] Clare, *Sketches*, p. 51.

non-essential possessions, and William Brown, who had been apprenticed to a pawnbroker in Sheffield remembered that ". . . I have known scores who have regularly pawned their Sunday clothes, bible, etc, every Monday morning, and redeemed them as regularly every Saturday . . .".[8] In addition, the Bible was important to the family as an agent of continuity from generation to generation. Several of the autobiographers make use of the record of births and deaths kept in the family Bible to reconstruct their own family trees. It was a practice which suffered with urbanization for as the families moved into the overcrowded cities, the family heirlooms, including the Bibles, were frequently lost. The Central Society of Education surveys in Marylebone reveal a much lower rate of possession of Bibles than in the rural areas.[9]

This pattern of ownership and use persisted in the majority of working class households throughout the nineteenth century. The possession of mostly ephemeral secular literature may have increased, but a survey of a Lancashire working class community in 1904 revealed a similar predominance of a small number of religious works.[10] Yet however small the libraries, and however unread the majority may have been, their existence at the beginning of the nineteenth century, together with the correspondingly high literacy rates,[11] constituted an essential foundation for the pursuit of knowledge. Most of the autobiographers could find at least some printed matter in their parents' homes, some of it fit for little more than helping them to learn to read, but much else, including the Old Testament, Milton and Bunyan, capable of firing their imagination and awakening an unquenchable appetite for all forms of literature. Furthermore, the evidence of seventeenth and eighteenth century spiritual autobiographies written by labouring men,[12] together with the activities of Stephen Duck and his successors,[13] suggest that there had always existed a minority of genuine readers in even the more isolated rural communities. The nineteenth century readers thus inherited both a background of book ownership and a tradition, albeit a narrow one, of serious reading. What was to change as the industrial revolution began to transform the lives of the working class was both the scale of their activity and the meaning that was attached to it. The way in which the tiny libraries were handed down from generation to generation suggests that the working class community in general, and not just the committed readers, had always possessed a certain reverence for the printed word. Now, however, there emerged a tradition of reading, of pursuing knowledge, which had at its centre, quite simply, a love of books.

This is brought out with great clarity if we look at the account given by Ben Brierley, a Lancashire weaver, of the formation of a mutual improvement society in Failsworth in the early 1840s. A small group of young working men met together in a little room in a building used by the local Sunday school. Typically the society decided that the main priority was the formation of a

---

[8] Brown, p. 18.

[9] *Central Society . . . First Publication*, pp. 339–42; *Second Publication*, pp. 250–56.

[10] R. D. Altick, op. cit., p. 246.

[11] See chapter one, pp. 7–8. High though they may have been, if the C.S.E. findings are accurate, more families must have possessed books than could actually read them.

[12] See especially Margaret Spufford's conclusion that by 1700, "illiteracy was everywhere face to face with literacy, and the oral with the printed word" (art. cit., p. 427).

[13] See chapter two, pp. 30–35.

library.[14] The first task was to make some bookshelves:

> We desked around the small room we had set aside for our exclusive use, and did other carpentry jobbing in quite a workmanlike manner. Like newly married people who look forward to important events we made our cradle before the child was born—we shelved a corner to accommodate what we had the presumption to call a library. But we had no books, nor had we yet the means of purchasing any. I remember the late Elijah Ridings once saying to me—"If I'd fifty pounds I'd go to Lunnon, an' buy a ton o' books"; what a magnificent spectacle that presented to me![15]

Eventually the room was ready, and the members waited impatiently for the time when they could acquire the first books:

> Supplies came at last, we had been subscribing our pennies weekly until the sum had amounted to something worthy of being invested in literature, and this was to be spent. My uncle, Richard Taylor, who lived near to the School, and was taking an active interest in our Society, was appointed to select a number of volumes from some of the old bookshops in Manchester. He had been a great reader, and was well up in not only literature but some of the sciences, so that we could depend on the choice he would make. I was one of two youngsters told off to carry the books when bought, and were we not proud of the appointment? Elated at the idea of seeing our empty shelves stocked we set out one Saturday afternoon to meet my uncle, who was employed in Manchester, taking with us a weaver's wallet in which to carry the books. The necessary purchases were made; our wallet filled until the weight of it made us stagger; but there being no other means of conveyance in those days, we had to struggle with it until we boarded the treasure in its proper place. It afterwards became a labour of love to cover the bindings, which we did with stout nankeen, so as to make them last for ever. This work accomplished we had a show night for friends, who, while they encouraged us in our undertaking, did not think we could have achieved so much in so short a time. From that nucleus our "library" grew until the shelves would no longer accommodate it; so we had an elegant book case made by a professional joiner, doing the painting and varnishing ourselves. I can see in memory the daub we made of that work. But it was a grand cabinet to us, and caused us to wonder if Manchester possessed anything like it.[16]

The period under review witnessed an enormous expansion in the amount of literature with which a section of the working class came into contact, yet the continual and inescapable tendency of their desire for books to far outrun their ability to satisfy it, and the dominant role that was attached to the power of the written word ensured that the books they did obtain were the subject of a special regard. The term "bibliophile" today carries connotations of aesthetic dilettantism which ill-accords with either the passion or the poverty of the

[14] Samuel Smiles, giving evidence to the Public Libraries Committee of 1849, summarized the general behaviour of the societies, and the general problem: "One of the first things they do is get a library together, but they have considerable difficulty in getting books . . ." *Report of the Select Committee on Public Libraries* (1849), p. 126, Q. 1984.

[15] Brierley, p. 35. For a similar account of artisans building their own furniture for study, see Farish, *Autobiography*, p. 46.

[16] Brierley, pp. 35–6.

members of the mutual improvement societies, but we have only to look at Ben Brierley and his friends applying their artisan skills to the tasks of building bookshelves and binding the precious volumes to see how the term becomes literally appropriate.

(ii)

As they looked back over their life-long struggle to acquire books, the auto-biographers were united in their conclusion that they had lived through an age of progress. "My great want was books", wrote Christopher Thomson of his youth, "I was too poor to purchase expensive ones, and 'cheap literature' was not then, as now, to be found in every out-o'-the-way nooking."[17] Thomson was born in the last year of the eighteenth century, as was another Yorkshire-man, James Watson, who recorded a similar transformation in the volume and cost of literature during the first half of the nineteenth century: "At that time there were no cheap books, no cheap newspapers or periodicals, no Mechanics' Institutions to facilitate the acquisition of knowledge".[18] William Lovett was born a year later, and grew up in an era which now seemed to lie on the further side of a great watershed: ". . . in looking back upon this period of my youth", he wrote, "and contrasting it with the present, and the advantages that young people have in the present age—in the multiplicity of cheap books, newspapers, lectures, and other numerous means of instruction—I cannot help regretting that I was so unfortunately placed; for, with a desire for knowledge I had neither books to enlighten nor a teacher to instruct".[19]

These statements require some qualification. Firstly, in this context cheap literature was a moral as well as an economic category. The autobiographers were not referring to the centuries-old tradition of chap-books which had been peddled around every town and village in the country at prices ranging from a farthing to sixpence. Although the network of chap-men was at last beginning to disintegrate,[20] many of the autobiographers relied upon the collections they found in their homes and perhaps supplemented by a few purchases of their own, for their introduction to secular literature. John Clare provides the best account of this world:

> These were such that came my way 6py Pamphlets that are found in the possession of every doorcalling hawker & on every bookstall at fairs & markets whose bills are as familiar with everyone as his own name shall I repeat some of them *Little Red Riding Hood, Valentine & Orson, Jack & the Giant, Long Tom the Carrier, The King & the Cobbler, Tawney Bear, The Seven Sleepers, Tom Hickathrift, Johnny Armstrong, Idle Laurence*, who carried that power spell about him that laid everybody to sleep—old *Mother Bunch, Robin Hood's Garland, Old Mother Shipton & Old Nixons Prophecys, History of Gotham* & many others shall I go on no these have memorys as common as Prayer books Poulters with the peasantry such were the books that delighted me & I saved all the pence I got to buy them for they were the whole world of literature to me and I knew of no other . . .[21]

[17] Thomson, p. 319. He was writing in 1847.   [18] Watson, p. 109.
[19] Lovett, p. 21.   [20] V. E. Neuburg, op. cit., p. 116.
[21] Clare, *Autobiography*, p. 19.

By the time Clare was growing up,[22] it was becoming less easy to encounter the travelling booksellers, although at least four of the autobiographers, Cameron, Love, Burn and MacKenzie, were involved in the trade in the early decades of the century, but in the towns the publishers of the broadsides and street ballads proved capable of responding to the growing demand for sensational reading matter. James Catnach was the first publisher to exploit this market on a mass scale, and in 1828 he reputedly sold in London alone, 1,160,000 copies of the *Last Dying Speech and Confession of William Corder, the Murderer of Maria Marten*.[23] In the 1830s and 1840s the Salisbury Square publishers consolidated the market for cheap literature, largely relying on weekly or fortnightly serial publications at a penny an issue.[24]

Secondly, the scale of the developments which took place in the decade which straddled the reform bill caused some of the autobiographers to underplay the innovations which preceded the explosion in the late twenties and early thirties. The history of improving "cheap literature" really begins in the Spring of 1792 when Tom Paine published Part Two of *Rights of Man*, and as well as issuing it in the same 3s. edition in which Part One had appeared, he also put out a 6d. edition of both parts. Its success was without precedent in the annals of British publishing. At the end of 1793 it seems generally accepted that 200,000 copies were in circulation,[25] and by 1809 Paine claimed a total circulation of 1.5 million for Part Two alone.[26] Pitt's war government eventually succeeded in suppressing all forms of radical literature, but within months of the final cessation of hostilities Cobbett had reduced the price of his *Political Register* from 12½d. to 2d. increasing its circulation from between 1,000 and 2,000 to between 40,000 and 50,000,[27] and instigated a new era of radical journalism. The achievement of Paine and his successors called into existence a second category of improving cheap literature, the purpose of which was to counteract the influence of radical writing on the working class population. The pioneer in this field was the Cheap Repository Tract Society which in the twelve months between March 1795 and March 1796 distributed an estimated 2,000,000 copies of moral tales and ballads, and gave the political and religious establishment its first lesson in the potential and techniques of mass propaganda.[28]

All the early developments in the provision of cheap literature raised acute problems of political and social morality. According to the category in question

[22] Clare was born on 13 July 1793.

[23] R. D. Altick, op. cit., p. 288; L. Shepherd, op. cit., pp. 72–5.

[24] The one autobiographer to treat this branch of publishing with some charity was Thomas Frost, who had at one point written for it. See *Forty Years Recollections*, ch. VI, "Popular Literature Forty Years Ago".

[25] See E. P. Thompson, *The Making of the English Working Class* (Harmondsworth, 1968), p. 117, and R. D. Altick, op. cit., pp. 69–72 for a discussion of the validity of the circulation figures which are also quoted in R. K. Webb, op. cit., p. 38.

[26] This figure, for which it is impossible to provide any accurate confirmation, includes Irish sales and European translations.

[27] M. L. Pearl, *William Cobbett. A Bibliographical Account of His Life and Times* (Oxford, 1953), p. 68.

[28] G. H. Spinney, "Cheap Repository Tracts: Hazard and Marshall Edition", *The Library*, 4th series, vol. XX (1940), pp. 301–2 and *passim*. The tracts were nominally sold at ½d. and 1d., though many were given away to captive audiences, such as workhouse inmates, charity school pupils, hospitals and prisons.

including the novels of Scott and the poetry of Byron.[49] The variety was a product of the large number of different sources upon which he had been dependent. These included a school library, chapel libraries, Sunday school teachers, a market stall, borrowing from friends, and eventually an artisans' library, which enabled him to acquire Scott and Byron. Each one of these outlets was created by a different set of circumstances, each one offered a limited type of literature.

The physical characteristics of books were also an important contributory factor. It is clear that the cost of certain types of books limited their initial acquisition to groups defined by a particular level of income, and that various chronological developments fixed the earliest point at which different categories of literature could be read. But books are extremely durable. Even the flimsy farthing chap-books sold by the eighteenth century hawkers were often kept for generations in households where they might represent the only secular literature, and provided the essential first primers for the young self-educator. The more substantial two and three decker novels, and works on science and political philosophy which were originally acquired by middle class readers, were, in the course of time, sold to secondhand bookshops, lent or given to servants or employees, bequeathed to libraries, lost or misappropriated. Consequently, even where the working class reader had access to an artisans' or chapel library, he would often find the most incoherent collection of literature which had been somehow acquired.[50] We might look, for instance, at the way in which Charles Shaw's dependence on a small Sunday school library in Tunstall, imparted a magnificent if involuntary scope to his education:

> I read *Robinson Crusoe* and a few other favourite boys' books, but there were not many there. After these the most readable book I could find was Rollin's *Ancient History*. I was somehow drawn by it. His narratives opened a new world, but I never supposed that world had anything to do with the one in which I was then living. It might have been a world whose development took place on some other planet. I regarded it as remote from Tunstall and England as those other worlds I read of in Dick's *Christian Philosopher*, which book I found in the library too . . . Then I read Milton's *Paradise Lost*, Klopstock's *Messiah*, and, later on, Pollock's *Course of Time*, and Gilfillan's *Bards of the Bible*. These books may look now a strange assortment for such a boy of fourteen or fifteen to read, but they were no assortment at all. They

[49] Thomson, pp. 64–5, 79–80, 319, 336–7, 339–40. John Clare similarly reported that, "My Library about now consisted of the following: Abercrombie's Gardener's Journal, 'Thomson's Seasons,' a shattered copy of 'Milton's Paradise Lost,' 'Ward's Mathematics,' 'Fisher's Young Man's Companion,' 'Robin Hood's Garland,' 'Bonnycastle's Mensuration' and 'Algebra,' 'Fenning's Arithmetic,' 'Death of Abel,' 'Joe Miller's Jests,' a 'Collection of Hymns' with some odd Pamphlets of Sermons by the Bishop of Peterborough" (Clare, *Sketches*, pp. 66–7).

[50] The Mechanics' Institute libraries, for instance, acquired large quantities of books by such means, although as George Dawson made clear, the gifts were not always appreciated: "The chief libraries for operatives are those of Mechanics Institutes and they are small. Many of the books are gift books, turned out of people's shelves, and are never used, and old magazines of different kinds, so that out of 1,000 volumes perhaps there may only be 400 or 500 useful ones" (Public Libraries Committee, p. 79. Q. 1212). In his *Manual*, B. F. Duppa described the resulting confusion: "The libraries of Mechanics' Institutions are accumulated in two ways, —by the gifts of friends, and by purchase from the common funds. Hence the varied and unconnected character of too many of them". B. F. Duppa, *A Manual for Mechanics' Institutions* (London, 1839), p. 50.

119

just happened to fall into my hands, and though I might have read more elementary and educative books, these could not have moved the passion in me which these other books did.[51]

Common to the autobiographers was an exuberant catholicism in their approach to literature, which is characterized by Thomas Cooper's proposed course of self-education:

> I thought it possible that by the time I reached the age of twenty four I might be able to master the elements of Latin, Greek, Hebrew, and French; might get well through Euclid, and through a course of Algebra; might commit the entire "Paradise Lost" and seven of the best plays of Shakespeare to memory; and might read a large and solid course of history, and religious evidences; and be well acquainted also with the current literature of the day.[52]

The Dundee Factory Boy claimed that while an apprentice shoemaker, he read, "books on nearly all the disputed questions in theology and metaphysics, books on history, belles letters, and science. I even read the celebrated Decline and Fall of the Roman Empire three times from beginning to end".[53] The particular combination of soaring ambition and undisciplined eclecticism was a reflection of the transformation in the availability of literature and the continuing inability of the readers to control their access to it. It led to heroic feats of learning but at the same time frequently caused considerable confusion both in the minds of individual readers and in the identity of the corporate activity of self-education.

(iii)

"The Pursuit of Knowledge under Difficulties" became one of the key terms in the debate over the purpose of self-education.[54] Its precise meaning varied according to the outlook of whoever was using it, yet as with several other such catch-phrases, the term gained wide currency because it referred to an inescapable characteristic of the experiences of the working class readers. As they attempted to read and sometimes to write, the autobiographers were faced with a wide range of "difficulties" imposed by the conditions in which they lived and worked. In most cases, the first steps in self-improvement were taken in the home, using literature already in the family's possession, and whilst in later life the readers would probably become involved in organizations which used some type of purpose built room, such as a school, or an upstairs room in a public house, the mainstay of their activity would remain private reading in the home. Here the obstacles were as varied as they were formidable. In the first instance, the would-be reader would have the utmost difficulty in finding any privacy and silence. John Harris, growing up in a large family near

---

[51] Shaw, p. 218. Between half and three-quarters of urban Sunday schools had libraries by 1840. T. W. Laqueur, op. cit., pp. 117–8.

[52] Cooper, pp. 57–8.

[53] Dundee Factory Boy, p. 64.

[54] See chapter seven for a discussion of the use of the term. It was the title of one of the major publications of the Society for the Diffusion of Useful Knowledge and Charles Shaw used it as the title of chapter thirteen of his autobiography.

Camborne described the circumstances in which he attempted to write his first verses:

> I wrote in the dear old chimney by the winter firelight, while my buxom brothers were shouting around me. And this was my only study, save the barn or the cowhouse. O how I longed for some obscure corner, where, with a handful of fire in the grate, and the smallest lamp upon the unplaned board, I might write my hymns in quiet. But this was denied me, and I often sat in my bed-room, with my feet wrapped in my mother's cloak, with a pair of small bellows for my writing desk.[55]

For those working men who escaped the worst of the slums, the growth of the new industrial towns had little effect on the size of their living accommodation;[56] nonetheless the working class family could count itself fortunate if it occupied as many as three rooms, and it was only the best of the new artisan dwellings which contained four.[57] The reading had to be done in the presence of other members of the household, and where the reader surmounted the discomfort, he was invariably left with a strong sense of the contrast between his activity and the customary pursuits of the rest of the family, a feeling which John Clare describes very clearly:

> Never a leisure hour pass'd me without making use of it; every winter night, our once unlettered hut was wonderfully changed in its appearance to a school room. The old table, which, old as it was, doubtless never was honoured with higher employment all its days than the convenience of bearing at meal times the luxury of a barley loaf, or dish of potatoes, was now covered with the rude beggings of scientific requisitions, pens, ink, and paper,—one hour, hobbling the pen at sheephooks and tarbottles, and another, trying on a slate a knotty question in Numeration, or Pounds, Shillings and Pence, . . .[58]

Many readers resorted to taking books into neighbouring fields in summers' evenings and on Sundays; and where this was not possible, waited until the rest of the family had finally gone to bed. One of the very few autobiographers who ever managed to acquire his own room in a house was Charles Shaw, and the pleasure which this gave him communicates better than any complaint the deprivation of his fellow readers:

> We had in our house a small room over an "entry". This "entry" afforded

---

[55] Harris, p. 29. J. A. Leatherland pleaded indulgence for the poetry which his autobiography prefaced on the grounds that, "Many of the compositions were written amid noise and bustle —in an apartment common to a whole family, or the din of a workshop—" (p. 39).

[56] In Leeds, the average amount of floor space of working class cottages actually increased slightly between 1790 and the 1830s. W. G. Rimmer, "Working Men's Cottages in Leeds, 1770–1840", *Thoresby Society*, vol. XLVI, 1961, pp. 179–82.

[57] Edwin Chadwick, *Report on the Sanitary Condition of the Labouring Population of Great Britain* (London, 1842, republished Edinburgh, 1965), pp. 82–4, and *passim; Second Report of the Commissioners for Inquiring into the State of Large Towns and Populous Districts* (1845), "Reponses to Questions for Circulation in Populous Towns and Districts", especially Q.51, "What number of families of the poorer classes, on average, inhabit each house?" Appendix, parts 1 and 2, *passim;* Stanley D. Chapman, *The History of Working Class Housing* (Newton Abbot, 1971), pp. 24–5, 97, 136–41, 146–50, 176–80.

[58] Clare, *Sketches*, pp. 48–9.

a passage from the street to the backyards of the cottages. This room was about three to four feet wide, the widest part being a recess near the window, the other part of the room being narrowed by the chimney. I got a small iron stove to warm the room on cold nights, and I fixed up a small desk against the wall, and two small shelves for my few books. I don't know what a university atmosphere is. I have dreamt of it, but I know when I entered this little room at night I was in another world. I seemed to leave all squalor and toil and distraction behind . . . My life there was strangely and sweetly above what it had been during the day. It was often from nine o'clock to half-past before I could enter this room after walking from my work and getting my tea-supper, the only meal since half-past twelve at noon.[59]

A separate problem was that of light. English agricultural cottages had always had inadequate windows, and those in Scotland were worse still. Somerville's parents, itinerant farm labourers in the Borders, and regular readers of religious literature, adopted the only practical solution: "My father and mother had a window (the house had none) consisting of one small pane of glass, and when they moved from one house to another in different parts of Berwickshire in different years, they carried this window with them, and had it fixed in each hovel into which they went as tenants".[60] Windows in the new housing in the industrial towns were limited firstly by the cost of glass which bore a heavy duty until 1845, and secondly by the window tax which was not repealed until 1851. Cottages of less than eight windows were exempt, but not so the tenements in the centre of the towns, which as a consequence were notoriously ill-lit. Some indication of the overall situation can be gained from the fact that between 1789 and 1844, the consumption of glass remained virtually unchanged, while the population nearly doubled.[61] Artificial lighting was confined to candles and rushlights;[62] there was very little gas lighting to be found in working class dwellings before 1850.[63] So the reader whose hours of work left only the late evening free during the week was once more forced to continue his studies amidst the rest of his family in the one room in the house which they could afford to light. Otherwise he ran the risk of ruining his eyesight[64] by reading with a single candle or a rushlight, which, as Adams remarked, "did scarcely more than make the darkness visible".[65] Thomas

---

[59] Shaw, p. 224. John Harris had to wait until he was 53 years old before he could afford to "build a little study for myself over our kitchen", and realize "what I had been anxiously desiring for a lifetime" (Harris, p. 62).

[60] Somerville, p. 3. See also Marjorie Plant, *The Domestic Life of Scotland in the Eighteenth Century* (Edinburgh, 1952), pp. 35–6.

[61] *First Large Towns Report*, pp. 115–166, 436–7; *Second Large Towns Report*, Appendix, part 2, pp. 134, 201–2; G. R. Porter, *The Progress of the Nation* (London, 1851), pp. 252–7.

[62] The performance of candles, which cost 1½d. each by 1838, was greatly improving during the '20s and '30s. William T. O'Dea, *The Social History of Lighting* (London, 1958), pp. 40–54; John Burnett, *A Social History of Housing, 1815-1870* (Newton Abbot, 1978), pp. 27–8.

[63] *Second Large Towns Report*, Appendix, Parts 1 and 2, answers to Q. 54, "Is gas light generally introduced into the shops or dwelling places . . . ?".

[64] Always supposing it was adequate in the first place. See Edward Rymer's account of the way his view of the world was transformed when he picked up a pair of old spectacles on a market stall (Rymer, p. 16).

[65] Adams, vol. 1, pp. 44–5. "It was almost as well," he added, "that the general body of the people could not read for persistent efforts to turn the advantage to account after sunset would almost certainly have ruined half the eyes of the country."

Wood, an apprentice mechanic, described the problems he faced in the dark evenings:

> Then, as to reading in winter I had to read by firelight excepting when I could afford a $\frac{1}{2}d.$ candle, which I used to save to read with in bed. I have read perhaps scores of times till 12.00 or 1 o'clock. There were no curtains to fire. There were no interruptions. A house with seven or eight children on one floor is a fine opportunity for the display of patience on the part of a "student" or an earnest reader. Get into bed for warmth and then the luxury of an unbroken reading was a treat that compensated for any privations, and lifted me for the time being into another world.[66]

The impact of the "difficulties" of the home environment was intensified by the changes that were taking place in the conditions of employment during this period. The hours of work both in agriculture and in the pre-industrial trades had always been long; rarely less than twelve and frequently as much as fourteen, especially during the summer months. But the size and organization of the economic units, together with the often irregular flow of work could provide occasional opportunities for both obtaining and reading literature. Alexander Somerville, for instance, owed his introduction to the world of books to meeting an old shepherd whilst at work "herding the cows in the wooded solitudes of the Ogle Burn".[67] Samuel Bamford, warehouseman to a cloth printer in Manchester at the beginning of the century, was able to make use of seasonal fluctuations in business to greatly increase the range of his reading: "As spring and autumn were our only really busy seasons, I had occasionally, during other parts of the year, considerable leisure, which, if I could procure a book that I considered at all worth the reading, was spent with such book at my desk, in the little recess of the packing room. Here, therefore, I had opportunities for reading many books of which I had only heard the names before . . .".[68] In the artisan workshops where discipline could be relaxed and where there might be friendly contact with older employees and masters who could better afford literature, there always existed the chance of coming by a book or an old periodical, and the workshops provided a unit for clubbing together to buy books and newspapers.

It is very difficult to arrange the distribution of opportunities in the pre-industrial trades into a single hierarchy. Those who worked alone enjoyed the benefit of privacy and a degree of control over the pace of their labour—James Hogg considered that for this reason a shepherd was better placed than a ploughman[69]—those who worked in groups enjoyed the advantage of conversation—Thelwall thought that mechanics must be more learned than shop

---

[66] T. Wood, p. 9. Brierley vividly recalled the dangers attendant on reading by firelight: "In the study of my favourite authors, I was not allowed a candle during winter nights, until my hair underwent a constant singeing process" (Brierley, pp. 31–2). See also Thomson, p. 67; Claxton, p. 15; Dundee Factory Boy, p. 64. In the '30s and '40s, a third of all house fires in London were caused by candles igniting curtains.

[67] Somerville, p. 38. James Hogg first heard of Burns when another shepherd repeated to him Tam O'Shanter (Hogg, p. 11).

[68] Bamford, *Early Days*, p. 280.

[69] Hogg, p. 11.

assistants.[70] Some trades, such as printing and bookbinding,[71] were obviously particularly suited to the pursuit of knowledge, and in general, a small, prosperous artisan workshop, with an established tradition of rational pursuits and in a trade which did not require heavy physical toil perhaps offered the most conducive surroundings, but a determined reader could almost always find some occasion to further his education during the hours of work. The servant John Jones, for instance, used to hurry through laying the dinner table that he might spend a few minutes looking at the contents of the dining room bookshelves,[72] and the anonymous Stonemason, then employed as a roundsman, taught his horse the route and thereafter read as he travelled.[73]

It would be wrong to over-romanticize the situation; the would-be reader still faced a great many problems. His fellow working men could vary widely in their character and tastes, and, as we shall see in chapter eight, there was often considerable tension between readers and non-readers. Free time outside the hours of work was extremely limited, and it is clear that those artisans who were impatient to educate themselves were forced to undergo great hardship. Thomas Cooper's account encompasses the range of devices which were adopted to cram in as much reading as possible during, in between, and after working hours; particularly common was the indigestive habit of simultaneously consuming food and knowledge:

> Historical reading, or the grammar of some language, or translation, was my first employment on week-day mornings, whether I rose at three or four, until seven o'clock, when I sat down to the stall. A book or a periodical in my hand while I breakfasted, gave me another half-hour's reading, I had another half-hour, and sometimes an hour's reading or study of language, at from one to two o'clock, the time of dinner—usually eating my food with a spoon, after I had cut it in pieces, and having my eyes on a book all the time. I sat at work till eight, and sometimes nine, at night; and, then, either read, or walked about our little room and committed "Hamlet" to memory, or the rhymes of some modern poet, until compelled to go to bed from sheer exhaustion—for it must be remembered that I was repeating something, audibly, as I sat at work, the greater part of the day—either declensions and conjugations, or rules of syntax, or propositions of Euclid, or the "Paradise Lost", or "Hamlet", or poetry of some modern or living author.[74]

Industrialization made it far more difficult to read whilst at work. The break-up of the domestic economy, the increased size of the industrial units, the divorce between master and employees, the greater discipline, and continuous mechanical process were factors which together confined nearly all self-education to after working hours and to the home. Two of the autobiographers, J. A. Leatherland and William Heaton had direct experience of the weaving trade both before and after industrialization. Leatherland began work in a ribbon factory, left at the age of twenty-four to work as a velvet

[70] Thelwall, pp. x–xi. He had, nonetheless, managed to read a good deal whilst working as a shop assistant, as did C. M. Smith (p. 10).

[71] See above, ch. 1. Ten of the autobiographers worked in these trades. See especially, the comments of Benjamin Stott, a bookbinder and poet (p. x).

[72] Jones, p. 173.   [73] Stonemason, pp. 50–51.

[74] Cooper, p. 59. He was working as a cobbler at this time. See also T. Wood, pp. 9–10; Carter, *Memoirs*, pp. 74–5, 144; Lowery, p. 63.

weaver in a small workshop containing just seven men, and then later in life was forced back into the ribbon factory as a recession hit the velvet trade. His summary of the relative advantages of the two sets of occupational conditions for those who wished to improve themselves is thus of particular interest:

> I found velvet-weaving a highly suitable occupation for the exercise of thought and meditation—much more so than my former employment. In the ribbon loom, the worker has to manage a number of pieces at once, every one of which requires his care and attention; but in velvet weaving the work is more under his command, and there is only one piece of work to superintend, and with good silk and use, the work becomes little more than mechanical, and affords scarcely any interruption to mental exercises. There is also far less noise attending the manufacture; and, owing to stopping every third time the shuttle is thrown across, to cut out the wire, the muscles are not kept in such constant motion. Some weavers of plain silk, place books before them to read whilst at work. I never could manage this with any good result. I think the secret of doing things well, is to do only one thing at a time. My plan, therefore, was to read at leisure intervals, and to ruminate on such reading whilst engaged in manual occupation. If in the course of my thoughts anything struck me particularly, I made a note of it in a memorandum book, which I kept by the side of my loom for the purpose.[75]

Heaton was a handloom weaver who worked at his loom in the small village of Luddenden a few miles west of Halifax until 1850, when he had to take a job in Crossley's Carpet Manufacture in Halifax. At the centre of his sense of loss was the destruction of the integration between his employment, his literary activity, and his contact with the countryside: ". . . but with all my discouragement I still persevered with my writings. It was when I was weaving at home, that I made the most progress with them. I frequently wish now for my churchyard cot and my busy loom; that I could walk in the fields at the close of the day and at my leisure hours. But it is all over; I must continue to work amidst the clatter of machinery".[76] Few of the self-educating factory workers abandoned their ambitions altogether, but they now faced enormous problems. ";The hours of labour in cotton mills, when I was a piecer," recalled William Aitken, "were so protracted that improvement of the mind was almost an impossibility."[77] As the movement of self-improvement gathered momentum so the process of industrialization to which it was a response ensured that in a purely practical sense the world of books became increasingly divorced from the world of occupation.

(iv)

Reading is a solitary activity, and many of the problems encountered by these men were created by the need to withdraw from the company of their families

---

[75] Leatherland, p. 12. See also the handloomweaver William Farish who ". . . with Walkingham's arithmetic, and a slate and pencil at my side . . . used to con over the problems as I worked the treadles" (*Autobiography*, p. 45).

[76] Heaton, pp. xxii–xxiii. See also the comments of the cotton piecer and poet, John Teer (p. iv).

[77] Aitken, 25 Sept., p. 3.

and friends, yet as they wrestled with their difficulties, so, inevitably, they began to make contact with other readers. A constantly recurring event in the autobiographies is a meeting with another working man who has embarked on a similar course of self-improvement. In every case the formation of a relationship with him is ascribed a central role in the course of the auto-biographer's pursuit of knowledge. The potential friend is introduced to the readership with a brief descriptive phrase which hardly varies. Christopher Thomson explains the basis of his contact with a fellow shipwright: "He was a reading man . . .";[78] John Clare meets "one Thomas Porter . . . who, being a lover of books, was a pleasant companion . . .";[79] Alexander Somerville comes across a stacker in the harvest, "James Wilson, who was a reader of books . . .", and later meets "Alick F—", who, "was no more than a stone-mason, working for weekly wages, but he was a reader, and also a thinker";[80] Thomas Cooper reaped great benefit from associating with Christopher MacDonald, whom he describes in a splendidly antithetical sentence: "He was a Methodist; but he was a reader and a thinker";[81] and Ben Brierley spots from afar a young man who "had the name of being a great reader".[82] Throughout this period the term "reader" had a resonance which extended far beyond its literal meaning. To have "the name of being a great reader", to be known in the community as a "lover of books", signified an individual who could be clearly distinguished from other working men by his outlook and behaviour. It was partly a matter of an attachment to the values of rational enquiry and moral improvement which we shall explore in the following chapters, and partly a matter of the physical and intellectual hardship which each self-educating working man experienced. As one reader came upon another, he recognized a man who not only shared his attitude and commitment, but who also had suffered and was still suffering the many privations which the pursuit of knowledge engendered. In a sense the very loneliness of the life of the reader made him all the more eager to embrace any available opportunity to make contact with another working man who had embarked on the same voyage.

There were a number of practical benefits to be gained from association. In the first instance, a fellow working man was an important source of books, particularly in the formative years. Charles Shaw, for instance, owed his ·introduction to self-education to a friendship he formed with a local potter:

This young potter I gratefully remember too, for another reason. His name was William Leigh. He was then, as in his after life, of studious habits, modest, and upright in all his ways, and whose life had much fragrance and sweetness in it. He found out, from seeing me reading at nights when he came to our house, that I was fond of reading, and up to the time of going to the work-house he regularly supplied me with books, and these were as precious as the bread he gave us. It was he who first opened to me the great world of literature . . .[83]

In the same way the Dundee Factory Boy described how his "early pursuit of

---

[78] Thomson, p. 78.   [79] Clare, *Sketches*, p. 71.   [80] Somerville, pp. 86, 124.
[81] Cooper, p. 45. For the Methodists and reading see below, pp.178–80.
[82] Brierley, p. 44.
[83] Shaw, p. 92. He later received invaluable assistance from his Sunday School teacher George Kirkham (pp. 138–40).

knowledge'' was stimulated by the books lent to him by an old shoemaker.[84] Once launched upon a course of self-improvement the problem of acquiring books remained, and indeed became more acute. New friendships could enable readers to pool such surplus monies as they possessed to buy an expensive volume,[85] or club together to subscribe to a newspaper or periodical,[86] or simply to widen the scope of their reading by borrowing each other's books. The more experienced reader could also be a vital source of guidance as the self-educator entered upon an unexplored field of knowledge. "I became acquainted with a young man," wrote William Dodd, "who was very kind in lending me books, and explaining any difficulty I might be labouring under in my studies. I shall never forget his kindness—he was to me like a brother."[87] Where the ignorance was mutual, there was much to be gained by the two men working out the problems together, as Ben Brierley found:

> My next-door neighbour, a married man, felt the want of a knowledge of arithmetic, through weaving a class of work that required a good deal of calculation. We agreed to exercise by our two selves. I was to lead the way from addition onwards, and very closely he followed me. It was from spring to autumn when these schoolings took place. Up by five 'clock every morning, except Sundays, we pegged at it until seven when we took to our looms.[88]

In a more general sense the friendships kept the working men going by providing a valuable source of psychological encouragement in times of particular difficulty or self-doubt. Thomas Cooper and his friend John Hough, for instance, each recognized the importance of their contact: "My friend Hough's conversation, on Saturday nights, was both a relief and an inspiration to me . . . With him I discussed questions relating to mind, religion, to history, and general literature; and these weekly conversations, as I returned to my reading and studies, gave a new impulse to thought and inquiry. He also used to say, 'You do me good. You freshen my mind weekly' ".[89]

The extent to which such relationships could overcome the problems facing the reader was always limited. William Lovett, for instance, formed a friendship with a fellow apprentice in Newlyn. They were brought together by a shared desire to remedy their lack of knowledge, but faced with the dearth of literature in their community, the two of them made no more progress than each separately. All they achieved was a pooling of their ignorance, and Lovett had

---

[84] Dundee Factory Boy, pp. 50–1. The three volumes which made the greatest impression were *Robinson Crusoe, Roderick Random,* and *Pilgrim's Progress.*

[85] For instance, J. A. Leatherland clubbed together with some like-minded velvet weavers to purchase, " 'Harris's Hermes', from which we gained some knowledge of the principles, elements and philosophy of language generally and of the English tongue in particular" (Leatherland, pp. 9–10).

[86] See above, p. 118.

[87] Dodd, p. 20. Timothy Claxton was given evening lessons by a journeyman carpenter (Claxton, p. 9) and John Clare received invaluable assistance from his friend John Turnill, who, although "far from a good writer himself", was "of a studious musing turn of mind and fond of books" and used to set the young Clare texts to copy out (Clare, *Sketches,* p. 19).

[88] Brierley, p. 33. See also P. Taylor, p. 80; Farish, *Autobiography,* p. 47; Frost, *Forty Years,* pp. 33–4.

[89] Cooper, p. 62. Hough was a draper and Dissenter. "He was, however, a broad general reader, had an excellent library, and made me welcome to the loan of every book in it that I desired to read" (p. 51).

to wait until he moved to London before his self-education could begin.[90] However, where conditions allowed a start to be made, then invariably the practical requirements of the reader encouraged him to seek out and co-operate with other working men at this basic level. The friendships were formed in all sorts of situations, some in the workplace, others amongst neighbours. They were unofficial, unstructured, and unrecorded save by the autobiographers. But it is here that we may most clearly see the relationship between the individual and social identity of the reader. The mutual improvement societies, the formal, institutional manifestation of the culture of self-improvement, were built upon this foundation. C. M. Smith's account of the formation of such a society in Bristol demonstrates how the informal meeting could develop into an organization possessing all the institutional attributes—rules, sanctions, rituals of behaviour, a financial structure, and property, even if it was only a rented room.

> One holiday afternoon, while strolling among Clifton's rocky scenery, I met with a young man . . . , to whom I had occasionally spoken before. He proposed to me to join a club of seven, which he was then endeavouring to organise with a view to mutual improvement. The plan was, to hire a room for three-and-sixpence a week, and to stock it with books, papers, and drawing-materials, each one contributing what he could. Subjects were to be discussed, essays written and criticised, the best authors read aloud and their sentiments subjected to our common remark. I joined at once without hesitation, and have congratulated myself that I did so to this day. We got a good room, with such attendance as we required, at the sum above named; and thus, for sixpence a week each, with an additional three-halfpence in winter time for firing, we had an imperfect, it is true, but still an efficient means of improvement at our command. Here we met nearly three hundred nights in the year, and talked, read, disputed, and wrote *de omnibus rebus et quibusdam aliis*, until the clock struck eleven. We had fines for non-attendance, and prizes, paid out of the fines, for the best-written productions.[91]

Such organizations played an important role in the lives of the readers and in the working class community, but they were mostly short-lived, and even as a member of a flourishing society the reader would continue his private studies. What translated individual endeavour into a culture in the sense of a social entity which existed as a distinct element within the culture of the working class as a whole was not so much the incidence of corporate activity as the simple recognition, with all that it entailed, of one reader by another.

(v)

Over his lifetime, an individual reader would experience considerable fluctuations in his capacity to isolate the surplus margin of cash, time and space which the pursuit of knowledge demanded. Apart from possible contact with literature at day and Sunday schools, the first opportunity for independent

---

[90] For details, see Lovett, pp. 21–2.
[91] C. M. Smith, pp. 14–15. See also the accounts by Peter Taylor and J. A. Leatherland of similar societies growing out of artisan workshops. (P. Taylor, p. 60, Leatherland, pp. 9–10).

action normally came in his late teens.[92] At this time an apprentice would begin to receive a small cash wage over and above his keep, and his time and resources would not be burdened by a family or the management of a business.[93] For those not bound as apprentices, the absence of overriding family commitments permitted the development of various forms of independent entrepreneurial action as a means of accumulating the crucial margin of a few spare pence. Ben Brierley for instance saved the money he needed for books by fetching water for an old pensioner and accompanying him on trips to Manchester.[94] More romantically, Alexander Somerville raised the four shillings he needed to buy *Hutton's Mensuration* by stabling and grooming the horse of a gentleman who was courting the "master's beautiful sister".[95] For William Dodd, working in a mill since the age of six, it was a case of waiting until, at the age of about twenty, his wage moved slightly ahead of the cost of his basic subsistence: "But having completed my second seven years of servitude (somewhat earlier indeed, than it is usual for work-men to have finished their first) I got advanced to 9s per week, and began to think myself well-to-do in the world, and could, by following a rigid course of economy, spare a shilling or two occasionally for the purchase of such books as I took a fancy to".[96]

The methods varied, and their success was always limited, but the conjunction of relative irresponsibility and slowly increasing earning power made late adolescence and early manhood an optimum period for the acquisition of books. "Here and there", wrote Thomas Frost of the 1830s, "might be a studious artisan who, before the cares and cost of a family pressed hard upon him, had acquired a quarto edition of Hume and Smollett, or Bloomfield's 'View of the World', with plate illustrations, in shilling numbers",[97] and such were the men who tended to form mutual improvement societies.[98] The frequency with which the organizations were made up by young men is also explained by their greater resistance to personal discomfort, by their energy, and by the innocence and perhaps immaturity of their ambition. Brierley identified the atmosphere of his first organization with great accuracy:

Aspiring to know more than could be taught me at the Sunday School in Hollinwood, I joined the one known as the "Old School", in Pole Lane, Failsworth . . . Here I found a number of congenial spirits, who, like myself, had grown out of their childhood, and were looking forward to becoming men. We banded ourselves together, and formed the nucleus of the present

[92] In his study of family earning patterns in Preston Anderson concluded that "There is no doubt . . . that children by their late teens did earn enough to support themselves and that many earned as much or nearly as much as they would ever earn, and more, often, than their parents" (M. Anderson, *Family Structure*, p. 129).
[93] See Claxton, p. 7; C. M. Smith, p. 14; Oliver, p. 16.
[94] Brierley, p. 32. He earned a penny a week for fetching water and 3*d*. for each journey to Manchester.
[95] Somerville, pp. 48–9. As a young servant, John Jones used the tips he received to subscribe to a library (Jones, p. 176).
[96] Dodd, p. 22. At this time he calculated that his expenses for board, lodging, and washing averaged 7*s*., leaving 2*s*. to spend on clothes and books. He was living away from his parents and was unmarried.
[97] Frost, *Forty Years*, p. 79.
[98] Samuel Smiles considered that the "Mutual Improvement Societies . . . are principally formed by young men" (Public Libraries Committee, p. 126).

Mechanics Institution, then existing under the name of the Mutual Improvement Society. Wonders were to be done by this body of aspirants to learned greatness; and some of them were accomplished.[99]

If they enjoyed none of his privileges, they shared something of the outlook of the more committed university student of our own day. This is not to say either that the mutual improvement societies were made up exclusively of those who were neither boys nor men, or that the individual self-educators abandoned the pursuit as they grew older, but there is a quality of youthful exuberance about the pursuit of knowledge which to some extent belies its traditional image of cautious sobriety.

Once into manhood, the effect of the home and working environment becomes less predictable. There was a wide range of factors which could at various times prevent or at least discourage the activity of self-improvement. These included the life-time earnings cycle of working class families,[100] periods on the tramp, loss of income through recession or unemployment, and family mobility into and around the rapidly growing industrial towns. These factors interacted with each other, with external factors such as the transient impact of a political crisis, and with the purely chance events such as the making and breaking of valuable friendships, in such a way as to prevent the emergence of a consistent pattern of behaviour.

The bias towards youth and the fluctuations in adult life are, however, merely modifications which have to be made to the general picture. For in relation to alternative forms of working class activity, it is the element of continuity which stands out as the major characteristic of the individual's pursuit of knowledge over his own lifetime. Men like Cooper and Gutteridge and Thomson and Younger are to be found at their books for decade after decade, ". . . blind Henry's Life of Wallace was the first book that stirred my mind, and set me on a career of reading and thinking that will only terminate with my life, or the complete prostration of my faculties . . ." wrote the Dundee Factory Boy: "Reader, always reverence the first book that excited in you the desire of self-culture, for when this desire is once kindled it ought not and cannot be extinguished."[101] Although, as we have seen, the difficulties facing the reader sooner or later forced him to make informal and formal contact with other working men, it remained the case that when friends were lost, and organizations declined, the process of self-education could be continued by the individual alone. If reading always led to social exchange it remained quintessentially a private activity which took place over time, and as such, an activity which more than any other could survive the fluctuating fortunes of the working man and the working class. Throughout the periods of disillusion and the periods of repression, the culture stood as a great flywheel, sustaining not only a tradition of values but one of active response to the developing industrial society.

[99] Brierley, p. 35. See also Shaw, p. 221.
[100] Anderson and Foster have applied Rowntree's concept of the poverty life-cycle to the mid-century working class populations of Preston, and Oldham, Northampton and South Shields, and have confirmed Rowntree's conclusion that the most prosperous periods for a family were before the birth of the first child and when the children were old enough to earn adult or near-adult wages. Conversely, the poorest period was when a family has young children (M. Anderson, *Family Structure* . . . , pp. 29–32; John Foster, op. cit., pp. 95–99).
[101] Dundee Factory Boy, p. 32.

(vi)

The pursuit of knowledge was and has remained a minority tradition within the working class. After half a century of rapid growth in both the availability of literature and the number of readers and their organizations, the bulk of the labouring population never set eyes on what the autobiographers would term "useful" books. No firm statistical statements can be made on the basis of the present source material,[102] but it is possible to isolate some characteristics of the size and occupational identity of the culture of self-improvement. For reasons which should now be evident, the more skilled the working man, and the larger the community in which he lived, the easier it was to acquire and read literature. Possession of the basic techniques of literacy had always been distributed by occupational status and in the middle of this period the proportion of tradesmen and artisans capable of signing a marriage register was about double that of labourers and servants.[103] Urban artisans would have greater opportunities to buy or borrow books, would find it much easier to form organizations, and the more skilled amongst them would enjoy significant advantages in income and housing conditions. But two important modifications need to be made to this picture. Firstly, despite all the disadvantages under which they laboured, a scattering of readers was always to be found in the ranks of the agricultural labourers, and these readers could themselves usually find kindred spirits in their communities. The pursuit of knowledge was not confined to the urban artisan, still less to the upper stratum of skilled men who came to constitute the aristocracy of labour during the mid-Victorian period. Secondly, as we shall see in chapter eight, a fundamental characteristic of the experience of the artisan readers is that they rarely found themselves in a situation in which their tastes and pursuits were shared by all those amongst whom they lived and worked. Occasionally we find a small workshop full of like-minded men, but the more common pattern is for the artisan reader to feel himself separated from and often in conflict with many of those who came from exactly the same occupational background.

The impact of the industrial revolution upon the pursuit of knowledge was far from straightforward. The innovations in printing and distribution transformed the volume and cost of literature and laid the foundation for the expansion in the number of readers and the range of their activities and organizations, but it was the continuing difficulties experienced by those who sought book knowledge which threw them together and led to the growth of a distinct culture of self-improvement. The concentration of the labouring population into larger groups enhanced the opportunities for gaining access to literature, and at the same time the development of the factory system made it even more difficult to integrate the activities of working and reading. The readers were amongst the most direct beneficiaries of industrialization, yet the most dramatic proliferation of material written either by or for the working

[102] Given the ephemeral character of so many of the mutual improvement societies, and the fact that so much reading was undertaken in private, it is doubtful whether it would ever be possible to arrive at any reliable figures, although John Foster has concluded that in Oldham, "By 1855 overall membership [of adult education societies] included perhaps one in ten of Oldham's younger workers" (John Foster, op. cit., p. 200).

[103] Lawrence Stone, art. cit., p. 110.

class was a product of the major crisis of the industrial society which saw the creation and the defeat of the first working class attempt to challenge the principles upon which it was based. The inescapable practical problems examined in this chapter ensured that the readers would be particularly sensitive to the changes which were taking place in the economic circumstances of their class, but the precise relationship between the pursuit of knowledge and the pursuit of bread and freedom was, as we shall see in the following chapter, very much open to debate.

Chapter Seven

The Idea of Useful Knowledge

It is possible to trace a tradition of serious reading in the labouring community which stretches back to at least as far as the end of the seventeenth century, but it is evident that under the influence of industrialization and urbanization, the pursuit of knowledge took on a new dimension. More working men read more books, and as they did so, it became necessary to redefine the role of literature in the pattern of class relations. The series of developments which commenced with the appearance of *Rights of Man* and culminated in the flood of publications and organizations in the 1830s posed a range of urgent questions for both the emergent working class and their new masters. What was to be the connection between reading and manual labour? What relevance had the skills of literacy to social mobility? What impact would the revolution in communications have on traditional popular culture? And, above all, was the pursuit of knowledge to be a means of reinforcing or undermining the edifice of political and economic power which the middle class was attempting to construct?

From the outset the middle class was reluctant to leave the resolution of these problems in the hands of the readers. The first reaction was one of repression, but by the 1820s its more enlightened sections were beginning to consider ways of channelling rather than damming up the forces of change. They were encouraged in their ambitions by the salient characteristics of those who embarked upon the pursuit of knowledge. The readers were unusually intelligent and articulate men who, through a combination of strength of character and favourable domestic and occupational circumstances had established sufficient control over their situation to permit the expenditure of time, energy and money on their intellectual development. As such, they bore a disproportionate responsibility for defining the ideology of the nascent working class, and leading the organizations in which it was embodied. At the same time their sobriety, self-discipline and commitment to rational inquiry and moral improvement led them towards the values and behaviour that were being promoted by their social superiors. The single act of recognizing the potential of the written word placed the readers simultaneously in the vanguard of their class and in close contact with the advanced forces of the middle class. For this reason it is in the dialogue between the middle class radicals and the working class self-educators that the relationship between the two classes is most transparent.

The problem for the middle class educators was one of communication; the problem for the historian is one of measuring their success. The campaign to win over the readers is easily recognizable and the failure of the major organizations involved to attract, still less retain the attention of those they set out to reach has been discussed in some detail.[1] Yet to measure the outcome of an attempt at communication solely in terms of attendance or sales is clearly insufficient. The real touchstone is the extent to which the ideology which the campaign embodied was accepted by the intended audience. The exchange can only be understood by means of a detailed comparative study of the pattern of ideas over a period of time.

Any act of communication presupposes the existence of a common language, but it was a singular characteristic of this particular dialogue that the argument was not over which term was the more appropriate, but over the definition of terms which both sides accepted as accurate descriptions. In this chapter we shall contrast the range of meanings the autobiographers attached to one of the most significant of these terms, the phrase "useful knowledge", with its application by the most important middle class agency of the period, the Society for the Diffusion of Useful Knowledge. In this way it may be possible to disentangle a little of the semantic confusion which surrounds the whole question of self-improvement and to reach a clearer understanding of the extent to which the working class conception of the uses of literacy was vulnerable to the aggrandizement of the middle class educators.

(i)

William Lovett is perhaps the most representative figure of all the autobiographers. He was born in the first year of the century, and after moving to London at the age of twenty-one, he immersed himself in the world of self-improvement, becoming a leading exponent of its ideology and playing a central role in most of the important working class organizations of the period, including co-operation, child and adult education, the war of the unstamped press, the working class political movements of the 1830s, and finally Chartism. The opening chapter of his autobiography stands as the prologue, covering his growing up in Newlyn and his early attempts to establish himself as a journeyman cabinet maker in London. The first sentence of chapter two summarizes the main characteristic of his life so far, and introduces what is to be the major theme of his life-history: "Owing to the many difficulties I had met with in the way of learning a trade by which to earn my bread, I had hitherto made very little intellectual progress".[2] It had been impossible to make contact with any literature in Newlyn, and he had arrived in London not only without money or friends, but without having served an apprenticeship in the trade he now wished to take up. However, the real business of his life was now about to begin: "That which first stimulated me to intellectual enquiry, and which laid the foundation of what little knowledge I possess, was my being introduced to a small literary association, entitled 'The Liberals', which met in Gerard Street,

---

[1] See R. K. Webb, *The British Working Class Reader, 1790–1848* (London, 1955); R. D. Altick, op. cit., pp. 269–77; Thomas Kelly, *A History of Adult Education in Great Britain* (Liverpool, 1970), chs. 8 & 11; J. F. C. Harrison, *Learning and Living* (London, 1961); David L. Robbins, *A Radical Alternative to Paternalism: Voluntary Associations and Popular Enlightenment in England and France 1800–1840* (unpublished York University Ph.D, 1974).
[2] Lovett, p. 34. He was now aged about twenty-three.

Newport Market. It was composed chiefly of working men, who paid a small weekly subscription towards the formation of a select library of books for circulation among one another".[3] This was the turning point, and it is of particular interest to see how Lovett describes the event:

> I now became seized with an enthusiastic desire to read and treasure up all I could meet with on the subject of Christianity, and in a short time was induced to join my voice to that of others in its defence whenever the question became the subject of debate; and often have I sat up till morning dawned reading and preparing myself with arguments in support of its principles. Political questions being also often discussed in our association, caused me to turn my attention to political works, and eventually to take a great interest in the parliamentary debates and questions of the day. In short, my mind seemed to be awakened to a new mental existence; new feelings, hopes, and aspirations sprang up within me, and every spare moment was devoted to the acquisition of some kind of useful knowledge.[4]

The idea which fired his imagination, the goal which inspired his actions, was the acquisition of "useful knowledge". In these two words—the object "knowledge", and the description, "useful"—Lovett summarizes the content and the purpose of the reading, the book collecting, the debating, the organizing and the writing which together made up his life as a self-improving working man.

The term was employed by the autobiographers to communicate a complex range of attitudes and aspirations, but its fundamental meaning is already apparent in the context of Lovett's reference. In themselves, the two words seem austere, but look again at his description of the impact of useful knowledge: "In short, my mind seemed to be awakened to a new mental existence, new feelings, hopes and aspirations sprang up within me ...". For Lovett, as for every other reader, the "use" of knowledge was nothing less than to effect a transformation in his consciousness and in his relationship with the external world. It is a phenomenon which we find whenever the autobiographers attempt to convey their feelings as they make their first contact with the world of books. Robert Story, for instance, read his first real book, Watts' *Divine Songs for Children*, with, "my heart burning with secret rapture. Its effect upon my mind was magical. It gave me the feeling of a new existence".[5] The shoemaker's daughter Mary Smith described how her earliest contact with literature, "awakened my young nature".[6] Ben Brierley found himself suddenly transported after meeting another reader: "It was in every sense a new light to me. I lived in another world than the one I was supposed to inhabit".[7] The Dundee Factory Boy's first book, "opened up a new world to me, and I longed for more mental food to satisfy the cravings of an awakened appetite".[8] When James Hogg discovered Burns, "I was delighted! I was far more than delighted—I was ravished!"[9] and Burns'

---

[3] *Ibid.*, p. 34.

[4] *Ibid.*, p. 35. For a description of a similar debating society, see Lowery, p. 72.

[5] Story, *Poetical Works*, pp. v–vi. Isaac Watts' *Divine Songs attempted in easy language for children* was continually reprinted in the first half of the century by publishers ranging from the SPCK to James Catnach.

[6] M. Smith, p. 33.   [7] Brierley, p. 44. See also Shaw, p. 92.

[8] Dundee Factory Boy, p. 31. See also Burn, p. 191.

[9] Hogg, p. 11. He was looking after sheep one summer when "a half daft man named James Scott, came to me on the hill, and to amuse me, repeated Tam o' Shanter".

effect on John Younger was, "an electrifier, I felt something as I suppose people will feel when going crazy".[10] "When I first plunged, as it were, into the blessed habit of reading," recalled Samuel Bamford, "faculties which had hitherto given but small intimation of existence suddenly sprang into action."[11] The discovery of useful knowledge amounted to a secularized conversion experience which left no part of the readers' lives untouched.

In their recognition of the potential of knowledge, and in their employment of the term "useful knowledge", to communicate that potential, the working men were not alone. "Useful knowledge" was a crucial component of the middle class language of reform during this period, and was enshrined in an institutional form by the creation of the Society for the Diffusion of Useful Knowledge on 6 November 1826.[12] The SDUK was the publishing wing of the concerted drive by middle class radicals in the 1820s and 1830s to break down the barriers of the country's educational system. It was founded just nine months after the official launching of the University of London, largely by the same group of men, and frequently met in its premises.[13] The secretary of the SDUK, a solicitor named Thomas Coates, was also the secretary of University College from 1831 to 1835. In Henry Brougham and his *Practical Observations Upon the Education of the People* the Society shared with the growing Mechanics' Institute movement a guiding spirit and a foundation text.[14] The Mechanics' Institutes were explicitly committed to the pursuit of "useful knowledge", and in turn the SDUK saw itself as the handmaiden of the movement and of all associated bodies involved in the field of adult education.[15] It assumed the responsibility on behalf of the Mechanics' Institutes for articulating their objectives, and assisting their progress by supplying them with suitable literature,[16] publishing a manual for forming and running Institutes,[17] and

[10] Younger, p. 121.

[11] Bamford, *Early Days*, p. 91.

[12] For an account of the founding meeting see *General Committee Minutes Book of the SDUK*, vol. 1, pp. 1–4. This was in fact the second attempt to get the Society off the ground. A committee of "The Society for Promoting the Diffusion of Useful Knowledge" had originally met in April 1825. See, "Society for the Diffusion of Useful Knowledge", *Westminster Review*, vol. XLVI, June 1827, pp. 225–244; Harold Smith, *The Society for the Diffusion of Useful Knowledge, 1826–1846. A Social and Bibliographical Evaluation* (Halifax, Nova Scotia, 1974), pp. 5–7.

[13] For the connection between the University and the SDUK, see Thomas Kelly, *George Birkbeck* (Liverpool, 1957), pp. 153–4, 160–3, 190–1; H. Hale Bellot, *University College London. 1826–1926* (London, 1929), pp. 91-6, 212.

[14] *Practical Observations upon the Education of the People addressed to the Working Classes and their Employers* was first published in 1825 and went through 20 editions in a year, Brougham giving the profits to the London Mechanics' Institute. In it he outlined the need both for Mechanics' Institutes and the launching of a scheme of cheap publications. See Chester New, *The Life of Henry Brougham to 1830* (Oxford, 1961), pp. 328–57.

[15] The object of the first London Mechanics' Institute was stated as "The instruction of the members in the principles of the Arts they practice, and in the various branches of science and useful knowledge", quoted in T. Kelly, *George Birkbeck . . .*, p. 88. For similar statements, see the rules of the York Mechanics' Institute quoted in J. F. C. Harrison, op. cit., p. 62, and the specimen "Objects of the Institution" provided in B. F. Duppa, *A Manual for Mechanics' Institutions* (London, 1839), Appendix 1.

[16] The Libraries of Useful and Entertaining Knowledge and successive SDUK publications were planned to meet the requirements of the Mechanics' Institutes and were supplied to them at a discount. For the perception of the requirements of the Institutes and the intention of meeting these, see *General Committee Minutes Book of the SDUK*, vol. 1, pp. 1–4; *Prospectus of the SDUK* (London, 1826), p. 2; Monica C. Grobel, *The Society for the Diffusion of Useful*

when, during the late 1830s, the movement began to lose momentum, investigating its failings and attempting to reorganize it.[18]

The significance of the SDUK, however, stretches beyond its relationship with the middle class educational initiatives. The lifetime of the Society, which was finally disbanded on 11 March 1846, straddled that of the great Whig reform ministries of Grey and Melbourne, and never before or since has an extra-governmental propaganda organization been so closely identified with the ruling politicians of the time. The SDUK committee,[19] which, in 1832, launched its most successful publication, *The Penny Magazine*, and planned *The Penny Cyclopaedia*,[20] included the serving Lord Chancellor, Paymaster General, Chancellor of the Exchequer, President of the Board of Trade, Lord Chief Justice, Secretary at War and Secretary to the Treasury, all either present or future cabinet ministers.[21] The Lord Chancellor was Henry Brougham, founder of the SDUK and the Chairman and guiding spirit throughout its lifetime. It was an organization dominated by politicians and, in the words of its final address, "The political circumstances of the time had much influence in producing its formation".[22]

The Society's *raison d'être* was communication. "The object of the Society", proclaimed the *Prospectus*, "is strictly limited to what its title imports, namely the imparting of useful information to all classes of the community, particularly to such as are unable to avail themselves of experienced teachers, or may prefer learning by themselves".[23] The audience was the working class and the communicators self-consciously represented the advance guard of the political and intellectual elite of the country. In his autobiography, Charles Knight, the Society's main publisher, dwelt at length on the calibre of the Committee, claiming that: "There was perhaps no society in England, with the exception

Knowledge 1826–46 (unpublished University of London M.A. thesis, 1933), pp. 693–5; Harriet Martineau, *The History of England during the Thirty Years Peace, 1816–1846* (London, 1849–50), vol. 1, p. 578.

[17] B. F. Duppa, op. cit., which contained a history of the Institutes, some trenchant criticism, and specimen rules and courses of lectures.

[18] Brougham and the SDUK organized the Association of London Mechanics' Institutes in 1839 in an attempt to co-ordinate activity, exchange ideas and reduce overlapping expenditure. The secretary of the Association was the ubiquitous Thomas Coates. See "Minutes of SDUK General Committee for 1839" in the *Ellis Collection*, and Thomas Coates, *Report of the State of Literary, Scientific, and Mechanics' Institutions in England* (London, 1841), pp. 1–17.

[19] The SDUK Committee had full responsibility for the Society's affairs, and until 1843, was self-perpetuating, electing members from the general membership when vacancies occurred. From June 1843, members were given "a voice" in the election of the Committee. Its size was flexible, but under the rules it was not to number less than 40 and not more than 60.

[20] The first issue of *The Penny Magazine* was on 31 March 1832. *The Penny Cyclopaedia* appeared on 2 January 1833.

[21] The ministers were respectively, Lord Brougham, Lord John Russell, Lord Althorp, Lord Auckland, Lord Denman, Sir John Cam Hobhouse and T. Spring Rice. Other past or future ministers on the Committee included Sir H. Parnell and Rowland Hill. A third of Melbourne's First Cabinet (5 out of 16 members) was on the Committee. By contrast, the Chambers brothers who ran the rival, and ultimately more successful, *Chambers Edinburgh Journal*, prided themselves on being quite independent of any other individual or group of individuals. See William Chambers, *Memoir of Robert Chambers with Autobiographical Reminiscences of William Chambers* (London, 4th edn., 1872), p. 238.

[22] *Address of the Committee of the Society for the Diffusion of Useful Knowledge. March 11, 1846* (London, 1846), p. 3.

[23] SDUK Prospectus, p. 1.

of the Royal Society, which could present such a knot of young men of high promise as were assembled at our committees in the earliest stages of their organisation".[24] Membership was confined to those who could afford £1 for an annual subscription or £10 for life membership.[25] Throughout the critical years of the new industrial society, the years which witnessed the Captain Swing rising, the Reform Bill crisis, the conflict over the New Poor Law, and the climax of Chartism, the SDUK was vigorously at work, pouring forth a flood of publications in an effort to win the minds of the most intelligent and articulate section of the working class to the kind of society which the Whig governments were trying to create.

The SDUK was first and foremost a society of idealists. It was founded on a resolute confidence in the actual and potential intellectual advance of the working class. According to the *Prospectus of the Penny Cyclopaedia*, "Within the last twenty years the elementary education of the working classes has been steadily advancing; and there are now hundreds of thousands of adults of both sexes, engaged in the various occupations of profitable industry, who are anxious to direct the powers of reading which they have acquired, to such employment of their leisure hours as may at once furnish amusements and instruction".[26] Whatever part the fear of working class rebellion played in the Society's activities there is no doubting the genuine commitment of its leaders to the value of knowledge for its own sake. In the first and most successful volume of the Library of Useful Knowledge, *A Discourse on the Objects, Advantages and Pleasures of Science*,[27] Henry Brougham outlined the philosophy which motivated the society and those who supported it:

> But the same bountiful Providence has endowed us with the higher nature also—with understandings as well as with senses—with faculties that are of a more exalted nature and admit of more refined enjoyments, than any the bodily frame can bestow; and by pursuing such gratification rather than those of mere sense, we fulfil the highest ends of our creation, and obtain both a present and a future reward. These things are often said, but they are not, therefore, the less true or the less worthy of deep attention. Let us mark their practical application to the occupations and enjoyments of all branches of society, beginning with those who form the great bulk of every community, the working classes, by what names soever their vocations may be called— professions, arts, trades, handicrafts, or common labour.[28]

This call must be placed in the context of its times, and in particular it must be contrasted with the inherited attitude of the ruling class towards the reading

---

[24] Charles Knight, *Passages of a Working Life During Half a Century* (London, 1864–5), vol. II. p. 125. See pp. 117–132 for his survey of the membership of the SDUK Committee, and H. Smith, op. cit., Appendix A. No women ever served on the Committee.

[25] In 1829 the number of annual subscribers topped 500, but thereafter there was a steady decline, until by 1843 there were fewer than 40. The fall was due at least in part to the impotence of the membership in the Society's affairs until 1843, and the fact that after its first year the Society attempted to balance its books on the publications alone, and therefore was not too anxious about the number of subscribers.

[26] *Prospectus of the Penny Cyclopaedia* (London, 1832), p. 1.

[27] It was published on 1 March 1827. By 16 December 1829 it had sold 33,100 copies, and by 1833, 42,000. M. C. Grobel, op. cit., p. 681; R. K. Webb, op. cit., p. 69.

[28] Henry Brougham, *A Discourse on the Objects, Advantages and Pleasures of Science* (London, 1827), p. 40.

habits of the working class. It was only seven years since the passage of the Six Acts which had attempted to repress all forms of working class political literature, and the Lord Chancellor at that time, Lord Eldon, was still in office.[29] The Society was founded partly in order to wage war on the still prevalent contempt towards the lower orders and mistrust of the power of knowledge, and throughout its lifetime was involved in constant skirmishes with the forces of religious and educational reaction within the ranks of the Whig and Tory parties. It was one of the earliest recognizable pressure groups and took part in a series of campaigns to repeal the Almanack Duty, the Newspaper Stamp, and to reduce the high cost of postage.

The final address of the Society identified the SDUK with a newly awakened spirit:

—a spirit which led to the successive foundation of University College, Kings College, and the University of London, and which had previously established the Mechanics Institutes; which overthrew the laws excluding Roman Catholics and Protestant Dissenters from the public service; which reformed the representation in spite of the utmost efforts of wealth and power; which broke the chain of slavery throughout the British Empire, and is still at work forwarding the best interests of the whole human race.[30]

The spirit was one of idealism and progress, and here the Benthamite radicals and the working class readers were occupying the same ground. "Every man is by nature endowed with the power of gaining knowledge, and the taste for it: the capacity to be pleased with it forms equally a part of the natural consti-tution of his mind",[31] asserted Brougham. "If the poor are indeed poverty stricken, the God of Creation 'who made nothing in vain' has endowed them with reason and sooner or later they will exercise it",[32] proclaimed Christopher Thomson, one of the most articulate and militant of the self-educators. There was a common belief in the humanity of the working man, and in the relevance of knowledge to his emancipation, and it was this belief which created the possibility of communication.

(ii)

The difficulties which faced the working class readers imparted certain basic characteristics to the culture of self-improvement, yet the debate over the meaning of "useful knowledge" rested on the abstraction of the concept from the pattern of activities, values and ideas which made up the life of the working man. A line was drawn round the notion of knowledge, and the protagonists were faced with the task of establishing its connection with the major areas of working class life. The most obvious problem was how the acquisition of useful knowledge was to relate to the occupational life of the readers. Would it enhance the value of their labour or alienate them from it? And how would it affect the workers' experience of the growing economic inequalities of the industrializing society?

[29] His long tenure came to an end in the following month with the formation of Canning's Ministry. After an interval of three years Brougham himself became Lord Chancellor.
[30] 1846 SDUK Address, p. 7.   [31] H. Brougham, *Discourse* p. 42.
[32] Thomson, p. 14.

Of the autobiographers, none was more conscious of the potential of knowledge than James Burn. In his *Autobiography of a Beggar Boy* he described his peripatetic childhood as the step-son of an alcoholic Scottish beggar, but by the time he came to set down his life story, he had behind him a career as a trade unionist, a radical politician in Glasgow during the Reform Bill crisis, and a member of the Board of Directors of the Manchester Unity of Oddfellows. He identified the turning point in his life, when he entered "upon the real voyage of life with something like a man at the wheel",[33] as the period during which he managed to settle down to a trade during his early twenties, and at last made contact with other literate working men. He described the event in the following terms:

> Up to this time I was not able to write my own name, and while I was serving my apprenticeship in Hexham I had no opportunities to learn. Thanks to my step-father, I could read a little, and never failed to turn it to account when I had the opportunity. During my stay in Hexham I had no means of seeing anything in the shape of literature; neither of the families in which I had lived possessed the most distant taste for reading, and as far as my memory serves me, I am not aware of having seen a book read in either of their houses. In the latter end of the year of 1826, a friend made me a present of an old edition of Chevalier Ramsay's *Life of Cyrus*. This little volume opened up to my inquiring mind a rich field of useful knowledge. The appendix to the work contained the *heathen mythology*: this part of the work completely fascinated me, and for a considerable time became my constant companion. I had now a continual craving to pry into the mysteries of literature.[34]

Here again we have the feeling of the transforming power of knowledge, but it is important to note the central characteristic of the "rich field of useful knowledge". By useful knowledge he meant book knowledge. And by book knowledge he meant, in any practical sense, useless knowledge. At that time Burn was learning to be a hatter, but although his apprenticeship had enabled him to begin to read and although he saw the two events as integral parts of the acquisition of a new identity as a respectable working man, the *Life of Cyrus* would not further his career as a hatter, and equally his increasing skill at his trade would never enlarge his understanding of the "mysteries of literature". At the level of practice, book knowledge and occupational knowledge were separate categories.

This was true even where the self-educator read whilst at work. Alexander Somerville was herding cows when first he learnt "anything of the world which is laid before us in books—anything of countries beyond our own—anything of other ages, and other classes of society".[35] For him book knowledge meant any knowledge that could not be picked up during the course of his daily routine.

[33] Burn, p. 123.

[34] *Ibid.*, p. 130. A. M. Ramsay's *The Travels of Cyrus* first appeared in English in 1727 and was continuously in print throughout the eighteenth century. The book followed the wanderings of its hero throughout the Ancient World and thereby introduced its readers to a wide range of classical history, mythology and theology.

[35] Somerville, p. 40. The three volumes which made the most impression on him at this time were Anson's *Voyage Round the World*, a book of Gospel Sonnets, and a collection of Burns' poems.

Yet still he employed the adjective "useful" to specify this type of literature: "About this time a parish library was established at Innerwick, and we got books from it. But the larger part of them were silly stories, of that silliest kind of literature—religious novels. Intermingled with these, however, were a few useful works of divinity, history, and biography".[36] Somerville saw no contradiction in this, for, as with every other autobiographer, he assumed a rigid distinction between the idea of "knowledge" and the idea of "skill". It is in the period of apprenticeship in particular that the autobiographers are able to point out the contrast between the separate channels of learning. John Younger was acutely conscious of it:

> I was now learning to work as a shoemaker's apprentice; but otherwise was sorely cramped in the means of following the bent of my natural tastes; and I made less progress in acquirements of general knowledge in these two years than in any two months previously. Not a germ further in school education, and without either example or enticing books, or other excitement to read; so except what was acquired in use of hand in shoemaking, these two years were a blank in as much as mind was concerned.[37]

C. M. Smith was introduced to books towards the end of his apprenticeship as a printer by a compositor in his workshop named Martin, who was "The means and medium of much pleasant and useful information to his companions".[38] By this time he was on the way to becoming fully qualified in a trade requiring great technical expertise, which commanded a high status and high wages,[39] and it is interesting to note the conclusion he drew from his first experience of literature: "I found out what Martin had before caused me to suspect, namely, that I knew nothing and had everything to learn".[40] From then onwards his pursuit of useful knowledge and his training as a printer occupied separate compartments of his life.

It is at this point that we discover the first major conflict between the perceptions of the working class self-educators and those of the middle class propagandists. The Mechanics' Institutes and the Society for the Diffusion of Useful Knowledge were founded on the assumption that the Industrial Revolution finally had broken down the barrier between the natural sciences and practical manufacture. The lesson which both organizations drew from the history of innovation over the preceding half century was that there was no branch of science that was not relevant to economic production, and conversely, there was no form of employment and, crucially, no working man, that was not capable of making a contribution to the body of science.[41] Henry Brougham explained the connection between practical skill and theoretical knowledge to the Manchester Mechanics' Institute in 1835: "Those men who are daily employed in handling tools, working amongst the very elements of

[36] *Ibid.*, p. 92.   [37] Younger, p. 103.   [38] C. M. Smith, p. 10.

[39] During the first half of the century the weekly rates for London compositors ranged from 33*s*. to 48*s*. a week, depending on the type of work. See A. L. Bowley, *Wages in the United Kingdom in the Nineteenth Century* (Cambridge, 1900), pp. 71–3.

[40] C. M. Smith, p. 14. See also the similar experience of another apprentice compositor, J. B. Leno (p. 9).

[41] For the assumptions and practices of the Mechanics' Institutes in this area see J. F. C. Harrison, op. cit., pp. 62–75; T. Kelly, *George Birkbeck* . . . , pp. 233–242; A. E. Dobbs, *Education and Social Movements 1700–1850* (London, 1919), pp. 170–183.

mechanical science, or always using mixtures of chemical drugs in a mechanical way are amongst the very persons whose situation is the best adapted in the world for actually making discoveries and inventing improvements".[42] In successive volumes of the Library of Useful Knowledge, covering such subjects as the discoveries of Francis Bacon, brewing, vegetable physiology, probability, the manufacture of iron, and natural philosophy, the Society attempted to provide a catalyst for the process by which the practice and meaning of the working man's labour was to be transformed.

In his *Discourse on the Object, Advantages and Pleasures of Science*, Brougham outlined three functions of science, the first and most significant of which was that "It makes men more skilfull, expert, and useful in their particular kinds of work by which they are able to earn their bread, and by which they are able to make it go far and taste well when earned".[43] In the autobiographies there are very few instances of artisans studying in order to make themselves better workmen. Somerville was at one time fired with the ambition of following an elder brother's footsteps and becoming a forester, and to that end he acquired a copy of *Hutton's Mensuration* to learn measuring and account keeping;[44] John Clare bought "Abercrombie's *Gardening*" to help him as a gardener for the Marquis of Exeter;[45] and we saw in the preceding chapter how Brierley and his neighbour studied arithmetic in order to be better able to manage the calculations required in weaving. Their attempts were largely ineffective and made little impact on their conception of the usefulness of knowledge.

The only autobiographer to uphold the connection between science and labour was Timothy Claxton. He had organized a pioneer mechanics' institute in London between 1817 and 1820, and in 1839, after the movement and its ideology had been fully developed by middle class supporters, he published *Hints to Mechanics*, in which he attempted to demonstrate by an account of his own life the truths expounded by men such as Brougham.[46] However his exposition of the relationship is not backed up with any specific examples of its application to his own trade as a whitesmith,[47] and both the practice of the autobiographers and what is known of the general situation of skilled artisans in this period suggests that his was a lone voice. The innovations in the techniques of production which had taken place by 1850 had yet to substitute book learning for the traditional method of acquiring a trade by practice and by

[42] Henry Brougham, "Address to the Members of the Manchester Mechanics' Institution July 31 1835", in *British Eloquence: Literary Addresses, 2nd Series* (London, 1855), p. 170.

[43] H. Brougham, *Discourse . . .*, p. 41.

[44] Somerville, pp. 44–6. The book must have been Charles Hutton, *A Treatise on Mensuration, both in theory and practice* (1st ed., Newcastle-upon-Tyne, 1770, 4th ed., London, 1812). The practical section covered the calculations used by land surveyors, bricklayers, masons, carpenters and joiners, slaters and tilers, plasterers, painters, glaziers, pavers, plumbers and, which was relevant to Somerville's needs, forestry workers. Nothing came of the venture, and he eventually escaped from his home by joining the army.

[45] Clare, *Autobiography*, p. 27. John Abercrombie wrote several manuals on gardening, including *Every Man his own Gardener* (1st ed., 1767, 21st ed., 1818) and *The Gardener's Pocket Journal* (1789, 14th ed., 1815).

[46] Claxton, ch. 1, pp. 1–37. For Claxton's work, see T. Kelly, *A History of Adult Education . . .*, p. 117.

[47] The most he could say was that his scientific experiments had given him "freedom of handling, inventing and improving" (p. 120).

example. There were no examinations and no recognized paper qualifications.[48] In his *Report on the State of the Literary Scientific and Mechanics Institutions*, Thomas Coates, the SDUK secretary, proposed that they should adopt a "plan of CERTIFICATES of proficiency after an examination" for the express purpose of making the courses more practically useful to working men,[49] but his idea was not followed up, and it was not until 1851 that the Pupil Teacher scheme began to send a few working men to training colleges where they might acquire teaching certificates. Industrialization undermined the institution of apprenticeship by simplifying the skills required in many occupations, but where the need for skill remained, or in some cases was increased, then these were still obtained by the traditional seven-year period of training.[50] Beyond a basic literacy and numeracy there was little abstract knowledge which an artisan could usefully gain outside the practice of his trade, and once qualified, the worker at the factory bench would find that the discipline, noise and monotony of the industrial process would make it very difficult to make any contact with what he would consider to be "knowledge". At a practical level, the experience of industrialization was driving apart rather than uniting the pursuit of knowledge and the pursuit of bread.

Brougham's second function of science was that, "It enables men to make improvements in the arts, and discoveries in philosophy, which may directly benefit themselves and mankind".[51] Here there was at least a possibility of a direct line of communication between the SDUK and its intended audience. There did exist a very small minority of working men who were not content with imbibing and expounding the received body of knowledge, but who attempted to undertake original scientific research. One of the most remarkable of these men was Roger Langdon, who lived out his life as a signalman and stationmaster in villages in Somerset and Devon.[52] He was fascinated by the developments in science, and combined his reading with his manual skills to construct a harmonium, a model village, a magic lantern and no less than four telescopes. In 1871 the stationmaster received the accolade of an invitation to read a paper on certain markings he had discovered on Venus before the Royal Astronomical Society. Many of the artisan autobiographers were proud of their manual skills and emphasized them in their writings, but the proportion whose position as craftsmen survived industrialization, and who were also interested in experimental science, was extremely small. Men like Langdon and Joseph Gutteridge, the Coventry ribbon weaver who built his own microscope and made a large collection of botanical and geological specimens,[53] were exceptional members of their community,[54] and as Gutteridge himself

[48] However, skilled workers frequently required "characters" when moving to a new job or seeking promotion, and in this respect a known involvement in the pursuit of knowledge might be of some practical value. This was particularly true of pledged teetotallers, who could advertise particular personal qualities and specific evidence of possessing them. See Brian Harrison, *Drink and the Victorians* (London, 1971), p. 97.

[49] T. Coates, op. cit., pp. 65, 66.

[50] For the training of the new industrial workforce, see Sidney Pollard, *The Genesis of Modern Management* (London, 1965), pp. 174–181.

[51] H. Brougham, *Discourse* . . . , p. 42.   [52] 1825–1894.

[53] Gutteridge, *passim*, especially pp. 87–9. See also below, pp. 172–4.

[54] The autobiographies of both men contain accounts of the superstitious amazement with which their astronomical knowledge was greeted by other working people (Langdon, p. 84; Gutteridge, pp. 104–6).

admitted, no amount of intelligence, skill and enthusiasm could make much headway against the practical problems faced by all working men.[55] In the nineteenth century world of science, the gifted amateur needed a university education and a substantial income if he was to make a serious contribution to the existing body of knowledge.

The third function, "the pleasure derived from mere knowledge, without any view to our own bodily enjoyments", was a restatement of the broad idealistic commitment to knowledge for its own sake, and thus Brougham ignored the question which must always be associated with the education of the labouring population, that of the relationship between the acquisition of knowledge and upward social and economic mobility. The members of the SDUK had in fact discussed the problem amongst themselves and their conclusion was embodied in the most successful volume in the Library of Entertaining Knowledge, George Craik's *The Pursuit of Knowledge Under Difficulties* which first appeared in 1830.[56] It is typical of the ambition and the idealism of the Society that it eschewed both the concern to retain a subservient and uneducated workforce which had characterized the work of establishment writers from the time of de Mandeville, whilst at the same time trying to avoid the emphasis on economic advancement which was later to be found in the more popular works of Samuel Smiles.[57]

In terminology borrowed wholesale from the political economists, the SDUK put forward a conception which ran parallel to, but apart from, capitalism. The great virtue of the pursuit of useful knowledge was that unlike the burgeoning industrial sphere it required neither capital nor competition. As Craik himself put it:

> In other pursuits, the most unremitting endeavours often fail to secure the object sought; that object being generally some worldly advantage, is equally within the grasp of other competitors, some one of whom may snatch it away before it can be reached by him who best deserves it. But in the pursuit of knowledge it matters not how many be the competitors. No one stands in the way of another, or can deprive him of any part of his chance, we should

[55] "To study the science (of geology) properly", he admitted, "a man must have time and means at his command and education as well as a natural inclination" (Gutteridge, p. 207). During one period of intense poverty he was forced to sell his entire collection of specimens to buy food for his family.

[56] G. L. Craik, *The Pursuit of Knowledge Under Difficulties*, 2 vols. (London, 1830–31). The popularity of the work far outlived the lifetime of the Society which commissioned it, and it was republished in 1844, 1845, 1858, 1865, 1880, 1881 and 1906. Craik also wrote *The Pursuit of Knowledge Under Difficulties, Illustrated by Female Examples* (London, 1847).

[57] Smiles' *Self-Help* appeared in 1859. Charles Knight was emphatic in his account on "the great distinction between the love of knowledge for its own sake, and the love of knowledge as the means of worldly advancement (which) may be traced very distinctly in the two popular volumes of Mr Craik and the equally popular 'Self Help' of Mr Smiles" (C. Knight, op. cit., p. 133). Smiles made much the same distinction in his autobiography, but he claimed to have been greatly influenced by Craik's book, much of which he knew by heart, and often regretted that the success of his industrial biographies tended to obliterate the non-materialistic side to his approach, which manifested itself both in his early career in Leeds and in his less well-known works, such as *The Life of a Scottish Naturalist, Thomas Edwards* (London, 1876); Samuel Smiles, *Autobiography* (London, 1905), pp. 222, 325–6. See two useful studies of the ambiguity of Smiles' thought, J. F. C. Harrison, "The Victorian Gospel of Success", *Victorian Studies*, vol. I, Dec. 1957, pp. 155–164; Kenneth Fielden, "Samuel Smiles and Self-Help", *Victorian Studies*, vol. XII, Dec. 1968, pp. 155–176.

rather say of his certainty, of success; on the contrary, they are all fellow-workers, and may materially help each other forward. The wealth which each seeks to acquire has, as it were, the property of multiplying itself to meet the wants of all.[58]

The spokesmen of the Society attempted to define a world in which the rules of political economy did not apply. Charles Knight wrote in the introduction to Carter's autobiography that, "It is beginning to be felt that knowledge is the common property of the human family—the only property that can be equally divided without injury to the general stock".[59] Whilst retaining the emphasis on the Puritan values of toil and duty, they hoped to allocate to working men an area of experience which could co-exist with capitalism rather than challenge its inescapable economic and social inequalities.

The Society attempted to communicate its message through the medium of the potted biography, to which it devoted a great deal of its slender resources, publishing not only Craik's *Pursuit*, but a *Gallery of Portraits*, a volume on *The Lives of Eminent Persons* in the Library of Useful Knowledge, and numerous biographical items in the *Penny Cyclopaedia* and *Penny Magazine*.[60] Eventually it launched an ambitious *Biographical Dictionary* in 1842, and the loss of £5,000 on the first seven half-volumes making up the letter *A* was the immediate cause of the Society's dissolution in 1846.[61] As in other areas of its communication, there was initially firm common ground between the Society and at least a part of its intended audience, and we can best discover how far this extended by concentrating on the presentation of just one of the heroes, Henry Kirke White. The outline of his life is briefly told. He was born in Nottingham in 1785, the son of a butcher. After a little elementary schooling he was set to work at a stocking loom at the age of fourteen. By this time he had developed a marked taste for literary pursuits, and eventually he managed to get himself articled to a local firm of solicitors, serving a preliminary two years in lieu of a premium. He taught himself Latin, and began to publish his poetry in the *Monthly Preceptor* and the *Monthly Mirror*. This attracted the attention of Capel Lofft, who arranged for the publication of a volume of poetry[62] which in turn brought him to the notice of Robert Southey and William Wilberforce, who admired not only his humble poetical skills but also his developing evangelical piety. Together with the Rev. Charles Simeon, his sponsors procured a sizarship at St. John's College, Cambridge, where he was to study for Holy Orders, but his health gave out, and at the end of his first year, in which he had shown the highest promise, he died of consumption aged just twenty-one. It was then that Southey's formidable publicity machine rolled into action. Within a year of White's death he published *The Remains of Henry Kirke White*,

[58] G. L. Craik, op. cit., vol. 1, p. 418.

[59] Carter, *Memoirs*, p. ix.

[60] A. T. Malkin, ed., *The Gallery of Portraits, with memoirs*, 7 vols. (London, 1833–6); (Various authors) *The Lives of Eminent Persons*, 13 parts (London, 1833). The subjects were typically diverse: Galileo, Kepler, Newton, Mahomet, Wolsey, Sir Edward Coke, Lord Somers, Caxton, Admiral Blake, Adam Smith, Niebuhr, Sir Christopher Wren, and Michelangelo.

[61] G. Long, ed., *Biographical Dictionary of the Society for the Diffusion of Useful Knowledge*, vols. 1–4 (London, 1842–44). Had the undertaking survived, it would have been far longer than the later *Dictionary of National Biography*. For an account of the financial problems, see the SDUK 1846 Address, pp. 10–11; H. Smith, op. cit., pp. 14–15.

[62] Henry Kirke White, *Clifton Grove* (London, 1803).

which contained a biography by Southey, tributary verses by numerous literary figures, including Byron, and the collected prose and verse of the late poet.[63] The book was an instant success, going through ten editions by 1823, and White was an obvious choice for Craik, who included an edited version of Southey's biography in *The Pursuit*. He would have devoted even more space to White, but, as he explained, ". . . it is probable . . . that most of our readers are acquainted with the narrative of his life which has been so delightfully written by Mr. Southey . . .".[64]

Several of the autobiographers certainly were familiar with the details of his life, and as Southey and Craik would have wished, held him up as an inspiration for their own activities. The butcher's son was at the forefront of Thomas Cooper's mind as he set forth on his self-education: "What though I could not get to Cambridge, like Kirke White, could I not study as hard as he studied, and learn as fast"?[65] Both John Harris and Mary Smith read the *Remains* "with great delight",[66] and Thomas Carter actually saved up a guinea to buy the book. It was, he said, "a large sum for one like myself to spend at one time in buying books: yet I had good reason to be satisfied; for the work was useful to me in the way of strengthening and confirming my habits of reading and observation".[67]

The appeal of the book lay primarily in the details of Southey's biography in which he painted a remarkably accurate and sympathetic picture of the difficulties experienced by a self-improving working man.[68] There is no doubt that the majority of its readership was drawn from the educated classes who were anxious to be assured that the tradition pioneered by Stephen Duck was still alive, but there were at least two genuine points of intersection between the preoccupations of the middle class educators and the working class readers. The first of these was the theme of self-discipline and self-denial which ran through the account. From Brougham's point of view, the promotion of these virtues was essential if the pursuit of knowledge were to coexist with the demands of industrialization. For the working men, the suffering and intense application displayed by White were inevitable concomitants of self-improvement and as such their presentation and celebration in the works of Southey and Craik would serve as an inspiration or a solace.[69] Furthermore, if the autobiographers rarely indulged in the degree of bathos displayed by many of the contributors to *The Remains*, there was a tendency, especially amongst those who wrote poetry, to take a perverse pleasure in the loneliness of reading and writing, and in the hostility they often encountered in their family or workplace. The second intersection is to be found in the attempt to isolate the pursuit of knowledge from the inequalities of class relations. It is quite clear that in this respect the

[63] Robert Southey, *The Remains of Henry Kirke White*, 2 vols. (London, 1807).
[64] *Ibid.*, p. 223.   [65] Cooper, p. 53.   [66] Harris, p. 46; M. Smith, p. 40.
[67] Carter, *Memoirs*, p. 188. See also Joseph Blacket, who wrote a "Monody on the Death of Henry Kirke White".
[68] See Robert Southey, *The Remains* (7th edn., London, 1818), vol. 1, pp. 1–38. He succeeded in previewing the majority of the problems and their solutions which were discussed in the previous chapter.
[69] Of the autobiographers, Thomas Cooper eventually wrote his own version of Craik, in which the emphasis was placed on the toil and struggle which the "peaceful achievements of science and benevolence" required. Thomas Cooper, *The Triumphs of Perseverance and Industry* (London, 1854).

SDUK had established a foothold in the experiences of the working class readers. "My actual world was bare enough and narrow enough," wrote Charles Shaw, "but in the world of books I had 'ample verge and room', could commune with those 'who rule our spirits', and hold my mean environment in some disdain when compared with the wealth and imagination poured at my feet."[70] As we saw in the previous chapter, the occupational and domestic circumstances of the readers permeated every aspect of the pursuit of knowledge, but in spite of this, part of the attraction of the world of books was precisely that it offered a much greater freedom than was to be found in any other area of their situation. In the short term at least, they could make virtually no impression on the conditions in which they lived and worked, yet the chance encounter with a stray copy of Shakespeare, or Milton, or Bunyan could transform their intellectual world almost instantly. They could never attain the standard of living of the ruling class, and they faced a long battle to gain a share of its economic and political power, yet already they had, like White, a limited access to its literature.

Beyond these two points, the distance between the patterns of behaviour projected in the potted biographies, and the actual experience recorded in the autobiographies, many of which were also written to encourage the pursuit of knowledge, begins to increase. Henry Kirke White had started life a trades-man's son; he had been befriended by the leading poets of the time and had ended his days an undergraduate at Cambridge. His career exemplified an assumption which was crucial to the SDUK's outlook, that in the pursuit of knowledge all men were equal and bound together in a common fellowship. It was a powerful myth and one which was capable of attracting men like Thomas Cooper. The examples of White and a handful of others, such as Samuel Lee, a carpenter who rose to become Regius Professor of Hebrew at Cambridge,[71] kept alive the dream, but the circumstances in which Cooper came close to realizing it only emphasised its unreality. While he was serving a two-year sentence for sedition and conspiracy in Stafford Gaol, the prison chaplain offered to get him into Cambridge on condition that he abandoned politics. Cooper indignantly refused to "degrade or falsify myself by making such a promise", and no other autobiographer was similarly tempted.[72] As the old grammar school systems, which had once offered a means of escape to a few fortunate and talented working men's children, became increasingly exclusive, the chances of a working man's child gaining sufficient formal education to enter a university, even supposing the fees could be found, dwindled into nothing.[73] Equally, as adults, the growth in the number of

[70] Shaw, p. 93.

[71] Lee was born in 1783 in the Shropshire village of Longnor. He was apprenticed at the age of 12 to a Shrewsbury carpenter. By the age of 25 he had taught himself Latin, Greek and Hebrew, and had made progress in Chaldee, Syriac, Samaritan, Persian and Hindustani. He was eventually noticed by the Church Missionary Society, who launched him on his academic career at the age of 30. He died in 1852.

[72] See Cooper, p. 257. He had been convicted for his part in the Chartist disturbances in the Potteries in 1842. Another autobiographer, J. A. Leatherland, claimed that a curate had once offered to get him into an unspecified college (Leatherland, p. 14).

[73] Samuel Bamford, who attended the junior section of Manchester Grammar School in the 1790s and was prevented from progressing to learn the classics by his father who could see little point in such knowledge, was the only autobiographer who even glimpsed the prospect of a ladder from manual labour to university (Bamford, *Early Days*, pp. 92–3).

working class readers, made it more difficult for them to find a welcome in the older middle class literary societies,[74] and in turn made them unwilling to participate in the mechanics' institutes which were set up to provide an organizational framework for the intellectual fellowship the Broughamites were attempting to create.[75] In practice the readers' experience of the economic and social inequalities of their society, together with the nature of their response to them, determined that the figure of Henry Kirke White remained a fantasy rather than a model they might hope to imitate.

However, if the readers could not become Anglican parsons, could they remain good cobblers, contented shepherds and fulfilled engineers? Could they be prevented from abandoning their labours in favour of less productive and possibly more disruptive forms of activities, or in favour of an attempt to raise themselves into the middle class? As we have seen, the SDUK, through a combination of idealism and pragmatism, had placed little emphasis on the role of knowledge as an instrument of individual economic mobility. Not only would this introduce a distasteful element of materialism into the concept of useful knowledge, the inevitable frustration which the aspiring readers would experience might increase the danger of disaffection from their labour and from the organization of production in general. Watt, Arkwright and Rennie do make an appearance in Craik's volumes, but they are lost in a sea of heroes taken from every possible culture and period. In turn, there is little evidence that the self-improving working men saw useful knowledge as a means towards industrial success. In a sense, such a finding is inevitable, given the original decision to exclude from this sample those who had moved up into the middle class during the period, but there are two reasons for believing this to be an accurate picture. Firstly, we find no reference to entrepreneurial figures whose careers the autobiographers attempted but failed to emulate in the same way that some dreamed of emulating that of White. Secondly, the last two or three decades of this period seem to represent a hiatus between the early period of industrial innovation where "uneducated" artisans could and did become successful entrepreneurs,[76] and the later growth of the managerial and white collar classes which were more closely identified with formal educational qualifications. In real terms the opportunities for working men to become upwardly mobile either by an institutional education or by gaining the equivalent by their own efforts, were at a nadir.[77]

---

[74] A few of the earlier autobiographers did gain acceptance in such societies, notably Thelwall, (p. xix), Hogg (pp. 23–4), and Carter (*Memoirs*, p. 215), but from the 1830s onwards, the autobiographers tended to participate only in organizations run by fellow working men.

[75] For the failure of the mechanics' institutes, see E. R. Royle, "Mechanics' Institutes and the Working Classes, 1840–1860", *The Historical Journal*, 1971, pp. 305–321.

[76] This phenomenon should not be over-estimated. In the words of Pollard "The number of genuinely self-taught geniuses was remarkably small in spite of the large space they occupy in the literature", though he concedes that the cotton industry had "unusually democratic origins". S. Pollard, op. cit., pp. 104, 105. For the general argument in this sentence, see pp. 104–159.

[77] For an isolated example of a process which was to become much more common later in the century, see the career of Hugh Miller, a self-educated mason from Cromarty, who after educating himself and publishing some poetry, was offered the post of "accountant" (bank-clerk) in a newly opened branch of the Commercial Bank of Scotland in his native town in the early 1830s. Hugh Miller, *My Schools and Schoolmasters* (Edinburgh, 1854), especially pp. 484–5.

The real question, as the SDUK correctly realized, was whether the readers could be persuaded to maintain their occupational and intellectual lives in a mutually supportive relationship. If the hope that self-improvement would make the readers more skilful workers had little chance of realization, it remained imperative that the pursuit of knowledge did not alienate the readers from the performance of their trades. This fear had been at the centre of the traditional hostility towards the education of the labouring classes, and if Brougham and his fellow radicals were to convert the ruling class to their outlook it was essential that reading and working should exist in a state of peaceful coexistence. Craik's volumes attempted to divert attention from any disruptive connections between the two spheres of activity by deliberately diffusing the cultural and temporal identity of the pursuit of knowledge. The 273 main characters ranged through Pythagoras, Archimedes, Julius Caesar, Peter the Great, Pascal, Galileo, Gainsborough, Giotto, Haydn, Mozart, Shakespeare and Arkwright. Similarly the notion of "difficulties" suffered the widest possible interpretation, referring not only to "obscure and humble situation" and "extreme poverty", but also to "defects of the senses or other natural bodily powers" and "blindness", and the problems faced by literary soldiers, literary merchants and "persons of rank or wealth".[78] However, the autobiographers were too aware of the particular details of their own difficulties to be deflected in this way, and there is no doubt that to many readers self-improvement offered the chance to escape from or at least alleviate the hardship of their lives as working men.

Initially there would be the opportunity to engage in spare-time work through the existing institutions of the dissenting churches. A number of the autobiographers became either lay preachers or Sunday school teachers.[79] This work was unpaid,[80] but at least it afforded an additional focal point in their lives, and, particularly in the case of local preachers, could be a means of conferring considerable status within the community. Then there were at least four areas in which the pursuit of knowledge might lead to taking up alternative full-time occupations of varying security and income. Firstly, there was a range of jobs which could be fashioned out of the practical requirements of the culture. Every reader was inevitably something of a part-time bookdealer—borrowing, lending, buying and selling the secondhand volumes—and several were tempted into trying to make a full-time business out of it.[81] Where the existing newsagents refused to stock the current radical literature, there was often no alternative but to go into business in competition, ordering the newspapers wholesale and retailing them to fellow members of the workshop or community. The shops run by men such as Watson, Dunning and Thomas Cooper then served as the physical centres of local political activity, although they were often uncertain forms of financial support for their owners. On the same principle, Alexander Somerville opened a combined coffee, beer and

[78] See, respectively, vol. 1, chs. 3, 16, 17, 18, 9, 10 and vol. 11, ch. 1.
[79] Arch, H. Carter, Cooper, Harris, Kitson, Oliver, Saville, Scott and Shaw were lay preachers; Basset, Bezer, Bowcock, T. Carter, Davis, Hanson, Harris, Heaton, H. Herbert, Hopkinson, Innes, Lovekin, Parkinson, J. Taylor and P. Taylor were Sunday school teachers.
[80] See particularly the account of Thomas Carter, who claimed that his work actually left him out of pocket (*Memoirs*, p. 166). The late eighteenth century schools often paid their teachers, but the practice was discontinued after 1800 (T. W. Laqueur, op. cit., pp. 91-2).
[81] See especially Leno, p. 76; Lovett, pp. 244-5; Bamford, *Early Days*, p. 311.

spirits shop,[82] James Burn a public house for members of his trade[83] and William Lovett a coffee shop which included a separate library.[84] Somerville's and Burn's ventures failed very quickly, but Lovett's lasted two years, and he was well satisfied with the experience: "But notwithstanding my want of success, I now look back upon those two years of my life with great pleasure and satisfaction, for during this period I gained a considerable amount of information, and was, I believe, the means of causing much useful knowledge to be diffused among the young men who frequented the place".[85]

Secondly, it was a fairly simple matter for a literate working man to set up his own school. In 1830, as much as two thirds of all elementary education was provided by unsystemized and unregulated private day schools.[86] It merely required that the would-be teacher should declare his front room to be a school, and for as long as he could retain the support of local parents, he was in business. At the end of the Napoleonic Wars, William Brown was paid off by the navy, and like many other ex-servicemen, found himself with no home and no trade. He wandered up the country, often begging for his living, until he fetched up in the Yorkshire village of Middleham where his landlady mentioned that "poor people's baines can get no larning". The former pawnbroker, cutlery salesman and ship's corporal seized the opportunity: "I wrote my terms, and published them at the market cross. I got a board and printed on it a Day School by William Brown, I placed this board in the window, I lay on a chaff bed on the floor having no bedstead; I had a board by the side, and another at the bottom, to prevent my rolling off. I got some sticks and boring some holes in the boards they served for forms by day . . . I soon got scholars to the number of sixteen".[87] "There can be no surprise excited at my 'keeping a school'," wrote another instant schoolmaster, the former shipwright and travelling actor Christopher Thomson, "anybody could make a schoolmaster. People must live; and as well to keep a school as do anything else; every sixpence will buy a loaf; and to be a schoolmaster is one of the few comfortable trades which require no previous training."[88] The useful knowledge which had been so painfully acquired could now be turned to practical advantage, as the Ashton-under-Lyne cotton piecer William Aitken discovered when he fell foul of the town's employers because of his involvement in the Ten Hours Campaign: "Being out of employment some time I was advised to commence a school, having diverted a deal of spare time to the acquisition of useful knowledge. I have been employed in that useful calling until now . . .".[89] The church schools

---

[82] Somerville, pp. 373–4; his capital was £250 collected on his behalf after a national controversy had been aroused over a flogging he had received whilst serving in the Scots Greys in 1832.

[83] Burn, pp. 145–6, 153. His public house, *The Hatters' Arms* became the meeting place for the first branch of the Manchester Unity of Oddfellows in the west of Scotland, and launched Burn on a career that led him to become Grand Master of the district and a member of the governing body of the national organization.

[84] Lovett, pp. 88–9. The coffee shop opened in 1834 in Greville Street, London.

[85] *Ibid.*, p. 88.   [86] See above, p. 101.

[87] Brown, p. 121. The venture prospered and Brown was still running his school when he wrote his autobiography twelve years later.

[88] Thomson, p. 207. He started his school in the south Yorkshire village of Tickhill in 1827, but he faced competition from an established national school, and although the venture kept his family alive through a difficult time, he subsequently returned to acting.

[89] Aitken, 25 September, p. 3. The school kept him until just before his death over thirty years later in 1869 but, according to his obituary, he never enjoyed real prosperity.

were making increasing efforts to supplant the private day schools and professionalize their own teachers, but they made slow progress, and in the meantime the occupation provided a welcome if ill-paid refuge for working men who were unable or unwilling to continue with their manual labour.[90]

Thirdly, there was the possibility of earning or at least supplementing a living by literary pursuits. Despite the famous examples, it had always been extremely difficult for a struggling poet to gain sufficient patronage to become a professional writer, and although four of the autobiographers, John Jones, James Hogg, John Clare and Willie Thom did receive substantial assistance,[91] the great majority of working class poets had to make their own way in the literary market place.[92] Here it was unlikely that the aspiring writer would ever make much money, but equally it required little or no capital or talent to get into print. The columns of radical and religious journals, and later family journals and local newspapers were open to working class poets, and it was quite possible for the more ambitious writers to publish their own work. In 1801 James Hogg took some sheep to market in Edinburgh, and finding himself with two days to spare, he wrote out some of the poems he had composed in his head whilst tending his flock and took them to the first printer he came across, meeting the cost out of the proceeds of the sale of his sheep,[93] and half a century later the tin-miner John Harris was able to experience the pleasure of publication simply by taking a poem he was particularly pleased with to a printer in the nearest town.[94] Complete volumes could be financed out of savings or by organizing a list of subscribers[95]—at least sixteen of these autobiographies were published by their authors[96]—and although the rewards were insubstantial, a small profit on the sale of some poetry or an essay on a topical subject could

[90] See also the Carlisle handloomweaver William Farish, who used his self-acquired "scholastic improvement" to escape from his declining trade into teaching (Farish, p. 48), and the teaching experiences of the shoemaker Thomas Cooper (pp. 100–102) and the compositor C. M. Smith (pp. 181 ff), and Mary Smith who spent her adult life in a variety of teaching ventures in Carlisle (pp. 97–298). See also above, pp. 101–3.

[91] Jones was discovered by Robert Southey, who published his poetry and the prefatory memoir. Hogg became acquainted with most of the major Scottish literary figures of his time, and in 1814 was given a small farm by his admirers. Clare was launched into London society in 1820, and received spasmodic patronage from various sources, particularly the Marquis of Exeter and Lord Fitzwilliam, but he was still living in poverty when he became insane in 1837. Thom's patron was a local gentleman, Mr Gordon of Knockespock, who, together with a group of Scottish merchants, paid him to settle in London, where, cut off from his background, he drank himself into poverty and a premature death.

[92] Those who succeeded, however, might now look forward to some recognition and assistance from the State towards the end of their lives. Cooper was given a State grant of £200 for his literary activities, Leno received £50 from the Civil List, Burn received two small grants from the Royal Literary Fund, Harris received £50 from the same source, £200 from the Royal Bounty Fund and two grants of £100 from the Civil List. John Clare was also awarded £50 from the Literary Fund (which had been established in 1780), and Gutteridge was sent £100 by W. E. Gladstone on receipt of his autobiography. For the relationship between working class poets and their patrons, see Martha Vicinus, op. cit., pp. 168–184.

[93] Hogg, p. 15.   [94] Harris, p. 56.

[95] For an account of the toil of collecting a list of subscribers, see Harris, p. 89, who concludes, "The struggle to get subscribers was just as bitter as blasting the rock in the mine, it being generally looked upon as a charity". See also Hogg, p. 17, Heaton, p. xxii.

[96] Those of Brown, Leatherland, Love, Plummer and Thomson by subscription, those of the Printer's Devil, Chatterton, Dale, Davis, Downing, Farish, Hanson, Heaton, H. Herbert, Mackenzie and White were apparently financed by the authors.

provide a welcome respite for the author's hard-pressed family economy.[97] In addition, there was the possibility of earning occasional sums of money through performing one's own or other writers' works. At the beginning of the century we find David Love and William Cameron making livings by composing, publishing, singing and selling ballads and broadsides,[98] and Christopher Thomson has left us with a marvellous portrait of the life of one of the last strolling players.[99] Although both professions were in decline, the proliferation of working class political and educational organizations opened up a new and much more respectable market for the part-time lecturer and poetry reader.[100]

Most of the literary activities offered little prospect of a permanent alternative to manual labour, but there was one area in which the self-educated working man might hope to become a full-time writer. The 1830s and 1840s were a period of great expansion and experimentation in the world of journalism. The barriers which now exist between printing, writing and publishing, between professional and amateur journalism, and between involvement in the spheres of politics and literature, were then of much less significance. For the aspiring working man the field was remarkably open in spite of the earlier attempts to repress radical literature. The range of possibilities is perhaps best illustrated by the career of Thomas Frost during the 1840s. Armed with no more than a stock of self-acquired knowledge, his skill as a compositor and a bequest of £25, he was able to earn his living by founding and editing a local newspaper in his native Croydon, launching a short-lived satirical magazine called *Penny Punch*, editing the Owenite *Communist Chronicle* and then his own *Communist Journal*, acting as a correspondent for *Lloyd's London Newspaper* and the *South Eastern Gazette*, and contributing to *Chambers Papers for the People*.[101] Throughout the period he was continually on the bread-line and had a growing family to support, but he was able to launch a series of publications with virtually no capital, and, what is of equal significance, see them all fail without being

---

[97] See, for instance, Burn p. 173, who bridged a crisis in his family affairs by realizing £5 on the sale of *A Historical Sketch of the Independent Order of Odd-fellowship of the Manchester Unity* (Manchester, 1845), and Carter, *Memoirs*, p. 195, who cleared a pile of bills hanging over the family by organizing the publication by subscription of a paper he had read to a local literary society. There were isolated examples of authors making very much larger sums—see Hogg, who made £300 out of the sale of a volume of poetry entitled *The Mountain Bard* (Edinburgh, 1807), and Frost, who sold 10,000 copies of an imitative version of Eugene Sue's stories, and the career of Ben Brierley whose "Ab-o'-th'-Yate" tales exploited the growing market for dialect literature in the third quarter of the century.

[98] Love, p. 14; Cameron, pp. 90–97 and *passim*.

[99] Between 1822 and 1832 he toured through the villages of South Yorkshire, Lincolnshire and Nottinghamshire, putting on the traditional bills of fare in which scenes from Shakespeare would be juxtaposed with one act farces and melodramas and interludes of singing, dancing and juggling. See also the account by the "clown and man monkey" Harvey Teasdale of his struggle to earn a living as a travelling comedian and early music hall artist during the 1840s and '50s (Teasdale, pp. 44–62). For the economic and social problems facing actors in the first half of the century see Michael Baker, *The Rise of the Victorian Actor* (London, 1978), pp. 18–81.

[100] The opportunities for professional poetry reciting increased rapidly after 1850 when the rise of dialect poetry created a new market amongst working class communities. See M. Vicinus, op. cit., pp. 50–1, 221–2. In his 70s, Bamford embarked on a career of public readings of his own material and also the poetry of Tennyson (for details, see Brierley, pp. 63–4). Cooper became virtually a full-time itinerant lecturer from 1849 onwards (Cooper, pp. 296–300, 318, 321–9, 344–6, 352–5). See also Leno, p. 37.

[101] Frost, *Reminiscences*, pp. 38–43; *Forty Years' Recollections*, pp. 13–76, 186–96.

permanently ruined. None of the other autobiographers, with the possible exceptions of Linton and Cooper, were quite as versatile, but many seized the opportunity to participate in one or more of these areas.[102] If the partial repeal of the Stamp Act in 1836 brought to an end the golden age of the unstamped newspaper, its final abolition in 1855 ushered in a phase of great expansion in local newspapers which, with no trade unions to control entry, could offer full or part-time employment to experienced working class writers.[103]

The fourth category of employment was what might be termed the professional agitator. Virtually every working class organization made use of written communication and as such was dependent upon the skills of literate working men. The earliest form of full-time advocacy on behalf of an institutional working class cause was provided by Methodism, and from the 1820s the scope and variety of such opportunities slowly increased. The co-operative movement gave William Lovett his first experience of professional working class activity when, as early as 1829, he gave up cabinet-making to succeed James Watson as storekeeper to the First London Co-operative Trading Association.[104] The 1839 Chartist Convention made use of full-time missionaries[105] and by 1851 the trade unions, the temperance movement and the friendly societies were all employing permanent officials.[106]

Thus, if there is little evidence that the working class readers pursued useful knowledge in order to make themselves more efficient workmen, or embryo capitalists, they were not prepared to confine their activity to a separate intellectual sphere, abstracted from the economic circumstances in which they lived and worked. Combining self-improvement and physical labour was desperately hard work, particularly if the reader was unskilled, or worked in a factory or in a declining domestic industry, and many seized the chance of supplementing or perhaps supplanting altogether their manual occupations. Willie Thom was not ashamed of being a handloomweaver, and harboured no aspirations of becoming a large employer, but equally he had few illusions about the life he and his family were forced to lead and eagerly grasped such patronage as he was offered, for, as he wrote, "I dream of making my 'escape' from the loom; and of being enabled to pull my little ones out from amongst 'folks feet' ".[107] The readers benefited from the opportunities created by their own community—parents who bought an education for their children, other

---

[102] See especially the journalistic careers of Leatherland (pp. 36–7), Cooper (pp. 112–172) and Brierley (p. 56).

[103] See the further career of Frost, who remembered that in the mid-1850s, "The number of newspapers published in the United Kingdom had increased so much since the repeal of the stamp duty that I felt encouraged . . . to aspire to the position of a journalist" (*Forty Years*, p. 239). But he also noted that the country journalist could earn only three-quarters of the wage of a bricklayer (p. 241). See also Alan J. Lee, *The Origins of the Popular Press in England 1855–1914* (London, 1976), pp. 104–115; G. A. Cranfield, *The Press and Society* (London, 1978), pp. 204–221.

[104] Watson, p. 112; Lovett, p. 41. He later became storekeeper at a co-operative in Greville Street, and opened his coffee shop in the same premises when the co-operative failed.

[105] J. T. Ward, *Chartism* (London, 1973), p. 118. See the experiences of Lowery, pp. 107–9, 129–35.

[106] B. Harrison, op. cit., pp. 147–57; H. Pelling, *A History of British Trade Unions* (London, 1963), pp. 42–4; P. H. J. Gosden, *The Friendly Societies in England 1815–1875* (Manchester, 1961), pp. 27, 36, 88–93.

[107] Thom, pp. 30–31.

153

readers who wanted books and newspapers, various organizations which required management—and from the absence of restrictions in occupations which later would be professionalized.

It is important to recognize the scale of the possibilities which existed during the first half of the century. To elaborate four distinct categories of employment is a little misleading, for it was the rule rather than the exception for the reader to try, at various times, aspects of more than one category, and then to return to his original trade. The common characteristic of all these occupations was insecurity of both tenure and income;[108] indeed involvement in political or trade union agitation could lead to complete loss of employment, either through blacklisting by local employers or, as no less than thirteen of these autobiographers discovered, imprisonment.[109] With the exception of the ministry in the dissenting churches, and lecturing for the temperance movement later in the period, none of the fields of employment offered the sort of career with which the working man could completely identify himself.[110] Men like Cooper and Lovett, who travelled the furthest from their manual occupations, and gained national prominence in the process, were involved in a variety of short term occupations, and consequently could only describe themselves as being of the working class rather than of this or that working class institution. Most of the occupations slightly enhanced the chance of achieving a move into the middle class, but none offered a secure route. The local government structure, which was to provide working men with the possibility of power and prestige in their neighbourhood, if not income, was as yet barely formed.[111] The extreme youth of the trades union bureaucracy, and the absence of a working class parliamentary party, deprived the self-educated man of the two major fields of permanent employment and the two great escalators to the ruling class. Nonetheless, the range of possibilities did allow some readers to become partially or intermittently independent of their manual labour, and these men constituted a sort of working class intelligentsia who had gained some very limited freedom to think and act in ways which did not necessarily coincide with the outlook and behaviour demanded by the middle class radicals.

[108] For instance William Lovett was paid less as a storekeeper to the First London Co-operative Trading Association than he could earn as a cabinet maker, and Thomson calculated that, "My individual amount of money support from the stage never averaged as much per week as 'the poor stone-breaker'" (p. 288).

[109] See especially the miner Edward Rymer, who calculated that he lost his job thirteen times as a result of his trade union activities. The prisoners were Bamford, Aitken, Lovett, Cooper, Teer, Watson, Bezer, Chadwick, Crowe, Hetherington, McCarthy, Thelwall and Hardy, the last two being acquitted of High Treason after spending a period in custody.

[110] Of the main group of autobiographers, Farish and Lowery identify themselves as temperance workers, and William Matthews lists sixty-three nineteenth century Methodist autobiographers.

[111] For early attempts by working men to become involved in municipal politics, see J. F. C. Harrison's account of "municipal Chartism" in Leeds: "Chartism in Leeds", in Asa Briggs, ed., Chartist Studies (London, 1959), pp. 86–8, 90–93. For an example of the opportunities which the later growth of the structure and the setting up of the school boards after 1870 would bring, see the career of Frederick Rogers, a self-educated London bookbinder, born in 1846, who became a school manager and rose to be an L.C.C. Alderman. Frederick Rogers, Labour, Life and Literature. Some Memories of Sixty Years (London, 1913). Ben Brierley also served for six years on Manchester City Council during the 1870s (Brierley, pp. 77–8). Foster found that one in five of the councillors in Oldham in 1890 came from working class backgrounds, and "of these almost all began their careers within the adult education, Sunday school, temperance orbit". John Foster, op. cit., p. 222.

(iii)

The application of the adjective "useful" to the notion of knowledge was an act not only of description but of discrimination. Underlying the qualification was the assumption that there existed knowledge which was *not* useful, and that it was possible to identify a type of book from which such non-useful knowledge might be obtained. In the autobiographies there is a keen sense of the stratification of the world of knowledge. Thomas Carter, whose diverse and zealous attempts to obtain literature were discussed in the previous chapter, explained that his initial problem was not so much a shortage of books, as the character of those which were available: ". . . my prevailing desire was to obtain some useful knowledge; consequently I was soon satiated with what was adapted only to please a vagrant or a sickly fancy. When I first began to read for amusement, I had, as has been hinted, access to but few books that were likely to be useful as well as entertaining".[112] John Bezer used the term as a touchstone for assessing the value of the education he received at Sunday school: "Now, that school did not even learn me to read; six hours a week, certainly not *one* hour of useful knowledge; plenty of cant, and what my teachers used to call *explaining* difficult texts in the Bible, but little, very little else".[113] For these men the significant event was not gaining the first knowledge but the first knowledge of a specific quality. Ben Brierley identified his particular moment: "I must confess that my soul did not feel much lifted by the only class of reading then within my reach. It was not until I joined the companionship of Burns and Byron that I felt the 'god within me' ".[114]

Every act of affirmation implied an act of rejection, and this was equally true for those who were attempting to influence the type of literature read by working men. The SDUK was preoccupied with the content as well as the cost of books. The final Address emphasized the duality of purpose which had been a constant theme throughout the Society's lifetime: "The Society's work is done, for its greatest object is achieved—fully, fairly, and permanently. The public is supplied with *cheap* and *good* literature to an extent which the most sanguine friend of human improvement could not, in 1826, have hoped to have witnessed in twenty years".[115] That the educators and self-educators should have had this much in common arose from a shared problem. Both sides were attempting to define the character of a literate culture which was being constructed on the foundation of one in which literature had played a much smaller part. The absence of established guidelines was the cause of much of the euphoria and ambition, but there was always present a sense of uncertainty, for both the SDUK and the autobiographers were well aware that the conditions which promoted their activity might also favour the forces represented by the Salisbury Square publishers.

Early in 1829, William Lovett, who was by now an established figure in the world of London working class radicalism, drew up a petition for the opening

---

[112] Carter, *Memoirs*, p. 28. The bulk of his "useless" literature was old chap-books, as was the case with John Clare who wrote of the same period in his life that "I deeply regret useful books was out of reach" (*Sketches*, p. 50). See also J. D. Burn's discussion of the categories of useful knowledge (Burn, pp. 197–8).
[113] Bezer, p. 157.
[114] Brierley, p. 32. See also Dundee Factory Boy, p. 31.
[115] 1846 Address of the SDUK, p. 13.

of the British Museum on Sundays. He included the text in his autobiography as an indication of his thinking at the time, and it provides one of the clearest statements of the basic ideology of the culture of self-improvement:

> Your petitioners suggest to your Honourable House . . . that if useful knowledge was extensively disseminated among the industrious classes, if they were encouraged to admire the beauties of nature, to cultivate a taste for the arts and sciences, to seek for rational instruction and amusement, it would soon be found that their vicious habits would yield to more rational pursuits; man would become the friend and lover of his species, his mind would be strengthened and fortified against the allurements of vice; he would become a better citizen in this world, and be better qualified to enjoy happiness in any future state of existence.[116]

It was in these broad terms that the readers approached the crucial problem of discrimination. The usefulness of categories of knowledge, and of the books which contained them, was to be assessed not in relation to the daily performance of the individual's trade, but rather according to their capacity to promote the pursuit of reason and to realize a set of moral goals.

Again there was common ground between the SDUK and the self-educators. The immediate object of Lovett's petition was perfectly acceptable to the Society, which between 1832 and 1836, made its own contribution to the cause by publishing guides to various parts of the British Museum in its Library of Entertaining Knowledge.[117] It shared the readers' basic commitment to reason and moral improvement, and addressed itself to the problems which beset the new culture with a similar sense of responsibility. Yet as it began to translate its ambitions into a series of publications, elements of paternalism and restriction began to manifest themselves. They were apparent, initially, in its general attitude to the reading patterns of the self-educators. As we have seen, there was a fundamental eclecticism in the approach of the readers, which was partly forced upon them, but which was also accepted as a positive value. Once they had discovered its existence, they approached the higher class of literature with the indiscriminate enthusiasm of a child let loose in a sweet shop. "During these years", Thomas Cooper recalled, "I was . . . reading anything and everything I could lay hold of."[118] "No specific plan was laid down for our guidance, nor any chains imposed on our daring young spirits", wrote the Dundee Factory Boy of a "select debating society" he formed with some friends: "We wrote papers on History, Literature, Religion, Theology and Metaphysics".[119] Charles Shaw mourned the passing of the spirit of these organizations:

---

[116] Lovett, p. 58.

[117] G. Long, *The British Museum: Egyptian Antiquities*, 2 vols. (London, 1832–6); Sir H. Ellis, *The British Museum: Elgin and Phigaleian Marbles*, 2 vols. (London, 1833); Sir H. Ellis, *The British Museum; the Townley Gallery*, 2 vols. (London, 1836). *The Penny Magazine* also contained numerous items on the Museum. Sir Henry Ellis was Principal Librarian of the British Museum from 1827 to 1856. Despite considerable agitation on the subject during the 1820s and '30s, the Museum was not opened to the public every day of the week until 1879, and Sunday opening was not achieved until 1896. See Edward Miller, *That Noble Cabinet. A History of the British Museum* (London, 1973), pp. 134–40, 256–7.

[118] T. Cooper, pp. 35–6. See also Thelwall, p. vii; Heaton, p. xvii; Clare, *Sketches*, pp. 22, 54; Harris, p. 100; Bamford, *Early Days*, p. 210.

[119] Dundee Factory Boy, pp. 70–71. For his equally ambitious private reading, see p. 64.

"The audacity and simplicity of young men in such societies in those days cannot be understood in these more disciplined days. 'The schoolmaster has been abroad' since then, and by examinations and even by 'cramming' has scared away all such lofty flights".[120] In this context, the SDUK was the prototype of all the schoolmasters who were later to impose themselves on the pursuit of knowledge. Those who taught in the elementary schools in this period could rarely exercise much influence over the higher levels of learning; their role was confined to providing, or failing to provide, the basic tools which the more able and determined amongst their pupils might use as they grew older. The SDUK, however, deliberately set out to give some order and shape to the explorations of the readers. Charles Knight described *The Penny Magazine*, which was the SDUK's response to the catholic tastes of its intended audience, as "the small optic-lens called *the finder*, which is placed by the side of a large telescope, to enable the observer to discover the star which is afterwards to be carefully examined by the most perfect instrument"[121], and the Society's hopes for its sister publication, *The Penny Cyclopaedia*, were expressed in a revealing image: "Those therefore, who expend their Weekly Penny on this work must in some degree consider that they are laying it in a Savings Bank of Knowledge".[122] However, where the SDUK hoped that knowledge would be acquired with the same caution and order that the businessmen accumulated profit, the readers remained unrepentant spendthrifts. Figuratively, and in the odd case literally, they went straight to the big telescope. They were childlike only in their innocence; they had no wish for their food to be chosen and chopped up for them: Milton, Hume, Homer, Paine, Scott, Culpepper, Gibbon and Bunyan were taken in whole.

The attempt to impose a curriculum might have had some chance of success, had not the Society's distrust of the judgement of its audience caused it to curtail drastically the range of subjects it was prepared to teach. The difficulty was not over the range of topics which were to be considered "useful"—the SDUK thought itself a true heir of the French Encyclopaedists, and as such was committed to the promotion of all branches of intellectual endeavour—but rather over the timetable for their acquisition. When it came to giving effect to its principles, it suddenly appeared that the immaturity of its pupils and of their culture was such as to render it advisable to discourage the reading of fiction and to postpone altogether the topic of politics.

The question of imaginative literature was posed early in the Society's history when a policy had to be adopted on the categories of knowledge to be covered by the Penny Magazine. Knight, who was to publish it, was for inclusion, but Brougham carried the committee against him. The decision put the publication at a permanent disadvantage against its closest rival, *Chambers Edinburgh Journal*, which carried some fiction in every number, and further

[120] Shaw, p. 222.
[121] Charles Knight, *Passages of a Working Life During Half a Century* (London, 1864–5), vol. II, p. 182.
[122] *Prospectus of the Penny Cyclopaedia* (London, ? 1832), p. 2. Knight's summary of the fortunes of the "Savings Bank of Knowledge" is somewhat ironic: "The chronic loss for eleven years, which was induced by the Cyclopaedia, and which fell wholly upon me, absorbed every other source of profit in my extensive business, leaving me little beyond a bare maintenance, without hope of laying for the future". He calculated the total deficit to be £30,788 (C. Knight, op. cit., vol. II, pp. 203–4).

diminished what little chance it had of reaching the homes of the working class. Brougham's attitude may have owed something to his Benthamite approach to the non-quantifiable areas of human experience,[123] but the major factor was a fear of the consequences of allowing the imagination of the working man to run free. With the exception of the religious allegories, virtually all the fiction which circulated in the traditional popular literature was now condemned, and despite the rapid growth in the circulation of novels amongst middle class readers, the Society dared not attempt to fill the gap. It would not publish light fiction, and unlike Matthew Arnold two decades later, it had no conception of using "culture", in the sense of the tradition of classic works of literature and the values they embodied, as a bulwark against the disintegrating forces of the age.[124] The nearest it came to an endorsement of any fiction was the seventeen titles which crept into the twenty-seven page reading list for Mechanics' Institutes contained in Duppa's *Manual*: "The unceasing seeking after such reading" cautioned Duppa, "is very distant from, and is rarely found in combination with a love for knowledge and a desire for improvement".[125] For most practical purposes, useful knowledge was disconnected from the imagination; moral improvement was to be achieved by the accumulation of facts.

Despite the very serious purpose of self-improvement, the approach of the working class readers was, in the first instance, much more relaxed. James Burn described what he gained from his reading: "From my own experience, I would say, that well selected books, not only furnish us with useful instruction, but they also convey to our minds a source of silent pleasure not to be found elsewhere".[126] The distinction between "useful" and "entertaining" knowledge around which the SDUK organized the publication of its treatises, had little meaning. All useful knowledge gave pleasure. There was, inevitably, great variation in the literary tastes of the autobiographers, and considerable uncertainty about the shape of the culture which they were attempting to create, but it is possible to isolate three basic assumptions which permeated their approach to literature. Firstly, the chap-book and broadside traditions which had entertained their forefathers and upon which many had cut their own literary teeth, were dying and should not be revived. Secondly, some replacement for this category of literature would have to be found; the appetite for fiction was natural and inextinguishable. Finally, any development must promote what Thomas Frost, in a brilliant essay on the popular fiction of the 1840s, termed, a "more wholesome and refined literature".[127] The working class readers possessed as much moral sensibility as their social superiors and were capable of responding to and being improved by the highest form of art. For proof of this point, the autobiographers needed to look no further than their own experience: "—Oh! John Milton! John Milton!" cried Samuel

---

[123] He summarized his thoughts on the matter in one of the Society's publications: "The peculiar action of the intellectual facilities, or of the feelings and passions, is not a subject of great extent. All we know of it is soon told, and there is but little variety in different individuals as far as it is concerned". *Political Philosophy*, 2 vols. (London, 1842–3), vol. 1, p. 5.

[124] See Matthew Arnold, *Culture and Anarchy* (London, 1869).

[125] B. F. Duppa, op. cit., pp. 49–50. He admitted, however, that it would be "inexpedient" to totally "exclude fiction from the libraries of working men".

[126] Burn, p. 191.

[127] Frost, *Forty Years*, ch. VI, "Popular Literature Forty Years Ago", p. 95.

Bamford, "of all the poetry ever heard, ever read, or recited by me, none has so full spoken out the whole feelings of my heart—the whole scope of my imaginings—as have certain passages of thy divine minstrelry".[128]

Whatever the SDUK's hesitation about matters of the imagination, its commitment to the connection between useful knowledge and reason seemed established beyond doubt. In his influential *Practical Observations*, Brougham had proposed that ". . . political, as well as other works, be published in cheap form, and in numbers",[129] yet by the time the SDUK had created the means of realizing such a possibility, those who managed its affairs were beginning to entertain serious doubts about the categories of facts which could be considered useful. Eventually, in the words of the 1846 Address, "the Society determined, with obvious prudence, to avoid the great subjects of religion and government".[130] Thus during the nineteen years of its existence, just three volumes of direct relevance to the political and economic issues of the day were published under the superintendence of the Society—Charles Knight's *Results of Machinery* and *Rights of Industry*, and Harriet Martineau's *Illustrations of the Poor Laws*.[131] In addition, it put out two short pamphlets on machine breaking and combinations, a brief administrative pamphlet on the Poor Laws,[132] plus Brougham's two volumes on political philosophy which treated the subject at a very general level. Otherwise the Society, which, as we have seen, was dominated by politicians then in power, remained silent throughout the most dangerous political crisis and the worst economic depression of the century.

The Society's virtual abdication of its proclaimed role as an instrument for winning the minds of the dissident working class intellectuals to industrial capitalism was mocked by the unstamped press[133] and condemned by its natural ally, the *Westminster Review*, which demanded a complete reversal of its priorities: "When the labouring population have been made to comprehend what influence is exercised by wages over their own happiness," it wrote in the aftermath of the Swing rising, "when they have learned in how much that rate depends on their own conduct, in how much on that of other men; when by this means (the only effectual means) they are made to see the necessity of a strict adherence to morality and the law, and are consequently made moral, and obedient, and easy in their condition, then is the time when we may hope to succeed in conveying a knowledge of those physical sciences in which also their welfare, as well as that of the community at large, is so greatly dependent".[134] But although the SDUK was itself highly critical of the Mechanics'

---

[128] Bamford, *Early Days*, p. 194.

[129] H. Brougham, *Practical Observations*, p. 4.

[130] 1846 Address of the SDUK, p. 4.

[131] Charles Knight, *The Results of Machinery* (London, 1831) and *The Rights of Industry, Capital and Labour* (London, 1831), both volumes in the "Working Man's Companion" Series, 1s.3d. each vol.; Harriet Martineau, *Poor Laws and Paupers Illustrated* (London, 1833–34), four tales, *The Parish, The Hamlet, The Town, The Lands End*, 1s. each vol.

[132] Henry Gawler, *Address to Labourers on the Subject of Destroying Machinery* (London, 1830), price 1d.; Henry Gawler, *Address to Workmen on Combinations to raise Wages* (London, 1831), price 1d.; R. A. Slaney, *Hints for the Practical Administration of the Poor Laws* (London, 1832).

[133] See in particular the commentary in the *Poor Man's Guardian*, 29 Sept. 1831; 14 April 1832; 18 May 1833, 22 June 1833. Also J. Wiener, *The War of the Unstamped* (London, 1969), p. 40.

[134] "The Society for the Diffusion of Useful Knowledge", *Westminster Review*, vol. XIV, April 1831, p. 369.

Institutes for failing to encompass politics,[135] it refused to reconsider its policy. By contrast, the self-educators read and discussed politics as a natural extension of their pursuit of useful knowledge. "With the desire for culture", wrote Adams, "there had come a passion for politics."[136] They developed an alternative conception of useful knowledge, and an alternative means of supplying it, a point which William Lovett made very clear in his auto-biography:

> . . . many of the cheap literary and scientific publications that were published during that period were started with the avowed object of "diverting the minds of the working classes away from politics", and of giving them "more useful knowledge". In fact a new class of literature sprang up for the first time in England avowedly for the millions, and has gone on increasing and extending its beneficial influence from that period to the present. To this cheap literature, and the subsequent cheap newspapers that resulted from our warfare, may be also traced the great extension of the coffee-rooms and reading rooms of our large towns and the mental and moral improvement resulting from their establishment.[137]

(iv)

An observer of the debate over the meaning of "useful knowledge" might be forgiven for concluding that to most intents and purposes the phrase was a contradiction in terms. It is doubtful whether the knowledge the SDUK attempted to communicate was of any use in lessening class tensions during the Society's lifetime, and the working class readers were both unwilling and unable to use knowledge to better their immediate economic conditions, although a few did manage to exploit their literary skills to gain some insecure independence from their manual labour. Yet both sides remained resolutely committed to the concept, and a number of interesting and perhaps even useful conclusions can be drawn from this attempt to establish the utility of book knowledge in an industrializing society.

The efforts of the SDUK, which at the outset possessed so many assets and so much ambition, were frustrated partly by the failure of its audience to listen, and partly by the failure of the Society to carry out a significant portion of its original prospectus. The first failure reflected the state of class relations in general, but the second was the product of a number of dilemmas inherent in this apparently self-confident and powerful vanguard of the rising middle class. The professed intention to communicate the political and economic ideology of the society the Whig governments were trying to create was undermined by three basic contradictions in the Society's situation. Firstly, the preponderance of active politicians in its ranks was a direct cause of the Society's political quietism. The impasse in which Brougham and his friends found themselves is a powerful reminder that the political elite was still seriously divided in its

---

[135] See B. F. Duppa, op. cit., p. 36 and T. Coates, op. cit., pp. 14, 24–5 for SDUK-sponsored criticisms of the movement's failure. See also J.F.C. Harrison, op. cit., pp. 74–9; T. Kelly *Adult Education*, pp. 127–9.
[136] Adams, vol. 1, p. 118.   [137] Lovett, pp. 62-3.

attitude towards the industrializing society, and this was true not only of relations between Whigs and Tories, but also within the Whig party itself, to which virtually all the SDUK's politicians belonged. Brougham was one of an articulate and successful group of Benthamite radicals, but as a member of the Whig government he sat in the company of men who distrusted him personally, and who were not prepared to allow him to further inflame the Tories or some sections of the Whig party by turning the SDUK into a personal propaganda machine.[138] Eventually he was forced to concede the distinction between useful and political knowledge, and set up the separate Society for the Diffusion of Political Knowledge in 1834. The membership of this society, limited to sixty, was now centered not on cabinet ministers but on leading radical reformers such as Edwin Chadwick and Nassau Senior, the two men most closely associated with the creation of the New Poor Law. The intention was to diffuse among the working classes "those facts and opinions upon which most men are agreed who consider public questions with calmness and the love of truth; and by discussing any questions which involve differences of opinion with the candour which can alone lead to the discovery of what is extensively and permanently beneficial".[139] It took over the superintendence of the *Companion to the Newspapers* and continued its policy of largely factual reporting of Parliamentary proceedings thought relevant to the progress of the mind,[140] but a proposed periodical called *The Citizen*, which was to instruct the population in its social and legal duties, did not appear. The Society disappeared from view after August 1836, and the field was left to the dissemination of non-political useful knowledge.

The second contradiction was that the Society's founders were committed to a belief in the role of market forces in promoting the diffusion of knowledge, and refused to rely either on government support, or on massive private donations and legacies in the manner of contemporary religious propaganda organizations, yet at the same time they were prepared to let their beliefs about the inadvisability of including politics or fiction wreck the long-term commercial chances of their publications. William Chambers identified the problem in his discussion of the Society's failure: ". . . if any reason be wanted, it probably lay in the fact that a society cannot, as a rule, compete with private enterprise".[141] As a propaganda organization, its finances were never strong enough to allow it to compete in sheer volume with, for instance, the SPCK

---

[138] The *Westminster Review* article specifically attacked Brougham for betraying his radical principles for the sake of gaining office from the aristocratic Whigs (see pp. 377–8). For a summary of Brougham's standing in the Whig party, see Llewellyn Woodward, *The Age of Reform 1815–1870* (2nd ed., Oxford, 1962), p. 56. As Brougham himself said in a speech in 1835, "I have never stood, at any period of my public life, either in this or in the other House of Parliament, otherwise than as the member of a minority, generally a minority inconsiderable in numerical force". *Speech on the Education of the People. House of Lords, May 21, 1835* (London, 1835), p. 4.

[139] For the creation of the SDPK, see the "Announcement" and "Prospectus" in Charles Knight's *Companion to the Newspapers*, No. 20, 1 Aug. 1834, pp. 167–8. See also R. K. Webb, op. cit., pp. 92–3; Robbins, op. cit., pp. 234–43.

[140] The most common feature was the republication of evidence from contemporary Select Committees. There was a very limited amount of actual comment on such controversies as the New Poor Law and Stamp Duties. See *Companion to the Newspapers (under the superintendence of the Society for the Diffusion of Political Knowledge)* Sept. 1834–Aug. 1836.

[141] William Chambers, op. cit., p. 278.

or the BFBS,[142] and as a commercial organization its publications were outsold not only by the Salisbury Square publishers, but, in the long run, by Chambers and the later household magazines of the early 1850s.

The third contradiction lay at the heart of the SDUK's identity. Just four years after its inception the Society was re-christened the "Steam Intellect Society" in Thomas Love Peacock's parody of the political economists.[143] The new title captured the obsession with science and communication, but obscured what was a less obvious but equally important characteristic, the strain of pure idealism running through the Society. The belief in knowledge as a force standing above all sectional conflict, capable of establishing the true equality of man and of fashioning a humanistic brotherhood devoted to the pursuit of the undisputed truths upon which the progress of man and society was to be founded, was at the root of its being. For this reason it instinctively drew back from those areas, such as religion and contemporary politics, where for the moment, the reception of any publication would destroy these basic tenets. The reason given for the initial decision not to publish works on religion and government was that these were subjects ". . . on which it was impossible to touch without provoking angry discussion"[144], and this argument seemed to be confirmed by the reaction to the first two volumes of Brougham's work on political philosophy.[145] The logic of this situation demanded that the worse the political crisis, the less enthusiastic was the Society to become involved. Here, as in their attitude towards the moral development of the working man, the idealism of their original stance was crippled by uncertainty and insecurity when it came to putting these ideals into practice. The extent to which the idealism eventually made a mockery of the hard-headed empirical ethos to which the society was supposedly committed is nowhere better illustrated than in the epitaph contained in the Society's final address. The success was conceptualized entirely in terms of the demonstration of "possibilities": "In the 'Library of Useful Knowledge', they showed the possibility of producing sound treatises on the principles of all branches of human inquiry, at prices theretofore unexampled in lowness. In the 'Library of Entertaining Knowledge', they proved that equal soundness of detail, but with a higher range of subjects than was usual in books of that class, might be introduced into works as cheap, intended for lighter reading".[146] The basic practical failure of the intended audience to buy and be converted by the cheap literature was accepted without a qualm.

[142] The Society received £4,760 in subscriptions and donations during the first seven years, but these dried up and by 1835 it was in severe financial difficulty and needed to raise a loan of £1,000 to keep going. A major item of expenditure was on books commissioned but found not suitable for publication. By contrast the SPCK was able to sustain a loss on its publications and through various grants, of almost half a million pounds between 1833 and 1853. The British and Foreign Bible Society raised £100,000 a year throughout the 1830s and '40s. M. C. Grobel, op. cit., pp. 695–727; "Auditors Statement of the Financial Affairs of the Society 30th June 1834 in the *Ellis Collection*; W. K. Lowther Clarke, *A History of the SPCK* (London, 1959), p. 151; B. Harrison, op. cit., p. 145.

[143] Thomas Love Peacock, *Crotchet Castle* (London, 1831, repub. London, 1964). See p. 29 for an onslaught on both the Society and its founder.

[144] 1846 Address of the SDUK, p. 4.

[145] *Ibid.*, p. 19.

[146] *Ibid.*, p. 14. For a restatement of the epitaph, see Henry Brougham, *Cheap Literature for the People. An address delivered in St. Georges Hall, Liverpool, October, 12th, 1858, in connection with the Meeting of the National Association for the Promotion of Social Science* (London, 1858), p. 4.

The principle that useful knowledge could mean cheap knowledge had been established, and like all true idealists, the men of the SDUK settled for the principle rather than any more tangible achievement.

Indeed, as we move on to consider the wider problem, the failure to communicate, it can be argued that just as the SDUK's message was curtailed by its idealism, so the readers were to a considerable extent insulated by their own strongly held ideals. In a later period, when books were of more relevance to apprenticeship and the performance of the skills demanded by advanced industrial processes, and where there existed a ladder to further education and the lower-middle class,[147] there would be some temptation to see useful knowledge as the handmaiden of the industrial society. As it was, the readers remained preoccupied with the values of rational inquiry and moral improvement, which they related to their experience of industrialization in such a way as to render them largely resistant to the higher levels of the ideology of the middle class radicals. The thread which held together the various aspects of the readers' conception of useful knowledge was the notion of independence. This was embodied in a rejection of the assumption which permeated the SDUK's essentially paternalistic stance, that useful knowledge was the discovery and the property of the ruling class, and that by embarking upon its pursuit the reader was necessarily identifying himself with the practices and the ideology of his social and economic superiors. Brougham outlined the attitude of both the SDUK and the Mechanics' Institutes in an address he gave to the Manchester Mechanics' Institution in 1835:

> One word more before I release you from what I have called this lecture of mine—one word upon the manner in which learning and improvement make their way in society. I think it must be admitted that it is always in one way, and that downwards. You begin by making the upper classes aware of the value of certain kinds of knowledge . . . then . . . the middle parts of the middle class get well acquainted with the subject and feel its importance . . . and they try, by their exertions and their money, kindly applied and judiciously bestowed, to spread to the class below them a little of the same feeling, the same love of learning, which they possess themselves; and so that lower class gets by degrees impregnated itself.[148]

But, as Thomas Frost explained, "Working men do not like to be treated like children, to have the books they shall read chosen for them".[149] If the choice frequently fell on works which belonged to a culture which had hitherto been the preserve of the educated classes, it was made by the reader himself, according to his own criteria. In every autobiography the desire for literature is presented as a spontaneous attribute of the working man, not as a taste which was handed down to him.

There was a powerful feeling that despite all the difficulties with which they were faced, the readers had within their grasp more freedom of action than in

---

[147] For recruitment into the slowly growing white-collar class during the second half of the century, see Gregory Anderson, *Victorian Clerks* (Manchester, 1976), pp. 11–15.

[148] Henry Brougham, "Address to the Members of the Manchester Mechanics Institution, July 31 1835", in *British Eloquence: Literary Addresses, 2nd Series* (London, 1855), pp. 180–2.

[149] Frost, *Forty Years*, p. 29. The context of this remark was a discussion of the failure of the Croydon Literary and Scientific Institution which drove out a large working class membership by excluding from its library works on politics and controversial theology.

any other sphere of their existence, with the possible exception of their family life, where again, the chances of fulfilment battled endlessly with a range of practical problems. As the shoemaker John Younger put it, "Upon the whole, I began . . . to regard my own mind as the only wealth of property I should ever possess in this world, and therefore I determined to take care of its health, whatever might be the servitude to which the attached body might be subjected".[150]

What Christopher Thomson described as "the free exercise of thought" was seen as a means of simultaneously transforming the moral state of the working man and emancipating him from the control of his social and economic superiors. He wrote with a mixture of scorn and pity of the plight of the unimproved working man: ". . . the free exercise of thought would have taught him self-dependence and moral elevation, instead of serfish cringing crumb-picking—the free exercise of thought would have taught him the advantage of sobriety over the debasing sensuality that sinks the man beneath the level of the brute—would have taught him *that* true wisdom which alone makes man the noblest work of God".[151] Debasement and dependence were symptoms of the same disease, and knowledge could set in motion the cure for both. But it had to be a certain sort of knowledge. By one means or another, the labouring population had always been subject to the ideas of those whom Thomson dubbed "the conventionally ordained professors of thought".[152] "The literacy acquired by a minority of agricultural labourers", wrote Joseph Arch, "had hitherto served only the ends of their masters: of course he might learn his catechism; that and things similar to it, was the right, proper, and suitable knowledge for such as he; he would be the more likely to stay contentedly in his place to the end of his working days."[153] *Useful* knowledge, was by definition, that knowledge which suited the interests of the working class readers. The qualification implied conflict,[154] and thus the attempt by the SDUK to promote a common conception broke down.

A clear and deliberate attempt to establish the hegemony of middle class values over the very young culture of self-improvement had failed, but in that failure we may distinguish a number of factors which will be of relevance for class relations in the second half of the century. Firstly, however absurd the SDUK's epitaph might appear in relation to its prologue, the middle class educators had learned an important lesson. This was that there was no room for hybrid semi-official, semi-commercial organizations. In one sense the SDUK was the last of the line of organizations pioneered by the Reeves Association of the 1790s. Brougham had tried to graft a commercial enterprise on to a government propaganda machine, and the result had done little to sustain the government in a period of great crisis and had very nearly ruined the publishers involved. Henceforth the objectives were to be realized through the market alone—and *Chambers Edinburgh Journal* was but the forerunner of a phalanx of successful cheap but morally uplifting journals—or through direct government

[150] Younger, p. 177.
[151] Thomson, p. 8.
[152] *Ibid.*, p. v.
[153] Arch, p. 25.
[154] See Richard Johnson, "Really useful knowledge", in John Clarke, Chas. Critcher and Richard Johnson, eds., *Working Class Culture* (London, 1979), pp. 75–102.

164

action, either in providing elementary education, with which Brougham had always been closely involved, or in the promotion of public libraries, to which the Society increasingly turned its attention in its declining years.

Secondly, despite its manifold failure to understand or respond to the needs of the working class readers, the SDUK had made a genuine attempt to supply what the readers were desperately seeking—cheap, good quality literature, and in retrospect a few of them looked back to the Society with some goodwill.[155] For most of the autobiographers, the early 1830s were the real watershed of the nineteenth century, partly because of the transformation in the availability of the better class of literature; however much he may have been ignored and even reviled at the time, Brougham's involvement in this transformation, and his struggle for working class education in the face of apathy or hostility from many of his Whig colleagues, was remembered.

Finally, although the common language concealed what was, at this time, a decisive difference of interpretation, we can see here the affinities in the commitment of the advance guard of both the middle and working classes to the values of rational inquiry and moral improvement which in the calmer years which followed the demise of Chartism were to be vital elements in the creation of a more peaceful pattern of class relations. If the coincidence of approach between the Broughamites and the readers which was traced at the beginning of this chapter makes the breakdown of communication the more striking, it also renders the subsequent amelioration of class tensions a little more comprehensible.

[155] See Plummer, p. xix, H. Herbert, p. 25; Thomson, p. 319.

Chapter Eight

Knowledge and Freedom

Samuel Bamford first "plunged . . . into the blessed habit of reading" whilst working as a warehouseman in Manchester during the first decade of the nineteenth century. As with many working class readers who were employed in workshops or small businesses, he frequently found an opportunity to add to his stock of book knowledge during the course of the working day: going about his duties, his mind might still be dwelling in the realm of literature. "Very often", he remembered, "whilst bending beneath a load of piece goods, as I carried them through the crowded streets, or wiping the sweat from my brow as I rested in the noon sun, would I be unconsciously wandering in my imagination in the free forest glades with Robin Hood, or 'Over some wide water'd shore' with Milton."[1] In this sentence Bamford summarizes the two basic characteristics of the pursuit of knowledge outlined in chapters six and seven. Firstly, the readers were brought together by their common experience of the manifold "difficulties" created by the need to earn a living and support a family, activities which could be grouped under the general heading of the pursuit of bread. Even if he did manage to acquire a copy of Milton, and to read or meditate upon his poetry during the hours of work, Bamford was always aware of the practical problems with which he was faced and the sacrifices which he had to make. The way in which the pursuit of bread conditioned and shaped the pursuit of knowledge ensured that by embarking upon a course of self-improvement, the reader would inevitably change his relationship with the society in which he found himself. Secondly, the outcome of the debate on the meaning of "useful knowledge" established that the primary attraction of the world of literature was that it offered the working class reader a limited but very real area of independence. Bamford had been unable to gain as much schooling as he had wanted, had watched helplessly as his family was decimated by smallpox, and had entered the labour market with few skills and very little prospect of economic advancement, but nothing could prevent him walking in the footsteps of Milton's *Il Penseroso*. In this sense, knowledge and freedom were synonymous, yet however abstract their initial conception, the readers' pursuit of knowledge was bound to affect their view of the world and their own position in it. When set in the context of the inherited structure of ideas, beliefs and practices, and the social, political and economic relations within which they lived, the freedom they sought had varied, and not always complementary, implications for the readers and their community.

[1] Bamford, *Early Days*, p. 195.

This chapter will examine some of the more creative and some of the more disruptive consequences of Bamford's blessed habit.

(i)

The readers, as we have seen, were encyclopaedic in their approach and their ambitions, but even an encyclopaedia must have divisions, and we can usefully distinguish five areas in which they discovered that book knowledge could further their emancipation. Firstly, the pursuit of knowledge offered the possibility of gaining freedom from the influence of non-rational beliefs. It is a safe generalization that the more literate a working man became during the first half of the nineteenth century, and the more useful knowledge he obtained through contact with formal literature, the more interested he became in the pre-literate forms of behaviour which were slowly disappearing from his culture. The autobiographers were drawn to the topic because they were both historians and representatives of the forces of historical change. It was impossible to describe the culture of their youth without reference to the pervasive presence of a bewildering variety of superstitious beliefs. Bamford devoted a considerable portion of *Early Days* to the "manners, legends and superstitions" of late eighteenth century rural Lancashire, and made no apology for doing so:

> The noticing of these supposed supernatural appearances may seem puerile to some readers. The suppositions in themselves may be so; but taken in connection with and, affecting as they did, in a degree, the minds and manners of the rural population of the period, they are of more consequence than may at the first glance be apparent. At all events, in giving account of a place and its inhabitants in past times, one cannot well refrain from alluding to whatever might have influenced their actions, any more than one can remain silent with respect to the actions themselves.[2]

In these accounts there is the feeling that the autobiographers have lived through a period which marked the end of a tradition which belonged not just to their parents' generation, but, literally, to time immemorial. "During all bygone time," wrote the Wigtonshire farm labourer Samuel Robinson, "including my early days, the belief was cherished in the existence of various kinds of beings of a middle class, friendly or hostile to man according to the class— fairy, brownie, fire or water kelpie etc.—as the case might be; and their existence, haunts, habits, and instances of good or evil tricks was the engrossing topic of conversation whenever a gossiping party met in the winter evening in Galloway, as in all other parts of Scotland; and the district was rich in such lore."[3] Although some of the tales may have originated in chap-books whose contents had been absorbed into the folk memory of the community, it was basically an oral tradition, passed down through the generations until it reached the ears of the autobiographers. "Many a time my hair has been made to stand erect at the recital of some tale of blood and murder," remembered James Burn, "and often has my young imagination been filled with wonder at

[2] *Ibid.*, pp. 33–4. See also pp. 27–38, 131–169.
[3] Robinson, p. 72. See also Donaldson, pp. 40–42; Hanson, p. 11; Mountjoy, p. 15; Shaw, p. 37; Harris, p. 39; T. Wood, pp. 1–2; Younger, p. 195; Oliver p. 85.

the fairy legend of a by-gone age. At that time the people on the Borders were proverbial for their superstitious notions."[4] Down in Lincolnshire, John Clare was receiving a similar education whilst scaring birds and weeding the crops in the company of old women, whose "memories never failed of tales to smoothen our labour; for as every day came, new Giants, Hobgoblins, and fairies was ready to pass it away".[5] These men were both fascinated by and distanced from this pattern of beliefs and customs because they themselves were the product of the erosion of the oral tradition which had sustained it.

As in other respects, the autobiographers were concerned not merely to measure change but to evaluate it. By discussing such matters, wrote Bamford, "we are enabled distinctly to perceive the great change which, in a few years, has taken place in the tastes and habits of the working classes: and seeing these alterations clearly set forth, we shall be better able to determine whether or not the labouring classes have been advancing in, or retrograding from, that state of mind, and that bodily habit, which are meant by the term, Civilisation".[6] The autobiographers' sense of progress was rooted in the history of their own psychological development. They had first encountered the supernatural world in their childhood, at a time when they were quite incapable of distinguishing between fact and fantasy, and whilst some of the tales had been merely entertaining, many, by accident or design, had deeply frightened their impressionable minds. Christopher Thomson received a thorough education in the local superstitions from his dame school teacher, whose stock of knowledge consisted of nothing but ghost stories, and throughout the remainder of his childhood his "fear-stricken imagination" was filled with "monsters" which his "spectacled old mistress" had conjured up.[7] The particular localities around the villages and small towns in which the great majority of these men grew up were so densely populated with supernatural beings that, as John Clare wrote of his native Helpston, it was impossible to travel more than half a mile in any direction without passing a spot where some apparition was "said to be seen by these old women or some one else in their younger days".[8] That most rational of working men, William Lovett, wrote at length of the terrors he experienced whilst travelling in the dark through the lanes around his home town of Newlyn, and admitted that ". . . the numerous stories regarding those nocturnal visitants told to me in infancy, reiterated in boyhood, and authenticated and confirmed by one neighbour after another, who had witnessed, they said, their existence in a variety of forms, riveted the belief in them so firmly in my brain, that it was many years after I came to London before I became a sceptic in ghosts".[9]

The autobiographers slowly and painfully escaped from the grip of superstition through their exploitation of the means of communication. It was necessary to make an intellectual and often geographical journey away from the structure of beliefs and practices of the communities in which they had grown up. Distance lent objectivity, and the pursuit of knowledge provided the weapons for defeating the irrational forces which imprisoned the minds of the labouring population. Reason rather than religion was the enemy of magic.

---

[4] Burn, p. 66. See also Tester, p. 3; J. Lawson, op. cit., pp. 47-52.
[5] Clare, *Sketches*, p. 48.   [6] Bamford, *Early Days*, p. 132.
[7] Thomson, pp. 35–6.   [8] Clare, *Sketches*, p. 56.
[9] Lovett, p. 11. See similar confessions by Burn (p. 68), and Robinson (p. 75).

Anthony Errington, one of the earliest and least literate of the autobiographers, is the only one to give an affirmative account of supernatural events, and his proud description of the three occasions on which he was called in by despairing housewives and managed to turn the milk into butter by a combination of prayer and a churning ritual provides a fine example of the way in which popular religion could reinforce rather than undermine the influence of superstition.[10] The acquisition of book knowledge made it possible to attack the power of the supernatural, and to provide alternative explanations for the natural phenomena which affected their lives. Having emancipated themselves, the readers could attempt to overthrow and perhaps replace the traditional wise men and cunning women who had for so long been the major source of "knowledge" in the community. "How pitiful it is", wrote Thomson, "that we should thus cheat ourselves, and put money into the purses of tricksters, who laugh at our ignorance. If the artisans will become 'wise men', they must exercise their judgement, maturing it by reading, and the science of the class-rooms, and then, as they become mind-enfranchised, will the jugglery of imposters be exploded, and a death-blow given to the trade of the WISE MAN."[11] Although the term is never used, the readers were putting forward a working class version of the Enlightenment, in which they themselves would be the new *Philosophes*.

The pursuit of knowledge also held out the prospect of achieving freedom from the influence over both the readers and the working class in general, of various forms of non-rational behaviour, the most significant of which was drunkenness. As in the response to superstition, the readers' commitment to the abstract principles of intellectual and moral improvement owed much of its vigour to the element of personal experience. Of the autobiographers, at least eleven had their childhoods blighted either by drunken fathers or by parents who ruined the family's finances by venturing into the drink trade,[12] and others saw friends or relatives killed by alcoholism. The careers and attitudes of many of these self-improving working men become much more comprehensible if attention is paid to their family background. When the great champion of the unstamped press, Henry Hetherington, came to set down an account of his formative years, there was only one event he wanted to write about:

At the time of his birth his parents were living in comparative comfort. His father was a master tailor employing on average eight or ten men, and his house was well furnished throughout. He was young, fond of company, and unfortunately a *good singer*; possessing little knowledge and no discretion.

---

[10] Errington, pp. 29–32. On the final occasion he "drew the cork and Breathed into it. I then took hold of the Handel. All was silent. And I said, 'Depart from Me, O all you that work Inequity and let the Poor of Our Lord Jesus Christ reign, in the Name of the Fauther, Sun and Holy goast.' I turned 3 times from me and the second time felt the butter, and turning 3 times back, it was heard by all present to flap-flap-flap on the Brickers" (p. 32). For other Northumberland cures for the problem, see M. C. Balfour, *Examples of Printed Folk-Lore concerning Northumberland* (London, 1904), p. 54, and Burn, p. 67. For the interpenetration of popular religion and magic in this period, see James Obelkevich, *Religion and Rural Society: South Lindsey 1825–1875* (Oxford, 1976), ch. VI; A. W. Smith, "Popular Religion", *Past and Present*, no. 40, July 1968, pp. 181–6.

[11] Thomson, p. 115.

[12] i.e. Bezer, Burn, T. Carter, Dundee Factory Boy, Dunning, H. Herbert, Hetherington, Leno, Love, J. Taylor and Thomson.

He soon determined to take a public house—the house from whence he called his workmen—the Robin Hood in Great Windmill Street. He sold off his business and all his furniture to raise the sum required, for the goodwill and stock, which amounted to about £1,600. This fatal step ultimately plunged his family into ruin. From that time forward his love of company, his unconquerable propensity for drink, effectually weaned him from his home; and his generosity of character and total want of judgement made him an easy prey to the host of drunken associates who continually beset him. His career was short. Dissipation threw him into a decline, of which he lingered three years, and death terminated his suffering before he had reached his thirty-eighth year; leaving his wife and four children overwhelmed with debt and misery to struggle through the world.[13]

The sequence of events varied from case to case. In some instances, the drinking habits of the father were a permanent drain on the family's material and emotional well-being, in others, drink was a direct cause of the father's death, or desertion, or even, as with the father of the Dundee Factory Boy, his transportation for killing a man in a drunken brawl. Two of the most active and articulate pursuers of knowledge, John Leno and Christopher Thomson, dwelt in some detail on the impact on their developing personalities of the scenes they witnessed in the public houses run by their parents. "A sense of shame and disgust comes over me whenever I refer back to this period of my life," wrote Leno, "and remember how my father was systematically fleeced, and how I used to be called on to amuse the fleecers, by my singing."[14]

As children, the essence of the autobiographers' experience was their help-lessness, their inability to influence the behaviour of those upon whom their security depended; as adults, the tension in their accounts is provided by their own exposure to the temptations and pressures generated by the culture of drink. Notwithstanding the generally high moral tone of these works, at least one of the autobiographers is known to have eventually drunk himself to death,[15] and there were a number who were more infirm of purpose, or perhaps merely more honest, than the rest and admitted to a life-long struggle against what James Bowd described as the "Easey Besetting sin".[16] A particular example is provided by James Burn, a man whose desperate search for respect-ability has to be set in the context of a childhood dominated by an alcoholic stepfather, and an adult life in which several ventures into the drink trade in Glasgow exposed him to moral and financial disasters from which he only just managed to escape.[17] For the majority, however, the most serious problem was that of defining the quality of their personal relationships with the less sober members of their class whom they encountered at work and in their recreations. Despite the complex and growing stratification of the working class, it was not

[13] Hetherington, pp. 3–5. He was born in 1792.
[14] Leno, p. 18. See also Thomson, pp. 47–51.
[15] i.e. Willie Thom, whose decline and death four years after the publication of his autobio-graphy, which had ended on a rising note of optimism about his personal circumstances, is described by Robert Bruce in, *William Thom, The Inverurie Poet–A New Look* (Aberdeen, 1970). The transported convict Snowden Dunhill was said by the editor of his autobiography to have "sunk into habitual drunkenness" since writing his life-history, "as a warning to others".
[16] Bowd, p. 296.
[17] For his public house ventures, see pp. 100–1, 117–8, 145, 147, 149–50, 153, 157, 161–3, 171.

possible to establish any form of cultural apartheid which might insulate the more respectable members from contact with those whose behaviour they deplored or feared, and any hostility towards excessive drinking caused a series of personal and ideological tensions which will be discussed later in the chapter.

The antagonism towards the culture of drink can thus be explained without reference to the middle class values with which it appeared to coincide. James Burn's summary of his general response to the problem spoke to the daily experiences and observations of all self-improving working men: "How humiliating it is," he wrote, "to see a man come down from the high and god-like dignity of his reason and leave his moral nature behind him that he may revel in madness!".[18] At the centre of the hostility, and the affirmation of an alternative way of life, was the notion of self-control. Drink could destroy a family before the eyes of the powerless child, and would deprive the adult of the capacity to resist exploitation by middle class interests. Eleven of the autobiographers were involved in the temperance movement, but most maintained an attitude of sympathetic detachment to the temperance movement, partly because it placed too much emphasis on the symptoms of a malaise whose roots lay in the living and working conditions of the labouring population,[20] and partly because it assumed that working men and women were so lacking in moral strength that total abstinence enforced by the pledge was the only means of preventing the decline into drunkenness.[21] The claim that the working class had the right to control their own lives could scarcely coexist with the surrender of personal judgement which the pledge entailed. In its way the movement was as much a threat to freedom as the force it claimed to oppose. James Hawker made the point with characteristic bluntness:

> I am not going to Condem drink. I might as well Condem My Gun Because some men Blow out their Brains. I admire a man or Woman who advocates Temperance but I don't always approve of the manner in which they do it. You cannot make a man Sober by force. Don't try. A man has as much Right to Drink as we have to abstain. This is a free country. We should allow everyone the same Liberty that we enjoy ourselves . . . I was always Ready to join any Party who stole a march on the rich Class by Poaching or Fishing. But not Drinking. As long as we do that we are strengthening the Hands of our Enemy and weakening our own.[22]

A more positive means of combating the evils of drink was through the provision of various forms of rational amusement, most of which were founded on the activity of reading. John Farn had at one stage been a full-time temperance lecturer but by the time he came to set down an account of his career in 1867, he had become critical of the techniques of the movement. In place of the obsession with the pledge, he argued,

---

[18] Burn, p. 50.

[19] i. e. Ayliffe, Blow, Cooper, Farish, Farn, H. Herbert, Lowery, Marsh, Scott, W. Smith and Wilson.

[20] See in particular Henry Price's angry exposition of the connection between bad housing and drinking (p. 73) and the sympathetic comments of Arch and Shaw on the way in which working conditions drove men to drink (Arch, p. 36, Shaw, p. 73).

[21] See Geoffrey Crossick, "The Labour Aristocracy and its values: a study of mid-Victorian Kentish London", *Victorian Studies*, 19 March 1976, p. 323.

[22] Hawker, pp. 24–5.

The promoters of temperance societies should be first and foremost in providing amusements for the people. Where labour is excessive, or carried on
under *depressing* conditions, amusement becomes one of the moral necessaries
of life. They should be first and foremost in the work of mental and moral
instruction by the establishment of cheap reading-rooms, libraries, and
literary institutions, and conversation meeting; by these, or a similar means
of counteraction, they may maintain their conquests from the army of
drunkards, and thus not find their labour in vain.[23]

The self-educator would have neither the time, money,[24] nor inclination to
indulge in excessive drinking. The pursuit of knowledge was the only way in
which the working class might escape the influence of non-rational forms of
behaviour without sacrificing their independence and self-respect.

The third freedom which might be approached by the readers was an
extension of the first. A minority of the autodidacts was not content with merely
hastening the demise of the body of superstitions, but sought through the
pursuit of knowledge to diminish the influence over their lives of the workings
of the natural world which so many of the superstitions had sought to explain.
Their imaginations were fired by the possibility of undertaking scientific
investigations into natural phenomena, and thereby emancipating themselves
from the centuries of folk wisdom and folk ignorance. At the outset, the small
groups of working class botanists, zoologists and geologists,[25] were, like many
of these autobiographers, simply men who enjoyed walking in the countryside
around their homes. Until the beginning of the second phase of urban expansion
in the 1880s, when the centres of some of the bigger cities began to be cut off
from the rural areas by rings of suburbs, the great majority of the industrial
workforce lived and worked in easy walking distance of unspoiled countryside.
This applied not only to those who worked in semi-rural industrial processes,
such as mining, but to those who were employed in the textile factories located
in the rapidly expanding northern towns.[26] The fields and moors around the
mines, potbanks and industrial centres were an obvious source of recreation at
a time when the provision of leisure facilities was failing to keep pace with the
growing urban population. Most were content to stroll with friends or their
family and enjoy the contrast with their working environment, but those who
were both more literate and of a scientific frame of mind, found in the surrounding countryside a huge, free laboratory where it was perfectly possible to
undertake genuine research. This was the golden age of the amateur scientist,

---

[23] Farn, p. 246. The temperance movement was alive to this criticism, and was attempting, with
generally limited success, to provide some alternative to alcohol centered recreations. See
Brian Harrison, op. cit., pp. 322–4; Peter Bailey, *Leisure and Class in Victorian England* (London,
1978), pp. 47–8.

[24] A point illustrated by the experience of many of the autobiographers, including Farish
(*Autobiography*, pp. 44–5) and Oliver (p. 17).

[25] For working class botanists in and around Manchester, see James Cash, *Where There's a Will
There's a Way: An Account of the Labours of Naturalists in Humble Life* (London, 1873)
pp. 10–135; Gwyn A. Williams, *Rowland Detrosier, A Working Class Infidel 1800–1834* (York,
1965), p. 16; *Report of the Select Committee on Public Libraries* (1849), p. 84. For working class
naturalists in the West Riding, see J. F. C. Harrison, op. cit., p. 49.

[26] As late as 1861, no provincial town except Newcastle had a municipal area in excess of 6,000
acres—about 9 square miles. David Cannadine, "Victorian cities: how different?", *Social
History*, no. 4, January 1977, p. 462.

and if there is little evidence of much personal contact between educated and self-educated botanists or geologists, these working men undoubtedly benefited from the greater availability of scientific publications, which, though still very expensive, might turn up now and then on second-hand bookstalls or the shelves of artisan libraries.[27] Thus William Heaton, a weaver from a village near Halifax, wrote of a flourishing group of like-minded men, who combined a love of nature with a passion for scientific investigation:

> I collected insects in company with a number of young men in the village. We formed a library, and bought a number of the best books we could find on the subject. As soon as the lovely rays of the summer's sun have shone over the hills of my native valley, have we wandered forth, especially on the Sabbath morning, by four o'clock, and have not returned till seven or eight at night; often having never tasted food all the day: we have brought shells, eggs and nests as well as insects home with us, and were as much, or more, pleased than if we had dined off the best. I believe I and a companion of mine (now no more) collected twenty-two large boxes of insects, one hundred and twenty different sorts of British birds' eggs; besides a great quantity of shells (land and fresh water), fossils, minerals, ancient and modern coins, and plaster casts of those coins we could not procure.[28]

It was the discovery of the world which lay beneath the superficial knowledge of nature that excited these men. Joseph Gutteridge, the Coventry weaver and naturalist, eventually decided to build his own microscope:

> By dint of perseverance and under many difficulties . . . I at last succeeded in making a powerful achromatic microscope with one-eighth inch, quarter inch, and half inch doublet objectives, buying nothing but the raw material from which to construct it, and also making all the tools for the purpose. I think of it now with much pleasure as the greatest triumph I ever achieved towards helping me to understand the various phases of matter and the myriad forms and functions of animalcular existence. It opened up a new world. It passed the utmost stretch of imagination to conceive that the mass of green filaments, which I had always conceived belonged to the Vegetable Kingdom, was endowed with life and motion, and with the power of pro-creating its kind . . . It would be almost impossible to describe the intense pleasure or the valuable instruction received from these examinations of the structure and functions of plant life. The wonders unfolded by this instrument enabled me to form more rational conclusions as to cause and effect . . .[29]

Such conclusions were necessarily limited, and opened up new difficulties which were beyond the capacity of these beginners to resolve, but set against the level of knowledge which had hitherto prevailed in their communities, the

---

[27] Two frequently mentioned works were James Sowerby's *English Botany* (37 vols. 1790–1814) and Nicolas Culpeper's *English Physicians and Complete Herbal* (1st edn., 1652 but available in this period in various revised editions). For the growth of the study of nature and the social tensions amongst English amateurs, see D. E. Allen, *The Naturalist in Britain* (London, 1976), chs. 4–8, especially pp. 164–7.

[28] Heaton, pp. xviii–xix. See also the Dundee Factory Boy's account of the "Zoological and Botanical Society" he formed with some friends in Dundee (p. 70).

[29] Gutteridge, p. 89. See also the use made by the Cornish miner Thomas Oliver of a microscope he saved up to buy (Oliver, pp. 60–61).

working class naturalists felt a sense of intellectual command over the natural world which was a source of deep satisfaction.

The discovery of the causes of previously inexplicable phenomena was at the centre of the fourth freedom which the pursuit of knowledge might promote. The naturalists constituted a distinct minority within the body of self-improving working men, but the dialectical relationship between superstition and rationality which informed their activities, had a more general application. The opening chapter of William Lovett's autobiography was designed to demonstrate his state of mind before he embarked upon the pursuit of knowledge and freedom. For this reason he dwelt in some detail, as we have seen, on the prevalence of superstitions in his native Newlyn, and on the influence they exercised over his mind. He and his friend were rendered defenceless by their lack of book knowledge: "Of the causes of day and night, of the seasons, and of the common phenomena of nature we knew nothing, and curious were our speculations regarding them. We had heard of 'the sun ruling by day, and the moon by night,' but how or in what way they ruled was a mystery we could never solve. With minds thus ignorant, persons need not be surprised that we were very superstitious".[30] Throughout his subsequent career of self-education Lovett retained a curiosity in scientific matters and eventually wrote a school textbook on elementary anatomy and physiology,[31] but the "causes" which useful knowledge enabled him to explore came to encompass the functioning of every aspect of class relations in the industrializing society. It was a short step from studying natural phenomena to gaining an insight into the consequences of man's growing ability to exploit them. William Dodd, who was being exposed to the full impact of the factory system, found that once he had begun to read books on "several branches of natural and experimental philosophy", much else began to become clear: ". . . in proportion as the truths of science were unfolded to my wondering sight, and the mists of ignorance chased from my mind, so the horrors of my situation became daily more and more apparent . . .".[32] Reading taught these men how to think, and, what was of equal importance, demonstrated in the face of the extensive dislocation and injustice of their daily experience, that it was possible to conceive and construct an ordered and justifiable pattern of living. During the time he worked in an Aberdeen weaving factory, Willie Thom was wholly dependent on books for such conception he had of an alternative way of life. During occasional breaks in the working day, he used to gather with a few like-minded weavers in the garden of an adjacent hospital: "There, of a summer day, we would meet—those of us who had a turn for reading—and gossip over all we knew of books and the outer world. Then came glimpses,—the only glimpses afforded us of true, and natural, and rational existence".[33]

For the first time it seemed possible that the uneducated might free themselves from the world view of the educated. As an indication of his new-found aspiration, Lovett included in his autobiography the text of an address he wrote as secretary of the London Working Men's Association in 1836:

. . . the floodgates of knowledge, which the tyrants of the world have raised

[30] Lovett, p. 22.
[31] i.e. *Elementary Anatomy and Physiology . . . With Lessons on Diet etc.* (London, 1851).
[32] Dodd, p. 19.   [33] Thom, p. 21.

174

to stem its torrent, are being broken down", he proclaimed, "We have tasted its refreshing stream; the mist of ignorance and delusion is past; we *perceive* the injustice practised on us, and *feel* the slavery from which we have *not yet power to free ourselves*. Our emancipation, however, will depend on the extent of this knowledge among the working-classes of all countries, on its salutory effects in causing us to perceive *our real position in society* . . .[34]

Nothing was possible unless the habit of intellectual deference was challenged. "Where you find ignorance among the working men," observed James Hawker, "you will find them inclining towards the Class. Where you find men who Toil, intelligent men, they incline towards trying to Better the condition of their fellows. One of the clearest proofs of this is seen in the way the Class tried to Keep the People ignorant and would do even today if they could Rob us of this blessing."[35] If working men could demystify the social, economic and political forces which controlled their existence, they would then be in a position to mount a real attack on the power of "the Class".

Finally, the pursuit of knowledge provided a range of essential tools for the pursuit of freedom. Those working men who had gained some command over the techniques of written communication could perform a variety of services for their community. The occasional letter needed to be spelt out for those who could not read, and many who might have been able to sign a marriage register would require assistance if ever they had to write to a lover, or a relative, or enter into official correspondence.[36] As we have seen, a number of these auto-biographers acted as scribes for less literate neighbours and friends,[37] and others were nominated to read out newspapers in public houses or workshops.[38] The range of "literary occupations" which were examined in the previous chapter, particularly preaching and teaching, were means by which readers applied their skills to the good of the majority, and some of the naturalists discovered that their small stock of scientific knowledge was sufficient to elevate them into the role of the local doctor.[39] Whatever the inclinations of the reader, the demands of the non-literate ensured that his own improvement would contribute to the wellbeing of those amongst whom he lived, and whilst some of the benefits he might confer were of limited value, others could make a vital contribution to the emancipation of the working class as a whole.

In the first instance, an attack on the localization of the working man's outlook was a prerequisite of any sort of class action. Joseph Arch, who eventually succeeded in organizing the first national agricultural labourers' union, saw the inability of his fellow labourers to move either physically or mentally from the situation in which they were born as the chief obstacle to progress. "Discontented as they were," he wrote, "they lacked the energy to

[34] Lovett, p. 98: "Address to the Working Classes of Belgium", Nov. 1836.
[35] Hawker, p. 91.
[36] The nineteenth century growth of the national and local government bureaucracy was gradually beginning to affect the lives of even the poorest members of the community. In the 1841 Census, for instance, schedules were distributed to every occupier who was expected to complete it before the enumerator called.
[37] See chapter three, p. 41.
[38] See Burn, p. 94; Carter, *Memoir*, p. 90; Price, p. 18; C. M. Smith, p. 118; Robinson, p. 47; Farish, *Autobiography*, p. 12.
[39] Gutteridge, p. 78; Love, p. 77. See also the experiences of the "Corn-Law Rhymer", Ebenezer Elliott: "Autobiography", *The Athenaeum*, 12 Jan. 1850, p. 48.

better themselves. They would grumble and complain by the hour, but they would not budge an inch from the place and position in which they found themselves. The fact was, very few of them could write a letter, so the majority were afraid to go from home, because they would not be able to communicate with their friends. This inert mass of underfed, overworked, uneducated men was stuck fast in the Slough of Despond.''[40] The growth of class consciousness came down to men like Arch, whose political activity until his mid-forties was confined to skirmishes with the various manifestations of privilege and power in his native village, first of all reading every scrap of literature he could lay his hands on, then travelling as an itinerant hedge-cutter and later as a lay preacher, and finally turning to his fellow working men and by example, encouragement, and education in the most diffuse sense of the term, trying to make them follow in his footsteps. Self-education meant enlargement of the working man's perspective, and as individuals within their particular communities, those who pursued knowledge acted as a window onto the outside world.

Secondly, the skills possessed by a self-educated working man were indispensable to almost any working class organization. In the course of his pursuit of knowledge the reader would add to his basic literacy a capacity to manage his slender resources so as to isolate the necessary surplus time and money, a familiarity with the various sources of books and with the distribution network of the radical press, an ability to follow sustained argument and debate abstract questions, experience as an organizer of mutual improvement societies, and finally, as was the case with all the autobiographers and most of the self-educators, the reader had to master the process of writing, whether in the form of lectures to gatherings of other self-educators, articles or letters for newspapers, poems for performance or publication, or, very occasionally, full-length books. A working man would rarely gain such attributes from his parents, his schooling, or his occupational training, although some might be acquired through participation in religious institutions. In the context of the daily pursuit of bread, these were artificial skills, but from the moment when the prototype working class organization dubbed itself a *Corresponding* society, virtually every form of organized advocacy of a working class cause was in some way dependent on them. An indication of the volume of writing which a single organization could generate is supplied by the career of the miners' organizer Edward Rymer, who calculated that during the course of thirty-seven years' work on behalf of his union he had composed 10,000 letters, reports and communications, and engaged in a correspondence which amounted to 35,000 letters, postcards, telegrams and circulars.[41] Behind every strike, demonstration, protest march and petition there would be committees, minutes, letters, broadsides and newspapers, and therefore, self-educated working men.

It was for this reason that when some political or industrial crisis occurred, the readers would be natural candidates for the posts of leadership and responsibility. As examples we may cite not only such national figures as Lovett and Cooper, both of whom commenced their careers in mutual improvement

[40] Arch, p. 40. See also p. 246.
[41] Rymer, p. 32. During this period he worked only intermittently as a full-time organizer, but nonetheless reckoned to have travelled 700,000 miles and to have been put to a personal cost of £700 through loss of wages and other expenses.

176

societies, but relatively insignificant individuals like the Kettering weaver J. A. Leatherland. He was a founder member of a mutual improvement society, had "won some local celebrity as a versifier", and early in 1838, had been joint winner of a locally organized essay competition on "The Best Means of Improving the Condition of the Working Classes". Although he had had no previous political experience, and was still only twenty-six years old when Chartism arrived in Kettering, he was by then a practised writer and was well known in the community, and was thus an obvious choice as secretary of the town's Chartist association.[42] Seven other autobiographers served in a similar capacity,[43] and very few of these men who engaged in the pursuit of knowledge avoided making a practical contribution to some manifestation of the cause of freedom, either as official or unofficial leaders, or as political writers and poets.[44]

(ii)

There is a fine sense of confidence and achievement in these accounts of the ways in which the readers sought to use book knowledge to enhance the freedom of themselves and their class. It was as if they had emerged from darkness into light, and as they stood blinking in the glare of their new-found world, almost anything seemed possible. Yet if we look more closely at these narratives, we begin to notice that the freedom which they sought generated a range of problems for which there were no easy solutions. The more honest the autobiographer, the more thorough his engagement with the pursuit of knowledge, and the more searching his analysis of its consequences, the wider is the range of dilemmas and uncertainties which he reveals.

The first major difficulty stemmed from the fact that the autodidacts were true freethinkers, in the literal sense of the term. Their approach implied not only hostility to the attempts by middle class educators to shape and discipline their activity, but, sooner or later, conflict with the structure of religious beliefs and practices within which they had frequently taken their first steps along the road to self-improvement. The booklists of the autobiographers abound with religious books and books on religion. Many were taught their letters by means of the Bible and their subsequent reading matter ranged from the classic works of Puritan imaginative literature, particularly *Pilgrim's Progress* and *Paradise Lost*, through to the Enlightenment Biblical critiques such as Paine's *Age of Reason* and Volney's *Ruins of Empires*. Their autobiographies are full of Biblical references and metaphor, reflecting a characteristic of their culture which, in Charles Shaw's view, marked it off from that of the generation which was growing up at the end of the century:

There was, too, a leaven of religious feeling in those days in the Pottery towns which it is difficult to realise in these days . . . I remember *The Potter's Examiner* (though I have never seen one for over fifty years) was

[42] Leatherland, pp. 9–19. See also Teer, p. iv.
[43] Adams, Cooper, Dunning, Leno, Lovekin, Lovett and Snowden.
[44] For the role of poetry and song in radical movements of this period see Bamford, *Passages*, vol. 1, pp. 110–11, 166–7; Cooper, p. 165; Leno, p. 49; Arch, pp. 97–9; Burn, p. 140; Y. V. Kovalev, ed., *An Anthology of Chartist Literature* (Moscow, 1956); Martha Vicinus, op. cit., pp. 57–134; Robert Colls, *The Collier's Rant* (London, 1977).

177

steeped in the forms and methods of biblical expression. I remember letters addressed to certain "masters" in the style of "The Book of Chronicles", but there was no license and no irreverence in this form of address. To the bulk of the readers of the *Examiner* the rebukes were all the more weighty and scathing because of the Biblical form in which they were presented.[45]

Without the literature, and, in many cases, the institutions of the Church, the autobiographers would never have discovered the world of learning, but once they had done so, the place of religion in their lives was bound to change.

At the outset, the traditional domination by religious works of the category of serious literature was undermined. The readers' awakened intellectual appetite could no longer be satisfied by the books which they inherited from their parents. "There were many things that I wished to know," wrote Thomas Carter, "upon which both the Bible and my other instructors were silent."[46] As soon as he was able, he began to acquire and read an ever wider variety of secular literature which inevitably diminished the presence of spiritual writings in his mental universe. Nonetheless, as far as is known, Carter remained an orthodox Christian, and it is important to distinguish between the layers of secularization which the pursuit of knowledge engendered. Many of the autobiographers experienced a growing number of personal and intellectual tensions in their religious life which might amount to a falling away of the intensity of their belief, but did not threaten their nominal and often practising commitment to Christianity. It was only a minority of the serious readers whose intellectual explorations, coupled with their reactions to the industrializing society, led them away from religious belief altogether.

Active participation in the Nonconformist churches had always demanded a basic reading ability, and those who became fully literate would find plenty of outlets for their skills. William Bowcock, "The Lincolnshire Drillman", wrote a traditional spiritual autobiography which recorded his conversion to Baptism and his subsequent life-long career of preaching, teaching and polemicizing, none of which would have been possible without the period of self-education he underwent in his late teens and early twenties.[47] Yet it is in the readers' relationship with, in particular, organized Methodism, that the disruptive influence of their activities becomes evident. At a purely practical level there would be competition for the readers' spare time, for, with increasing work discipline during the rest of the week, Sunday provided the main opportunity for self-improvement. Several of the autobiographers were introduced to the habit of serious reading through their participation in the affairs of their chapel and then found their attendance dropping away as they wanted to spend more time with their books. "Methodists had a suspicion that I was sceptical," remembered Cooper, "because I had ceased to attend public worship. They did not understand that the chief reason was, that I might gain one whole day for study, weekly."[48] The real problem, however, was not so much the timing as the content of the readers' activities. Wesley had been deeply committed to both promoting and disciplining the pursuit of knowledge, and had sought to

[45] Shaw, pp. 192–3.   [46] Carter, *Memoirs*, p. 38.

[47] Bowcock, *passim*. He was "Particular Baptist" and belonged to congregations in Pinchbeck, Gosburton, Fleet and Boston, in the Lincolnshire Fens.

[48] Cooper, p. 71. See also Thomson, pp. 65–6 and below, and, for similar difficulties with the Anglican Church, see Clare, *Autobiography*, p. 32; Elliott, op. cit., p. 48.

resolve any conflict between these two goals by publishing a sufficient volume of approved literature to satisfy his increasingly literate followers.[49] After his death, the continued growth in the size of the movement and in the availability of secular literature could only exacerbate the latent tension. From his standpoint as a loyal Anglican, John Clare could safely mock the local Methodists' hostility to the poetry which had transformed his outlook,[50] but for those within the movement, the consequences of its censorious attitude towards imaginative literature were more serious. Christopher Thomson's career as a self-educator owed a great deal to his membership of a Methodist Sunday school and the small library it possessed.[51] His appetite whetted, he began to enlarge the range of his reading, and his chapel attendance declined. Inquiries were made into the causes of his absence, and eventually a bench of class leaders pronounced,

> . . . that "if I did not at once, and unconditionally, renounce all books, except such as they should approve of, I was for ever lost!" At that sentence I paused, and wept; the iron mandate was driven into my soul, and after a long self-struggle, I renounced my connection with all bodies who would prescribe the free range of thought in matters of such vital importance. Although I lingered with them some time after, from the very moment of that unchristian sentence I belonged to myself and God.[52]

There were several good reasons why Thomson's class leaders should so mistrust "the free range of thought". Apart from the straightforward question of mental distraction, too much emphasis on book knowledge threatened to upset the fragile balance between rational inquiry and anti-intellectual revivalism which lay at the heart of the Methodist approach to Christian faith. There were, as we have seen, a minority of autobiographers who continued to organize their interpretation around a pattern of sin and conversion, but the majority kept their distance from such periods of religious fervour as they might have experienced. Thomas Cooper, a man whose restless energy and high intelligence constantly drove him to conclusions which others lacked either the insight or the courage to reach, provided the most succinct account of the alienation many of the readers felt from the more emotional side of religious belief. He joined a group of Methodists and became convinced of his guilt, but after a period of "anguish and sorrow", he had second thoughts:

> I began to grow weary of creeping into corners twenty times a day to repent for sin—for I thought I was always sinning—and of believing myself again forgiven. I shrunk from the practice, at last in sheer disgust; but neither did that bring ease of mind. I began, gradually, to get back to my music and my reading; but some of the members of the Society—poor men who knew little of books, but who found happiness in prayer, and in hearing others read and preach about the goodness of God,—demurred to my reading any book but the Bible, unless it was a "truly religious book".[53]

---

[49] See Isabel Rivers, art. cit., pp. 192–4; R. D. Altick, op. cit., pp. 35–8; E. P. Thompson, op. cit., pp. 40–51.

[50] Clare, *Sketches*, p. 58. The Methodist weaver who lent him his first copy of Thomson's *The Seasons* explained its battered condition by saying that " 'twas reckoned nothing by himself or his friends".

[51] He mentions acquiring from it Boyle's *Travels*, *Robinson Crusoe* and *Phillip Quarl*.

[52] Thomson, p. 66.   [53] Cooper, pp. 38–9. See also Lovett, p. 22; C. M. Smith, p. 147.

One of Methodism's great strengths had long been its capacity to attract "poor men who knew little of books",[54] and it is no surprise that they should feel considerable antipathy to self-confident intellectuals like Cooper. There was, moreover, a real danger that those who set no limits to their intellectual enquiries would sooner or later fall into heresy. Thomas Oliver, a Cornish tin-miner, underwent the standard process of self-education and moved easily into the role of lay preacher in his local Methodist community. His learning and skill as a communicator fitted him for the post, which he greatly enjoyed, but his reading and scientific studies continued alongside his preaching, and eventually caused him to question publicly the doctrines of free-will and eternal damnation. What is notable here is not the congregation's subsequent censure, but their preacher's indignant response: "I felt disgusted that I was prevented from using the highest function of the brain, viz. free thought, and I felt determined to resign my preaching, which I did".[55] Oliver, Thomson, and, at this stage, Cooper, continued to think of themselves as Christians, as did the great majority of the autobiographers, but, whether or not they were involved in direct conflict, their self-education embodied a distinct process of secularization. Thomson, who dedicated his autobiography to "Fellow workers in the holy cause of Self-Elevation", is perhaps the clearest example of the transference of the language of religion to the pursuit of knowledge. He and his fellow workers were concerned with the self rather than the soul, and in turn their autobiographies recorded the history of their moral and intellectual development in concepts which were borrowed from rather than dependent upon their religious belief.

Amidst these varieties of belief, there were a handful whose free thought turned them into Freethinkers. It is impossible to provide a full explanation of why some of the readers lost their faith altogether, but in most cases the precipitating factor seems to have been a conjunction of intellectual enquiry and practical experience of suffering and injustice. No reader could avoid at least a flirtation with Biblical criticism. Their commitment to the rational investigation of all natural phenomena, together with the well-established connection between radicalism and infidelism, particularly as represented in the person and writings of Tom Paine,[56] ensured that at some point they would find themselves casting a questioning glance at received religious texts. It was partly a matter of reading the Bible more closely, and partly of engaging with those works which attacked it. Despite the Church's attempt to draw a firm distinction between religious and infidel works, all would be included in Lovett's "enthusiastic desire to read and treasure up all I could meet with on the subject of Christianity".[57] Paine, Voltaire and Volney would undermine the readers' religious deference,[58] and secularism, as distinct from a passive disbelief, was always an intensely literary activity. However, the catalyst which transformed spiritual insubordination into outright rebellion was, in these autobiographies, the apparent failure of Christianity to provide an adequate

---

[54] See E. J. Hobsbawm, *Primitive Rebels* (Manchester, 1959), pp. 131–4.

[55] Oliver, p. 56.

[56] See Edward Royle, *Radical Politics 1790–1900, Religion and Unbelief* (London, 1971), pp. 17–37; G. A. Williams, op. cit., *passim*.

[57] Lovett, p. 35.

[58] See, for instance, Linton, pp. 17–18; C. M. Smith, p. 10.

response to the cruelty and inequity of the industrial society. The physical and moral degradation of their families and the communities in which they lived could no longer be equated with the notion of a just and benevolent Deity. Cooper's period of real doubt commenced with his shocked discovery of the state of the starving Leicester stockingers, an event which drove him simultaneously into political radicalism and religious scepticism,[59] but the most coherent account of this process is provided by the Coventry ribbon weaver Joseph Gutteridge. He had read and pondered Voltaire's *Dictionary of Philosophy* and Paine's *Age of Reason*, but remained unconvinced until a prolonged period of family poverty and ill-health finally destroyed what was left of his faith:

> Fast merging into the materialistic tendencies of the age, the struggle for existence was a stern lesson. Others got on in the world without any seeming effort, whilst I struggled and strove with honest intention to make headway without avail. It seemed that God was very unjust and partial in keeping from me the means to sustain the life He had given. Conceiving myself to be a creature of circumstances, I was fast losing the power of free agency and falling into a state of unbelief in the Providence of God.[60]

Gutteridge's response was not the superficial reaction of an embittered man, but a crisis of faith as profound and agonizing as any suffered by the major Victorian intellectuals. He wrote:

> For several years succeeding 1845, I experienced a most severe trial. My mind was so much exercised with these doubts and fears respecting the great mystery of a life hereafter, that existence itself became a torment almost unbearable, and I often longed that I might drink of the water of Lethe to drown in oblivion the memory both of the past and present. Such a state of mind could not have continued much longer without merging into madness. The direful effect produced in my home and on the health of my faithful and loving wife no words can express. Were it in my power I would cheerfully give up ten years from my life to compensate for the misery wrought in my home circle by this state of semi madness and uncertainty.[61]

He eventually found his way back to a generalized belief in a divine presence, as did Cooper, but their spiritual journeys, and those of men like the Leicestershire Chartist Joseph Sketchley, who finally abandoned his Catholicism after ten years of reading and thinking had convinced him that "its claims were incompatible with human liberty and human dignity",[62] highlighted the threat to religious belief and practice which was inherent in the readers' commitment to pursuing knowledge to whatever destination it led them.

The second dilemma faced by the readers was that the form of intellectual freedom they had realized embodied an element of withdrawal from the world in which they found themselves. Where the pursuit of knowledge could lead to an investigation of their physical and ideological environment, it could also encourage a retreat from a reality which was becoming increasingly transparent.

---

[59] Cooper, pp. 259–60. His religious crisis reached its climax while he was serving a prison sentence for his political activities. See also Farn, p. 245.

[60] Gutteridge; pp. 79–80. See also Susan Budd, *Varieties of Unbelief* (London, 1977), pp. 104–123; Edward Royle, *Victorian Infidels* (Manchester, 1974), pp. 107–125.

[61] Gutteridge, p. 84.   [62] Sketchley, p. 21.

The process was set in motion by the practical difficulties faced by the self-educators. As we noted in chapter six, although readers would sooner or later need to make contact with each other if they were to make the most of their limited opportunities, their activity demanded as much privacy as they could obtain. The entry into the realm of literature was frequently accompanied by a rejection of the reader's previous associates. Such was certainly the case with the apprentice compositor William Adams:

> One Sunday afternoon the usual call was made for a ramble in the fields. Word was sent to the callers that their old companion was not going to join them. I heard from an upper room, not without a certain amount of tremor, their exclamations of surprise. They wandered off into the fields in one direction; I, with a new companion, wandered off into the fields in another. My new companion was Young's "Night Thoughts". The old companions were never joined again. A new life had begun.[63]

There is a suggestion that some of the readers were naturally shy or lived in isolated surroundings, and had turned to literature to compensate for their loneliness; William Heaton, for instance, explained that, "Having no brothers, and only one sister, who was married prior to my mother's death, I found my companions in books".[64] But most were faced with a straightforward decision as to whether to spend their time with people or books, and were driven by their ambition to choose the latter. "I would stick like a limpet to my books of an evening", remembered Joseph Arch, " 'Not an idle minute' was my rule. There were no slack half-hours for me, no taking it easy with the other lads."[65]

What had begun as a response to a practical problem developed into an integral part of the image of the self-improving working man. His intellectual appetite awakened, Cooper envisaged his new role: "How rich I was, with ten shillings per week, to buy food and clothes—now all this intellectual food was glutting me on every side! And how resolute I was on becoming solitary, and also on becoming a scholar!".[66] Those who wrote or only read poetry were particularly prone to this form of self-dramatization. Ben Brierley, who by the time he wrote his autobiography had become older and wiser and could afford to mock the absurdities of his youth, dubbed the syndrome "Mooning with the Muses",[67] and described its essential characteristics: "I had begun to take solitary walks on summer evenings in company with Burns and Lord Byron. I could recite all the choice passages in 'Childe Harold', and repeat all the more popular songs of the gifted ploughman. I was aspiring to be a poet myself, and went so far as to adopt the 'Byron tie' and try to look melancholy".[68] As John Harris immediately recognized, Poetry and social intercourse were antithetical: "This [writing poetry] was my life-work for the weal of humanity, and by his help I would perform it, renouncing the noisy multitude for silence and the shades".[69] All the readers were fired by the possibility of making contact with not just the writings but the personalities of the great literary figures, and the influence of the popular notion of the lifestyle of the Romantic poet can be seen at work in many of these autobiographies.

[63] Adams, vol. 1, pp. 107–8. See also Dodd, p. 20; Harris, p. 34; Clare, *Autobiography*, p. 15.
[64] Heaton, p. xviii. See also Hopkinson, p. 10.   [65] Arch, p. 33. See also Farn, p. 197.
[66] Cooper, p. 53.   [67] Brierley, p. 33.   [68] *Ibid.*, p. 31.
[69] Harris, p. 48. See also Carter, *Memoirs*, p. 32.

There is a strain of sheer foolishness in this behaviour, as the autobiographers often admitted, but the sense of isolation which is present in their accounts was sustained by two very real forces. In the first instance, the range of beliefs and activities which became associated with the pursuit of knowledge set in motion a permanent crisis of personal relations between the readers and those with whom they lived and worked. Many of these writers, as was suggested in chapter two, retained the spiritual autobiographers' intention to morally improve their readership through the presentation of their life-histories, and this objective inevitably implied a degree of superiority over those who required this guidance. The Kettering staymaker and poet John Plummer, for instance, wrote that it was his desire, "to share, in common with numerous other toilers in the good work, the high and noble task of inculcating the doctrines of Temperance, Prudence, Morality and Education amongst those of our fellow-workers who so bitterly need such teachings . . .".[70] Committed to a pastime which demanded at least intermittent solitude and was largely irrelevant to the immediate problems of earning a living, the readers expounded a set of values and attitudes which were explicitly hostile to many features of the traditional culture of the labouring population.

The attack on non-rational forms of belief and behaviour, as exemplified by superstitions and excessive drinking, was bound to bring the self-improving working men into conflict with those whose lives were still subject to their influence, however much sympathy they might feel for them. This was particularly true in the case of their antagonism to patterns of alcoholic consumption which were embedded in many aspects of social exchange in the community. As soon as he embarked upon the pursuit of knowledge the reader would begin moving away from drink-centered forms of recreation. "I seldom visited the public-houses now", recalled Heaton, "the poetical ideas which I was striving to cultivate gave me a distaste for the ale-house and its company."[71] Intemperance was the dominant feature of an entire structure of irrational and morally corrupting behaviour from which the reader was attempting to emancipate himself. When Christopher Thomson entered a shipwright's workshop as an apprentice to his father, he found that he had little in common with his companions:

From the first I was discontented with the business; young and unthinking as I was, there was no comfort for me with such dare-devil companions. My attention was turned to books, to drawing, to questions of political moment, to the theatres, but above all, to the flowery fields and the green country. Few of my pursuits found a response in the breasts of my every-day associates; their tastes were of the lowest grade; their conversation generally disgusting; their books, the obscene trash raked up from the pest-holes that unfortunately may be found in every town; their amusements being card-playing, tossing with half-pence, and other low modes of gambling, with drinking, smoking and chewing tobacco.[72]

[70] Plummer, p. xxxiv. Even the unrepentant poacher James Hawker was attempting to change the ways of those who "are to much Eaten up with Drink and Gambling" (p. 75).
[71] Heaton, p. xviii.
[72] Thomson, p. 72. He later described the trade of sawyers in which he worked for a while as "generally a drunken class" (p. 173). See also H. Herbert, pp. 21, 52; Downing, p. 104; Hanson, p. 18; Farish, *Autobiography*, p. 29; Lowery, pp. 82–3.

What needs to be stressed here is that such problems would be encountered and recorded even by a man like Thomson, who was passionately committed to the elevation of the working class as a whole, and that it was extremely difficult for any self-improving working man to avoid them. Although the status, traditions, and material circumstances of the urban skilled artisan were the most conducive to the pursuit of knowledge,[73] the activity was far from limited to this section of the working class, and conversely, the army of the unimproved was by no means confined to the ranks of the unskilled. James Burn, who had spent his youth amidst the very lowest strata of society, regarded his late entry into a skilled trade as the major turning point in his search for respectability, but the hatter's workshop in which he was now employed scarcely represented a haven of sobriety: "During my apprenticeship, many of the elder journeymen were little better than half savages; one part of their time was spent in working like slaves, and the other in drinking like madmen. I have seen as many as seven stand-up fights among a shop of men before noon in one day".[74] It might be expected that the delicate sensibilities of the poet J. A. Leatherland would be threatened by an enforced move from a small weavers shop to a factory: "Those who are unacquainted with factory life", he complained, "can form but little idea of the cruel and brutal treatment, the systematic annoyances, the taunts, jeers, and blows, inflicted upon those that happen to be weaker than the rest, or do not choose to conform to the usages that prevail",[75] but what comes through in these accounts time and again is that the reader would be fortunate not to encounter such tensions wherever he worked. It sometimes happened that a small workshop would be entirely populated by like-minded men who supported each other's endeavours to educate themselves, but it was much more common for the reader to come into conflict not just with unimproved individuals, but with a structure of practices and customs which were an integral part of the work routine, and were accompanied by sanctions designed to enforce conformity.[76] If life in the workshops rarely reached the depths of degradation which were to be found in many of the factories, the routines of drinking were more rigidly defined and the tight-knit groups of journeymen would be better able to discipline those who stood out against them, as for instance, Henry Price discovered when his fellow cabinet makers threatened to put him "in Coventry" when he decided to set his face against their "Boosing Customs".[77]

There is evidence that the artisan workshops were slowly becoming more sober and respectable,[78] and there may well have been a much greater degree of cultural homogeneity amongst the "aristocracy of labour" which emerged during the third quarter of the nineteenth century,[79] but all these autobi-

[73] See above, ch. 6, pp. 123–4.   [74] Burn, pp. 156–7.
[75] Leatherland, p. 32. See also Gutteridge, p. 28; T. Wood, p. 11; Dodd, pp. 10–11.
[76] See Brian Harrison, op. cit., pp. 39–40.
[77] Price, p. 65. He particularly objected to being sent out to buy the beer for the drinking sessions. See also the similar experiences of the cabinet maker James Hopkinson (pp. 21–2, 32, 57–8), and the observations of another cabinet maker, William Lovett (p. 31).
[78] Particularly in the autobiography of Francis Place, op. cit., pp. 16, 51, 57, 82.
[79] See G. Crossick, op. cit., ch. 7; R. Gray, op. cit., pp. 99–115. Both writers describe a large degree of cultural cohesion amongst the artisan élite, though Gray admits that his "absence of data enabling us to correlate class situation and cultural patterns at an individual level" means that, "The analogies of occupational differences in culture and life-style has therefore

ographers who embarked upon the pursuit of knowledge defined their values and aspirations in opposition to the unimproved behaviour of members of their community with whom they were in daily contact. There is a constant tension at the level of both ideology and personal relations between the two groups to which it is clear that both sides contributed. The less literate chapel-goers censured the intellectual inquiries of the readers amongst them; those who retained a firm belief in the supernatural responded to the scepticism of the learned by regarding their learning as just another form of superstition;[80] and those whose work and leisure revolved around drink reacted with vigour to those whose words and actions implied criticism of their way of life. Some of the autobiographers fought against the isolating forces, others made little attempt: "As to choosing companions from among my fellow-workmen", wrote the tailor Thomas Carter, "it was wholly out of the question; for, although I took care to be upon civil terms with every one of them, as indeed I was bound to do, yet this was a very different matter from making them my associates when out of the workshop. I respected some of them as fellow-craftsmen and shopmates, but I knew not one whom I could choose as a friend. Their habits, language and modes of thinking were alike quite uncongenial with my own, and 'how can two', not to mention a greater number, walk together, except they be agreed? Thus I was a solitary being . . .".[81]

Carter, who suffered from a sense of isolation all his life, was accustomed to turn to nature for solace and poetry for self-expression. A central attraction of useful knowledge had always been its capacity to abstract the reader from the realities of his situation. "Books! books! books! was my continual cry", wrote John Plummer, lamed by a childhood illness, ". . . and I was always begging or borrowing them of the neighbours: and naturally so, for they enabled me, for the time, to forget my affliction, and converse, as it were, with the authors whose works came under my notice."[82] The intellectual transformation could be a means of furthering the freedom of themselves and their class, but equally it could encourage a retreat from a world rendered even more unattractive by their pursuit of knowledge. Of particular significance here were the twin influences of nature poetry and natural theology.

All the autobiographers read poetry, and a surprising number tried their hand at composition, including the sizeable band of published poets in their ranks. Poetry fulfilled a diverse range of functions, but common to many of those who took a serious interest in this form of self-expression was an endorsement of a view of the poet and his subject matter which owed much to the Romantic movement. James Burn, whose taste had been awakened by the traditional Scottish ballads told to him in his youth and subsequently developed by wide reading, began his definition of the role of the poet by explaining their supposed mental instability:

to be of a probabilistic type", and this evidence would suggest that the emergence of this cohesion was a slower and more painful process than has often been assumed.

[80] John Clare wrote of his mother that "superstition went so far with her that she believed the higher parts of learning was the blackest arts of witchcraft, and that no other means could attain them" (*Sketches*, p. 46). Thelwall discovered that the inhabitants of the Welsh countryside to which he retreated believed that he could "conjure", and that he walked in the woods by night "to talk with evil spirits" (p. xxxvii). See also Plummer, p. xvii.

[81] Carter, *Memoirs*, pp. 130–1.   [82] Plummer, p. xvii.

We cannot enjoy any great amount of excitement, without suffering a corresponding depression. The madness of poets may thus, in some measure, be accounted for. I am firmly convinced, that no man can be a poet, in the true sense of the term, whose heart and soul is not fairly engaged in it. His imagination must feel the electric influence of creative power, and his fancy must be for ever on the wing. His appreciation of the beauties of nature must be far above that of the common herd; and above all, he must feel within himself those passions that for ever agitate humanity in its tenderest parts.[83]

The poet, "in the true sense of the term", was set apart from his community by the intensity of his sensibility and sought his inspiration far away from the towns in which an increasing proportion of the working class population lived. Nature now appeared as a refuge from urban society, a repository of values and ideals which could be opposed to the working man's experience of industrialization.

The essence of its appeal was caught in the writings of Robert Burns and James Thomson, who, together with Milton, were the most frequently cited poets in the autobiographies. Burns' popularity rested on the capacity of his readership to identify themselves with the man as well as his verses. Samuel Bamford never forgot the sensation of reading a volume of his life and writings whilst working as a porter and warehouseman in Manchester:

There he was, a tall, stooping, lank haired, weather browned, dreamy eyed, God-crowned, noble minded, ploughman. And this, too, was of his writing, of his soul uttering; this "Lass o' Ballochmoyle" was one strain of his never dying melody! If this really be so, if this be indeed his poetry, what can these sensations possibly be, which awaken within me whenever I read a true poet's verse; these strange and undefined emotions which have brooded o'er my heart ever since I knew what love and poetry were. If these expressed sensations of the noble poet peasant constituted his imperishable wreath, what could these unexpressed but somewhat identical feelings of mine be, save poetry without the form—a spirit without the body. What then—methought—if I tried to throw them into form? what if I dared essay to give them utterance in verse?[84]

Bamford was one of many whose poetical aspirations were kindled by Burns, and the most quoted and imitated of his works was *The Cotter's Saturday Night*. This poem was a celebration of the family economy of a Scottish agricultural labourer in which the emotional and material functions were in perfect harmony. Parents and children were shown returning from their various labours to enjoy an evening of domestic contentment. It was a picture far from the reality of a man like the Kendal woollen spinner William Dodd, who quoted four stanzas of the poem in his autobiography, adding the comment that, "All who have been in a manufacturing town, will recollect the disgusting scenes that are to be witnessed there on a Saturday night".[85] Late eighteenth century rural Scotland was real enough, but sufficiently distant for English artisans and

---

[83] Burn, p. 194. See also Martha Vicinus, op. cit., pp. 140-58.

[84] Bamford, *Early Days*, pp. 289-90. One of the autobiographers, Anthony Errington, claimed to have met the great man in the Dog and Duck public house near Gosforth (pp. 23-4).

[85] Dodd, p. 40.

186

factory workers to hold up Burns' description as an ideal which it was becoming increasingly difficult to locate in their own experience.

James Thomson's *The Seasons* was completed in 1730 and was republished almost continuously for over a hundred years.[86] The sustained popularity of the work can be largely explained by the two innovations which Thomson introduced to the Augustan pastoral tradition within which he was writing. He was the first major pastoral poet to recognize the presence of agricultural labourers as producers of wealth in the rural economy, and despite his presentation of a wholly idealized relationship between landowners and their employees, a subsequent working class readership could find in his scenery toiling men with whom they might identify themselves. What attracted those whose occupations were being transformed by industrialization was Thomson's representation of the integration of the ordered rhythm of nature and the annual or diurnal round of agricultural employment, which he contrasted with the growing discontinuity of urban life:

> But now those white unblemished minutes, whence
> The fabling poets took their golden age,
> Are found no more amid these iron times,
> These dregs of life! Now the distempered mind
> Has lost the concord of harmonious powers
> Which forms the soul of happiness; and all
> Is off the poise within: the passions all
> Have burst their bounds; and Reason, half extinct
> Or impotent, or else approving, sees
> The foul disorder.[87]

At a time when industrial capitalism and the factory machine were imposing a new and artificial discipline on the pattern of work, Thomson's vision of a wholly natural relationship between the passage of time and the performance of labour was extremely seductive.

Alongside his depiction of nature as a realm of social order, Thomson hinted at an alternative view of nature as the repository of those moral values which were being corrupted by the new society. Thomas Carter wrote of *The Seasons* that, "With the exception of the Bible, I know not that I ever read any other book so attentively and regularly. Its beautiful descriptions of nature were delightful to my imagination, while its fine moral reflections—its earnest disuasives from vice—and its persuasive exhortations to virtue, were, as I believe, greatly instrumental in promoting my best interests".[88] By the time John Thelwall came to publish his autobiography in 1801, the polarization between a countryside peopled at most by a solitary shepherd or ploughman and the oppressive materialistic centres of population had become much

---

[86] The British Library holds 90 separate editions of the poem published between 1730 and 1851, and this does not include editions of Thomson's complete works. For the popularity of *The Seasons* in the early nineteenth century, see R. D. Altick, op. cit., p. 257.

[87] James Thomson, *The Seasons and The Castle of Indolence*, ed. James Sambrook (Oxford, 1972), *Spring*, lines 272–281. For a discussion of Thomson's treatment of the idea of change and the contrast between urban and rural life, see Ralph Cohen, *The Unfolding of The Seasons* (London, 1970), ch. 3; A. D. McKillip, *The Background of Thomson's Seasons* (Minneapolis, 1942), pp. 26–35; Raymond Williams, *The Country and The City* (London, 1973), pp. 68–71.

[88] Carter, *Memoirs*, p. 75.

sharper. Retreating from the legal and physical battering he had received from
Pitt's government and loyalist mobs, Thelwall had settled in a small Welsh
village on the banks of the Wye, where he hoped that the twin influences of
nature and poetry would salve his wounds: "Such a retreat could not but
appear, to an enthusiastic imagination, as a sort of enchanted dormitory, where
the agitations of political feeling might be cradled to forgetfulness, and the
delicious day dreams of poesy might be renewed".[89] This tendency to view
nature through the Romantic lens persisted long into the century. It was
partly sustained by another intellectual tradition which was given its definitive
statement at much the same time, natural theology.[90]

Most of the autobiographers reached maturity in the pre-Darwinian age, and
although it was possible for the reader's study of natural science to undermine
his faith altogether, it was often the case that nature provided some shelter for
those who could find little evidence of Christian values or behaviour in the
industrial centres. Joseph Gutteridge, whose religious crisis owed much to his
sense of economic injustice, was set on the road back to belief when his micro-
scopic investigations convinced him that, "a Power existed behind Nature
unknown to physical law".[91] Viewed through "an atmosphere polluted with
smoke belched from a thousand chimneys", nature might well seem to a man
like the Manchester poet Benjamin Stott to be possessed of a "sublime and
varied face".[92] Christopher Thomson, another of those who had great difficulty
in integrating his intellectual and religious pursuits, still found that he could
talk "with God in Nature's calm solitudes".[93] The countryside in which many
had been raised and which most could still see, became the last spiritual refuge.
Charles Shaw, for whom the contrast between his book knowledge and his
economic experience seemed almost unbearable, described the heightened
significance of the fields around the pot-banks:

> I remember well the aching tumult in my own heart after this meeting, the
> sense of a malignant confusion of all things. Yet I remember, too, the flowers
> in the valley only a few hundred yards away from that throbbing centre of
> passion. I thought also of the singing of the birds in Braddow Wood, but here
> were men yelling with hate of those they regarded as their oppressors. I knew
> these things meant two different worlds—one belonging to the God the
> Father about whom I read every Sunday in the Sunday school; and the
> other world belonging to rich men, to manufacturers, to mine-owners, to
> squires and nobles, and all kinds of men in authority.[94]

A final dilemma to which many of the autobiographies drew attention, is
that the pursuit of knowledge could have the effect of fragmenting and weaken-
ing the culture which the readers inherited. Amidst their celebration of the

[89] Thelwall, p. xxxvi.
[90] Willliam Paley's *Natural Theology, or Evidences of the Existence and Attributes of the Deity Collected from the Appearance of Nature* (London, 1802).
[91] Gutteridge, p. 91.
[92] Stott, p. x.
[93] Thomson, p. 388.
[94] Shaw, p. 35. The "meeting" was a union meeting at which the editor of the *Potters' Examiner* had spoken at length on the hardships of the potters, which "were contrasted with awful emphasis, with the well-fed tyranny they had to endure and support". See also Younger, p. 344; Harris, p. 65; Dundee Factory Boy, p. 32; H. Herbert, pp. 60, 158–9; Dodd, p. 20.

creative and liberating implications of their activity, it is possible to detect elements of regret and confusion. Accompanying the attack on superstition, for instance, there is often to be found an awareness that with their disappearance, popular culture was losing something of its vitality. Few men welcomed the release from the influence of the supernatural more than the former beggar-boy, James Burn, but he realized that his community might have to pay a price for its emancipation: "When ghosts, fairies, and witches cease to live in the belief of a people, the character of such a people will lose much of its poetry".[95] Burn was referring here to the general imaginative life of his people, but there was the particular problem of the fate of the orally transmitted poetry which had embodied and sustained so much of the belief in ghosts, fairies and witches. Interest in folk song had begun to develop amongst the educated classes towards the end of the eighteenth century,[96] and a leading figure of the movement, Walter Scott, employed one of these autobiographers, the Ettrick shepherd James Hogg, to collect material for him. Hogg's chief source was his own family, particularly his mother, and once he had realized how vital and how threatened was this tradition, he himself began to record and write imitations of the ballads he had listened to as he grew up.[97] The only other working man who is known to have participated in what was at this stage very much the pastime of those who had no direct experience of the cultural heritage of the early nineteenth century working class, was another poet and autobiographer, John Clare. He not only gathered together the ballads he heard from his parents and neighbours, but is thought to have been one of the very first collectors to attempt to set down the music to which they were sung.[98]

Other autobiographers who shared the concern of Hogg and Clare tried to cope with the problem by drawing a distinction between superstitions, which represented all the negative aspects of traditional culture, and customs, which were seen as the positive elements of the pre-industrial way of life. Their attitude towards the declining body of semi-religious, semi-pagan festivals was linked to their nostalgic view of nature and the seasons. Whatever its origins, the calendar of events and observances embodied the right of free-born Englishmen to order their labour and recreation according to their own traditions and not the demands of employers and machines. Some of the autobiographers could do no more than include in their accounts a record of customs which had disappeared during their life-times,[99] but others made an attempt to stem the tide of change. When that most committed autodidact Christopher Thomson settled down in Edwinstowe, a village on the edge of Sherwood Forest, he duly catalogued the customs which had been finally destroyed by the enclosures, and then encouraged the mutual improvement society he had set up in the village to try to revive them. "We were no longer

[95] Burn, p. 195.

[96] See Peter Burke, *Popular Culture in Early Modern Europe* (London, 1978), pp. 3–22.

[97] Hogg, pp. 61–8. See also Edith C. Batho, *The Ettrick Shepherd* (New York, 1969 edn.), chs. 2 and 3. Hogg's *Memoir* first appeared as the preface to *The Mountain Bard; consisting of Ballads and Songs founded on Facts and Legendary Tales* (Edinburgh, 1807). For a more detailed discussion of these points, see David Vincent, "The Decline of the Oral Tradition in Popular Culture", in Robert Storch, ed., *Popular Culture in Modern Britain: Persistence and Change* (London, 1982).

[98] Margaret Grainger, *John Clare: Collector of Ballads* (Peterborough, 1964).

[99] See especially Bamford, *Early Days*, ch. xv; Adams, vol. 1, ch. VI.

enjoying the days in which true Saxon blood made the Foresters' hearts beat merrily", he explained, "O no! those days were changed for the all-work and all taxes' days, when such horse-work, and empty pockets for half a bread loaf, had made the sons of Johnny Bull very melancholy boys indeed. Our ancient 'feast week' had dwindled into a mere public-house visiting, with only a few exceptions. In the autumn of 1841, a few of our villagers determined on attempting to restore the faded jollifyings which characterized the care-despising foresters, who made this village feast of days of yore, a thing to be remembered."[100] As Thomson's description of the second and last of these feasts indicates, the format was a curious mixture of supposed tradition and the newly developed principles and practices of self-improvement: "The memory of the Poets was reverenced; the memory and eternal renown of Robin Hood, honoured; and Science, Art, and Moral Worth were hailed on by approving sentiments".[101] Further north, in the village of Failsworth on the edge of Manchester, Ben Brierley was involved in a similar attempt to resuscitate what he called "the pageant" of the Wakes and the rushcart.[102] Here again the essentially artificial revival lasted only two years before collapsing for the last time. The bizarre meeting between Robin Hood and "Science, Art and Moral Worth" exemplified the difficulty which faced the readers. Their knowledge, their science, their moral worth, had been gained with the aid of those forces, urbanization, the spread of communications, which were doing so much to impoverish their inherited culture. They represented change, and were ill-equipped to prevent it.

The readers were better suited to the role of innovators than antiquarians, yet even in their enthusiastic exploitation of the constructive potential of the written word, we can discover a significant degree of uncertainty. At the outset, the ambition and independence of the self-educators collided with their in-experience and inadequate education. The range of literature to which they might now gain access could be simply overwhelming. Cooper's description of the course of self-education he mapped out for himself in his early twenties, covering four languages, mathematics, memorizing all of *Paradise Lost* and seven plays of Shakespeare, was followed by an account of the succeeding nervous breakdown.[103] Astonishing feats of learning were achieved, but all too often the readers found themselves led up one blind alley after another by their inability to discriminate effectively between the heterogeneous collection of literature which fell into their hands. "Unfortunately, I never acquired much in the way of knowledge," confessed Charles Shaw, "As I have since found out, I was on the wrong tack, and had no one to guide me."[104] It was a new world, and the explorers were frequently lost.

The readers were deeply unsure about the question of language. John Clare had begun to both read and write, when he was brought up short by a chance encounter with a school primer:

> Borrowing a school book of a companion having some entertaining things in it both in prose and verse, with an introduction by the compiler, who doubtless like myself knew little about either (for such like affect to give advice to others while they want it themselves), in this introduction was rules

---

[100] Thomson, p. 345. [101] *Ibid.*, p. 367. [102] Brierley, pp. 46–7.
[103] Cooper, p. 58. [104] Shaw, pp. 224–5. See also T. Wood, p. 9.

both for writing as well as reading. Compositions in prose and verse; where stumbling on a remark that a person who knew nothing of grammar was not capable of writing a letter nor even a bill of parcels, I was quite in the suds, seeing that I had gone on thus far without learning the first rudiments of doing it properly. For I had hardly said the name of grammar while at school. But as I had an itch for trying at everything I got hold of, I determined to try grammar, and for that purpose, by the advice of a friend, bought the "Spelling Book" as the most easy assistant for my starting out. But finding a jumble of words classed under this name, and that name and this such-a-figure of speech and that another-hard-worded-figure, I turned from further notice of it in instant disgust. For, as I knew I could talk to be understood, I thought by the same method my writing might be made out as easy and as proper. So in the teeth of grammar I pursued my literary journey as warm as usual . . .[105]

Clare's problem was familiar to all the readers. At issue here was how the self-educated working man was to connect the speech forms which he had learnt from his parents and in which he still communicated with his neighbours, with the forms of standard English which he increasingly encountered in his reading. Where Clare stands apart from his fellows is in his bold solution to the dilemma. Almost alone of the autobiographers he found a way of infusing his native oral tradition with his wide reading of the great literature of the preceding three centuries, and forged a literary style which was genuinely appropriate to his experience. His fellow ballad collector James Hogg, who stood with one foot in the folk culture of the Borders and the other in the sophisticated world of the Edinburgh salons, at times achieved a similar unity, and as he gained confidence, attempted to play off one culture against the other in a series of elaborate literary charades.

Elsewhere, we find much less confidence. Many turned to grammar books and became yet more doubtful about the value of the dialect in which they spoke. For instance, we find two of the most famous and influential working class leaders of the period commencing their voyages of self-improvement by going to considerable lengths to divest themselves of their regional accents. When William Lovett arrived in London he possessed a Cornish accent but no useful knowledge, and immediately set about remedying these twin defects with the aid of "Lindley Murray's Grammar".[106] Thomas Cooper, who lacked the excuse of geographical mobility, inevitably took the matter to extremes. Having decided it was impossible to commune with the classics in a Lincolnshire accent, he learnt to "pronounce with propriety" in the same way as he might learn a foreign language, and described the impact of his action on the community in which he was still working as a cobbler:

Now, to hear a youth in mean clothing, sitting at the shoemaker's stall, pursuing one of the lowliest callings, speak in what seemed to some of them almost a foreign dialect, raised positive anger and scorn in some, and amaze-

[105] Clare, *Sketches*, pp. 68–9. "the suds" are fen water, or a bog.
[106] Lovett, p. 34. Lindley Murray's *English Grammar adapted to the different classes of Learners* (York, 1795) had gone through 54 editions by 1846. See also William Cobbett's *A Grammar of the English Language In a Series of Letters. Intended for the Use of Soldiers, Sailors, Apprentices and Plough Boys* (London, 1818) for which Cobbett claimed sales of 100,000 by 1834.

ment in others. Who was I, that I should sit on the cobbler's stall and "talk fine"! They could not understand it. With Whillock and my intellectual friends I had conversed in the best and most refined English I could command; but I had used our plain old Lincolnshire dialect in talking to the neighbours. This was all to be laid aside now, and it took some courage to do it.[107]

These men derived their courage from two sources. Firstly, they were strongly tempted by the notion that there existed a single body of classical literature, made up of the works of men of genius of all ages, which embodied the eternal literary and spiritual values. This almost metaphysical regard for the great poets and authors reinforced the readers' inclination to use their book knowledge to transcend the day-to-day realities of their existence—John Harris, for instance, remembered how, on first encountering Shakespeare, "The bitters of life changed to sweetness in my cup . . ."[108]—and amidst the uncertainties of their new culture strengthened their hope that it would be possible to establish new moral standards in the face of the flood of sensationalist literature that was pouring from the presses. Secondly, in their constant struggle against the non-rational forms of belief and activity, it was all too easy to associate dialect with those forms of behaviour from which they were striving to emancipate themselves, and conversely there was a tendency to identify polite language with the respectability which they sought to attain. Many of the autobiographers reserved their use of the dialect which they themselves must have spoken for reporting the speech of those unimproved members of their community from whom they now wished to distance themselves.[109]

There was not, and never had been, a wholly independent working class literary culture. Despite the wide variety of regional dialects, and the well-established connection between language and social status, most working men, no matter how illiterate or non-literate, would have been familiar, either as listeners or readers, with that fount of classical English, the King James Bible. The supposedly indigenous literary forms, such as chap-books and ballads, had a complicated history, and it is clear that they had been neither written, published nor even read solely by members of the labouring population. The ballads, indeed, provide a particularly good example of the way in which the imaginative life of the popular culture had been developed over the centuries by the absorption of the literature brought to it by chap-men operating from distant towns. As a minority of the working class now began to make contact with the major figures of what they properly regarded as a common literary tradition, particularly Bunyan, Milton and "our Shakespeare" as Christopher Thomson called the man whose plays he had spent ten years of his life performing to the villagers of the north-east Midlands,[110] it seemed possible that through the agency of the serious readers, the entire working class culture might be further

---

[107] Cooper, pp. 56–7.   [108] Harris, pp. 62–3.

[109] See, for instance, C. M. Smith's sudden employment of West Country speech patterns when he wished to communicate his intellectual contempt for a group of "benighted villagers" listening to a hell-fire Methodist Preacher (p. 147), Lowery's similar use of the Cornish dialect in his account of the politically ignorant town crier of St. Ives (pp. 131–2), and Burn's comments on the "primitive simplicity" of cockney (p. 58).

[110] See above, p. 152 "Many a time have I felt my soul light up with a pure and holy fire at the altar of our Shakespeare", he wrote (p. 101).

enriched. In many areas this process could be seen taking place, nowhere more so than in the poetry and songs which were an integral part of all the major protest movements of the period. The writings and, in most cases, the personalities of Byron, Shelley, Bunyan, Wesley, Milton and Shakespeare were incorporated into a lively new radical culture which played an important part in uniting and sustaining the world's first mass working class movement.[111] The ability of the Chartists to synthesize politics and literature was encapsulated in the title of the volume which Cooper edited on behalf of his Association in Leicester, *The Shakespearean Chartist Hymn Book*.[112] Yet there was a constant danger that through their contact with what Brierley called the "higher class of literature", the readers would become separated from the broader culture of their community. The problem was brought to a head over the question of dialect, where, as Cooper's youthful experiments demonstrated, the readers were liable to fall into a state of cultural schizophrenia. In general, the autobiographies of the readers are weakened by their authors' hesitancy about language. Almost all were written in standard English, and very few succeeded in conveying the vitality of the speech forms which contained so much of their experience. The conventions of publication may have been a factor here. John Clare whose two autobiographies were not published in his lifetime, suffered continual interference from editors who insisted on correcting the syntax of his poetry, and there is evidence that at least one of the autobiographies, the posthumously published life of the Scottish ballad singer William Cameron, had been tidied up.[113] But few of the literate autobiographers took advantage of the forms of publication which might be subject to their control to attempt to combine their newly acquired literary sophistication with their inherited oral tradition, and as a result there is a major division between the handful of dialect manuscript memoirs of men who had read very little, and the majority of published works by self-educated men, who, with a few notable exceptions,[114] kept the speech forms of their community very much at arm's length. The dialect autobiographers gain in vigour and directness of expression, but lack the range of experience and insight which the readers possess.

(iii)

The pursuit of knowledge left no area of the readers' lives untouched. The record left by these autobiographers provides a minutely detailed picture of the hopes and fears, triumphs and difficulties of working men who were

[111] See Y. V. Kovalev, "The Literature of Chartism", *Victorian Studies*, vol. II, 1958, pp.122–6; Albert K. Stevens, "Milton and Chartism", *Philological Quarterly*, vol. 11, 1933, pp.377–88; Philip Collins, *Thomas Cooper, The Chartist: Byron and the Poets of the Poor* (Nottingham, 1969); M. Vicinus, op. cit., pp. 57–134.
[112] Published in Leicester in 1843. See Cooper, p. 165.
[113] See the Preface by the editor, John Strathesk.
[114] Particularly Samuel Bamford, forerunner of the Lancashire dialect revival of the third quarter of the century. He used dialect for much of the reported speech in his two autobiographies, and appended a brief glossary to *Passages*. He later published some short stories in dialect and an essay on the subject in *Walks in South Lancashire and on its Borders* (Blackley, 1844) and edited and republished John Collier's *A View of the Lancashire Dialect* . . . (1st edn. 1746; Manchester, 1850). Another Lancashire autobiographer, Ben Brierley, wrote numerous dialect tales between 1870 and 1894 featuring the activities of "Ab-'o'-th'-Yate".

experiencing a profound transformation in their way of life. The evidence of this group of individuals strongly suggests that the complexity of the implications of their actions cannot be reduced to variations in personal circumstances or temperament. Too often we find the same men performing apparently contradictory roles. No one, for instance, was more critical of, or more isolated from his fellow craftsmen than the tailor Thomas Carter, yet when a dispute occurs between the journeymen and the master tailors, it is to him they turn to present their case.[115] No poet was more enamoured of the Romantic view of nature than the miner John Harris, yet his first published poem is, "a polemical dialogue between a workman and his master. This was written soon after a strike for wages among some of the dissatisfied miners in a portion of my own district.".[116] And there is, of course, that most extravagant man, Thomas Cooper, whose kaleidoscopic career refracts almost every aspect of this topic. Such inconsistencies as stand forth from these accounts must be traced back to the nature of the freedom they sought. J. B. Leno, the Uxbridge printer, poet and politician, at one point turns to address his class: "You are endowed with the power of thinking—what for? I ask, if you are not sensitive to the importance of obeying the conclusions to which they lead you?".[117] It was because the readers possessed just this sensitivity that their conclusions were so varied, and, at times, so ambiguous. Their attempt to use book knowledge to emancipate themselves and their class from the influence of irrational beliefs and behaviour caused many difficulties in their relations both with unimproved members of their class and those features of their inherited culture which sustained much of the independence and vitality of their way of life. They encountered a range of social and intellectual pressures which encouraged them to withdraw from the realities of the world in which they found themselves, yet their learning and their skills were indispensable to the emerging working class. No two men displayed the same pattern of responses, but equally none followed a straight, untroubled path towards the goal of self-improvement.

The readers were and have continued to be a minority of their class. Their common experience of the practical difficulties with which they were faced bound them together as a distinct unit within the working class, and permits historians to treat them as a discrete element in the development of class relations in this period. Yet in spite of the sometimes divisive and destructive consequences of their pursuit of knowledge, they remained working men, both in occupation and outlook. The more determined the reader, the more sharply was he made aware of the material deprivation of his class. Wherever his intellectual explorations took him, he could never forget that as he read he was sitting up late at night after his family had gone to bed, or stealing ten minutes from his working day, or denying himself food or recreation. If books could constitute a means of escaping from the harshness of everyday life, in much the same way that drink could provide a temporary release for the unimproved, they would also, unlike alcohol, sooner or later force the reader to see more clearly at least some aspects of the position of his class. The uneducated readers rejected the utilitarian conception of useful knowledge put forward by middle class educators, and, as we have seen, were always able to locate their commitment to moral and intellectual improvement in the history of their personal development. They did not need to borrow values and aspirations from another

[115] Carter, *Memoirs*, p. 169.   [116] Harris, p. 55.   [117] Leno, p. 89.

class, and there is little evidence that they did so. The ambiguity and confusion which is often revealed in the autobiographies owed less to the proximity of the readers' activities to middle class patterns of behaviour and more to their relationship to the pre-industrial popular culture. The mould of that culture was being cracked and broken by the rapid development of every form of communication and the readers were those who made the most determined effort to harness the forces of change. It was in this sense that they may be seen as representative of their class as a whole. As they explored the consequences of the decline of the oral tradition and pushed forward the process of secularization, they were engaging with developments which eventually would permeate every aspect of their 'culture. By placing themselves in the vanguard of change the readers were bound to experience the full effect of the dislocation which it was causing.

There is evidence that they failed to come to terms with some of the implications of their actions, but in view of the scale of the opportunities which were opened up in this period, particularly in the second quarter of the century, this is scarcely surprising. The practical hardship, and the social and intellectual difficulties which have been discussed at various points in Part Three, to some extent belie the confident image which the self-improving working men often presented to outside observers, but in the end it was the affirmative, constructive content of their actions which leaves the deepest impression. These men were convinced that book knowledge could be used to transform the quality of their own lives and that of their class as a whole, and their autobiographies bear striking witness to their life-long attempts to translate their belief into reality. There seems little justification for regarding self-improvement as the "Achilles Heel" of working class militancy.[118] To do so is to both overvalue and devalue the pursuit of knowledge. Not even the most optimistic reader ever regarded the acquisition of useful knowledge and the forms of behaviour and outlook which it generated as being anything more than a precondition, an essential tool for the full emancipation of themselves or their class. If nothing else their continued experience of the material and emotional deprivation examined in the second part of this study, was evidence of the practical limitations of the most single-minded and successful pursuit of knowledge. It is clear that the self-improving working men made an essential contribution to the developing ideology and organization of the working class, and that in the context of an intensification of class hostility, the most sober and rational working men could find themselves in conflict with the law, as the careers of many of the autobiographers demonstrate. There seems no reason to suppose that if these men and their successors had ceased to read books and seek their moral and intellectual improvement, the amelioration of class relations after 1848 would not have taken place. At the same time the readers would argue that liberation comes in many forms, that in the pursuit of knowledge they had discovered a deeply satisfying area of freedom, and that in the midst of the confusion and oppression of their times, this was an achievement worthy of some celebration.

[118] The phrase is Harold Perkin's, from *The Origins of Modern English Society 1780–1880* (London, 1969), p. 289. For a more sophisticated presentation of this thesis, see Trygve R. Tholfsen, *Working Class Radicalism in Mid-Victorian England* (London, 1976).

Chapter Nine

Past and Present

Charles Shaw, the "old Potter", wrote *When I was a Child* in order that a new generation should not forget, ". . . the living, burning and agonising experience of those who lived sixty to seventy years ago".[1] If the memory of that experience was allowed to die, the achievements of those who had suffered so much would count for nothing. "We glibly talk of 'better times' ", he protested, "but this hurrying and superficial generation seldom thinks that these times are richer for the struggles and blood of those who went before them, as the early harvests of the plains of Waterloo were said to be richer after the carnage of the great battle fought there."[2] His autobiography was sustained by the dual conviction that he could only understand himself as an individual in the dimension of time, and that his readership could not hope to comprehend or exploit its present if it ignored or misinterpreted its past.

As they sought to come to terms with the process of change, the autobiographers were faced with the question of whether or not the society in which they were now living represented an advance over the society into which they had been born. On the whole, the prevailing tone was optimistic; the autobiographies were founded on a sense of progress. Many of their authors joined with Shaw in attacking any tendency to romanticize the past. "These were some of the good old times of which we hear people speak about", wrote William Aitken in conclusion to his account of his childhood, "but we may thank God that we have been delivered from such enormities."[3] The poacher James Hawker was characteristically forthright: ". . . It is often said the agricultural labourer seemed a Deal Happier 60 years ago than what they seem to Day. Well, we know there are many men Better off in Prison than what they are out. But they would Rather be out. The Labourer 60 years ago was merely a Serf".[4] Although, as was noted in the previous chapter, the urban workers sometimes looked back to what they imagined was once a better life in the country, the autobiographers were rarely nostalgic about the basic features of the past they had actually experienced.

The most usual criteria for measuring progress were the mutually supportive forces of intellectual and political freedom. Those who were most concerned

---

[1] Shaw, p. 133.   [2] *Ibid.*, p. 36.   [3] Aitken, 25 Sept., p. 3.
[4] Hawker, p. 76.

with the evils of child labour in the early decades of the century made reference to the beneficial influence of factory legislation, but there was little direct comment on the basic question of material prosperity. Rather, the autobiographers focussed their attention on the extent to which the working man's control over his situation had increased during his lifetime. The slow but apparently inexorable advance towards the vote, together with the rapid improvement in the network of communications, which included the printed word, the railways and popular education, were placed at the centre of the historical process. Alexander Somerville's faith in progress was founded on four pillars:

> Universal enfranchisement, railways, electric telegraphs, public schools (the greatest of the moral levers for elevating mankind named last—because last to be advocated, which should have been first); these are some of the elements of a moral faith, believing in the universal brotherhood of mankind, which I daily hold, and never doubt upon; which I believe will as certainly be realised, as I believe that *good*, and not *evil*, was the object of all creation, and is the end of all existence.[5]

Twenty years later William Lovett was able to look back on ". . . the progress of knowledge among our people by means of the press, the school and the rail . . .".[6] His contemporary James Watson described his youth as a time when, ". . . there were no cheap books, no cheap newspapers or periodicals, no Mechanics' Institutes to facilitate the acquisition of knowledge. The government was then in the hands of the clergy and aristocracy, the people, ignorant and debased, taking no part in politics, except once in seven years, when the elections were scenes of degradation and corruption".[7] A central theme of Thomas Frost's life-history was, ". . . the progress which has been achieved during that time in all that tends to the moral and intellectual dignity of humanity".[8] "When I began", concluded Joseph Arch, "the farm labourer had nothing. Now he has the political telephone of the vote, his Board Schools, his County Councils, his Parish Councils."[9]

This was very much a collective view of progress. Those of the autobiographers who had taken part in the struggle for knowledge and freedom obviously derived personal satisfaction from describing the success of their endeavours, but throughout the concern was with the advancement of the class rather than the individual. There is, in the end, little evidence that in embracing the art-form of the autobiography they were distancing themselves from the aspirations of their class, or standing aside from the culture in which they had spent their lives. At the same time, a life-history is not a general history, and it is possible to identify a number of conflicts which arose between the private and public perspective on the passage of time.

As a category of source material, autobiographies draw attention to the sheer diversity of human experience. The infinite variation in the patterns of occupational and family life, and in the forms and fortunes of attempts at self-improvement and self-expression which are to be found in these works serve as a necessary reminder that the shared experience of particular material and

---

[5] Somerville, p. 361.   [6] Lovett, p. 14.   [7] Watson, p. 109.
[8] Frost, *Recollections*, p. 28. See also Oliver, p. 11; Farish, *Autobiography*, p. 11; Thomson, p. 108; Gutteridge, pp. 273–4; Sutton, p. 18; Robinson, pp. 37–8.
[9] Arch, p. 403. See also Rymer, p. 20.

ideological forces did not produce identical life-histories. This point was established in chapter three at the end of a discussion of love and bereavement, but its application is not confined to the family. The less command an individual could exercise over his productive and reproductive life, and the greater his vulnerability to the workings of the labour market, to ill-health and to death, the less stable was every aspect of his existence. The more the outline of his life was determined by market forces, the more its detail was determined by luck, good or bad. Jobs were found or lost, children lived or died, all that was certain was uncertainty. As the worker's economic power increased, so did his capacity to gain some independence of blind fate, but as the artisan autobiographers constantly emphasized, the most skilled and prosperous labouring man rarely enjoyed prolonged security. It is something of a paradox that the middle and upper classes, whose lives exhibited a more regular pattern through their greater command over the means of existence, should have received the attention of the majority of biographers, whilst the working class, who not only constituted the bulk of the population but whose lives were more diverse, should have been the subject of only a handful of such studies. This comparative neglect is partly a product of a reaction against supposedly middle class forms of historiography, and partly a reflection of the poverty of the available source material, and it is to be hoped that the collection and examination of these autobiographies will accelerate the growing interest in the biographies of working men and women.[10]

It was inevitable that those whose lives were dominated by the struggle for existence, who were least successful in establishing some fleeting control over their material circumstances, should have been less concerned to speculate about the general progress of their class. At the end of their days they were more likely to be preoccupied with the increasing practical difficulties which beset all working men as their strength declined and their families dispersed. Such was the case with the itinerant cutler and occasional poet James Murdoch, whose memoir ended with its author in his mid-fifties, confined by a bedridden wife to a village too small to provide him with an adequate living. His autobiography was written less as a celebration of his life's achievements than as a last attempt to stave off destitution.

Those autobiographers still writing in the religious tradition, whose accounts were organized around their spiritual development, could encompass their increasing hardships without difficulty. *The Life, Experience and Correspondence of William Bowcock, the Lincolnshire Drillman* reached its conclusion as its author lay dying of cancer of the jaw.[11] Although he made no attempt to conceal his physical pain, he could present the experience as a culmination rather than a denial of his life's progress. Those, however, whose narratives centred on their struggle for intellectual and political emancipation, found the task less easy. The most dramatic failure to connect a belief in the advance of mankind with

[10] The number of satisfactory full-length biographies of nineteenth century working men is still limited, although A. R. Schoyen's *The Chartist Challenge* (London, 1958) and F. B. Smith's *Radical Artisan, William James Linton 1812–97* (Manchester, 1973) show what can be done. There is, however, an increasing volume of shorter biographies, particularly in John Saville and Joyce M. Bellamy, eds., *Dictionary of Labour Biography*, vols. 1– (1972–) and Joseph O. Baylen and Norbert J. Gossman, *Biographical Dictionary of Modern British Radicals*, vol. 1, 1770–1830 (Hassocks, 1979).
[11] Bowcock, pp. 149–50.

mounting personal misfortune was that of the former spinner and teacher William Aitken, who in his fifty-sixth year began to write his life-history for publication in the *Ashton-under-Lyne News*. The third chapter appeared on page three of the issue of Saturday, 2 October, 1869 and contained several ringing declarations of faith in the power of reason, and in the ultimate success of the demand for the vote. On page eight there was published his obituary followed by a report of the inquest into his suicide the previous Monday. The only clue to this act was provided by his wife, who gave evidence of depression caused by ill-health which had recently forced her husband to give up work. Two further chapters had been completed before his death, and these give no indication of the growing private despair which had accompanied his public confidence.

The narratives of past struggles were also full of tensions between a sense of progress and one of personal difficulty or uncertainty. It was not only that the pursuit of knowledge and freedom frequently entailed great sacrifice on the part of the individual and often his unfortunate family as well, but that the process of moral and intellectual improvement generated a series of dilemmas and conflicts—many of which were discussed in the second half of chapter eight. Common to most of the problems faced by self-improving working men was the difficulty of establishing satisfactory personal relations with those amongst whom they lived and worked. These men had compounded the inevitable disruption caused to the communities of the labouring poor by the trans-formation in the pattern of labour and the move from the country into the towns, by adopting values and forms of behaviour which were often in direct conflict with both their inherited culture and the practices and outlook of the majority of their class. The organizations which were developed to enhance the pursuit of knowledge and freedom were usually short-lived and provided insubstantial support to men whose commitment demanded at least inter-mittent rejection of the company of family and friends. Many found the bitter conflicts over such matters as drinking habits and forms of religious belief extremely painful, and others suffered from a sense of disorientation as they responded to the upheavals in their world by exploiting new forms of com-munication.

Unless they retained a strong identification with their class and a clear grasp of its place in the organization of production, they were always vulnerable to the suggestion that the gulf between their faith in progress and their continuing private troubles could be explained by shortcomings in their character or judgement. James Burn's *Autobiography of a Beggar Boy* described his odyssey from his early life as the illegitimate step-son of an alcoholic beggar and pedlar to his goal of respectability. Along the road he realized many ambitions, including entry into a skilled trade, his self-education and subsequent develop-ment of a considerable natural talent as a writer, and his elevation to positions of leadership in his trade union, in working class radicalism in Glasgow during the Reform Bill crisis, and in the Oddfellows movement. The publication and favourable reception of his autobiography in 1855 seemed to set the seal on his achievement, yet the interpretation which it contained was deeply flawed by his inability to come to terms with the series of economic reverses and ideological disputes which had dogged his adult life as a self-improving artisan. Having entered both his trade and the rapidly expanding industrial city of Glasgow at a comparatively late age, he always felt something of a stranger, and it is clear that his relentless search for respectability, combined with the long-term decline of his trade and the rapidly changing pattern of working class politics in the 1830s and '40s, undermined what chance he had of finding a home. His pursuit of reason and moral improvement could not prevent endless occupational setbacks, and eventually alienated him from the vigorous political culture of the city. He remained committed to the goals which had drawn him forwards, and had no doubt that the condition of his class had shown a major advance during his lifetime, yet amidst his celebration he confessed that, "at the end of fifty years I am more disappointed in myself than I have been in all the world beside".[12] Burn's situation was unusually complex, but his basic problem had to be faced by all the more literate autobiographers as they sought to reconcile their individual experiences with their general conclusions about the nature of historical change.

It was only to be expected that so large and inexperienced a group of writers should display considerable variation in their response to the challenge of the form of the autobiography. It was one thing to reject the spiritual autobiographers' essentially subjective view of the outside world, and it was quite another to achieve a successful interpretation of the life-long interaction between the individual and the society in which he had lived. For most of these men and women, their autobiographies represented their first and only venture into sustained prose composition, and it is not surprising that they should find the task of resolving the conflicts and contradictions of their past experience extremely difficult. Yet they remained committed to the view that the only way in which the self and the world could be understood was historically, and in the end there were a number of convincing reasons why they should reach a verdict that their lives were evidence of a forward movement in history.

In the first instance, although these autobiographies record a wide range of physical and emotional hardships many of which have been discussed under the headings of their family life and their pursuit of knowledge, it needs to be emphasized that they also constitute a record of an immense variety of private pleasures, some trivial, others deeply satisfying. The historiography of the working class has inevitably been influenced by the fact that the labouring poor were frequently only visible when their discontent spilled over into active protest, and one of the abiding virtues of this form of source material is that it allows working men and women to present a more complete picture of themselves. At times the pleasures are recorded in order to measure and evaluate some greater pain; elsewhere, as I indicated in chapter two, they are paraded before the reader that he might be entertained and that he might broaden his knowledge of the complexity and wealth of the working class culture. In some of the autobiographies the stream of anecdotes takes over the accounts and allows the writers to escape what must always have been the difficult task of recounting the suffering in their lives, but in the majority they contribute to a more balanced and convincing account of their past. Their presence was essential for the discussion in part two, where a central theme was that the emotional satisfactions and material demands of the working class family

[12] Burn, p. 172.

existed in a complex relationship in which the areas of love and emotional support could both survive and offer some limited compensation for the widespread deprivation. No man suffered more, both in his family life and in his intellectual endeavours, than the Coventry ribbon weaver Joseph Gutteridge, yet the title he gave to his autobiography, *Lights and Shadows in the Life of an Artisan*, was a perfectly accurate description of its contents.

The picture was rarely completely black and the majority of the autobiographers were encouraged by their attempts to improve themselves and their class, and in particular by their discovery of the uses of the written word. The connection between knowledge and freedom has been discussed at some length in the preceding three chapters, but a central conclusion was that the industrial revolution was bringing with it the means by which working men could eventually overcome the evils it was causing. In the sphere of education, and in the pursuit of useful knowledge, the exploitation of the new means of communication offered the possibility of harnessing the forces of change to the interests of the emerging class. Largely because of the prevailing relationship between literacy and the organization of production, the acquisition of book knowledge at school and as adults was undertaken for largely non-instrumental reasons, and the problems facing the readers together with the demand for their skills which existed amongst the non-literate, ensured that the emphasis remained upon the element of collective enterprise, in spite of the latent pressures towards division and isolation. The intellectual freedom they had gained and the more tangible freedoms they had moved towards with its aid, constituted a measurable advance in the independence of themselves and their class.

The autobiographies were a final form of communication, in some cases the crowning achievement of a long career of employing the techniques of literacy, in others the first and last venture into an unfamiliar mode of expression. They presupposed the possibility of a dialogue between the writer and a wider audience, which need not necessarily be confined to his family or his class. In this sense they must be seen as both a product of and a contribution towards the amelioration of class relations during the second half of the century. Their view of progress did not necessarily lead them into the arms of the Liberal Party. The idea that an industrial revolution is an essential step on the road towards the emancipation of the working class was fundamental to nineteenth century Marxism; a man like the Uxbridge compositor, poet and Chartist, J. B. Leno, could live on to meet William Morris and welcome the revival of socialism in the 1880s. As we have seen, the readers were resistant to the suggestion that useful knowledge and the values which it engendered were held on licence from their social superiors, and in the context of the increasing tensions in the economic sphere in the 1830s and '40s, their commitment could lead them into direct confrontation with the middle class. But from the very beginning there had existed a market for the life-histories of men whose belief in reason and enthusiasm for good literature suggested that the culture of the new working class might not be as alien as it so often appeared, and there is no doubt that many of the mid-century autobiographers were sensible of the welcome their life-histories would receive. In calmer waters, the pursuit of knowledge did offer common ground between the classes, ground which might yield a more fruitful harvest than Brougham and his associates raised in the

1830s, and its leading working class protagonists, particularly Lovett and Cooper, did become heroes to the class in whose interest both had once been imprisoned. For their part it was not difficult for those who had striven so hard for intellectual and political freedom to convince themselves that society was becoming more rational and that enfranchisement was at hand. The actions and ambitions recorded in these autobiographies did not in themselves cause the relaxation of class tensions in the 1850s and beyond, but it can be argued that the existence of that record, the existence of the communication, did play some part in it.

Although some of the autobiographies were written as an intervention in a battle the author was still waging, the majority were written in old age when reflection seemed more appropriate than action. This undoubtedly assisted the exchange between the classes, an old man always seems less dangerous than a young one, and it is of course true that the older the autobiographer, and the more distant he was from the experiences and conflicts which had formed his outlook, the less representative he was of the rising generation who had to formulate a new response to a changed world. Yet any attempt to change the present embodies a view of the past, and the true relevance of these auto-biographies to the second half of the century is that they yield some insight into what was known and believed about the events of the first half. The working class had few history books other than these autobiographies, no historians other than those who remembered and the few who wrote.

The final, and perhaps most convincing reason why the autobiographers believed that some progress had been made by the labouring poor during their lifetime was the simple fact that they had been able to write an autobiography. This book began with the opening lines of James Bowd's brief memoir. In his second paragraph, the Cambridgeshire farm labourer introduced his family: "For my descent then it was of a low inconsiderable Generation my father's hous beign of that Class of people that are so Lightly esteemed".[13] It was because that same class of people had now formed a larger estimation of themselves that these life-histories were written. The autobiographies were sustained by and in turn transmit a deep sense of pride in the way of life they describe.

[13] Bowd, p. 293.

Bibliography

I. Working Class Autobiographies 1790–1850

Editions subsequent to the first are only given where a later edition has been used for this study.

William Edwin Adams, *Memoirs of a Social Atom*, 2 vols. (London, 1903).

William Aitken, "Remembrances and the Struggles of a Working Man for Bread and Liberty", *Ashton-under-Lyne News*, 18 and 25 Sept., 2, 9 and 16 Oct., 1869.

Isaac Anderson, *The Life History of Isaac Anderson* (n. d.)

Joseph Arch, *Joseph Arch, The Story of his Life. Told by Himself*, edited with a preface by the Countess of Warwick (London, 1898).

George William Ayliffe, *Old Kingston: Recollections of an Octogenarian from 1830 and Onwards with Reminiscences of Hampton Wick* (Kingston-upon-Thames, 1914).

Samuel Bamford, *Early Days* (London, 1849); *Passages in the Life of a Radical*, 2 vols. (3rd edn., London, 1844).

(Josiah Basset), *The Life of a Vagrant or the Testimony of an Outcast to the Value and Truth of the Gospel* (London, 1850).

Janet Bathgate, *Aunt Janet's legacy to her nieces: recollections of humble life in Yarrow in the beginning of the century* (3rd edn., Selkirk, 1895).

(William Bayzand), "Coaching in and out of Oxford, From 1820 to 1840 by A Chip of the Old Block", *Oxford Historical Society*, vol. 47 (1905), pp. 267–309 [MS. written c. 1884].

(John James Bezer), "The Autobiography of one of the Chartist Rebels of 1848", *Christian Socialist*, 6 Sept.–13 Dec. 1851, republished in David Vincent, ed., *Testaments of Radicalism* (London, 1977), pp. 153–87.

Joseph Blacket, "Autobiographical Letter", in *Specimens of the Poetry of Joseph Blacket, with an account of his Life, and some introductory observations* (London, 1809).

John Blow, *Autobiography* (Leeds, 1870).

William Bowcock, *The Life, Experience, and Correspondence of William Bowcock, the Lincolnshire Drillman. Written by Himself* (London, 1851).

James Bowd, "The Life of a Farm Worker", *The Countryman*, vol. LI, no. 2 (1955) [MS. begun 1889].

Benjamin Brierley, *Home Memories and Recollections of a Life* (Manchester, 1886).

William Brown, *A Narrative of the Life and Adventures of William Brown* (York, 1829).

James Dawson Burn, *The Autobiography of a Beggar Boy*, edited with an introduction by David Vincent (London, 1978) [1st edn., 1855].

Mrs. Burrows, "A Childhood in the Fens about 1850–1860", in Margaret Llewelyn Davies, ed., *Life as We Have Known It, by Co-operative Working Women* (1931).

Robert Butler, *Narrative of the Life and Travels of Serjeant Butler. Written by Himself* (Edinburgh, 1823, 3rd edn., Edinburgh, 1854).

William Cameron, *Hawkie, The Autobiography of a Gangrel*, edited by John Strathesk (Glasgow, 1888) [MS. begun 1840].

Harry Carter, *The Autobiography of a Cornish Smuggler, 1749–1809*, edited with an introduction by John B. Cornish (Truro, 1894) [MS. written 1809].

(Thomas Carter), *Memoirs of a Working Man* (London, 1845); *A Continuation of the Memoirs of a Working Man* (London, c. 1850).

John Castle, "Memoirs", in A. F. J. Brown, ed., *Essex People 1750–1900* (Chelmsford, 1972) [MS. written 1871].

W. H. Chadwick, "Reminiscences", *Bury Times*, 24 Feb. 1894.

(Daniel Chatterton), *Biography of Dan Chatterton, Atheist and Communist, by Chat* (London, 1891).

James Child, "An Autobiography of James Child", MS., transcribed by F. V. Child [MS. begun 1913].

John Clare, "The Autobiography, 1793–1824", in J. W. and Anne Tibble, eds., *The Prose of John Clare* (London, 1951); *Sketches in the Life of John Clare. Written by Himself and Addressed to his Friend John Taylor esq.*, edited by Edmund Blunden (London, 1931) [MS. written 1821].

Elspeth Clark, "97th Birthday Reminiscences", *Elgin Courant*, 19 Sept. 1941.

Timothy Claxton, *Hints to Mechanics on Self-Education and Mutual Instruction* (London, 1839).

Thomas Cooper, *The Life of Thomas Cooper, written by himself* (London, 1872).

Robert Crowe, *Reminiscences of an Octogenarian* (New York, c. 1902).

R. D., "Autobiography", in *Autobiographies of Industrial School Children* (London, 1865), pp. 11–14.

Nathaniel Dale, *The Eventful Life of Nathaniel Dale with recollections and anecdotes . . .* (Kimbolton, c. 1871).

Thomas Davies, *Short Sketches from the life of Thomas Davies* (Haverfordwest, n.d.) [MS. written c. 1887].

Edward G. Davis, *Some Passages from My Life* (Birmingham, 1898).

William Dodd, *A Narrative of the Experiences and Sufferings, William Dodd, A Factory Cripple, Written by Himself* (London, 1841).

(Joseph Donaldson), *Recollections of an Eventful Life Chiefly Passed in the Army. By a Soldier* (Glasgow, 1825).

James Downing, *A Narrative of the Life of James Downing (A Blind Man) late a Private in his Majesty's 20th Regiment of Foot. Containing Historical, Naval, Military, Moral, Religious and Entertaining Reflections. Composed by Himself in easy Verse . . .* (London, 3rd edn., 1815).

"Dundee Factory Boy", *Chapters in the Life of a Dundee Factory Boy*, edited by J. Myles (Dundee, 1850).

Snowden Dunhill, *The Life of Snowden Dunhill, Written by Himself; Giving a particular account of his early years; his marriage; his various robberies; prosecution by Mr. Bernard Clarkson; sentenced to the Hulks; released therefrom and commences a fresh course of crime; tried a second time, and sentenced to transportation. Also an account of his wife and children* (5th edn., Howden, 1834).

Thomas Dunning, "Reminiscences of Thomas Dunning", in David Vincent, op. cit., pp. 119–146 [MS. written c. 1890].

Anthony Errington, "Particulars of my life and transactions", MS., transcribed by P. E. H. Hair [MS. written 1823].

William Farish, *The Autobiography of William Farish—the struggles of a handloom weaver with some of his writings* (?, 1889); *Reminiscences of an old Teetotaller* (Liverpool, 1890).

John C. Farn, "The Autobiography of a Living Publicist", *The Reasoner*, 16 Sept.– 23 Dec. 1857.

Thomas Frost, *Forty Years' Recollections, Literary and Political* (London, 1880); *Reminiscences of a Country Journalist* (London, 1886).

(William Green), *The Life and Adventures of a Cheap Jack by One of the Fraternity*, edited by Charles Hindley (London, 1876).

Joseph Gutteridge, *Lights and Shadows in the Life of an Artisan* (Coventry, 1893).

"Bill H-.", *The Autobiography of a Working Man*, edited by The Hon. Eleanor Eden (London, 1862).

Richard Hampton, *Foolish Dick: An Autobiography of Richard Hampton, the Cornish Pilgrim Preacher*, edited by S. W. Christophers (London, 1873).

George Hanby, *Autobiography of a Colliery Weighman* (Barnsley, 1874).

William Hanson, *The Life of William Hanson Written by Himself* (*In his 80th Year*) (Halifax, 1883).

Thomas Hardy, *Memoir of Thomas Hardy, Founder of, and Secretary to, the London Corresponding Society for Diffusing Useful Political Knowledge among the People of Great Britain and Ireland and for Promoting Parliamentary Reform, From its Establishment in Jan. 1792 until his arrest on a False Charge of High Treason On the 12th of May 1794. Written by Himself* (London, 1832), reprinted in David Vincent, op. cit., pp. 31–102.

John Harris, *My Autobiography* (London, 1882).

James Hawker, "The Life of a Poacher", MS., published as, Garth Christian, ed. and intro., *A Victorian Poacher. James Hawker's Journal* (Oxford, 1978).

Joseph Haynes, "The Life of Joseph Haynes . . ." MS. [written c. 1913].

George Healey, *Life and Remarkable Career of George Healey* (Birmingham, c. 1890).

William Heaton, *The Old Soldier; The Wandering Lover; and other poems; together with A Sketch of the Author's Life* (London, 1857).

George Herbert, *Shoemaker's Window. Recollections of a Midland Town before the Railway Age*, edited by Christiana S. Cheney (Oxford, 1948) [MS. written 1898–1900].

Henry Herbert, *Autobiography of Henry Herbert, a Gloucestershire Shoemaker, and Native of Fairford* (Gloucester, 1866).

Henry Hetherington, MS. Autobiography, Holyoake Collection, no. 216.

James Hogg, "Memoir of the Author's Life", in *The Mountain Bard* (1807).

James Hopkinson, "Memoirs", published as, Jocelyne Baty Goodman, ed., *Victorian Cabinet Maker, The Memoirs of James Hopkinson 1819–1894* (London, 1968) [MS. begun 1888].

Moses Horler, *The Early Recollections of Moses Horler*, edited by Mabel Frances Coombs and Howard Coombs (Radstock, 1900).

Catherine Horne, "Recollections", *Bury Times*, 18 Nov. 1911.

William Innes, "Autobiography of William Innes", in David Dickson, ed., *Memorials of a Faithful Servant, William Innes* (Edinburgh, 1876).

Arthur Jewitt, "Passages in the Life of Arthur Jewitt up to the year 1794", MS. [written 1844–9].

William Johnston, *The Life and Times of William Johnston, Horticultural Chemist, Gardener and Cartwright, Peterhead; written by himself . . .*, edited by Reginald Alenarley (Peterhead, 1859).

John Jones, "Some Account of the Writer, written by himself", in *Attempts in verse . . . With some account of the writer, written by himself, and an introductory essay on the lives and works of our uneducated poets, by Robert Southey, Poet Laureate* (London, 1831).

John Kitson, "Scetch . . . of my Life", MS. [written c. 1854].

Roger Langdon, *The Life of Roger Langdon, told by himself* (London, 1909).

William Lawrence, *The Autobiography of Sergeant William Lawrence, a hero of the Peninsular and Waterloo Campaigns*, edited by G. N. Bankes (London, 1886).

J. A. Leatherland, *Essays and Poems with a brief Autobiographical Memoir* (London, 1862).

John Bedford Leno, *The Aftermath: with Autobiography of the Author* (London, 1892).

Joseph Lingard, *A Narrative of the Journey to and from New South Wales, including a seven years' residence in that country* (Chapel-en-le-Frith, 1846).

William James Linton, *Memories* (London, 1895).

Robert Loisan, *Confessions of Robert Loisan, alias, Rambling Bob* (Beverley, ? 1870).

David Love, *The Life, Adventures and Experience of David Love* (Nottingham, 1823–4).

Emanuel Lovekin, "Some notes of my life", MS. [written c. 1895].

William Lovett, *Life and Struggles of William Lovett In his Pursuit of Bread, Knowledge & Freedom, with some short Account of the different Associations he belonged to & of the Opinions he entertained* (London, 1876).

Robert Lowery, "Passages in the Life of a Temperance Lecturer Connected with the Public Movements of the Working Classes for the last Twenty Years, By One of Their Order", *Weekly Record of the Temperance Movement* 15 April 1856–30 May 1857, reprinted in Brian Harrison and Patricia Hollis, ed. and intro., *Robert Lowery, Radical and Chartist* (London, 1979).

Lucy Luck, "A Little of my Life", *London Mercury* Nov. 1925–April 1926, reprinted in, John Burnett, ed., *Useful Toil* (London, 1974), pp. 68–77.

William Mabey, "A History of the life of William Mabey written from memory at 82 years of age", MS. [written c. 1930].

Charles H. McCarthy, *Chartist Recollections. A Bradfordian's Reminiscences* (Bradford, 1883).

Allan McEwan, *A Short Account of the Life of Allan M'Ewan, Late Sergeant 72nd Highlanders. Written by himself for the benefit of his children* (Dumbarton, 1890).

Peter MacKenzie, *A Short Account of Some Strange Adventures and Mishaps in the Strange Life of a Strange Man* (Elgin, 1869).

John Donkin McNaughton, *The Life and Happy Experience of John Donkin M'Naughton, written by himself* (Stokesley, ? 1810).

George Marsh, "A Sketch of the Life of George Marsh, A Yorkshire Collier 1834–1921", MS. [written 1912].

Jonathan Martin, *The life of Jonathan Martin of Darlington, Tanner, Written By Himself* (Darlington, 1825).

Robert Maybee, *Sixty-eight Years' Experience on the Scilly Islands* (Penzance, 1884).

Joseph Mayett, MS. Autobiography [written c. 1830–39].

George Miller, *A Trip to Sea from 1810 to 1815* (Long Sutton, 1854).

Alex Mitchell, *The Recollections of a Lifetime* (Aberdeen, 1911).

Timothy Mountjoy, *Sixty-two years in the Life of a Forest of Dean Collier* (1887), reprinted in *Hard Times in the Forest* (Coleford, 1971).

James Murdoch, *The Autobiography and Poems of James Murdoch, known as 'Cutler Jaimie'* (Elgin, 1863).

Hamlet Nicholson, *An Autobiographical and full historical account of Hamlet Nicholson In his opposition to Ritualism at the Rochdale Parish Church. Also an account of his work in the Conservative Interest from 1832 to 1892, together with Other Personal Narratives* (1892).

John Nicol, *The Life and Adventures of John Nicol, Mariner* (Edinburgh, 1824).

Thomas Oliver, *Autobiography of a Cornish Miner* (Camborne, 1914).

George Parkinson, *True stories of Durham pit-life* (London, 1912).

John Plummer, *Songs of Labour, Northamptonshire Rambles and other Poems (with an Autobiographical Sketch of the Author's Life)* (London and Kettering, 1860).

Henry Edward Price, "Diary", MS. Autobiography [written 1904].

"Printer's Devil", *Memoirs of a Printer's Devil; Interspersed with Pleasing Recollections, Local Descriptions, and Anecdotes* (Gainsborough, 1793).

Henry Quick, *The Life and Progress of Henry Quick of Zenor, written by himself* (Penzance, 1872).

Samuel Robinson, *Reminiscences of Wigtonshire about the Close of Last Century* (Hamilton, 1872).

Edward Allen Rymer, *The Martyrdom of the Mine or A 60 Years' Struggle for Life Dedicated to the Miners of England, 1898* (Middlesborough, 1898).

Jonathan Saville, *Memoirs of Jonathan Saville of Halifax Including his Autobiography*, edited by Francis A. West (3rd edn., London, 1848).

James Scott, *Autobiography of James Scott, Stotfield* (? 1883).

(Charles Shaw), *When I Was a Child by An Old Potter* (London, 1903).

Joseph Sketchley, "Personal Experiences in the Chartist Movement", *Today*, no. 7 (July 1884).

(Charles Manby Smith), *The Working-Man's Way in the World: being the Autobiography of a Journeyman Printer* (London, c. 1853).

Mary Smith, *The Autobiography of Mary Smith, Schoolmistress and Nonconformist. A Fragment of a Life. With letters from Jane Welsh Carlyle and Thomas Carlyle* (London and Carlisle, 1892).

William Smith, "The Memoir of William Smith", edited by Barry Trinder, *Shropshire Archaeological Society Transactions*, vol. LVIII, pt. 2 (1965–8), pp. 178–85 [MS. written 1904].

John Snowden, "The Career of a Humble Radical", *Halifax Courier*, 6 Sept. 1894.

Alexander Somerville, *The Autobiography of a Working Man* (London, 1848).

Robert Spurr, "Autobiography", published as, R. J. Owen, ed., "The Autobiography of Robert Spurr", *Baptist Quarterly*, vol. 26 (April 1976), pp. 282–8.

"Stonemason", *Reminiscences of a Stonemason, By a Working Man* (London, 1908).

Robert Story, *Love and Literature; being The Reminiscences, Literary Opinions and Fugitive Pieces of A Poet in Humble Life* (London, 1842); "Preface", in *The Poetical Works of Robert Story* (London, 1857).

Benjamin Stott, *Songs for the Millions and other Poems* (London, 1843).

"Suffolk Farm Labourer", "Autobiography of a Suffolk Farm Labourer With Recollections of Incidents and Events that have occurred in Suffolk during the Sixty Years from 1816 to 1876", ed. "Rambler", *Suffolk Times and Mercury*, 2 Nov. 1894–16 Aug. 1895.

William Sutton, *Multum in parvo; or The Ups and Downs of a Village Gardener* (Kenilworth, 1903).

John Taylor, *Autobiography of John Taylor* (Bath, 1893).

Peter Taylor, *The Autobiography of Peter Taylor* (Paisley, 1903).

Harvey Teasdale, *Life and Adventures of Harvey Teasdale, the Converted Clown and Man Monkey: with his Remarkable Conversion in Wakefield Prison. Written by Himself* (20th edn., Sheffield, 1881).

John Teer, *Silent Musings* (Manchester, 1869).

(W. H. L. Tester), *Holiday Reading. Sketches of La Teste's Life on the Road* (Elgin, 1882).

John Thelwall, "Prefatory Memoir", in *Poems Chiefly Written in Retirement* (Hereford, 1801).

William Thom, *Rhymes and Recollections of a Hand-Loom Weaver* (London, 1844).

Christopher Thomson, *The Autobiography of an Artisan* (London, 1847).

(John D. Tough), *A Short Narrative of the Life, and Some Incidents in the Recollection, of an Aberdonian, nearly eighty years of age* (Aberdeen, 1848).

James Watson, "Reminiscences", *The Reasoner*, vol. 16 (5 Feb. 1854), reprinted in David Vincent, op. cit., pp. 107–111.

Henry White, *The Record of My Life: An Autobiography* (Cheltenham, 1889).

Benjamin Wilson, *The Struggles of an Old Chartist: What he knows, and the part he has taken in various movements* (Halifax, 1887), reprinted in David Vincent, op. cit., pp. 193–242.

John Wood, *Autobiography of John Wood, an old and well-known Bradfordian, Written in the 75th Year of his Age* (Bradford, 1877).

Thomas Wood, *The Autobiography of Thomas Wood, 1822–1880* (1956) [MS. written 1878].

"A Working Man", *Scenes from my Life, By a Working Man*, with a preface by the Rev. Robert Maguire, M.A. (London, 1858).

James D. Wright, *Steeple Jack's Adventures, Being the Recollections of James D. Wright, The Original Steeple Jack* (Aberdeen, n.d.).

John Younger, *Autobiography of John Younger, Shoemaker, St. Boswells* (Kelso, 1881).

II. Other Autobiographical Works

F. Atkins, *Reminiscences of a Temperance Advocate* (London, 1899).

St. Augustine, *Confessions*, trans. R. S. Pine-Coffin (Harmondsworth, 1971).

Alexander Bain, *Autobiography* (London, 1904).

Samuel Bamford, *An Account of the Arrest and Imprisonment of Samuel Bamford, Middleton, on suspicion of High Treason Written by Himself* (Manchester, 1817).

George Barnes, *From Workshop to War Cabinet* (London, 1923).

John F. Bayliss, ed. *Black Slave Narratives* (New York, 1970).

John Binns, *Recollections* (Philadelphia, 1854).

Ulrich Bräker, *The Life Story and Real Adventures of the Poor Man of Toggenburg*, edited by Derek Bowman (Edinburgh, 1970).

Henry Broadhurst, *The Story of his life from Stonemason's Bench to a Treasury Bench, Told by Himself* (London, 1901).

John Buckley, *A Village Politician; the Life-story of John Buckley*, edited by J. C. Buckmaster (London, 1897).

John Bunyan, *Grace Abounding to the Chief of Sinners* (London, 1969 edn.).

John Burnett, ed. *Useful Toil* (London, 1974).

Thomas Burt, *Thomas Burt, M.P., D.C.L., Pitman and Privy Councillor, An Autobiography* (London, 1924).

William Chambers, *Memoir of Robert Chambers with Autobiographical Reminiscences of William Chambers* (London, 4th edn., 1872).

Mary Collier, *Poems, on Several Occasions . . . with some remarks on her life* (Winchester, 1762).

James Dunn, *From Coal Mine Upwards* (London, 1910).

George Edwards, *From Crow Scaring to Westminster* (London, 1922).

Ebenezer Elliott, "Autobiography", *The Athenaeum*, 12 Jan. 1850.

Wolfgang Emmerich, ed. *Proletarische Lebensläufe*, 2 vols. (Reinbeck bei Hamburg, 1974, 1975).

Olaudah Equiano, *The Interesting Narrative of the Life of Olaudah Equiano, or Gustavus Vassa, the African, written by himself* (1789).

Arise Evans, *An eccho to the voice from heaven. Or a narration of the life, and manner of the special calling, and visions of Arise Evans . . .* (1652).

W. H. Fitchett, ed. *Wellington's Men, Some Soldier Autobiographies* (London, 1900).

John Green, *Vicissitudes of a Soldier's Life* (London, 1827).

Lilias Rider Haggard, ed. *I Walked by Night, Being the Life and History of the King of the Norfolk Poachers* (London, 1935).

John Harris, *Recollections of Rifleman Harris*, edited by H. Curling (London, 1848).

John Hodge, *Workman's Cottage to Windsor Castle* (London, 1931).

G. J. Holyoake, *Bygones Worth Remembering*, 2 vols. (London, 1905).

William Hutton, *The Life of William Hutton . . .* (2nd edn., London, 1817).

Thomas Jackson, ed. *The Lives of early Methodist Preachers Chiefly written by themselves*, 3 vols. (London, 1837–8).

Charles Knight, *Passages of a Working Life During Half a Century*, 2 vols. (London, 1864–5).

John Langley, *Always a Layman* (Brighton, 1976).

Tom Mann, *Tom Mann's Memoirs* (London, 1923).

Hugh Miller, *My Schools and Schoolmasters* (Edinburgh, 1854).

George Mitchell, "Autobiography and Reminiscences of George Mitchell, 'One from the plough' ", in Stephen Price, ed. *The Skeleton at the Plough, or the Poor Farm Labourers of the West* (London, c. 1875).

Will Paynter, *My Generation* (London, 1972).

Francis Place, *The Autobiography of Francis Place*, edited by Mary Thrale (Cambridge, 1972).

Robert Roberts, *The Classic Slum* (Manchester, 1971); *A Ragged Schooling* (Manchester, 1976).

Frederick Rogers, *Labour, Life and Literature. Some Memories of Sixty Years* (London, 1913).
Adam Rushton, *My Life as Farmer's Boy, Factory Lad, Teacher and Preacher* (Manchester, 1909).
Samuel Smiles, *Autobiography* (London, 1905).
Silas Told, *An Account of the Life and Dealings of God with Silas Told* (London, 1786).
Thomas Tryon, *Some Memoirs of the Life of Mr. Tho: Tryon, late of London, merchant: written by himself* (1705).
John Whiting, *Persecution Expos'd in some Memoirs relating to the Sufferings of John Whiting* (1715).
Thomas Whittaker, *Life's Battle in Temperance Armour* (London, 1884).

III. General Primary Material

Samuel Bamford, *The Dialect of South Lancashire, or, Tim Bobbin's Tummus and Meary with His Rhymes and an enlarged Glossary of Words and Phrases chiefly used by the Rural Population of the Manufacturing District of South Lancashire* (Manchester, 1850); *Walks in South Lancashire and on its Borders* (Blackley, 1844).
Benjamin Brierley, *Ab-o'-th'-Yate at Knott Mill Fair* (Manchester, 1870).
Henry Brougham, *A Discourse on the Objects, Advantages and Pleasures of Science* (London, 1827); *Practical Observations upon the Education of the People addressed to the Working Classes and their Employers* (London, 1825); "Speech on the Education of the People", House of Lords, 21 May 1835 (London, 1835).
John Bunyan, *The Pilgrim's Progress* (Penguin edition, 1965).
Robert Burns, *The Poems and Songs of Robert Burns*, edited by James Kinsley (Oxford, 1968).
James Cash, *Where There's a Will There's a Way: An Account of the Labours of Naturalists in Humble Life* (London, 1873).
Central Society of Education, *First, Second and Third Publications* (London, 1837–9).
Edwin Chadwick, *Report on the Sanitary Condition of the Labouring Population of Great Britain* (London, 1842).
Thomas Coates, *Report of the State of Literary, Scientific, and Mechanics' Institutions in England* (London, 1841).
Thomas Cooper, ed. *The Shakespearean Chartist Hymn Book* (London and Leicester, 1843).
Thomas Cooper, *The Triumphs of Perseverance and Enterprise* (London, 1854).
G. L. Craik, *The Pursuit of Knowledge Under Difficulties*, 2 vols. (London, 1830–1).
Stephen Duck, *Poems on Several Occasions* (London, 1736).
B. F. Duppa, *A Manual for Mechanics' Institutions* (London, 1839).
R. G. Gammage, *The History of the Chartist Movement*, edited with an introduction by John Saville, (London, 1969).
E. C. K. Gonner, "The Early History of Chartism 1836–39", *English Historical Review* (1889).
William Jones, *The Jubilee Memorial of the Religious Tract Society* (London, 1850).
"The Journeyman Engineer" (Thomas Wright), *Johnny Robinson*, 2 vols. (London, 1867).
Charles Kingsley, *Alton Locke* (London, 1850).
Charles Knight, *The Old Printer and the Modern Press* (London, 1854).
Joseph Lawson, *Letters to the Young on Progress in Pudsey during the Last Sixty Years* (Stanningley, 1887).
W. J. Linton, "Who were the Chartists?", *Century Magazine*, vol. 23 (January 1882).
(James Lockhart), "Autobiography", *Quarterly Review*, vol. XXXV (28 December 1826).
William Lovett and John Collins, *Chartism* (London, 1840).
Henry Mayhew, "Home is Home, Be It Never So Homely", in Viscount Ingestre, ed., *Meliora, or Better Things to Come* (London, 1853).
Thomas Love Peacock, *Crotchet Castle* (London, 1831).

Frank Peel, *The Risings of Luddites, Chartists and Plug Drawers* (Heckmondwike, 1880).

The Penny Cyclopaedia.

The Penny Magazine.

G. R. Porter, *The Progress of the Nation* (London, 1851).

Report of the Select Committee on Public Libraries, PP. 1849, XI.

Samuel Smiles, *The Life of a Scottish Naturalist*, Thomas Edwards (London, 1876); *Self-Help* (London, 1859).

"Society for the Diffusion of Useful Knowledge", *Westminster Review*, vol. XLVI (June 1827).

S.D.U.K., *Address of the Committee of the Society for the Diffusion of Useful Knowledge*, 11 March 1846 (London, 1846); *General Committee Minutes Book*; *Prospectus of the Society for the Diffusion of Useful Knowledge* (London, 1826).

Robert Southey, *The Remains of Henry Kirke White*, 2 vols. (London, 1807).

Joseph Spence, *A Full and Authentick Account of Stephen Duck* (London, 1731).

James Thomson, *The Seasons and the Castle of Indolence*, edited by James Sambrook (Oxford, 1972).

Ann Yearsley, *Poems on Several Occasions* (London, 1785).

IV. Secondary Material

M. H. Abrams, *The Mirror and the Lamp* (New York, 1953).

D. E. Allen, *The Naturalist in Britain* (London, 1976).

W. O. B. Allen and Edmund McClure, *Two Hundred Years: The History of the Society for Promoting Christian Knowledge 1698–1898* (London, 1898).

Richard D. Altick, *The English Common Reader* (Chicago, 1957).

Gregory Anderson, *Victorian Clerks* (Manchester, 1976).

Michael Anderson, *Family Structure in Nineteenth Century Lancashire* (Cambridge, 1971); "Marriage Patterns in Victorian Britain: An Analysis Based on Registration District Data for England and Wales, 1861", *Journal of Family History*, vol. 1 (Aug. 1976); "Sociological history and the working class family: Smelser revisited", *Social History*, 3 (Oct. 1976).

Philippe Aries, *Centuries of Childhood* (Harmondsworth, 1973).

Peter Bailey, *Leisure and Class in Victorian England* (London, 1978).

Michael Baker, *The Rise of the Victorian Actor* (London, 1978).

John Barrell, *The Idea of Landscape and the Sense of Place; an approach to the poetry of John Clare* (Cambridge, 1972).

Edith C. Batho, *The Ettrick Shepherd* (New York, 1969 edn.).

John W. Blassingame, *The Slave Community* (New York, 1972).

Robert Bruce, *Willie Thom, The Inverurie Poet—A New Look* (Aberdeen, 1970).

Susan Budd, *Varieties of Unbelief* (London, 1977).

Peter Burke, *Popular Culture in Early Modern Europe* (London, 1978).

John Burnett, *A Social History of Housing 1815–1970* (Newton Abbot, 1978).

Duncan Bythell, *The Handloom Weavers* (Cambridge, 1969).

Stanley D. Chapman, *The History of Working Class Housing* (Newton Abbot, 1971).

John Clarke, Chas Critcher and Richard Johnson, eds. *Working Class Culture* (London, 1979).

W. K. Lowther Clarke, *A History of the SPCK* (London, 1959).

Ralph Cohen, *The Unfolding of 'The Seasons'* (London, 1970).

Frances Collier, *The Family Economy of the Working Classes in the Cotton Industry* (Manchester, 1964).

Philip Collins, *Thomas Cooper, The Chartist: Byron and the Poets of the Poor* (Nottingham, 1969).

Robert Colls, *The Collier's Rant* (London, 1977).

Peter Coveney, *The Image of Childhood* (Harmondsworth, 1967).

Geoffrey Crossick, *An Artisan Elite in Victorian Society* (London, 1978); "The Labour Aristocracy and its values: a study of mid-Victorian Kentish London", *Victorian Studies*, vol. XIX (March 1976).
Marjorie Cruikshank, *History of the Training of Teachers in Scotland* (London, 1970).
Paul Delany, *British Autobiography in the Seventeenth Century* (London, 1969).
O. J. Dunlop, *English Apprenticeship and Child Labour* (London, 1912).
Clive Emsley, *British Society and the French Wars 1793–1815* (London, 1979).
R. English, "The Price of the Novel, 1750–1894", *The Author*, vol. V (1894).
Kenneth Fielden, "Samuel Smiles and Self-Help", *Victorian Studies*, vol. XII (December 1968).
John Foster, *Class Struggle and the Industrial Revolution* (London, 1974).
P. H. J. H. Gosden, *Self Help* (London, 1973).
Margaret Grainger, *John Clare: Collector of Ballads* (Peterborough, 1964).
Antonio Gramsci, *Selections from the Prison Notebooks*, edited and translated by Quintin Hoare and Geoffrey Nowell Smith (London, 1971).
Robert Q. Gray, *The Labour Aristocracy in Victorian Edinburgh* (Oxford, 1976).
Brian Harrison, *Drink and the Victorians* (London, 1971).
J. F. C. Harrison, *Learning and Living 1790–1960* (London, 1961); "The Victorian Gospel of Success", *Victorian Studies*, vol. 1 (December 1957).
Christopher Hill, "The Norman Yoke", in John Saville, ed., *Democracy and the Labour Movement* (London, 1954).
E. J. Hobsbawm, *Labouring Men* (London, 1968).
Keith Hollingsworth, *The Newgate Novel 1830–1847* (Detroit, 1963).
Patricia Hollis, *The Pauper Press* (Oxford, 1970).
Pamela Horn, *Education in Rural England 1800–1914* (Dublin, 1978); *The Victorian Country Child* (Kineton, 1974).
I. M. L. Hunter, *Memory* (Harmondsworth, 1964).
Louis James, *Fiction for the Working Man* (Harmondsworth, 1974).
M. G. Jones, *The Charity School Movement* (Cambridge, 1938).
P. J. Keating, *The Working Classes in Victorian Fiction* (London, 1971).
Thomas Kelly, *George Birkbeck* (Liverpool, 1957); *A History of Adult Education in Great Britain* (2nd edn., Liverpool, 1970).
Y. V. Kovalev, ed. *An Anthology of Chartist Literature* (Moscow, 1956); "The Literature of Chartism", *Victorian Studies*, vol. II (1958).
T. W. Laqueur, *Religion and Respectability, Sunday Schools and Working Class Culture 1780–1850* (New Haven, 1976).
John Lawson and Harold Silver, *A Social History of Education in England* (London, 1973).
Q. D. Leavis, *Fiction and the Reading Public* (London, 1932).
Alan J. Lee, *The Origins of the Popular Press in England 1855–1914* (London, 1976).
Georg Lukacs, *History and Class Consciousness* (London, 1971).
Phillip McCann, *Popular education and socialisation in the nineteenth century* (London, 1977).
Neil McKendrick, "Home Demand and Economic Growth: A New View of the Role of Women and Children in the Industrial Revolution", in Neil McKendrick, ed., *Historical Perspectives: Studies in English Thought and Society* (London, 1974).
William Matthews, *British Autobiographies* (California, 1955).
Hans Medick, "The proto-industrial family economy: the structural function of household and family in the transition from peasant society to industrial capitalism", *Social History*, 3 (October 1976).
Edward Miller, *That Noble Cabinet, A History of the British Museum* (London, 1973).
John C. Morris, *Versions of the Self* (New York, 1966).
Victor E. Neuburg, *Popular Literature* (Harmondsworth, 1977).
Chester New, *The Life of Henry Brougham to 1830* (Oxford, 1961).
James Obelkevich, *Religion and Rural Society: South Lindsey 1825–1875* (Oxford, 1976).
Anthony Oberschall, *Empirical Social Research in Germany 1848–1914* (Paris, 1965).

William T. O'Dea, *The Social History of Lighting* (London, 1958).

James Olney, *Metaphors of Self* (Princeton, 1972).

Iona and Peter Opie, *Children's Games in Street and Playground* (Oxford, 1969).

R. B. Outhwaite, "Age at Marriage in England from the Late Seventeenth to the Nineteenth Century", *Transactions of the Royal Historical Society*, 5th Series, XXXIII (1973).

Roy Pascal, *Design and Truth in Autobiography* (London, 1960).

M. L. Pearl, *William Cobbett. A Bibliographical Account of His Life and Times* (Oxford, 1953).

H. Pelling, *A History of British Trade Unions* (London, 1963).

I. Pinchbeck and M. Hewitt, *Children in English Society*, vol. II (London, 1973).

Marjorie Plant, *The English Book Trade* (London, 1965).

Sidney Pollard, *The Genesis of Modern Management* (London, 1965).

Michel Ragon, *Histoire de la Littérature Prolétarienne en France* (Paris, 1974).

R. W. Rich, *The Training of Teachers in England and Wales during the Nineteenth Century* (Cambridge, 1933).

Eric Richards, "Women in the British Economy since about 1700. An Interpretation", *History*, (Oct. 1974).

H. P. Rickman, ed. *Meaning in History* (London, 1961).

Isabel Rivers, " 'Strangers and Pilgrims': Sources and Patterns of Methodist Narrative", in J. C. Hilson, M. M. B. Jones and J. R. Watson eds., *Augustan Worlds* (Leicester, 1978).

Edward Royle, "Mechanics Institutes and the Working Classes, 1840–1860", *The Historical Journal* (1971); *Radical Politics 1790–1800, Religion and Unbelief* (London, 1971); *Victorian Infidels* (Manchester, 1974).

Raphael Samuel, *Village Life and Labour* (London, 1975).

Michael Sanderson, "The grammar school and the education of the poor, 1796–1840", *Journal of Educational Studies*, vol. II, no. 1 (Nov. 1962); "Literacy and Social Mobility in the Industrial Revolution in England", *Past and Present*, 56 (1972).

Roger Schofield, "Dimensions of Illiteracy 1750–1850", *Explorations in Economic History*, vol. 10, no. 4 (Summer 1973).

Leslie Shepherd, *The History of Street Literature* (Newton Abbot, 1973).

Edward Shorter, *The Making of the Modern Family* (London, 1976).

Neil Smelser, *Social Change in the Industrial Revolution* (London, 1959).

Harold Smith, *The Society for the Diffusion of Useful Knowledge, 1826–1846. A Social and Bibliographical Evaluation* (Halifax, Nova Scotia, 1974).

T. C. Smout, "Aspects of Sexual Behaviour in Nineteenth Century Scotland", in A. Allan Maclaren, ed., *Social Class in Scotland* (Edinburgh, 1976).

G. H. Spinney, "Cheap Repository Tracts: Hazard and Marshall Edition", *The Library*, 4th Series, vol. XX (1940).

Margaret Spufford, "First steps in literacy; the reading and writing experiences of the humblest seventeenth century spiritual autobiographers", *Social History*, vol. 4, no. 3 (Oct. 1979).

Gareth Stedman Jones, *Outcast London* (Oxford, 1971).

S. H. Steinberg, *Five Hundred Years of Printing* (Harmondsworth, 1974).

Albert K. Stevens, "Milton and Chartism", *Philological Quarterly*, vol. II (1933).

Lawrence Stone, *The Family, Sex and Marriage in England, 1500–1800* (London, 1977); "Literacy and Education in England 1640–1900", *Past and Present*, 42 (1969).

Mary Sturt, *The Education of the People* (London, 1967).

Trygve R. Tholfsen, "The Intellectual Origins of Mid-Victorian Stability", *Political Sciences Quarterly*, vol. LXXXVI (1971); *Working Class Radicalism in Mid-Victorian England* (London, 1976).

Dorothy Thompson, "Women and Nineteenth-Century Radical Politics: A Lost Dimension", in Juliet Mitchell and Ann Oakley, eds., *The Rights and Wrongs of Women* (Harmondsworth, 1976).

E. P. Thompson, *The Making of the English Working Class* (Harmondsworth, 1968).

E. P. Thompson and Eileen Yeo, eds., *The Unknown Mayhew* (Harmondsworth, 1973).

Paul Thompson, *The Voice of the Past* (Oxford, 1978).

J. W. and Anne Tibble, *John Clare: A Life* (London, 1972).

Asher Tropp, *The School Teachers* (London, 1957).

Rayner Unwin, *The Rural Muse* (London, 1954).

Martha Vicinus, *The Industrial Muse* (London, 1974).

J. T. Ward, *Chartism* (London, 1973).

David Wardle, *English Popular Education 1780–1970* (Cambridge, 1970); *The Rise of the Schooled Society* (London, 1974).

Owen C. Watkins, *The Puritan Experience* (London, 1972).

R. K. Webb, *The British Working Class Reader, 1790–1848* (London, 1955).

E. G. West, *Education and the Industrial Revolution* (London, 1975).

H. N. Wethered, *The Curious Art of Autobiography* (London, 1956).

Joel H. Wiener, *A Descriptive Finding List of Unstamped British Periodicals, 1830–1836* (London, 1970).

Gwyn A. Williams, *Rowland Detrosier, A Working Class Infidel 1800–1834* (York, 1965).

Raymond Williams, "Base and Superstructure in Marxist Cultural Theory", *New Left Review*, 82 (1973); *The Country and the City* (London, 1973); *Culture and Society* (Harmondsworth, 1963).

Anthony S. Wohl, ed. *The Victorian Family* (London, 1978).

V. Unpublished Dissertations

Monica C. Grobel, *The Society for the Diffusion of Useful Knowledge 1826–46* (M.A. thesis, University of London, 1933).

David L. Robbins, *A Radical Alternative to Paternalism: Voluntary Associations and Popular Enlightenment in England and France 1800–1840* (Yale Univ. Ph.D., 1974).

Bernard Sharratt, *Autobiography and Class Consciousness. An Attempt to Characterise Nineteenth Century Working Class Autobiography in the Light of the Writer's Class* (Ph.D. thesis, Cambridge University, 1974).

Index

Dunhill, Snowden, 170
Dunning, Thomas, 44n, 65n, 89, 97, 118n, 149, 169n, 177n

Edinburgh, 151, 191
Education, 8, 12, 31, 33, 39, 52, 66, 67, 70, 72, 79, 80, 81, 89, 93–107, 138, 141, 145, 148, 150–1, 157, 165, 183, 198, 202. *See also* Schools, Teachers
Eldon, Lord, 139
Elliott, Ebenezer, 175n, 178n
Engels, Frederick, 23
Engineers, 49, 62, 67, 68n, 123, 148
Errington, Anthony, 7, 21, 37–8, 62, 69n, 84, 105, 169, 186n

Factory Acts, 74, 99, 102, 198
Family economy, 12, 39, 40, 44, 52–3, 58, 60, 62–86, 93, 94–7, 94, 104, 106, 107, 152
Farish, William, 28, 66n, 71, 92n, 95n, 100n, 118n, 125n, 127n, 151n, 154n, 171n, 172n, 175n, 183n, 198n
Farn, J. C., 18n, 82n, 93, 94, 95, 97n, 171–2, 181n, 182n
First London Co-operative Trading Association, 153
Franklin, Benjamin, 37
Freethought, Secularism, 180–1
French Revolution, 26
Friendly Societies, 53, 140, 150n, 152n, 153, 200
Frost, Thomas, 25, 27, 114n, 127n, 129, 152–3, 158, 163, 198

Gammage, R. G., 28
Genius, concept of, 32–3
Glasgow, 140, 170, 200
Goethe, Johann Wolfgang von, 14n, 36
Grace Abounding to the Chief of Sinners, 16–17
Gramsci, Antonio, 10–11, 36
Green, William, 22–3, 24, 73n, 96
Grief, see Death
Gutteridge, Joseph, 47, 49, 50, 51, 52n, 53n, 68n, 74, 89, 102, 130, 143–4, 151n, 173, 175n, 181, 184n, 188, 198n, 202

"H., Bill", 7n, 23, 47, 49, 55n, 56, 67
Halifax, 25, 28, 51, 93, 125, 173
Hampton, Richard, 81n, 100n
Hanby, George, 69n

Handloom-weavers, 52–3, 62, 64, 67, 69, 71, 75–6, 78, 80, 92, 95, 111, 124–5, 127, 142, 145, 151n, 153, 177, 184, 202
Hanson, William, 9, 17, 51, 54, 58, 89n, 96n, 149n, 151n, 167n, 183n
Hardy, Thomas (of the London Corresponding Society), 25–6, 27, 28, 29, 44n, 154n
Harris, John, 14, 21, 55, 56n, 69n, 90n, 94–5, 96–7, 98, 100, 104, 120–1, 122n, 146, 149, 151, 156n, 167n, 182, 188n, 192, 194
Hatmaking, 68n, 69, 140, 150, 184
Hawker, James, 21, 49, 81, 171, 175, 183n, 197
Hawkers, 5, 7, 24, 45, 113, 119
Haynes, Joseph, 9, 56
Heaton, William, 43n, 52n, 90n, 96, 124–5, 149n, 151n, 156n, 173, 182, 183
Herbert, George, 95n
Herbert, Henry, 55n, 57n, 102n, 104n, 149n, 151n, 171n, 183n, 188n
Hetherington, Henry, 65, 154n, 169–70
Hexham, 69, 140
History, working class sense of, 11–12, 19, 24–9, 36–7, 168, 197–203; inadequacy of formal record, 25–8
Hogg, James, 14, 34, 64, 104, 117n, 123, 135, 148n, 151, 152n, 189, 191
Holyoake, George, 27
Hopkinson, James, 14, 17, 47, 53n, 68, 82n, 89, 149n, 182n, 184n
Horler, Moses, 41n, 69n
Home, Catherine, 8, 40
Hutton's Mensuration, 129

Illegitimacy, 43
Ill-health, Sickness, 1, 52, 54, 59, 65–6, 78, 87, 92, 166, 181, 185, 199–200
Imprisonment, 50, 69, 147, 154, 181n, 203
Industrial novels, 23
Infidelism, 180–1
Innes, William, 48n, 100n, 149n

Job-finding, 50, 53, 66–8, 71–2, 75, 85
Jones, John, 31, 34, 94, 101, 124, 129n, 151
Journalists, 9, 23, 59, 152–3

Kettering, 177, 183
Kingsley, Charles, 2, 29
Kitson, John, 51, 149n